Transpositions

For my nieces and nephews

Transpositions

On Nomadic Ethics

Rosi Braidotti

polity

First published in 2006 by Polity Press

Polity Press
65 Bridge Street
Cambridge CB2 1UR, UK

Polity Press
350 Main Street
Malden, MA 02148, USA

ISBN: 0-7456-3595-4
ISBN: 0-7456-3596-2 (pb)

A catalogue record for this book is available from the British Library.

Typeset in 10 on $11\frac{1}{2}$ pt Palatino
by SNP Best-set Typesetter Ltd, Hong Kong
Printed and bound in Great Britain by MPG Books Ltd, Bodmin, Cornwall.

The publisher has used its best endeavours to ensure that any URLs for external websites referred to in this book are correct and active at the time of going to press. However, the publisher has no responsibility for the websites and can make no guarantee that a site will remain live or that the content is or will remain appropriate.

Every effort has been made to trace all copyright holders, but if any have been inadvertently overlooked the publishers will be pleased to include any necessary credits in any subsequent reprint or edition.

For further information on Polity, visit our website: www.polity.co.uk

Contents

Acknowledgements

I want to express all my gratitude to my publisher John Thompson and the staff at Polity Press, for their unfailing support and sound professional advice. I wish to thank the Robert Schuman Centre at the European University Institute in Florence, for awarding me a Jean Monnet Fellowship in 2001 and a Jean Monnet Chair Visiting Professorship in 2002 and 2003. My special thanks to Yves Meny for his enlightened leadership, to Luisa Passerini and Dawn Lyon.

The Dutch Research Organisation (NWO) awarded me a personal grant to support my sabbatical leave in 2001; the Arts Faculty of Utrecht University, especially the Institute for Culture and History (OGC) granted me a semester leave at a time of great financial constraints. Special thanks to Wiljan van den Akker, Frans Ruiter, Maarten Prak and Dean Hans Bertens. My recurrent visiting professorship at the London School of Economics 1999–2002 provided stimulating contacts and discussions with Anne Phillips, Henrietta Moore, Claire Hemmings and Tony Giddens. My gratitude also to Alan Schrift of Grinnell College in the United States, for making possible the last quiet weeks in 2004 when I could revise the manuscript.

Sincere thanks to my research assistants Marta Garro, Hester Vons, Silvia Panzironi and Eva Midden for their enthusiasm and dedication well beyond the call of duty.

To my closest staff members Trude Oorschot, Annabel van Baren and Marlise Mensink for their support and professionalism. To my colleagues Rosemarie Buikema, Gloria Wekker, Sandra Ponzanesi and especially to Berteke Waaldijk, whose friendship I treasure. I acknowledge many generations of students, whose passionate discussions and sharp minds I thoroughly enjoyed, especially Mischa Peters, Sarah Bracke, Joana Passos, Rutvica Andrijasevic, Maayke Botman, Edyta Just, Marta Zarzycka, Jeannette van der Sanden and Iris van der Tuin.

Claire Colebrook was unfailing in providing feedback and support. Bolette Benedictsen Blaagaard gave me thoughtful and incisive comments in the final stages. Harry Kunneman remained a privileged interlocutor throughout. Keith Ansell-Pearson, Arnaud Villani, Yves Abrioux, Judith Butler and Costas Boundas were generous with their comments. I thank the artist Natasha Unkart for granting permission to reproduce one of her striking photographs on the book cover.

I acknowledge with deep affection and gratitude my sister Giovanna, a Ph.D. in molecular biology who made contemporary genetics intellectually attractive and accessible to me. Thanks also to my best friend Annamaria Tagliavini, because she taught me that silence does not equate loss and distance need not spell absence.

The book is dedicated to all my nieces and nephews. They are, on the Australian side of the family, Noah, Luca and Ely Haas-Harris, and on the Dutch side, Jip, Lisa, Else, Bop, Joska, Casper and Felix Smelik. May their existence be transposed into happiness and peace.

To my partner Anneke Smelik for our blissful life together.

The Author and publisher would like to thank the following for permission to reproduce epigraphs in the book:

Blackwell Publishing Ltd., from Zygmunt Bauman in *Postmodern Ethics*, 1933.

Cambridge University Press, from Freidrich Neitzche in *Human all too Human, A Book for Free Spirits*, 2nd. Edition. Edited by R. J. Hollingdale, Introduction by Richard Schacht, 1944; and from Marilyn Strathern in *After Nature*, 1992.

Excerpt from THE DIARY OF VIRGINIA WOOLF, Volume II, 1920–1924, copyright © 1978 by Quentin Bell and Angelica Garnett, reprinted with permission of Harcourt, Inc.

The Diary of Virginia Woolf, edited by Anne Olivier Bell, published by Hogarth Press. Reprinted with permission of The Random House Group Ltd.

Indiana University Press, from Judith Halberstaum and Ira Livingston in *Posthuman Bodies*, 1995.

Random House for the extract from *Virginia Woolf* by Hermione Lee, published by Chatto and Windus, 1996.

Serpent's Tail Ltd., from Kathy Acker, *Bodies of Work*, 1988.

Every effort has been made to contact copyright holders, but in some cases this has proved impossible.

PROLOGUE

Transformations

Introduction

We who dwell in post-industrial societies live in a world that is not only geno-centric (Fausto-Sterling 2000: 235), but also lucratively and unjustly so. In this book, I want to address the ethical temperature or fibre of our era, also known as the technologically driven historical phase of advanced capitalism. The project is motivated by the concern that the desire for social justice and progressive transformation, which is one of the salient manifestations of our ethical consciousness, seems to be dwindling today. Times are definitely no longer a-changing.

Nothing expresses this cultural climate better than the media's insistence on celebrating, with unsuppressible glee, 'the end of ideologies'. For the last twenty years I have sat through regular waves of celebration of the multiple deaths of every available 'ideology'. So much so, that I am almost tempted to define ideologies as movements that never cease to end. When will a new one actually start? The emphatic reiteration of the decline of 'ideology' finds its latest incarnation in the 1989 fall of the Berlin Wall. It translates into a one-way political model, namely that all programmes of change have exhausted their historical function, especially Marxism, communism, socialism and feminism. Hence people can now relax and carry on with the normal task of minding their own business. A hasty and fallacious historical dismissal of social reformism and critical radicalism results in the reassertion of the banality of self-interest, as a lesser and necessary evil. This moral apathy is constitutive of neo-conservative political liberalism in our era.

Donna Haraway stresses the quasi-monopoly exercised upon our cultures by: 'the status of bio-technology in the transition from the economics and the biologies of the Cold War era to the New World Order's secular theology of enhanced competitiveness and ineluctable market forces' (Haraway 1997: 90). Alain Touraine (2001) describes this phenomenon as 'la pensée unique',[1] that is to say a *de facto* hegemony of a neo-liberal orthodoxy which denies 'the existence of autonomous social actors capable of influencing political decision-making' (Touraine 2001: 1). Arguing forcefully that globalization has not dissolved our collective capacity for political action, and wary of any facile rejection of globalization *per se*, Touraine calls for renewed social criticism. Resistance is needed against the new master narratives, which entail American hegemony of the world markets and the specific brand of USA-based fundamentalism, which targets the Islamic world under the cover of the 'clash of civilizations'. Cultural identities and global capital are the key terms of the current political economy and they need to be turned into active spaces of resistance.

Paradoxes, however, multiply all along the way. Post-industrial culture triumphantly asserts the end of ideology defined as the desire for social justice and attempts to fulfil a conservative's favourite fantasy of an immutable and unmovable 'human nature', allegedly best catered for by advanced capitalist services (Fukuyama 2002). This same culture, however, simultaneously frustrates the very conservative dreams it so perversely aroused. Contemporary society is in fact fascinated to the point of obsession by all that is 'new'. It pursues change with maniacal faith in its beneficial side-effects. It disrupts the very social fabric and the modes of exchange and interaction which were established by industrial culture. The much-celebrated phenomenon of globalization and its technologies accomplishes a magician's trick: it combines the euphoric celebration of *new* technologies, *new* economy, *new* lifestyles, *new* generations of both human and technological gadgets, *new* wars and *new* weapons with the complete social rejection of change and transformation. In a totally schizophrenic double pull the consumerist and socially enhanced faith in the *new* is supposed not only to fit in with, but also actively to induce, the rejection of in-depth changes. The potentially innovative, de-territorializing impact of the new technologies is hampered and tuned down by the reassertion of the gravitational pull of old and established values.

Issues related to technology, more specifically to bio-technologies, are consequently central to my concerns and they form the main thread through the book. The convergence between information and communication technologies on the one hand, and bio-technologies and genetic engineering on the other, is one of the major social manifestations of the current status of the subjects in advanced, post-industrial societies, situated as they are in a state of dispersion and fragmentation.

Times of fast changes, such as those taking place in the so-called advanced societies, reveal the paradox of continuing archaism on the one hand and hyper-modernism on the other. In some ways, the defining

---

[1] Translation: 'The one-way thought'.

feature of our age is the high level of anxiety, exhilaration, fear or optimism. They are directly related to the speed and range of the social changes themselves, which in turn are a function of the availability and access to the new technologies. Genetics and bio-technologies are making people nervous about their DNA and their organic capital. Anxiety runs more and more to the surface of things. In such a context, politics can be described not merely as the government of the polis, but also in terms of the management of insecurity. The ongoing changes are currently packaged in modes of social representation which alternate between the euphoric and the apocalyptic. This is in keeping with a manic-depressive logic which cannot fail to affect also the scholarship that deals with contemporary techno-cultures. Studies of technology swing from utopianism to gloom while in mainstream culture negative modes of representing the technological artefact as potentially threatening monstrous others recycle classical gothic themes (Braidotti 2002).

The political climate of this historical context can be best summed up in terms of capitalism as schizophrenia. Deleuze and Guattari (1992) analysed this double pull in contemporary cultures as a conflict between, on the one hand, the rising demands for subjective singularities, or autonomy and, on the other hand, the conservative re-territorialization of desires for the purpose of commercial profit. This is reflected in the schizoid paradox of the compulsive consumerism of mass culture, where all the emphasis falls on the quest for 'personalized' or 'itemized', custom-made specifications and commodities. This achieves a disastrous dual effect; it reasserts individualism as the unquestionably desirable standard, while it reduces it to brand names and to logos. It also pushes commercial profit-making to the innermost boundaries of subjectivity itself, making 'I shop therefore I am' the leading refrain of our times. This is one of the reasons for the contemporary mix of archaic attachment to 'safe' notions and the fear of losing them, on the one hand, and the euphoric celebration of technological innovation on the other.

Keith Ansell-Pearson (1997a) argues that grand narratives have come back into fashion, and that they tend to stress the inhuman character of the current evolution of the human species, through interface with intelligent machines. 'A new mythology of the machine is emerging and finds expression in current claims that technology is simply the pursuit of life by means other than life' (Ansell-Pearson 1997a: 203). He adds that such a vision is both philosophically and politically naïve as it rests on a simplistic model of bio-technological evolution. Such grand narratives reflect 'the dynamics of contemporary hyper-colonialist capitalism' (1997a: 203), one which conflates change with novelty, speed with simple acceleration and sells 'entropic modernization in its most imperialist guise'. A hierarchical fantasy of vertical perfectibility, the technologically mediated quest for immortality and for disciplined and acquiescent subjects, has gained widespread currency. In opposition to this master narrative, which corresponds to what Donna Haraway calls 'the informatics of domination', I want to stress the relevance of a materialist, nomadic philosophy of becoming, as an alternative conceptual framework, in the service of a sustainable future. The political cartographies I present in chapters 2 and 3 respond to this need. These cartographies also raise an important set of ethical questions. On the analytic front: what means do social and cultural critics have at their disposal in order to make sense of and account for the structural paradoxes of a historical era? On the more normative front, the question is: what are our hopes of finding adequate ways of expressing empowering alternatives and of having them socially enacted? How does this consumerist and socially enhanced emphasis on the *new* fit in with the rejection of in-depth changes? How do they join forces in reiterating old and established viewpoints? What are our hopes of finding adequate ways of handling them?

Amidst such cacophony of conflicting fears and desires, punctuated by public exposures of emotions in the 'intimate public sphere'(Berlant 1997), it is important to focus seriously on the notion of political passions, and to stress a rigorous vision of affectivity. Nomadic subjectivity involves a materialist approach to affectivity and a non-essentialist brand of vitalism. These constitute a concrete answer to the contemporary flair for (alternatively) nostalgia or euphoria for commercialized emotions. More specifically, in chapter 4 I will explore vitalistic ethics and alternative modes of desire which attempt to stress positivity and not lack. As no discussion of ethics is complete without dealing with negativity, in chapter 5 I will discuss specifically the darker, more death-bound elements of the positive ethics of becoming which I defend throughout this book.

This project consists in transposing the ethical implications of nomadic subjectivity. The subject of postmodernity is caught between humanistic expectations of decency and dignity and the growing evidence of a posthuman universe of ruthless power-relations mediated by technology. I will reposition the subject amidst the 'new' master narratives that aim at restoring traditional, unitary visions of the self in the neo-liberal model, so as to be able to passionately pursue the quest for alternatives. I will concede from the outset that the non-unitary subject is ever prone to pressures that pull him or her in many potentially contradictory directions at once: nothing is played out in advance. Nomadic subjectivity is a contested space of mutations that follow no technological directives and no moral imperatives. What kind of ethics is possible for such a subject is the question this book attempts to address as an open challenge.

Non-unitary subjectivity here means a nomadic, dispersed, fragmented vision, which is nonetheless functional, coherent and accountable, mostly because it is embedded and embodied. This book deals with the implications of this vision in terms of accountability, and ethical and political agency. The book will explore the possibility of a system of ethical values that, far from requiring a steady and unified vision of the subject, rests on a non-unitary, nomadic or rhizomatic view. The notion of 'sustainability' is the central point of reference, which I will explore with a number of concrete examples of ethics drawn from the fields of environmentalism, feminism, anti-racism, and the studies of science and technology. I will supplement these emblematic cases with critical reflection on the making of ethical subjects. This includes a discussion of the conditions that are most conducive to cultivating and sustaining the desire for change and in-depth transformation of the dominant, unitary vision of human subjectivity, while avoiding the twin pitfalls of relativism and of nihilistic self-dissipation.

About transpositions

The term 'transpositions' has a double source of inspiration: from music and from genetics. It indicates an intertextual, cross-boundary or transversal transfer, in the sense of a leap from one code, field or axis into another, not merely in the quantitative mode of plural multiplications, but rather in the qualitative sense of complex multiplicities. It is not just a matter of weaving together different strands, variations on a theme (textual or musical), but rather of playing the positivity of difference as a specific theme of its own. As a term in music, transposition indicates variations and shifts of scale in a discontinuous but harmonious pattern. It is thus created as an in-between space of zigzagging and of crossing: nonlinear, but not chaotic; nomadic, yet accountable and committed; creative but also cognitively valid; discursive and also materially embedded – it is coherent without falling into instrumental rationality.

Evelyn Fox Keller, in her brilliant study of the life and work of Barbara McClintock (1983), argues that 'transposition' refers to processes of genetic mutation, or the transferral of genetic information, which occur in a non linear manner, which is nonetheless neither random nor arbitrary. This is set in opposition to the mainstream scientific vision that tends to define the gene as a steady entity that transmits fixed units of heredity in an autonomous and self-sufficient manner and genetic variation as random events. Transposable moves appear to proceed by leaps and bounds, but are not deprived of their logic, or coherence.

Central to transpositions is the notion of material embodiment; in the case of genetics, McClintock highlights the decisive role played by the organism in framing and affecting the rate and the frequency of the mutations. Transpositions occur by a carefully regulated dissociation of the bonds that would normally maintain cohesiveness between the genes, which are laid out in a linear manner on the chromosome. McClintock shows that as a result of the dissociative impact, a mutation occurs that splits the chromosome into two detached segments. The rate of the mutation of these 'jumping genes' is internally determined by the elements of the cell itself, and thus is not pre-written in the gene. The notion of trans-position emphasizes the flexibility of the genome itself. This implies that the key to understanding genetics is the process itself, the sequence of the organized system. This can be traced *a posteriori* as the effect of the disso-ciative shifts or leaps, but these controlling agents remain immanent to the process itself and are contingent upon the rearrangements of the ele-ments. In other words, genetics information is contained in the sequence of the elements, which in turn means that the function and the organiza-tion of the genetic elements are mutable and interdependent.[2]

Consequently, as Hilary Rose put it ever so wittily: 'DNA, far from being the stable macho molecule of the 1962 Watson–Crick prize story, becomes a structure of complex dynamic equilibrium' (Rose 2001: 61). Nobody and no particle of matter is independent and self-propelled, in nature as in the social. Ultimately, genetic changes are under the control of the organisms, which, under the influence of environmental factors, are capable of affecting the reprogramming of the genetic sequence itself.

As if it were capable of 'learning from experience', the organism defined as the host environment of the genetic sequence plays an interactive and determining role in the transmission of genetic information. Haraway sums it up brilliantly: 'A gene is not a thing, much less a master molecule, or a self-contained code. Instead, the term "gene" signifies a mode of durable action where many actors, human and non-human meet' (Haraway 1997: 142).

Transposition is a scientific theory that stresses the experience of crea-tive insight in engendering other, alternative ways of knowing. McClin-tock and Keller do not alienate scientific methods, but rather use them to demonstrate – albeit *a posteriori* – what they knew already. Resting on the assumption of a fundamental and necessary unity between subject and object, the theory of transpositions offers a contemplative and creative stance that respects the visible and hidden complexities of the very phe-nomena it attempts to study. This makes it a paradigmatic model for sci-entific knowledge as a whole, particularly feminist epistemologies, notably the critique of dualistic splits. It also shows affinity with spiritual practices like Buddhism, not in a mystical mood, but in a cognitive mode.

What is the relevance of the notion of transpositions for this book? Multiple and complex, transpositions occur on many levels at once. Firstly, this work applies, expands and develops the ethical and political implica-tions of some of the arguments exposed as cartographies in *Metamor-phoses*. The relationship between the two books is neither linear, as in cause and effect, nor does it fall between the fundamental–applied distinc-tion; they are interlinked, while each maintains its singular profile. Their interconnection is a transposition, that is to say a creative leap that pro-duces a prolific in-between space.

[2] I thank my sister Giovanna for these insights into contemporary genetics.

Secondly, the term 'transposition' refers to mobility and cross-referencing between disciplines and discursive levels. I rely on transposable notions that drift nomadically among different texts – including those I authored myself – while producing their own specific effects. Transposable concepts are 'nomadic notions' that weave a web connecting philosophy to social realities; theoretical speculations to concrete plans; concepts to imaginative figurations. Trans-disciplinary in structure, transposable concepts link bio-technology to ethics and connect them both with social and political philosophy. Moreover, I will inject feminism, anti-racism, environmental and human rights as an extra booster of theoretical energy and then let nomadic flows of becoming run loose through them all.

Thirdly, the notion of transposition describes the connection between the text and its social and historical context, in the material and discursive sense of the term. The passion that animates this book is a concern for my historical situation, in so-called advanced, post-industrial cultures at the start of the third millennium. A kind of *amor fati* motivates me, not as fatalism, but rather in the pragmatic mode of the cartographer. I am seeking modes of representation and forms of accountability that are adequate to the complexities of the real-life world I am living in. I want to think about what and where I live – not in a flight away from the embodied and embedded locations which I happen to inhabit. In *Metamorphoses* I argued that, if you do not like complexities you couldn't possibly feel at home in the third millennium. *Transpositions* enacts this notion by proposing creative links and zigzagging interconnections between discursive communities which are too often kept apart from each other. To name but a few significant ones: bio-technologies and ethics and political agency; the omnipresence of a state of crisis on the one hand and the possibility of sustainable futures on the other; the practice of nomadic politics of difference versus technological monoculture; the creative potential of hybrid subjectivity, in opposition to new and more virulent forms of ethnically fixed identities; cartographic accounts of locations and normative stances. Ultimately: post-structuralism and ethical norms or values.

More specifically, I will transpose nomadically from philosophical theory to ethical practice. Loyal to the feminist politics of locations, I remain committed to the task of providing politically informed maps of the present, convinced of the usefulness of a situated approach as a critical tool to achieve an enlarged sense of objectivity and a more empowering grasp of the social. Politically, a cartographic method based on the politics of locations results in the recognition that not one single central strategy of resistance is possible (Grewal and Kaplan 1994; Patton 2000; Massumi 1992b). A heterogeneous style of politics is needed instead, based on centrelessness. As a corollary, this implies a variety of possible political strategies and the non-dogmatic acceptance of potentially contradictory positions. A scattered, weblike system is now operational, which defies and defeats any pretence at avant-garde leadership by any group. Resistance being as global as power, it is centreless and just as non-linear: contemporary politics is rhizomic.

This book tracks the zigzagging transpositions of multiple differences across the global landscape of a mediated world. The concrete socio-economic conditions of advanced capitalism, the so-called 'global-economy', with its flows of commodities and the mobility of goods, is one of the factors responsible for the collapse of mono-centred systems and of binary modes of opposition between centre and periphery. The poly-centred, multiple and complex political economy of late postmodernity is nomadic in the sense that it promotes the fluid circulation of capital and of commodities. In this respect, it favours the proliferation of differences, but only within the strictly commercial logic of profit. My nomadic vision of subjectivity, on the other hand, is strictly non-profit (Braidotti 1994; 2002). It aims to provide a rigorous account both of the mobile subject-positions that are available in late postmodernity, and also of modes of resistance and alternative to the profit–minded values of today. I rely on transposable notions to account adequately for the fast-moving processes of change and for the overlapping complexities of place and time.

I will investigate the creative force of transpositions in the framework of new power relations and explore its potential as the grounds for a new political ontology. Such a creative move takes the form of a qualitative leap. It does not trust the mechanistic determinism of the genes and memes (*pace* Dawkins 1976). Nor does it rely on the reassuring linearity of a divinely ordained evolutionary teleology (*pace* Teilhard de Chardin 1959). It is rather the case that this qualitative or creative leap takes the form of a change of culture: a transformation not only of our schemes of thought, but also of our ways of inhabiting the world. Such a radical change, rooted in the immanent structure of the subject, requires a lucid understanding of the topology and ethnology of the interconnections that link us to our social and organic environment. In other words, it is an eco-philosophy of belonging and of transformations.

Transformative ethics

An ethics of sustainability, based on these interconnections, will conse-quently form the main structure of my argument. This transformative ethics includes a critical or reactive and an affirmative or active phase. On the critical side, the issue at stake is the critique of tradition, i.e. which forces, aspirations or conditions are likely to propel us out of the inert repetition of established habits of thought and self-representation. On the affirmative side, the issue is how we can cultivate the political desire for change or transformation, for actively willing and yearning for positive and creative changes. How can we link the issue of desire, as a structural force that entails both ethical and erotic elements, with the question of socio-political forces and power-relations?

Lest my passion for transformations may lead to a seemingly hasty dismissal of attachment to traditional values, I will discuss this issue at length in chapter 1. In defence of the desire for change or transformation, I will argue that the force of habit is indeed little more than inertia, that is to say a reactive type of affect. 'Habits' are a socially enforced and thereby 'legal' type of addiction. They are cumulated toxins which by sheer uncreative repetition engender forms of behaviour that can be socially accepted as 'normal' or even 'natural'. The undue credit that is granted to the accumulation of habits lends exaggerated authority to past experiences. *Transpositions* addresses the question of which forces, desires or aspirations are likely to propel us out of traditional habits, so that one is actually yearning for changes in a positive and creative manner. This leads to the classical political question: What makes people want to change? How do you motivate them to change? How can we account for the political desire for transformation to occur? How can we link the issue of desire – its structure, which entails both erotic and political elements – with sustainable ethics?

This approach calls for a style that adequately expresses the process in a non-linear manner. A philosophical style is a way of shifting the very foundations of the corporate identity of philosophy. Against the traditional definition of this discipline in terms of cognitive mastery and normative power, I want to call for a radical scrambling of its codes. The catalogue of alternative modes of postulating the self–other interaction is broad: the placenta as a non-dialectical dyad; the figuration of the parasite; the cloned animal; the leaping gene; hybrid complexity, diasporic displacements and cosmological resonance. These figurations are steps towards a non-linear rendition of the subject in its deep structures. It is a kind of transposition, a way of revisiting, reclaiming and relocating a crucial shift in the process of becoming subjects.

Transposing is a gesture neither of metaphorical assimilation nor of metonymic association. It is a style, in the sense of a form of conceptual creativity, like a sliding door, a choreographed slippage, a drifting away that follows a trajectory which can be traced *a posteriori* and thus be made accountable. Like a weather map, genetic printing or digital tracking, an account can be made of what will have been – in the first instance – a fluid flowing of becoming.

Transposing between the cartographic and the normative, this book will ask time and time again: 'So what, then?' What if the subject is 'trans', or in transit, that is to say no longer one, whole, unified and in control, but rather fluid, in process and hybrid? What are the ethical and political implications of a non-unitary vision of the human subject? How does this vision express and reflect the complexities and contradictions of contemporary culture and cultural politics? This is in some ways the philosophical question *par excellence*: it provokes and thus invites serious questioning, while injecting into the debate a healthy dose of debunking. I shall do my best to follow this thread while giving ample space in this book to a more normative dimension of thought in terms of the ethics of sustainability. This rigour in both intent and content will not prevent my flair for paradoxes from striking healthy blows to the philosopher's *esprit de serieux*. This talent is needed more than ever, for these are strange times indeed, and strange things are happening.

1

Translations: Transposing Moral Debates

The greatest crimes against humanity (and by humanity) have been perpetrated in the name of the rule of reason, of better order and greater happiness.

Zygmunt Bauman, *Postmodern Ethics*

The older morality, namely Kant's, demands from the individual those actions that one desires from all men. It is a theory like that of free trade, which assumes that a general harmony would have to result of itself, according to innate laws of melioration.

Friedrich Nietzsche, *Human, All Too Human*

BEYOND MORAL PHILOSOPHY

Ever since Dostoevsky had the unfortunate idea of proclaiming that 'if God is dead, then anything goes', the threat of moral and cognitive relativism has been hanging over any project that shows a concerted effort at displacing or decentring the traditional, humanistic view of the subject. This pessimistic attitude strikes both a contradictory and an inconsistent note. In this chapter I therefore put to the test the pretentious belief that only a liberal and humanistic view of the subject can guarantee basic elements of human decency: moral and political agency and ethical probity. In opposition to this belief, which has little more than long-standing habits and the inertia of tradition on its side and is extremely popular also in feminist circles, I will argue that a nomadic and post-humanistic vision of the subject can provide an alternative foundation for ethical and political subjectivity.

Philosophical nomadism rests on a cartography of our historical condition that highlights the relevance of a non-unitary vision of the subject. This sets poststructuralist ethics against the dominant, mostly Anglo-American traditions of moral philosophy. There seems to be a consensus that, as Todd May (1995) points out, morality as a field of inquiry and moral philosophy as a discipline do not score highly in poststructuralist philosophy or in Continental French philosophy as a whole. This is no reason, however, to move against it the lazy charges of moral relativism and nihilism. One only has to look across the field of French philosophy: Deleuze's ethics of *amor fati*, Irigaray's ethics of sexual difference, Foucault's search for the ethical relationship, Derrida's and Levinas's emphasis on the receding horizons of alterity – to be fully immersed in ethical concerns. Ethics in poststructuralist philosophy is not confined to the realm of rights, distributive justice, or the law, but it rather bears close links with the notion of political agency and the management of power and of power-relations. Issues of responsibility are dealt with in terms of alterity or the relationship to others. This implies accountability, situatedness and cartographic accuracy. A poststructuralist position, therefore, far from thinking that a liberal individual definition of the subject is the necessary precondition for ethics, argues that liberalism at present hinders the development of new modes of ethical behaviour.

The charge of relativism is especially serious and persistent, as shown by Sokal and Bricmont's attack on poststructuralism (1998). They tried an 'experiment' by submitting to a fashionable American journal, *Social Text*, a parody of the type of work a 'postmodernist' would write, to see whether they would publish it. The article, jargon-ridden and brimming with absurdities, was accepted and published. The authors, revealing the hoax, provoked reactions in the academic press. They went on to extend their negative criticism not only to the whole area of so-called 'French postmodernism', but also to any discipline other than mathematics and physics. The main line of their attack is the charge of epistemic, cognitive and moral relativism, namely the idea that in the poststructuralist mindset, modern science is nothing more than a 'myth', a 'narration', or a 'social construction' among many others. Single-handedly erecting the paradigms of the natural sciences to untouchable heights of universal value, these authors go on to attack the 'linguistic turn' for its alleged 'evaporation of reality' (Gellner 1992) and scientific inaccuracy. Among others, this aggressive position denies the historical existence of a solid tradition of French epistemology and rationalist philosophy of science, which runs from Bachelard, Koyré and Canguilhem right into the work of Foucault and Deleuze. Sokal and Bricmont – two scientists whose main publications are as jargon-ridden, obscure and incomprehensible as those of all high-level specialists in any field of scientific endeavour – make manifest the general image of poststructuralism as a relativist philosophy. Adding insult to injury, they subsequently proceed to legislate on the fundamental rules of the scientific game in such a way as to suit their disciplinary backgrounds and personal preferences.

Crucial to this discussion is the notion that responsibility, in the cognitive and moral sense, is best served by individualism. In her work on feminist ethics, Susan Parsons (1992) outlines the enormous appeal and importance of the notion of individualism in moral philosophy. She analyses it in terms of rational control in the form of a choice of behaviour that is in keeping with one's standards and is not swayed by passions or over-involvement. In so far as 'rational behaviour is understood to be the control of choices by transcendence of the emotions, it aims at reaching practical conclusions by calculating the best means of carrying out one's general principles' (Parsons 1992: 383). It can thus be held to be a universal principle. What is universalizable about it is that it can serve as the basic premise for some practical syllogism that can guide the moral choices of all moral agents.

What is central to liberalism is Kantian moral universalism, i.e. the belief in a necessary link to the epistemological and knowledge-related aspects of this tradition of moral thinking. It joins consciousness with rationality in the pursuit of universal moral norms, by making objectivity a crucial concept. Feminist critics of this tradition have stressed precisely its limited applicability, as opposed to the universal pretension. They have also commented on the genderization of the notions of reason, objectivity and of the universal itself, which are biased in favour of the masculine.

Feminist poststructuralists go even further into this critique than other schools of feminist thought. Ethical accountability is closely related to the political awareness of one's positions and privileges. Poststructuralist ethics is consequently concerned with human affectivity and passions as the motor of subjectivity, not so much with the moral content of intentionality, action or behaviour or the logic of rights. Alterity, otherness and difference are crucial terms of reference in poststructuralist ethics. Todd May, for instance, argues forcefully that an ethical standpoint is built into Deleuze's anti-representational position. The anti-representationalism consists in rejecting the critical function of judgement as the model for philosophical inquiry. The Kantian model of the judge of reason is overthrown by Deleuze in favour of values which are 'contingently grounded and politically infused' (May 1995: 14). Deleuze rejects moral judgements in favour of an ethics of forces and affects.

The generation of French neo-Nietzscheans (Schrift 1995) goes much further into a radical critique of dominant morality and of the ways in which it affects intellectual life and scientific production. Pursuing the critique of power in/as discourse (Foucault), the rejection of the dogmatic image of thought (Deleuze) and the implicit masculinism (Irigaray) of representational thought, they argue that the power to impose on people representations of themselves, or of others on their behalf, is intrinsically oppressive. The thinker or philosopher is neither the judge, nor the priest nor the umpire of reason. Therefore, the thinker's appointing himself or herself to the position of having to represent others is rejected by poststructuralist philosophers as an oppressive and abusive move. Rather than dismissing this anti-representationalism as relativism, I see it instead

as a profoundly ethical position, which rejects the arrogant power that
intellectuals and scholars award themselves as the guardians of truth.

What Irigaray's ethics of sexual difference and Deleuze's ethics of
nomadic sustainability indicate is that the proper object of ethical inquiry
is not the subject's moral intentionality, or rational consciousness, as much
as the effects of truth and power that his or her actions are likely to have
upon others in the world. This is a kind of ethical pragmatism, which is
attuned to the embodied materialism of a non-unitary vision of the subject.
Todd May sums it up quite clearly: 'By undercutting the pretensions of
humanism, poststructuralists hope to draw our attention to the many
small, contingent and often dispersed practices that contribute to who we
are and to our concept of ourselves as primarily self-constituting beings'
(May 1995: 71). Ethics is therefore the discourse about forces, desires and
values that act as empowering modes of being, whereas morality is the
established sets of rules. Philosophical nomadism shares Nietzsche's dis-
taste for morality as sets of negative, resentful emotions and life-denying
reactive passions. Deleuze links this with the Spinozist ethics of affirmation to produce a very accountable and concrete ethical line about joyful
affirmation. More of this in chapters 4 and 5.

As D. W. Smith (2000) rightly signals, this also affects Deleuze's relationship to Kantian ethics. Although Kant is not one of Deleuze's favourite
thinkers, he praises Kant's integrity in pursuing the task of critique as the
main aim of philosophical inquiry and in applying critical thought to
reason itself. Kant, somewhat paradoxically, paves the way for the purely
immanent critique of reason, which Deleuze also pursues. He overthrows
the Kantian project of transcendence and the centrality of consciousness,
replacing it with his dynamic and rhizomic subject-in-becoming.

In moral philosophy, however, one touches Kant at one's risk and peril.
Thus, in her attack on poststructuralist theories in general and the feminist
ones in particular, Sabina Lovibond (1994) expresses her concern at the
loss of moral authority that is entailed by a non-unitary vision of the
subject. Relying on Kantian philosophy, Lovibond raises the question
whether 'an ironic or suspicious attitude to the regulative ideals of rational
discourse' (1994: 65) allows us to make any normative judgement on any
issues at all. Convinced that the rejection of the Enlightenment-based
categories, such as 'emancipation' or 'progress', leaves us in a moral
limbo, Lovibond also questions the interpretations of Nietzsche by postmodern philosophers, whom she argues misread his critique and make it
far more radical than the texts allow. The key notion, predictably, is the
extent to which in a Nietzschean perspective – just as much as for Foucault,
Deleuze and other poststructuralists – ethical conduct is linked to knowledge and to cognitive states. Morality, in this perspective, concerns an
orientation towards truth and is as much an epistemological as an ethical
endeavour. Although she is concerned by the element of rationalist aggression implicit in this attitude, Lovibond is more worried by the rejection

of authorities and masters. Dismissing the Deleuzean argument against totalitarian structures and the persistence of micro-fascism, she appeals to notions of the integrated personality and stable representations of both reality and the self. Lovibond also opts for a broader, post-metaphysical acceptance of universal systems.

The Kantian agenda is restated as the only relevant one left after the debris of postmodernism, distinguishing between rationality and rationalism, morality and moralism in order to rescue the moral and cognitive power of universal reason. I would instead take the very opposite road and attempt to read poststructuralist philosophy in its own terms, rather than reducing it to the standards of a system of thought – in this case the Kantian tradition – that shares so little of its premises. Ethics relates to the anti-representational roots of contemporary poststructuralist philosophy and entails the critique of liberal individualism and its replacement by a nomadic view of subjectivity. The ethics of nomadic subjectivity rejects moral universalism and works towards a different idea of ethical accountability in the sense of a fundamental reconfiguration of our being in a world that is technologically and globally mediated.

UNIVERSALISM

My argument will move further in this section: moral philosophy is of hindrance, not of assistance, in dealing with the ethical complexities of our times. Let us take the case of moral universalism, one of the most vocal advocates of which is Martha Nussbaum. Nussbaum defends the need for universal values as a remedy for what she perceives as the fragmentation and the relativistic drift of poststructuralist philosophies. In opposition to such evils, Nussbaum posits her own brand of humanistic cosmopolitanism. This is also presented as an alternative to nationalism and ethnocentrism, which plague the contemporary world, and to the prevailing American attitude of ignorance of the rest of the world. For Nussbaum, the cosmopolitan exemplifies the abstract universalism as the only stance that is capable of providing firm foundations for moral values, such as compassion and respect. Nussbaum's recent work (1999a) reads as if she had claimed the monopoly over such basic values of human decency by allocating them exclusively to the philosophical tradition which she happens to represent: American liberal individualism.

Nussbaum's position is explicitly individualistic and it barely conceals a strong nostalgia for fixed identities, steady locations and ties that bind. Nussbaum's attachment to liberal bourgeois notions of the individual also implies the acceptance of the dualistic opposition between self and other, which remains unproblematic in Nussbaum's moral universe. This self-assurance is inconsistent with Nussbaum's work on the centrality of the emotions and passions (1986) and hence the vital importance of negotiating the boundaries between self and other in a non-violent manner. For Nussbaum, the individual can only be conceived as either part of a global entity – family, state, nation, humanity, the cosmos – or, on the contrary, as splintered off and atomized. In turn, Nussbaum's line positions language as an instrument of communication and banks on human affectivity – especially the qualities of identification and empathy – as the only possible moral bridges between the various atomized particles. This position does not split or open, but rather solidifies the subject. An individualistic position thus clashes with Nussbaum's cosmopolitan claims.

In his comparative reading of Nussbaum's brand of cosmopolitanism with Adrienne Rich's transnational feminist ethics, Homi Bhabha (1996) expresses some pertinent criticism of the former. Questioning the sign and value attributed to 'humanness' in Nussbaum's notion of the 'cosmopolitan' in the framework of global relations of power, Bhabha critiques the notion of the 'self' that is implicit in this position. As a spatial notion, it sets 'the self at the centre of a series of concentric circles that move through the various cycles of familial, ethnic and communal affiliations, to the largest one, that of humanity as a whole' (Bhabha 1996: 200). This produces a profoundly provincial brand of universalism: 'provincial', in a specific, early imperial sense. Nussbaum too readily assumes the 'givenness' of a commonality that centres on a particular image of the 'empathetic self' as it generates the 'cosmopolitan' concentric circles of equal measure and comparable worth. Playing his own politics of locations, Homi Bhabha challenges Nussbaum's backward-looking philosophical genealogy of Stoicism and Kant, by stressing the urgency to think about the ethical challenges of today's world – namely structural injustices, ecology, food supply and population. This amounts to disrupting Nussbaum's homogeneous definition of a community in terms of commonality of beliefs, norms and values. Choosing instead to emphasize the locations and specific problems of refugees, migrants, victims of global disruptions caused by war and ecological disasters, Bhabha questions the traditional sense of commonality that drives Nussbaum's cosmopolitanism.

By contrast, Adrienne Rich's work displays, according to Bhabha's analysis, 'an affective and ethical identification with "globality", premised on the need to establish a transhistorical "memory"' (Bhabha 1996: 201). Aware of the traumatic impact of specific historical events, such as the Holocaust, slavery, war, migration and diaspora, Rich activates a countermemory of places and times which respects the singularity of each historical event, thus avoiding easy parallelisms. This produces in Rich's work a deep sense of respect, identification and accountability. It has to do with a shared sense of 'a common humanity' ('We' are in *this* together), rendered through the poetic medium of memory. In Bhabha's reading the subject that sustains Rich's project does not instantiate the commonality of history and culture (*pace* Nussbaum) as much as the effort to revisit that history and account for it. Rich's project turns history into the transcription of traumatic events. Historical consciousness is a great connector among subjects who share it. It is a form of intervention that enacts accountability for the transnational places we all inhabit in late post-modernity. Bhabha defines this subject in terms of a fundamental restlessness, a 'translational' space: 'an interstitial temporality that stands in contention with both the return to an originary "essentialist" self-consciousness as well as a release into an endlessly fragmented subject-in-process' (Bhabha 1996: 204). This 'translational' brand of cosmopolitanism is set in opposition to Nussbaum's 'concentric cosmo-politan' and hence is a corrective to her provincial brand of universal values. In this shift, a unitary and 'home-bound' subject gets redefined in terms of multiple belongings, non-unitary selfhood and constant flows of transformation.

Nussbaum poses her provincial brand of cosmopolitanism as an alter-native to poststructuralism and feminist postmodernist theories, with a quality of over-zealous passion that does not do justice to either her erudi-tion or her philosophical competence. *Cultivating Humanity* (1999a) is a very influential statement in favour of a neo-liberal American appropria-tion of classical European humanism, mostly ancient ideals in education, culture and society. This strikes me as an eminent example of the practice that Eric Hobsbawm describes as 'the invention of traditions', which is 'essentially a process of formalization and ritualization, characterized by reference to the past, if only by imposing repetition' (Hobsbawm 1983: 4). There is, of course, a long-established tendency to identify US academic life with classical European 'high culture', but in Nussbaum's case the terms of this appropriation are not questioned. Thus, questions such as 'why neo-liberal humanism?' and 'why now?' are not even raised. Given that the publication of Nussbaum's pro-humanist manifesto was imme-diately followed by her virulent and – in my assessment – below-the-belt attack against feminist poststructuralist Judith Butler (Nussbaum 1999b), these are legitimate questions which cannot be waved away even by Nussbaum's passionate conviction that whatever she writes is endowed with immediate self-evidence. Nussbaum's philosophy rests on two basic assumptions, which run against the tenets of philosophical nomadism: firstly an unquestionable appeal to the authority of the history of philo-sophy and secondly the exercise of philosophical reason as a moral crusade.

This philosophical tradition is obviously at the antipodes of poststruc-turalist philosophy: Nussbaum's self-assertive brand of liberal individualism has little in common with the materialist theories of sub-jectivity proposed by those same philosophers whom she dismisses as relativist. For Foucault, Deleuze, Derrida and Irigaray, the critique of liberal individualism is a fundamental starting point and their main priority is how to rethink the interconnection between the self and society in a non-dualistic manner. They are especially concerned with disentan-gling the subject from the confining structures of Marxist theory. Of great relevance here is also the dialogue with the psychoanalytic theory of language, which historicizes and therefore politicizes the process of subject formation. According to poststructuralist psychoanalysis, language is what one is made of: it is an ontological site that defies rational let alone individual control. Thus, to suggest that it is a 'tool' is a humanist form of arrogance that does not help either the moral plan of bringing humanity together, nor the task of the social critic. Psychoanalysis also smashes any illusion of atomized individuality by embedding the subject in the thick materiality of a symbolic system of which language is the most available source. This allows for subtler analyses of the interaction between self and society and among different selves than liberal, ego-based psychology.

The specular double of the issue of universalism is the charge of alleged relativism that is moved against all who dare to question it. This charge is upheld by diehard champions of European rationality against postmodern thought, such as Gellner (1992), but is also rife within feminist theory.

Were it the case that the crisis of rationality and the loss of power and prestige of philosophy were merely the side-effects of poststructuralism and dated back to the 1960s radicals, the problem could easily be solved. That, however, is doing them too much honour: the crisis of philosophical reason has long-standing historical roots. Not unlike the debate on essentialism (Fuss 1989), the polemic over relativism has little to offer in the way of substantive issues.[1] Following the provocative stance proposed by Clifford Geertz (1984), I am more interested in the ways of thinking and the values that are proposed by the 'anti-relativists'. On closer scrutiny, these turn out to be authoritarian values, which attempt to stifle the opposition and hinder experimentalism with alternative approaches. Moral universalism activates the spectre of relativism as a force of intimidation and discouragement.

Consequently, two issues arise: the first is that, contrary to the panic-stricken universalists, an ethics worthy of the complexities of our times requires a fundamental redefinition of our understanding of the subject, and not a mere return to a more or less 'invented tradition'. Contrary to those who fear that the proliferation of micro-discourses will result in a realistic drift into nihilism, I see this process as productive of new and more adequate accounts of our being-in-the-world. Secondly, feminism, of all social movements, has been most eloquent and innovative in the production of new visions of the subject and new values. Contemporary feminist philosophy has a more general range of applications then ever before: it has a universalistic reach, if not a universalistic aspiration. It just so happens that feminist universalism is grounded, partial and accountable, according to the micro-political model also favoured by poststructuralism.

---

[1] For a scholarly analysis of this issue, see Barbara Herrnstein-Smith (1988).

On historical accountability

Nussbaum's unargued *assertion* of the universal value and validity of concepts like humanism, justice and American-style liberalism, has one formidable thing going for it: historical tradition. The historical sedimentation of these values gives them the appearance of self-evidence. Nussbaum fails to address the historicity of her position. Even more problematic are the implications of this debate for the practice of philosophy. In philosophical nomadism, the history of philosophy is not approached in a vacuum or out of context, but as a highly specific and therefore socially accountable event. Thus, the authoritative nature of the appeal to the history of philosophy is challenged. This is quite evident in the work of the poststructuralist philosophers Irigaray, Foucault and Deleuze. All of them engage critically, passionately and often violently with 'The History of Philosophy' and its complicity with forms of structural exclusion. Foucault's critique of discourse as power is also a quarrel with the classical institution of philosophical learning. Irigaray's mimetic dialogues with the masters of metaphysics is a way of interrogating the institutionalization and canonization processes by which dead white men become legislators of human truths. More radically still, Deleuze's meandering itinerary in and out of historical texts is constitutive of his anti-Oedipal philosophy.

Against Nussbaum, therefore, I would appeal here to the need to respect cultural differences among different traditions of philosophy and to defend poststructuralism as radical critique of both the institutional power and the corporate identity of philosophy, as well as the explicit role it plays in upholding eurocentrism. Furthermore, the mere appeal to the authority of experience and history, as well as the sovereignty of the humanist tradition, is an ineffectual way of dealing with the complexities of our times. The fast rate of change, as well as the paradoxical power relations of late postmodernity are such as to require more accurate cartographies and a higher degree of conceptual creativity on the part of critical thinkers. On this point, I am in agreement with Benhabib who defines feminist theorists as 'brokers in the complex renegotiation of sexual difference and new collective identities' (Benhabib 1999: 357).

The debate about the history of philosophy also illustrates the conservative appeal to the authority of tradition – as embodied in an institutionalized disciplinary practice, and experienced as a comforting identity-forming 'habit'. Such habits are forms of legal addiction and critical theory should be disintoxicated from them through the injection of destabilizing creative thoughts that provoke some movement. I prefer to think of the relationship to the history of philosophy along the more humble but also intellectually more stimulating ways that both Jenny Lloyd and Gilles Deleuze taught me. I have often been struck by how similar Lloyd and Deleuze are on this point: both eminent Spinoza scholars, they never stopped questioning the history of philosophy. They did so, however, almost like a form of

apprenticeship towards their own philosophical style. When Deleuze
argues that learning to think philosophically is like learning to use colours
in painting – and that the history of philosophy is the necessary background training for the use of colour – he is elevating the question of 'style'
to a conceptually central position. This goes hand in hand with his conviction that philosophy today can only be the creation of concepts, i.e. creativity, not truth, is the issue at stake. It is the humble, patient, concrete and
pragmatic pursuit of the singular, in all its complexity and diversity. Such
a seemingly paradoxical assertion only makes sense if one remembers that
it assumes a nomadic, i.e. non-unitary, vision of the subject as a multi-
layered and dynamic entity. Philosophy is the construction of immanent
singular subjects and of perceptions, concepts and figurations that would
do justice to their complexity.

For Deleuze the history of philosophy is the most abstract branch of
this discipline – very analogous to a portrait gallery of great thinkers, who
need to be 'studied' and approached carefully. What I find convincing in
Deleuze and absent in Nussbaum is the idea of cultivating an approach,
that is to say a style of thinking, in a self-reflexive mode. An emphasis on
complexity does not mean a free fall into boundlessness. Similarly, from
the flexibility and multi-facetedness of the non-unitary subject it does not
follow, either logically or politically, that relativism is the only option. Just
because there is not one single centre it does not follow that all is in a state
of relativistic chaos.

For instance, Lloyd never disengages her own work of analysis and
commentary on historical texts from something akin to an intellectual
autobiography. Each philosopher marks, quite literally, a moment of
being. Some last longer than others; none is ever a quick fix. Philosophy
banks on the long term, and is aware of the selective and partial structure
of memory. Deleuze's statement that teaching philosophy is like compos-
ing a musical score again comes to mind here. Cultivating an approach,
like trying to learn a musical score, requires some powers of listening,
some deep respect for the text and its effects. It is about duration, repetition and thus, ultimately, about movement. Difficult texts get illuminated
over time, with the build-up of experience and under the motivation of
endless frustrations. A good philosophical course, but this is actually true
of any discipline, is a living tune that goes on resonating. You just can't
put it down or get it out of your mind. Understanding requires passion
as much as intelligence, emotion as much as erudition. I shall return to
this in chapter 4.

The question of Europe as or in philosophy

In Continental philosophy, one can hardly separate the actual discipline
from its history. This makes philosophical issues constitutive of European

identity. Ever since the Second World War and especially in France, powerful critiques have been developed of the institution of philosophy, of its discursive and social prestige and the role it played in sustaining both the Enlightenment ideals and also oppressive, exclusionary and discriminatory modes of thought. Episodes that are central to European history, such as colonialism, fascism and the persistence of anti-Semitism and racism, not to mention the continuing marginalization of women in the practice of scientific research, mainstream scientific theory and practice, and other forms of citizenship, have made necessary a critique of the power of philosophy.

It is difficult to underestimate the relevance of the question of Europe in or as philosophy. 'Europe' is a philosophical notion and, conversely, philosophical discourse has played a major role in constructing European identity. Central to this is the notion of 'difference' as disparagement, which is constitutive of both European identity and of a philosophical tradition which defines the Subject in terms of Sameness, that is to say as coinciding with a set of qualities and entitlements. Thus, Subjectivity equates with consciousness, rationality and self-regulating ethical behaviour. Such a view implies a dialectic of Others, which are defined in terms of negative difference and function as the specular counterpart of the Subject. These are sexualized, racialized and naturalized others.

In so far as difference spells inferiority, it acquires both essentialist and lethal connotations for people who get branded as 'others' and reduced to the status of disposable bodies. They become slightly less human and consequently more mortal than those who fall under the category of 'Sameness'. The fact that difference as disparagement is constitutive of the self-asserting power of Sameness makes it a foundational concept. Because the history of difference in Europe has been one of lethal exclusions and fatal disqualifications, it is a notion for which feminists and other critical intellectuals have made themselves accountable. I will expand on this in chapters 2 and 3.

Philosophy is played out on this dialectical juxtaposition of Sameness and specular Otherness and it thus implicitly raises issues of power, exclusion and disqualification. This also means that the question of the Subject, of His identity and of His function in the pursuit of philosophical truth is very central and it touches upon the very purpose and social relevance of the discipline of philosophy and is intrinsic to the exercise of critical thought.

This issue became all the more poignant and ethically urgent in the aftermath of the moral and political bankruptcy of Europe after the Second World War and Nazism. The critical analysis of this period has seen different and often conflicting practices of critical theory, emerging mostly from the German and French schools. There is not much love lost between them, of course (as often has been the case in the history of Western philosophy), but a great deal of cross-fire, little cross-reference and much polemic.

That mutual hostility damaged an already impoverished European philosophical landscape. It may be worth remembering here that historically the United States became the main beneficiary of the forced exodus, also known as the great intellectual migration of European Jewish communist, gay and other dissident intellectuals who opposed fascism and Nazism. The United States thus emerged from the war with a respectable human capital of radical thinkers, some of whom – like Adorno and Brecht – returned to Europe, whereas others – Arendt, Marcuse, Hirschman – stayed on. It is no understatement to say that Continental Europe, on the other hand, emerged from the war as a philosophical wasteland. Only the return of the previously exiled dissident, mostly Marxist, Jewish, or communist intellectuals, helped to ensure the continuity of a tradition of critical thought which had been violently and forcefully truncated by fascism. This is too complex an issue for me to deal with adequately here, but let me just say that in the post-1989 era after the end of the Cold War it has finally become possible, as well as necessary, to think the geopolitics of European philosophy with more freedom and lucidity than had been the case before.

Fascism marked a violent disruption in the history of European philosophy: by the end of the Second World War Europe had chased away, or brutally murdered, the thinkers who had invented and developed critical theory, notably Marxists, psychoanalysts and those who practised Nietzschean affirmative ethics (as opposed to the fascistic distortion of his work). Throughout the post-war period the context of the Cold War and the opposition of the two blocs, which kept Europe and the world split and dichotomized, did not facilitate the resurgence of those critical theories. Their reimplantation back into the Continent, which had eradicated them with such violent self-destruction, entailed a discussion of the long shadow of fascism and Nazism upon European cultural and intellectual history. This theme had been put on the agenda after the Second World War by the Marxist and anti-fascist resistance, and it became a crucial point for the poststructuralist generation and its critique of totalitarianism in all its forms. In this regard it is significant that the poststructuralists reappraised as heralding the philosophy of critical modernity those very thinkers – especially Marx and Freud – whom the Nazis had banned. The case of Nietzsche deserves more consideration than I can grant it here.[2]

We need a far more detailed study of the effects of geopolitics and international relations upon the institutional practice of philosophy. This genealogical account would be extremely useful in order to historicize, contextualize and thus assess the changes that have come over philo-

[2] For an enlightening philosophical analysis, see Schrift (1995).

sophical thought since the end of the Cold War, as well as in the project of European integration. Just as critical philosophy in Europe after fascism could only be on and of the Left, inspired by anti-fascism and Marxism, so there is no such thing in Europe as a right-wing feminist: the two terms are mutually exclusive. It also follows that critical theory could not avoid issues of European identity and the crisis of European humanism, in so far as it attempted to face up to Europe's role in developing fascism and triggering the Second World War. This alone is a major point of difference with the Anglo-American philosophical tradition.

The first generation of post-war critical philosophers started the analysis and critique of the role of European philosophy in the demise of European identity and values with and after fascism. Zygmunt Bauman shares this point of departure. If we acknowledge that the modern age has reached, in the historical phase of postmodernity, 'its self-critical, often self-denigrating and in many ways self-dismantling stage' (Bauman 1993: 2), the ethical theories of the past begin to appear like blind alleys. Modernity reached an aporetic moral condition by marching under the twin banners of universality and firm foundations. The former subjects everyone to the exceptionless rule of law, while the latter declares foundations to be the coercive powers of the state. The opposition between the two and the claim of rational individualism leads to an aporetic impasse, the worst examples of which are revolutionary violence and totalitarianism. These threaten the common good and undermine the autonomous responsibility of the moral self, while proclaiming loudly the need for clear and stable values. This historical position opens up 'the possibility of a radically novel understanding of moral phenomena' (Bauman 1993: 2). Emphasizing the continuing relevance of issues such as 'human rights, social justice, balance between peaceful co-operation and personal self-assertion, synchronization of individual contact and collective welfare' (Bauman 1993: 4), Bauman insists on the need to develop new and original ways of dealing with these questions within the horizon of postmodernity. Lamenting the facile association of the postmodern era with the demise of ethics, Bauman stresses instead the specific ethical challenge represented by postmodernity. This can be summed up as an increased degree of self-examination, the loss of the grandiose illusions that drove modernity to excess and a renewed sense of sobriety in setting social and moral goals. Postmodernity is modernity without illusions.

Challenging the Kantian equation of moral and legal laws, Bauman stresses the gratuitousness, the lack of self-interest and hence the profoundly non-rational nature of many moral choices which are made for the good of the world. This essential gratuitousness defeats the logic of means–end reasoning, the economist's calculations of profit and loss, which is so central to mainstream morality. Bauman criticizes the (false) universalism that consists in imposing on all a will from above. The postmodern ethical project stresses instead the primacy of ethics over politics in the constitution of the subject. The main point of Bauman's passionate plea for a renewal of ethics is the rejection of the vulgar idea that the postmodern condition leads to relativism and nihilism. The postmodern approach is, rather, the rediscovery of a sense of historical accountability. The issue of power is central to Bauman's thought, which situates ethics as the critique of the conflation of value with state powers. He also attacks the universalizing claims of state powers and the nationalist ideologies that invent traditions and claim territories for real or fictional nation-states. Bauman is equally scathing, however, against the neo-tribalism of the many self-appointed prophets who capitalize on nationalism and other forms of cultural essentialism. Instead of such cast-iron convictions based on newly reinvented foundations, he calls for the moral self to accept 'the inherent and incurable ambivalence in which the responsibility cast it and which is already its fate, still waiting to be recast into its destiny' (Bauman 1993: 15).

The discussion about the ethical implications of European history for the philosophical discussion of the dialectical and binary relationship between self and other shifts to France in the post-Second World War period. France acted as the regenerator of a self-reflexive and critical Continental philosophy of the subject, alongside the Frankfurt School, the Yugoslav school of Marxism and the southern European, mostly Italian, brands of 'Euro-communism'. This has a great deal to do with the moral stature of France in the resistance to the Nazi aggressors. This historical role is currently being reappraised in the light of new evidence that has emerged from archives since 1989, which I cannot adequately cover here. Suffice it to say that France has played this historical role of the motor for European self-reflexivity, which has resulted in a somewhat inflated association of French thought with 'radicalism' and even subversion. It is important to re-establish a link between this tradition of philosophical radicalism and anti-fascism as a historical and intellectual movement. French philosophy from Sartre to Deleuze plays a central role in this discussion.

The generation that came of age politically in 1968 introduced a radical critique of the by then untouchable systems of thought which had founded and guided critical theory before, during (albeit in exile) and after European fascism – namely Marxism and psychoanalysis and their respective reliance on Hegel. The poststructuralists called for a creative reappraisal of the key texts of these traditions, in opposition to the orthodox and canonical interpretations on Marx and Freud that were defended respectively by the (Western) European communist parties and by the International Psychoanalytic Association. The new forms of philosophical radicalism developed in France in the late 1960s are a vocal critique of the dogmatic structure of communist thought and practice. It included a critique of the alliance between philosophers like Sartre and Beauvoir and the French Communist Party – at least until the Hungarian insurrection of 1956. In response to the dogma and the violence, the generation of the poststructuralists appealed directly to the subversive potential of the texts of Marxism and psychoanalysis, so as to recover their anti-institutional roots. Their radicalism was expressed in terms of a critique of the humanistic implications and the political conservatism of the institutions that embodied Marxist and psychoanalytic dogma. Contrary to today's revisionist thinkers who flatly equate communism with Nazism, the poststructuralists respect the specificity of these historical events. They did not reject the bulk of Marx and Freud, but rather endeavoured to recover and develop the radical core. In their view, the crux of the problem was the theory of the subject which is implicit in these theories: under the cover of the unconscious, or the bulk of historical materialism, the subject of critical European theory preserved a unitary, hegemonic and royal place as the motor of human history. This is the implicit humanism that triggered the criticism of thinkers like Foucault, Irigaray and Deleuze (to name only my favourite ones). The rejection of humanistic assumptions therefore took the form of unhinging the subject, freeing it respectively from the dictatorship of a libido dominated by Oedipal jealousy, and from the linearity of a historical *telos* which had married reason to the revolution, both of them vowing violence.

This reappraisal of the founding texts of the critical theory tradition within Europe coincided with the explosion of the new social movements of the 1960s and 1970s, especially the women's movement, in a historical context of decolonization and progressive dislocation of Europe's hegemonic hold over world affairs. Post-colonialism is one of the major expressions of the historical condition of postmodernity.

The radical philosophies, which later will become labelled as 'poststructuralism', represent a moment of great theoretical creativity. They repossess the Marxist and psychoanalytic texts, promoting the importance of open-ended reinterpretation of the actual theories (Coward and Ellis 1977). Althusser and Lacan, the founding figures of this historical development, broke from existentialism by heralding a 'return' to the materialist roots of continental critical philosophy, via a radical reading of Marxism and psychoanalysis as critiques of the unitary subject of humanism. It was not a straightforward turning back, of course, but a more complex foundational gesture, which coincided also with a change of generation.

The issue of European consciousness is built into critical philosophy. The most prominent figure of May 1968, for instance, now very active in the European Parliament, Danny Cohn-Bendit, is almost the embodiment of a whole – till then frozen – slab of European history: Franco-German background, anti-fascist family background; Jewish, intellectual. The shadow of the Holocaust and the events of the Second World War was noticeable in the events of May 1968: 'Nous sommes tous des juifs allemands' ('We are all German Jews') chanted the students in Paris, while those in Prague put flowers into the mouths of the guns of the Soviet Red Army, which had just invaded and squashed their spring of hope and liberation. This is the 68-generation. The same generation chanted 'Power to the imagination!' and elected John Lennon's 'Imagine' to the status of an anthem. This is Europe's equivalent to the Californian flower power movement; Europe's continuing saga of structural privilege and unmentionable misery, internal divisions and endless production of pejorative differences. This is also, however, a whole new story waiting to be told and dying to be revealed.

The political culture of the European left in the 1960s and 1970s was one of sustained ambivalence towards the United States. On the one hand American culture had emerged from the Second World War not only morally and politically triumphant, but also enriched by the largest concentration of anti-fascist Marxist intellectuals in the 'free' world – as a result of the great exodus of Jewish and Marxist scholars and thinkers. This was enough to inflame the imagination of the European youth of the day, who looked to the United States for inspiration about dissidence, civil rights and civil resistance. California was especially important, with its 'flower power', 'black is beautiful' and 'sisterhood is powerful' political movements. On the other hand, considering the continuing division of Europe during the Cold War years, and especially after the effect of McCarthy's witch-hunt against left-wing sympathizers, a militant brand of anti-Americanism became *de rigueur* in the European Left.

Central to this brand of anti-Americanism was the resentment against the presence of nuclear warheads in the NATO bases scattered across what was then Western Europe. The issue of anti-nuclear peace movements cannot be underestimated as a factor that marked the post-war European generations. For a while, the resistance against the war in Vietnam provided a rallying point across the two shores of the Atlantic and as such it can be considered a defining moment in post-war political culture. The long shadow of Hiroshima and Nagasaki, however, also needs to be taken into account in this discussion. This infamous display of war violence shocked the world and dispelled a great deal of the capital of good will which the United States had accumulated after defeating Nazism. The 'post-nuclear' predicament, as it was to be known later, opened an era of insecurity on an unprecedented global scale. The fact is that science and technology, in the nuclear era, far from becoming factors that improve humanity's condition, have turned into threats to our common survival and put scientific rationality to the test. It is not exaggerated to say that the nuclear standoff and the 'balance of terror' between the United States and the Soviet Union after the Second World War combined with the trauma of the Holocaust to make the post-war generations in Europe very sceptical about the liberating powers of science and technological reason. It also inscribes pacifism as one of the features of the

European left. Cornel West describes the critical theories of post-war Europe as follows: 'These diverse and disparate theories – all preoccupied with keeping alive radical projects after the end of the Age of Europe – tend to fuse versions of transgressive European modernisms with Marxists or post-Marxist left politics and unanimously shun the term "postmodernism" '(1990: 26).

In the *Abécédaire* (1996), Deleuze speaks of the European Left of the 1960s and 1970s in terms of a specific sensibility, a creative imaginary and a desire for change that constitutionally clashes with the guardians of the *status quo*: the judges and managers of truths and the clarity fetishists.[3] Deleuze distances himself from both the nefarious illusion of revolutionary purity, which engenders violence and the universalistic utopian element of Marxism, which inflates the intellectual to the role of representative of the masses. In a much more grounded and ascetic tone, Deleuze sets the desire for transformations or becomings at the centre of the agenda. Politics is ultimately a matter of existential temperature, of passions and yearning. It is about engendering and sustaining processes of 'becoming' – a concept that is central to philosophical nomadism. This specific sensibility combines a strong historical memory with consciousness and the desire for resistance. It rejects the sanctimonious, dogmatic tone of dominant ideologies, Left or Right of the political spectrum, in favour of a production of joyful acts of transformation.

Poststructuralism is historically embedded in the crisis of European humanism, the critique of phallocentrism and the dislocation of European hegemony (see chapter 2). It is also just as firmly rooted in the critique of American imperial tendencies and military power.

The philosophical generation that proclaimed the 'death of man' was simultaneously anti-fascist, post-communist and post-humanist; it led to the rejection of the classical definition of European identity in terms of humanism, rationality and the universal. The philosophies of sexual difference, expressed by Irigaray, Cixous and others, through the spectrum of the critique of dominant masculinity, also stress the ethnocentric nature of European identity and the need to open it up to the 'others within' in such a way as to relocate diversity as a structural component of European subjectivity. Best expressed in Julia Kristeva's idea of becoming 'foreigners to ourselves' (1991), this deconstructed vision of the European subject is active also in Irigaray's thought about Eastern philosophy (1997) and in Cixous's reappraisal of her Algerian Jewish roots (1997). Gayatri Spivak is the key figure in creating a junction between the early poststructuralist deconstruction of the powers of sameness in European philosophy, and the vocal emergence of new post-colonial subjects who do not recognize the centrality of the historical inevitability of European hegemony.

---

[3] With thanks to Gayatri Spivak for this formulation.

Anthony Appiah (1991) reminded us of the need not to confuse the 'post' of post-coloniality with the 'post' of postmodernism, but to respect instead the specific historical locations of each. The work of Michel Foucault, Jacques Derrida (1997), Massimo Cacciari (1994) and Gilles Deleuze (Deleuze and Guattari 1980), to name but a few contemporary European philosophers, points strongly in this direction. The work of the opposition to these philosophers, be it Ernest Gellner or, for that matter, Martha Nussbaum, on the other hand, takes the form of the rejection of the very idea of a crisis of European humanism, let alone its historical decline.

The poststructuralist approach builds on the psychoanalytic notion of an open-ended or non-unitary subject activated by desire. Deleuze and Guattari especially take the instance of the unconscious not as the black box, or obscure god, of some guilt-ridden subject of lack, but rather as a receptor and activator of gratuitous forms of unprogrammed interconnections. This situates sensuality, affectivity, empathy and desire as core values in the discussion about the ethics of contemporary non-unitary subjects. Equally central to this generation of philosophers is the focus on power as both restrictive (*potestas*) and productive (*potentia*) force. This means that power formations, previously know as 'ideology', are expressed in systems of representation, narratives and modes of identification. These are neither coherent nor rational, and their makeshift nature, far from diminishing their effectiveness, is crucial to their hegemonic power. The awareness of the instability and the lack of coherence of the narratives that compose the social text, far from resulting in a suspension of political and moral action, becomes for the poststructuralists the starting point to elaborate a form of political resistance suited to the paradoxes of this historical condition. For instance, in relation to the issue of European hegemony, the crisis of European humanism and the shift in geopolitical relations towards a post-colonial, transnational world-order, a poststructuralist approach is quite distinct.

In a more sardonic vein, Spivak turns the tables on the deconstruction of ethnocentrism by suggesting that this high level of self-reflexivity is merely Europe's exacerbated expression of its discursive hegemony in the mode of a weakened or decentered subjectivity. Thus paradoxically, Western philosophical culture announces a lasting state of 'crisis' as the preferred mode of perpetuating itself. For Spivak the 'crisis' of European identity has become the *modus vivendi* of Western philosophers and its chosen manner of silencing the vocal minorities that crowd the margins of the globalized world. Gayatri Spivak comments (1992):

Given the international division of labor of the imperialist countries, it is quite appropriate that the best critique of the European ethico-politico-social universals, those regulative concepts, should come from the North Atlantic. But what is ironically appropriate in postcoloniality is that this critique finds its best staging outside of the North Atlantic in the undoing of imperialism.

I do not share Spivak's cynical dismissal of critiques of Eurocentrism by European philosophers. They highlight one of the central paradoxes of the postmodern historical condition – one which pitches centre versus periphery in a manner so complex and so perverse as to require that we think the simultaneity of potentially contradictory social effects. The response to this challenge is neither the exaltation of neo-universalism, nor the retreat into relativism, but rather a neo-materialist discursive ethics based on non-unitary subjectivity and hence on multiple forms of accountability. Poststructuralist philosophers provide such a response.

This includes humble and sincere accountability for historical aspects of European culture, like colonialism and fascism, which are in open contradiction with Europe's stated beliefs in humanist ideals and rational principles. Donna Haraway sums up admirably this mixture of affects:

> Shaped as an insider and an outsider to the hegemonic power and discourses of my European and North American legacies, I remember that anti-Semitism and misogyny intensified in the Renaissance and the Scientific Revolution of early modern Europe, that racism and colonialism flourished in the travelling habits of the cosmopolitan Enlightenment and that the intensified misery of billions of men and women seems organically rooted in the freedoms of transnational capitalism and technoscience. But I also remember the dreams and achievements of contingent freedoms, situated knowledges and relief of suffering that are inextricable from this contaminated triple historical heritage. I remain a child of the Scientific revolution, the Enlightenment and technoscience. (Haraway 1997: 3)

The fact that thinking is a nomadic activity, which takes place in the transitions between potentially contradictory positions, does not make it a view from nowhere. To be nomadic or in transition, therefore, does not place the thinking subject outside history or time. Thinking may not be topologically bound, especially in the age of the global economy and telematic networks, but this does not make it ungrounded. Postmodernity as a specific moment of our historicity is a major location that needs to be accounted for. A location is an embedded and embodied memory: it is a set of countermemories, which are activated by the resisting thinker against the grain of the dominant representations of subjectivity. A location is a materialist temporal and spatial site of co-production of the subject, and thus anything but an instance of relativism. Locations provide the ground for accountability. I will pursue this approach in the next two sections.

A CARTOGRAPHY OF GLOCAL POWERS

All other differences aside, moral philosophy and poststructuralist ethics rest on fundamentally different cartographies of power. I do not think it acceptable, in the age of globalization, to raise any issues related to ethics or to morality independently of considerations of power and power relations. Power as *potestas* (hindering) or as *potentia* (enabling); power as a circulation of complex and dynamic, albeit contradictory, effects, simply cannot be left out of the discussion on ethics and values. At times contemporary moral philosophy comes across as comfortably installed in a consensus about the context free nature of its deliberations. As a materialist nomadic feminist philosopher, however, I want to stress the urgency of rewriting issues of power, of economic and geopolitical exclusion and of modes of production and reproduction at the heart of the ethical agenda.

The socio-economic conditions of advanced capitalism resulted in a global form of post-humanism: the traditional unitary subject-position has become displaced under the contradictory pressure of global, post-industrial social relations. The most distinctive trait of contemporary culture and society is the convergence between different and previously differentiated branches of technology. This reflects also the trans-disciplinary or nomadic structure of contemporary scientific thinking (Stengers 1997). The distinction between bio-technologies and genetic engineering on the one hand and information and communication technologies on the other is untenable. They are equally co-present in driving home the spectacular effects of contemporary technological transformations, especially in terms of their impact on the gendered human subjects, who are the focus of my inquiry. All technologies have a strong 'bio-power' effect, in that they affect bodies and immerse them in social relations of power, inclusion and exclusion (Bryld and Lykke 1999). Thus, cyborgs, in the sense of bodies that are technologically mediated, include not only the high-tech, fit bodies of jet-fighters, or of cultural icons from Hollywood, but also the anonymous masses of underpaid and exploited bodies of mostly women and children in off-shore production plants and in those increasing pockets of underpaid labour within advanced economies, who fuel the technologically driven global economy (Braidotti 2002).

Globalization, however, encompasses many other, less glamorous aspects: the rise of religious extremism in a variety of forms, including Christian fundamentalism, entails a political regression of the rights of women, homosexuals and all sexual minorities. Significant signs of this regression are the decline in reproductive rights and the rise of sexual violence. The increase in poverty, especially among women, and the disparity in access to the new technologies is another feature of the contemporary cartography. Bodily politics shifts accordingly with the simultaneous emergence of cyborgs on the one hand and renewed forms of vulnerability on the other. Thus, great epidemics have returned: Ebola, TB, HIV – so much so that health has become a public policy and security issue as well as a human rights concern.

The point is that the global economy does not function in a linear manner, but is rather web-like, scattered and poly-centered. It is not monolithic, but an internally contradictory process, the effects of which are differentiated geopolitically and along gender and ethnicity lines, to name only the main ones. This creates a few methodological difficulties for the social critic, because it translates into a heteroglossia of data which makes both classical and modernist social theories inadequate to cope with the complexities. We need to adopt non-linearity as a major principle and to develop cartographies of power that account for the paradoxes and contradictions of the era of globalization, and which do not take shortcuts through its complexities.

My position is pragmatic: we need schemes of thought and figurations that enable us to account in empowering and positive terms for the changes and transformations currently on the way. We already live in emancipated (post-feminist), multi-ethnic societies with high degrees of technological intervention. These are neither simple, nor linear events, but rather multi-layered and internally contradictory phenomena. They combine elements of ultra-modernity with splinters of neo-archaism: high-tech advances and neo-primitivism, which defy the logic of the excluded middle. Contemporary culture and institutional philosophy are unable to represent these realities adequately. They favour instead the predictably plaintive refrains about the end of ideologies, run concurrently with the apology of the 'new'. Nostalgia and hyper-consumerism join hands, under the expressionless gaze of neo-liberal restoration. The unitary vision of the subject cannot provide an effective antidote to the processes of fragmentation, flows and mutations, which mark our era. In ethics, as in many others fields of contemporary social endeavour, we need to learn to think differently about ourselves and our systems of values, starting with adequate cartographies of our embedded and embodied positions.

My own cartography of the globalization process would definitely involve the following: it is one of the distinctive traits of advanced capitalism (Beck 1992, 1999); it extends beyond the nation-states (Giddens 1994; Dahrendorf 1990; Appadurai 1994); it is head-less and centre-less, yet hegemonic (Grewal and Kaplan 1994); mobile and flexible, yet fixed and very local (Sassen 1994); inherently violent and ruthless, thus prone to self-destruction (Dahrendorf 1990); as a system, it is illogical and without an end-point, aiming only at self-perpetuation (Negri 1981); it has produced the paradox of simultaneously contradictory effects, namely the homogenization of commodity culture in terms of consumerist practices, coupled with huge disparities and structural inequalities. In the West this has resulted in promoting a transformation of the private sphere and a feminization of the public sphere (Giddens 1994). It promotes multiculturalism as a marketing strategy, while reiterating racialized stereotypes (Gilroy, 2000). It is embedded and supported by a major technological revolution, in the fields both of bio-technologies and of information technologies. They in turn result in the compression of the time-space continuum of modernity (Castells 1996).

On a more conceptual level, postmodernity as a historical moment marks the decline of some of the fundamental premises of the Enlightenment, namely the progress of mankind through a self-regulatory and teleologically ordained use of reason and of scientific rationality allegedly aimed at the 'perfectibility' of Man. The emancipatory project of modernity entails a view of 'the knowing subject' (Lloyd 1985) which excludes several 'boundary markers' also known as 'constitutive others'. These are: the sexualized other, also known as women, the ethnic or racialized others and the natural environment. They constitute the three interconnected facets of structural otherness or difference as pejoration, which simultaneously construct and are excluded in modernity (Beauvoir 1949; Irigaray 1974; Deleuze and Guattari 1980). As such they play an important – albeit specular – role in the definition of the norm, the norm-al, the norm-ative view of the subject. More specifically, they have been instrumental in the institution of masculine self-assertion (Woolf 1938), or the 'Logic of the Same' (Irigaray 1974). To say that the structural others of the modern subject re-emerge in postmodernity amounts to making them into a paradoxical and polyvalent site. They are simultaneously the symptom of the crisis of the subject, and for conservatives even its 'cause', but they also express positive, i.e. non-reactive alternatives. It is a historical fact that the great emancipatory movements of postmodernity are driven and fuelled by the resurgent 'others': the women's rights movement; the anti-racism and de-colonization movements; the anti-nuclear and pro-environment movements are the voices of the structural Others of modernity. They also inevitably mark the crisis of the former 'centre' or dominant subject-position. In the language of philosophical nomadology, they express both the crisis of the majority and the patterns of becoming of the minorities. In the next two chapters I will analyse this phenomenon in terms of processes of 'becoming': becoming-woman or sexualization, becoming-other or radicalization and becoming-animal/earth, or naturalization. The whole point about becomings consists in being able to tell the difference between these different flows of mutation. As I will argue throughout this book, the criterion by which such difference can be established is ethical and its implications political as well as cultural.

POST-HUMANISM

It is against the background of such a conservative social climate, that I want to challenge the monopoly that Anglo-American moral philosophy seems to claim over discussions on norms and values and to criticize it in the context of bio-technological societies. I would like to propose a more balanced kind of interaction between moral philosophy and poststructuralist ethics by making a special case for sustainable nomadic ethics to be accepted as a relevant and viable partner in this debate. We need new sets of translations across different philosophical cultures so as to rearrange the present segregation of discourses. Transpositions of ideas, norms, practices, communities and theoretical genealogies have to be allowed and even encouraged. This necessarily addresses corporate interests and pre-established divisions of labour, such as that between Anglo-American moral philosophy and the Continental poststructuralist tradition.

One of the most pointed paradoxes of our era is precisely the clash between the urgency of finding new and alternative modes of political and ethical agency on the one hand, and the inertia and self-interests of neo-conservatism on the other. The latter, as Fukuyama shows, promotes at best a general commitment to the 'new' that is little more than a rhetorical gesture, considering the pressure that vested interests are placing on reasserting individualistic neo-liberal values and power-relations. In this context, I want to side firmly with the technological forces, but against the liberal individualistic appropriation of their potential. Let me instead emphasize the liberatory and transgressive potential of these technologies, against the predatory forces that attempt to index them yet again onto a centralized, white, male, heterosexual, Eurocentric, capital-owning, standardized vision of the subject (Deleuze and Guattari 1972a; 1980). Moreover, in defending this position, I want to propose an alliance with moral philosophy from the angle of poststructuralist ethics. Such an alliance is based on the mutual respect of the specific philosophical features and traditions of each position. It is high time we moved beyond the ritualized and facile attacks against non-unitary philosophies of subjectivity, in order to take on the far more serious conceptual and political challenges of our times. I want to think through and alongside these challenges, not in order to play them back onto the classical humanistic subject position, but to explore their diversity and to develop adequate non-unitary, nomadic and yet accountable modes of envisaging both subjectivity and human ethical interaction.

The political economy of affects in advanced postmodernity needs to be taken into account, especially the fear of catastrophe or the imminence of a fatal accident. This 'eco-philosophical' dimension is very acute in contemporary culture and related forms of subjectivity. The predicament of the impending catastrophe that used to be represented by the nuclear threat nowadays has shifted to the imminent threat of ecological disaster, genetic mutation or immunity breakdown. As Brian Massumi put it in his analysis of the political regime of advanced capitalism (Massumi 1992b), in post-industrial global systems, the accident is virtually certain, its unfolding merely a question of time. This is a permanent and all-pervasive form of insecurity about the capacity of the present to sustain itself, and thus to engender the conditions of possibility for a sustainable future. It is important to live up to this insight, without precipitating paranoia or frenzy, which is the manic-depressive mode favoured by our culture. The first step to take is to confront the challenge of our historicity, thus resisting the traditional move that disconnects philosophical thought from its context. This move entails the assumption of responsibility or accountability so that one can engage actively with the social and cultural conditions that define one's location. The ultimate aim is to negotiate spaces of resistance to the new master narratives of the global economy. The second step entails the need to rethink affects in a less frenzied or paranoid mode than contemporary techno-culture allows: a more neutral manner. The bodily materialism that is promoted by philosophical nomadism offers some powerful alternatives to both the neo-determinism of the geneticists, the euphoria of their commercial and financial backers, and the techno-utopianism of their academic apologists.

A primary example of the political economy of fear is provided by one of the most vocal champions of contemporary conservative or neo-liberal restoration: Francis Fukuyama. He perpetuates his lifelong crusade against the French postmodern 'relativists', perfecting the perverse talent that consists in twisting every theory or event to make them fit the foregone conclusion about the inevitability of capitalism as the highest level of world historical progress and human evolution. The evidence provided by contemporary science (molecular biology, genetics and neurology) adds new ammunition to Fukuyama's clash of conceptualizations of the subject. Deterministic and firmly in favour of evolutionary psychology and the testosterone-driven theory of human evolution, the campaigner grabs another opportunity to bash the social constructivism of the Left and installs the belief in universal human genetic traits. A conservative pan-humanist neo-liberalism is the result of Fukuyama's attempt to both evoke and deny the complexities of contemporary techno-culture. Wary of the subversive potential of genetics, Fukuyama aims at containing it and framing it within the traditional values of the status quo: masculine authority, control of the young, the women and the ethnic others. The state needs to regulate the technologies of 'Life' according to these allegedly liberal principles, so as to allow for 'free choice', but within set limits: 'the kinder, gentler eugenics that is just over the horizon will then be a matter of individual choice on the part of parents and not something that a coercive state forces on its citizens' (Fukuyama 2002: 87). The neo-conservative thinker combines a rigid definition of scientific rationality with the fluidity of liberal individualism. This amounts to combining the worst of both systems in a nostalgic approach to contemporary techno-culture. To call all this 'humanism' merely adds insult to injury.

My quarrel with humanism, in such a context, has to do with the limitations of its own historical relevance in the present context. In other words, I do not have an implicit mistrust if its tenets, be it in the secular version of the Renaissance ideal, in the more Protestant version of humanist tolerance or in the universalistic mode of human rights. Classical humanism needs to be reviewed and opened up to the challenges and complexities of our times. I want to put my own conviction to the test, by addressing some concrete issues in the light of a politics of life defined as *bios/zoe* power, which opens the possibility of the proliferation of highly generative post-humanities.

My position in favour of complexity promotes a continuing emphasis on the radical ethics of transformation and it shifts the focus from unitary to nomadic subjectivity, thus running against the grain of contemporary neo-liberal conservatism. This rejects individualism, but also asserts an equally strong distance from relativism or nihilistic defeatism. A sustainable ethics for a non-unitary subject proposes an enlarged sense of interconnection between self and others, including the non-human or 'earth' others, by removing the obstacle of self-centred individualism. This is not the same as absolute loss of values, it rather implies a new way of combining self-interests with the well-being of an enlarged sense of community, which includes one's territorial or environmental interconnections. This is an ethical bond of an altogether different sort from the self-interests of an individual subject, as defined along the canonical lines of classical humanism. It is a nomadic eco-philosophy of multiple belongings.

This also affects the question of universal values. Contemporary science and bio-technologies affect the very fibre and structure of the living, creating a negative unity among humans. The Human Genome Project for instance unifies all the human species in the urgency to organize an opposition against commercially owned and profit-minded technologies. Franklin, Lury and Stacey refer to this situation as 'panhumanity' (2000: 26), that is to say a global sense of interconnection between the human and the non-human environment, as well as among the different subspecies within each category, which creates a web of intricate interdependencies. Most of this mutual dependence is of the negative kind: 'as a global population at shared risk of global environmental destruction and united by collective global images' (2000: 26). There are also positive elements, however, to this form of postmodern human interconnection. Franklin *et alia* argue that this re-universalization is one of the effects of the global economy and it is part of the recontextualization of the market economy currently under way. They also describe it in Deleuzian terms, as the 'unlimited finitude', or a 'visualization without horizon' and see it as a potentially positive source of resistance.

The paradox of this new pan-humanity is not only the sense of shared and associated risks, but also the pride in technological achievements and in the wealth that comes with them. In a more positive note, there is no doubt that 'we' are in *this* together. Any nomadic philosophy of sustainability worthy of its name will have to start from this assumption and

reiterate it as a fundamental value. The point, however, is to define
the 'we' part and the *this* content, that is to say the community in its
relation to singular subjects and the norms and values for a political eco-
philosophy of sustainability. The state of the debates on these issues in
fields as diverse as environmental, political, social and ethical theories, to
name just a few, shows however a range of potentially contradictory positions. From the 'world governance idea' to the ideal of a 'world ethos'
(Kung 1998), through a large variety of ecological brands of feminism, the
field is wide open. In other words, we are witnessing a proliferation of
locally situated universalist claims. Far from being a symptom of relativism, they assert the radical immanence of the subject. They constitute the
starting point for a web of intersecting forms of situated accountability,
that is to say an ethics. The whole point is to elaborate sets of criteria for
a new ethical system to be brought into being that steers a course between
humanistic nostalgia and neo-liberal euphoria. An ethics of sustainable
forces that takes life (as *bios* and as *zoe*) as the point of reference not for
the sake of restoration of unitary norms, or the celebration of the master
narrative of global profit, but for the sake of sustainability. I will return
to this in chapters 4 and 5.

This general and widespread call for new global values, popularized
in terms of the global civil society, lends strength to my main argument:
namely, that such a web of localized universalisms and glocal claims to
rethink the fact that 'we' are in *this* together, would benefit from and also
help implement a non-unitary vision of the ethical subject. In disagreement with the humanistic vision of unified consciousness as the supervi-
sor and owner of the truth about subjectivity, I offer a nomadic alternative
of a sustainable ethical subject as a way of radicalizing the humanistic
vision. We need to join forces against the swelling tide of the neo-
deterministic, neo-liberal master narratives of this early part of the third
millennium.

Instead of falling back on the sedimented habits of thought that past
tradition has institutionalized, I would like to propose a leap forward into
the complexities and paradoxes of our times. Whatever concept or practice of a new pan-humanity we may be able to come up with, can only be
a paradoxical mixture, which projects humanity in between a future that
cannot be guaranteed, and a fast rate of progress, which demands one.
What is ultimately at stake in this, as we shall see in the last two chapters
of this book, is the very possibility of the future, which is to say a sustainable present.

CONCLUSION: THE TRIUMPH OF *ZOE*

A crucial intersection of concerns about bodies and post-human embodiment emerges at the heart of contemporary subjects. They produce several

multi-layered discourses. I shall review them in details in the next two chapters. For now, let me stress the extent to which the management of Life in a post-human mode has taken centre stage in the political economy of advanced capitalism. This includes the proliferation of practices, both scientific and social, which go beyond human life. Contemporary genetics and bio-technologies are central to this shift towards post-human ideas of 'Life' or 'Zoe', the non-human. The mutual interdependence of bodies and technologies creates a new symbiotic relationship between them. Cyborgs, or techno-bodies, are the subject of our prosthetic culture in a complex web of dynamics and technologically mediated social relations. This inaugurates an eco-philosophical approach to nomadic subjectivity, and hence also new ecologies of belonging. In the case of Deleuze and Guattari it also marks a radical critique of anthropocentrism in favour of the recognition of the entanglement of material, bio-cultural and symbolic forces in the making of the subject. I shall discuss 'bio-centred egalitarianism' and the notion of life forces, in chapter 4.

What 'returns' with the return of Life and of 'real bodies' at the end of postmodernism, under the impact of advanced technologies, is not only the others of the classical subject of modernity: woman/native/nature. What returns now is the 'other' of the living body in its humanistic definition: the other face of *bios*, that is to say *zoe*, the generative vitality of non- or pre-human or animal life. Accordingly, we are witnessing a proliferation of discourses that take 'Life' as a subject and not as the object of social and discursive practices.

Life is half-animal, non-human (*zoe*) and half-political and discursive (*bios*). *Zoe* is the poor half of a couple that foregrounds *bios* as the intelligent half; the relationship between them constitutes one of those qualitative distinctions on which Western culture built its discursive empire. Traditionally, the self-reflexive control over life is reserved for the humans, whereas the mere unfolding of biological sequences is for the non-humans. *Zoe* stands for the mindless vitality of Life carrying on independently of and regardless of rational control. This is the dubious privilege attributed to the non-humans and to all the 'others' of Man, whereas *bios* refers to the specific social nexus of humans. That these two competing notions of 'life' coincide on the human body turns the issue of embodiment into a contested space and a political arena. The mind–body dualism has historically functioned as a short-cut through the complexities of this question, by introducing a criterion of distinction, which is sexualized, racialized and naturalized. Given that this concept of 'the human' was colonized by phallogocentrism, it has come to be identified with male, white, heterosexual, Christian, property-owning, standard-language-speaking citizens. *Zoe* marks the outside of this vision of the subject, in spite of the efforts of evolutionary theory to strike a new relationship to the non-human. Contemporary scientific practices have forced us to touch the bottom of some inhumanity that connects to the human precisely in the immanence of its bodily materialism. With the genetic revolution we can speak of a generalized 'becoming infrahuman' of *bios*. The category of 'Life' has accordingly cracked under the strain.

In his unfinished magnum opus *The History of Sexuality*, Michel Foucault targets the notion of 'life' as one of its central concepts and attempts an analysis of this regime in terms of 'bio-power'. The regimes of modern government need to simultaneously include and control the biological, generative, living forces of the very people (*demos*) who constitute the social sphere (*polis*) of democratic regimes. According to Foucault, ever since modernity the aim of political power has been to control and thus govern the individual as representative of the species. This is shown by relatively recent phenomena such as population statistics, the control of reproductive and sexual behaviour, public health, mental as well as physical, and the gradual elimination of anomalies, defects and malfunctions among the population. A political technology of disciplining the bodies of the population has come into being, which takes the individual as a stand-in for the perpetuation of the species. According to Foucault regimes of 'bio-power' aim to include as fully controlled elements the very vital forces that, per definition, escape political control. The maternal feminine and hence the woman's body is a central player in this new negotiation of the boundaries with the powers of life (as *bios*/*zoe*). The fact that Foucault, in his chronic androcentrism, fails to see this obvious point while discussing the reproduction of the species, reflects poorly upon his work. Deleuze and Guattari on the one hand, and Irigaray and feminist theory on the other, travel much further down this road.

The political status of the individual as responsible for the survival of the species, that is, as an evolutionary and genetic unit, has been redefined by the post-nuclear predicament that concretizes the possibility of species extinction. Hence Foucault's famous formulation: 'For millennia man remained what he was for Aristotle: a living animal with the additional capacity for political existence; modern man is an animal whose politics calls his existence as a living being into question' (Foucault 1976: 188). The paradox of bio-political regimes is therefore that they unfold onto the question of death in the sense of elimination, exclusion and ever worse, extermination or extinction. The politics of bio-power affect those who are allowed to survive as well as those who are doomed to perish. It is a rather brutal regime of gradual, all-pervasive selection, which takes the form of distributing and controlling the forms of entitlement to 'life' understood as survival and perpetuation. As such, bio-power provides the grounding for a new political ontology.

A new generation of thinkers has taken over from where Foucault left off. For instance, Nicholas Rose (2001) suggests that bio-politics has become by now the dominant regime of control of bodies through a system of integrated scientific discourses and social mechanisms. As a consequence, argues Rose, Foucault's analysis needs to be updated nowadays and reinscribed into the political economy of risk management and security enforcement, which requires a responsible bio-citizen as the basic unit of reference. Rose defines this shift to a new 'ethopolitics' as a sort of generalized and largely self-implementing form of bio-political citizenship. Whereas work inspired by Foucault remains within the frame of Kantian responsibility and rational judgement, new reflections on the vitality of life following Deleuze and Guattari call for a radical revision of the very notion of life (Colebrook 2004). It is in this context that I situate my own work.

Giorgo Agamben plays different variations on the theme of *bios/zoe* by assimilating *zoe* to the economy of non-life in the sense of a failure of humaneness. More specifically, it refers to the human body's capacity to be reduced to non-human states by the intervention of sovereign power. *Zoe* is consequently assimilated to death in the sense of the corpse, the liminal bodily existence of a life that does not qualify as human. Agamben is the heir to Heidegger's thought on finitude; what he calls 'bare life' is 'the rest' after the humanized 'bio-logical' wrapping is taken over. 'Bare life' is that in you which sovereign power can kill. It is the body as disposable matter in the hands of the despotic force of power (*potestas*). 'Bare life' inscribes fluid vitality at the heart of the mechanisms of capture by the state system. Agamben is sensitive to the fact that this vitality, or 'aliveness', is all the more mortal for it. Pertaining to the Heideggerian tradition he stresses the tragic aspects of modernity: the cruelty, violence, wars, destruction and disruption of traditional ways. Agamben's 'bare life' marks the negative limit of modernity and the abyss of totalitarianism that constructs conditions of human passivity.

The position of *zoe* in Agamben's system is analogous to the role and the location of language in psychoanalytic theory: it is the site of constitution or capture of the subject. This 'capture' functions by positing as an *a posteriori* construction, a prelinguistic dimension of subjectivity which is apprehended as 'always already' lost and out of reach. *Zoe* – like Lacan's pre-discursive, Kristeva's *chora* and Irigaray's maternal feminine – becomes for Agamben the ever-receding horizon of an alterity, which has to be included as necessarily excluded in order to sustain the framing of the subject in the first place. This introduces finitude as a constitutive element within the framework of subjectivity. It also fuels an affective economy of loss and melancholia at the heart of the subject (Braidotti 2002). This view is linked to Heidegger's theory of Being as deriving its force from the annihilation of animal life. Agamben perpetuates the philosophical habit of taking mortality or finitude as the trans-historical horizon for discussions of 'life'. The fixation on Thanatos – which Nietzsche criticized over a century ago – is still very present in critical debates today. It often produces a gloomy and pessimistic vision not only of power, but also of the technological developments that propel the regimes of bio-power. I beg to differ from the habit that favours the deployment of the problem of *bios/zoe* on the horizon of death, or at the liminal state of not-life, or in the spectral economy of the never-dead. Instead, let me stress the generative powers of *zoe* by turning to the Spinozist ontology defended by Deleuze and Guattari (1972a; 1980).

No reason other than the sterility of habit justifies the emphasis on death as the horizon for the discussions on the limits of our understanding of the human. Why not look at the affirmative aspects of exactly the same issue? Speaking from the position of an embodied and embedded female subject I find the metaphysics of finitude a myopic way of putting the question of the limits of what we call life. It is not because Thanatos always wins out in the end that it should enjoy such conceptual high status. Death is overrated. The ultimate subtraction is after all only another phase in a generative process. Too bad that the relentless generative powers of death require the suppression of that which is the nearest and dearest to me, namely myself. For the narcissistic human subject, as psychoanalysis teaches us, it is unthinkable that life should go on without my own vital being-there. Freud was the first to analyse the blow that death inflicts on the fundamental narcissism of the human subject. The process of confronting the thinkability of a life that may not have 'me' or any 'human' at the centre is actually a sobering and instructive process. This is the very start for an ethics of sustainability that aims at shifting the focus towards the positivity of *zoe*.

By contrast to the positioning of *zoe* as the liminal condition of the living subject, its 'becoming corpse' so to speak, I want to think both the positivity of *zoe* and its being 'always already' there. This occurs in opposition to the Heideggerian legacy on finitude and death. It also rejects the reference to a linguistic model of interpretation that rests on the fundamental rules of metaphor of metonymy. As such it partakes of and is in turn constituted by the very dialectics of sameness and difference that I am committed to overcoming. Moreover, this model imposes the primacy of a representational way of thinking, which is inadequate given the schizoid and intrinsically non-linear structure of advanced capitalism. Representational thinking and the linguistic turn are outdated models to account for the kind of subjects we have already become. Instead, I opt for a neo-materialist, embodied and embedded approach. The key to this conceptual shift is the overturning of anthropocentrism as the bottom line of the critique of subjectivity. Poststructuralism initiated this critique by declaring, with Foucault, the 'death' of the humanistic subject of knowledge. Nowadays we are experiencing a further stage in this process and, as the rhizomic philosophies of Deleuze and Guattari point out, we are forced to confront the inbuilt anthropocentrism which prevents us from relinquishing the categorical divide between *bios* and *zoe* and thus makes us cling to the superiority of consciousness in spite of our poststructuralist scepticism towards this very notion. The monist political ontology of

Spinoza can rescue us from this contradiction, by pushing it to the point of implosion. Through the theory of nomadic becomings or plane of immanence, the subject is dissolved and re-grounded in an eco-philosophy of multiple belongings. This takes the form of a strong emphasis on the pre-human or even non-human elements that compose the web of forces, intensities and encounters that contribute to the making of nomadic subjectivity. The subject is an ecological entity.

Zoe refers to the endless vitality of life as continuous becoming. Guattari and Simondon refer to this process as a transversal form of subjectivity or 'trans-individuality'. This mode of diffuse yet grounded subject-position achieves a double aim: firstly it critiques individualism and secondly it supports a notion of subjectivity in the sense of qualitative, transversal and group-oriented agency. Lest this be misunderstood for epistemological anarchy, let me emphasize a number of features of this cartography that takes life as the subject of political discourse. The first main point is that the technological body is in fact an ecological unit. This *zoe*-techno-body is marked by the interdependence with its environment through a structure of mutual flows and data transfer that is best configured by the notion of viral contamination (Ansell-Pearson 1997a), or intensive interconnectedness. This nomadic eco-philosophy of belonging is complex and multi-layered.

Secondly, this environmentally bound subject is a collective entity, moving beyond the parameters of classical humanism and anthropocentrism. The human organism is an in-between that is plugged into and connected to a variety of possible sources and forces. As such it is useful to define it as a machine, which does not mean an appliance or anything with a specifically utilitarian aim, but rather something that is simultaneously more abstract and more materially embedded. The minimalist definition of a body-machine is an embodied affective and intelligent entity that captures, processes and transforms energies and forces. Being environmentally bound and territorially based, an embodied entity feeds upon, incorporates and transforms its (natural, social, human, or technological) environment constantly. Being embodied in this high-tech ecological manner means being immersed in fields of constant flows and transformations. Not all of them are positive, of course, although in such a dynamic system this cannot be known or judged *a priori*.

Thirdly, such a subject of *bios*/*zoe* power raises questions of ethical urgency. Given the acceleration of processes of change, how can we tell the difference among the different flows of changes and transformations? To answer these questions I shall develop a sustainable brand of nomadic ethics. The starting point is the relentless generative force of *bios*/*zoe* and the specific brand of trans-species egalitarianism, which they establish with the human. The ecological dimension of philosophical nomadism consequently becomes manifest and, with it, its potential ethical impact. It is a matter of forces as well as of ethology.

Fourthly, the specific temporality of the subject needs to be rethought. The subject is an evolutionary engine, endowed with her or his own embodied temporality, in the sense of both the specific timing of the genetic code and the more genealogical time of individualized memories. If the embodied subject of bio-power is a complex molecular organism, a bio-chemical factory of steady and jumping genes, an evolutionary entity endowed with its own navigational tools and an inbuilt temporality, then we need a form of ethical values and political agency that reflects this high degree of complexity.

Fifthly, and last, this ethical approach cannot be dissociated from considerations of power. The *bios/zoe*-centered vision of the technologically mediated subject of postmodernity or advanced capitalism is fraught with internal contradictions. Accounting for them is the cartographic task of critical theory and an integral part of this project is to account for the implications they entail for the historically situated vision of the subject (Braidotti 2002). The *bios/zoe*-centred egalitarianism that is potentially conveyed by the current technological transformations has dire consequences for the humanistic vision of the subject. The potency of *bios/zoe*, in other words, displaces the humanistic vision of consciousness, which hinges on the sovereignty of the 'I'. It can no longer be safely assumed that consciousness coincides with subjectivity, nor that either of them is in charge of the course of historical events. Both liberal individualism and moral universalism are disrupted at their very foundations by the social and symbolic transformations induced by our historical condition. Far from being merely a crisis of values, this situation confronts us with a formidable set of new opportunities. Renewed conceptual creativity and a leap of the social imaginary are needed in order to meet the challenge. Classical humanism, with its rationalistic and anthropocentric assumptions, is of hindrance, rather than of assistance, in this process. Therefore, as one possible response to this challenge, I propose a post-humanistic brand of non-anthropocentric vitalism as an affirmative and productive force.

In the following two chapters I will outline my cartography of the emergence of *zoe*-power by following the ongoing transformations. These are occurring on the axes of classical 'difference', which are currently being transposed into lines of 'becoming'. Sexualization, racialization and naturalization transpose into becoming-woman/other/animal/earth, under the impact of emergence of 'Life' as a subject of political and ethical concern.

2

Transactions:
Transposing Difference

The human body itself is no longer part of 'the family of man', but a zoo of posthumanities.

> Judith Halberstam and Ira Livingston, *Posthuman Bodies*

If bio-diversity is thought good for other species and for the global ecosystem, why not for the human species and its bio-cultural ecosystems?

> Lucius Outlaw, *On Race and Philosophy*

There are more telephone lines in Manhattan than in all Sub-Saharan Africa.

> Zillah Eisenstein, *Global Obscenities*

INTRODUCTION

This chapter fulfils both an illustrative and a normative function by focusing on the transpositions occurring on two modes of becoming: woman and other. In the next chapter I will pursue this analysis by looking at the rest of the sequence: becoming-animal and imperceptible. I will provide a cartography of current debates on the social transformations induced by our technologically mediated world. This cartography supports my thesis that a nomadic, non-unitary vision of the subject, far from preventing ethically relevant statements, is a necessary precondition for the expression of an ethics that reflects the complexities of our times. I want to argue further that this ethics renews the emphasis on embodiment and immanence and hence contributes to an enlarged sense of rooted and accountable universals.

The three modes of transformative becoming that structure my analysis map out the location of what used to be the 'constitutive others' of the unitary subject of classical humanism. They mark respectively the sexualized bodies of women, the racialized bodies of ethnic or native others, and

There is always something deadening about the drive for "poverty" (understood broadly) as a precondition of thought.

the naturalized bodies of animals and 'earth others'. They form the inter-connected facets of structural otherness defined as a hierarchical scale of pejorative differences which takes its bearing from the centre or standard of Sameness. The interaction centre–periphery; same–other; particular–universal has shifted under the impact of globalized postmodernity. It no longer corresponds to a dialectical model of opposition, but rather follows a more dynamic, non-linear and hence less predictable pattern, which composes a zigzagging line of internally contradictory options. The 'others' are not merely the markers of exclusion or marginality, but also the sites of powerful and alternative subject-positions. Thus, the bodies of others become simultaneously disposable commodities and also deci-sive agents for political and ethical transformation (Braidotti 2002). To think the simultaneity of these opposite projects in a non-dialectical or nomadic mode of interaction requires a shift of perspective and adequate cartographies. To understand it as an ethical principle, we need creativity and trust in the future.

Post-industrial societies make 'differences' proliferate to ensure maximum profit. I want to explore how this logic of multiplying differ-ences triggers a consumerist or vampiric consumption of 'others', meaning new forms of micro-, infra- and counter-subjectivities. The unity of the subject of humanism is exploded into a web of diverse discourses and practices. This phenomenon, however, seems to leave miraculously unscathed the centuries-old forms of sexism, racism and anthropocentric arrogance that have marked our culture. The transformation of the axes of sexualized, racialized and naturalized difference form intersecting pat-terns of becoming. They compose a new political economy of otherness and are therefore of great ethical and political relevance.

BECOMING-WOMAN: TRANSPOSING SEXUAL DIFFERENCE

Global gender politics

At the end of postmodernism, as I announced in the prologue, new master-narratives have arisen: the inevitability of 'free' market economies as the historically dominant form of human progress and biological essen-tialism, under the cover of genetics, new evolutionary biology and psy-chology. They help define the salient features in contemporary gender politics and they constitute a disjunction, not a synthesis. The mainstream master discourse of neo-liberal post-feminism rests on the new genetic social imaginary and it marks the return of the most classical forms of economic and social discrimination. As Franklin (2000: 188) put it:

> We are currently witnessing the emergence of a new genomic govern-mentality – the regulation and surveillance of technologically assisted

genealogy. This is necessitated by the removal of the genomes of plants, animals and humans from the template of natural history that once secured their borders, and their re-animation as forms of corporate capital, in the context of a legal vacuum.

The 'post-feminist' wave has merged with neo-conservatism in gender relations, producing a mild effect of 'gender trouble' in the social division of labour between the sexes. Most men pay lip service to gender mainstreaming, while the new generations of corporate-minded businesswomen disavow any debt or allegiance to the collective struggles of women. 'Gender mainstreaming' turned out to be an anti-feminist mechanism that increased differences in status, access and entitlement among women. Post-feminist neo-liberalism is pro-capitalist and hence it considers financial success as the sole indicator of the status of women. Social failure is accordingly perceived as a lack of emancipation, which implies that social democratic principles of solidarity are misconstrued as old-fashioned welfare support and dismissed accordingly. The post-feminist master narrative reintroduces the syndrome of 'the exceptional woman', which was in place before the women's movement introduced more egalitarian principles of interconnection, solidarity and teamwork. The pernicious part of this syndrome is that it fosters a new sense of isolation among women and hence new forms of vulnerability.

Post-feminism also entails some formidable lapses of the historical memory: it engenders a revisionist approach that turns into feminist heroines women who had explicitly rejected or kept their distance from the women's movements. This includes strong individual personalities, mostly artists, such as Louise Bourgeois, Yoko Ono or Madonna. It can also empower public figures who happen to be women, like Madeleine Albright, Benazir Bhutto, Margaret Thatcher or Condoleeza Rice. This trend becomes more problematic, however, when it flattens out all other political considerations, as in the reappraisal of right-wing women. The most blatant case to date is that of the German Nazi supporter and filmmaker Leni Riefenstahl who, as shown in her autobiography (Riefenstahl 1992), suffered from the genius complex. A film director and artist of great talent, Riefenstahl rode the historical wave of Hitler's movement to her best advantage, filming masterful works such as *The Triumph of the Will* and *Olympia*. After the fall of the Nazis, she was singled out for the denazification programme and her work was banned for a long time. It may well be that – as a woman – she was made to pay for her mistakes far more than Martin Heidegger and other unrepentant Nazis. Nevertheless, I feel moral repulsion and strong political opposition to a single-minded reappraisal of this character solely on the ground of gender politics. Riefenstahl's fascist aesthetics perpetuates both the myth and the practice of white supremacy under the spurious guise of the emancipation of women (Gilroy 2000). It is unacceptable to disengage feminist politics and genealogies from the issue of race, ethnicity, domination, exclusion or the fight for democracy. Individualism pushed to the extreme breeds horror.

Post-feminist liberal individualism is simultaneously multicultural and profoundly ethnocentric. It celebrates differences, even in the racialized sense of the term, so long as they confirm to and uphold the logic of Sameness. Condoleeza Rice, a right-wing woman of colour, or Pim Fortuyn, a conservative Dutch gay politician, are emblematic examples of the repositioning of former 'others' within the precinct of masculine authority. Gender politics in neo-liberal discourse is complicitous with a discourse about white supremacy, where the term 'white', like all racialized signifiers, has no biological grounding, but indexes access to power and entitlement. The dominant discourse nowadays is that 'our women' (Western, Christian, white or 'whitened' and raised in the tradition of secular Enlightenment) are already liberated and thus do not need any more social incentives or emancipatory policies. 'Their women', however (non-Western, non-Christian, mostly not white and not integrated into white society, as well as alien to the Enlightenment tradition), are still backwards and need to be targeted for special emancipatory social actions or even more belligerent forms of enforced 'liberation'. This simplistic position reinstates a world-view based on colonial lines of demarcation. It fails to see the great grey areas in between the doubly pretentious claim that feminism has already succeeded in the West and is non-existent outside this region. The in-between degrees of complexity are the only ones that matter and they should be put at the centre of the agenda. The key point, however, is that women's bodies function in this discourse as bearers of authentic ethnic identity, and as indicators of the stage of development of their respective civilizational fault-lines.

Because of the structural injustices built into the globalization process, the current geopolitical situation of women is more polarized than ever. The imaginary surrounding the alleged 'clash of civilizations' (Huntington 1996) is explicitly gendered. It features at centre stage the ruling couple of an allegedly emancipated, ageing and liberated Western world, the emblem of which is the 'soft' and 'feminized' European Union. The EU is opposed to the 'masculine' US partner supervising the war of civilizations through its military power and its supreme contempt of international law. In opposition to them is a more virile, youthful and masculine non-Western world, of which Islamic culture is the standard-bearer.

Such a caricature of global power relations is postulated and fought out on women's bodies: one of the recent emblems of this is the Burka-clad bodies of the Afghan women in whose defence an anti-abortionist, arch-conservative and anti-feminist president, George W. Bush, cynically claimed to launch one of his many commercially driven wars of conquest. Sexual difference has returned to the world stage in a fundamentalist and reactionary version. In a context of global war, racism and xenophobia, this type of gender politics results in mutual and respective claims about authentic and unitary female identity on the part of the 'liberated' West and its allegedly traditionalist opponents. This is a play of specular and belligerent fundamentalisms: one with a post-industrial and the other with a pre-industrial face. They compose a single phenomenon that is best understood in terms of the resurgence of imperial sovereignty (Hardt and Negri 2000). It fails to take into account the precious, patient and pragmatic work accomplished by the women's movements in the world over the last thirty years, and especially in the non-Western world, such as RAWA (Revolutionary Association of Women of Afghanistan).

The genetic social imaginary

The second dominant master narrative of today concerns the social genetic imaginary, in the framework of the bio-technological revolution. The work of Franklin, Lury and Stacey (2000) is especially relevant to this discussion, as it focuses on the process of globalization for a critique of Western science and technologies. They argue that the era of the global economy can best be described as the cannibalization of nature by a global market, they also argue that this process is being matched by an increased sense of reterritorialization and consequently a re-invention of nature. They speak of a 'transmagnification' of nature (2000: 19), which is being refigured and revitalized by being completely saturated with technological culture, while also resisting it. Nature is more than the sum of its marketable appropriations: it is also an agent that remains beyond the reach of domestication and commodification. I refer to this surplus vitality of living matter in terms of *zoe*, as opposed to the discursive production of meanings of life as *bios*. I will expand on this in the next chapter.

Franklin argues that contemporary genetic-driven societies euphorically associate the genetic code or DNA with marketable brand names. The genetic materials (like stem cells) become data banks of potentially profitable information and are commercialized as such. The very widespread practice of patenting and enforcing intellectual property rights as a standard way of doing scientific research demonstrates the point. What this means concretely is that scientific research, which is still reputed and funded as 'fundamental', results in applied technological innovations. The case of genetically modified organisms in food production is a glaring example of this practice.

In a very powerful twist to her argument, however, Franklin shows that the genetic social imaginary cuts two ways and if 'nature' has been transformed by technology, then the contamination also works in reverse. Thus, contemporary car engineering, for instance, is visually marketed in a genetic format, which stresses the industrial transmission of inherited traits through careful selection and manufacturing of strengths and weaknesses. This commercialized version of social Darwinism adds a touch of irony to the widespread idea of the 'next generation' of electronic gadgets, computers, cars or whatever. The basic equation at work in the social genetic imaginary is that the DNA results in marketable brand names, so that your genes are, literally, your capital.

The new bio-technologies of 'Life' (as both *bios* and *zoe*) are expanding fast. They also structure the labour force and forms of production, mostly through enforced flexibility. Agriculture, grains and seeds; food-production and animal-breeding; the new frontiers of medicine, including genetic and foetal medical interventions; the widespread phenomenon of the traffic in organs and body-parts, and the growing industry of genetic engineering and farming of organic tissues and cells are part of this phenomenon. The new technologies consequently have a direct impact on the most intimate aspects of existence in the so-called 'advanced world', from technologically assisted reproduction to the unsustainable levels of consumerism and the commercial exploitation of genetic data for the purpose of health and other types of insurance. Last, but not least, are the implications for contemporary warfare and the military-industrial complex.

The convergence of bio-technologies with the new information and communication technologies, backed by the Internet, is a major factor in inducing a radical revision of body-politics. 'Bio-power' has become a mainstream form of management of genetic or molecular politics (Rose 2001). The work of Foucault on the discursive production of contemporary embodied subjects is the relevant background to this discussion. Foucault demonstrates not only the constructed structure of what we call 'human nature', but also its relatively recent appearance on the historical scene, which makes it coextensive with forms of social control and disciplining. Haraway's work also starts from the assumption that 'life as a system to be managed, a field of operations constituted by scientists, artists, cartoonists, community activists, mothers, anthropologists, fathers, publishers, engineers, legislators, ethicists, industrialists, bankers, doctors, genetic counsellors, judges, insurers, priests, and all their relatives – has a very recent pedigree' (Haraway 1997: 174). Haraway argues that contemporary science has moved beyond Foucault's bio-power and has already entered the age of 'the informatics of domination', which is a different regime of visualization and control.

Deleuze and Guattari analyse this notion of power over life in their seminal work on capitalism as schizophrenia. They provide the single most coherent analysis of materialist vitalism, or 'Life' in a post-anthropocentric vein. I will explore this notion in chapters 4 and 5. Deleuze argues that the representation of embodied subjects is no longer visual in the sense of being scopic, in the post-Platonic sense of the simulacrum. Nor is it specular, in the psychoanalytic mode of redefining vision within a dialectical scheme of oppositional recognition of self and/as other. It has rather become schizoid, or internally disjointed; contemporary societies are immersed in this logic of boundless circulation and thus are suspended somewhere beyond the life and death cycle of the humanist vision of the self. It is consequently necessary to try to account for contemporary embodied subjects in terms of their surplus-value as visual commodities that circulate in a global circuit of cash flow known as the 'information society'. Much of this information is not knowledge-driven, but rather media-inflated and thus indistinguishable from sheer entertainment. Today's capital is spectral (Derrida 1994).

In *Metamorphoses* I argued that the gender politics of techno-bodies has undergone a paradoxical evolution. In modernity in fact, the machinic body-double was both genderized and eroticized – like the robot in Fritz Lang's *Metropolis* or the virile locomotives in Eisenstein's cinema. In postmodernity, however, this ratio changes: electronic and digital machinery are figures of complexity, mixture, hybridity and interconnectivity. As such they are not associated with either gender, nor are they particularly sexualized: they mark instead a space of sexual indeterminacy, undecidability or transsexuality. I analysed these traits in terms of the fantasy of the flight from the body, which I see as one of the tendencies of advanced cultures. This is echoed by the fantasy of stepping 'beyond gender', which is conveyed both in the dominant molar mode by the social imaginary about cyborgs and in the more radical minoritarian mode by feminist, queer and other counter-cultures. This blurring of the boundaries of sexual difference, in the sense of a generalized androgynous drive, is characteristic of post-industrial societies. J. F. Lyotard (1988) singles it out as one of the defining features of the postmodern condition – queering identities is a dominant ideology under advanced capitalism. In keeping with the paradox outlined above, however, this sexually indeterminate or transsexual social discourse goes hand in hand with the return of sexual polarizations and stricter gender roles, both in the West and in the rest. The schizoid double-pull of simultaneous displacement and refixing of binary gender oppositions is one of the most problematic aspects of contemporary political culture. It is also the key to its vehement anti-feminism, in that it erodes the grounds for the affirmation and the empowerment of embodied and embedded feminist political subjects.

In this context, the maternal function and hence the reproduction of the human in its bio-cultural mode has become simultaneously disengaged from the female body – because of the bio-technological intervention, also know as 'the desire to be wired'. It has also, however, been re-naturalized in a number of paradoxical variations ranging from religious convictions to secular affirmations of the theme of 'proud to be flesh'. These paradoxical patterns reflect the schizophrenic double-pull I have analysed before. On the one hand the maternal feminine is reinserted into a reinvented natural order that reaffirms the phallocentric system. On the other hand, the maternal is successfully inscribed into the techno-industrial market of alternative modes of reproduction. The simultaneous occurrence of opposite effects defeats the logic of the excluded middle and fits in with the manic-depressive alternation of euphoria and melancholia, which is the political economy of affectivity in advanced capitalism.

Feminist theory is not immune from this: the euphoric celebration of a brave new world of artificial reproduction is balanced by the attempts to reinvent a traditional feminine as holistic, healing and anti-technological. The distinction euphoria/nostalgia is internal to and hence it cuts across the feminist community, making its politics and values more complex. The pull towards traditional or reactive values (molar, sedentary, linear, static) is balanced by a more progressive and active drive towards more innovative solutions (molecular, nomadic, dynamic). The molar line of reterritorialization and the multiple lines of becoming trace altogether divergent patterns. Keeping these two lines well distinct qualitatively, while respecting the simultaneity of their occurrence, is an analytic necessity, albeit a challenging one. Where they differ, as we shall see in chapters 4 and 5, is on ethical grounds.

The return of the body

One of the effects of bio-technologies and the genetic social imaginary is the return of discourses and practices about 'real bodies'. Techno-bodies are more than ever immersed in sites of power, and contemporary politics is prone to massive phenomena of exclusion in so far as cyborgs are inscribed in the cash-nexus, which is not immune to racism and traditional power-relations. Moreover, if it is the case that the human body, and hence also the maternal feminine (the matrix), are now inscribed in the techno-industrial and military apparatus, it follows that they are neither metal nor flesh, but rather a highly contested social space, traversed by capital flows and hence power relations. Complexity and paradoxes are the challenge facing political subjects today. The representation and interpretation of techno-bodies therefore express fully the paradox of the contemporary subject, namely of a body that is invaded by technology, is bombarded by visual bits and bytes of information but also feels horror, pain and despair at these fundamental invasions of what used to be called his or her bodily integrity. Methodologically, the return of 'real body' in its thick materiality spells the end of the linguistic turn in the sense of the postmodernist over-emphasis on textuality, representation, interpretation and the power of the signifier. More on this in the next chapter.

The renewed emphasis on the materiality of corporeal bodies is especially strong in three areas of contemporary feminist theory: the first is the wave of Deleuzian feminism that emphasizes immanence (Buchanan and Colebrook 2000; MacCormack 2000); becomings (Grosz 1999a; Gatens and Lloyd 1999; Gatens 1996; Braidotti 1994 and 2002); and a new political ontology (Olkowski 1999).

The second is feminist science studies, which is quite separate from the humanities and social sciences and argues for a new epistemological paradigm (Wilson 1998; Franklin et al. 2000; Barad 2003). They refer to a different feminist genealogical line, which bypasses high postmodernist feminist theory – and hence psychoanalytic and semiotic criticism – emphasizing instead the epistemological tradition. The key figures are Margulis and Sagan (1995) but also Keller (1992) and Harding (1991). In this tradition, as in many others, Haraway (1997) provides both a focal point and a measure of consensus and cohesion.

The third is the new 'micro-political' form of feminist theory that is emerging at present, combining science studies with references to Guattari's notion of transversal subjectivity as well as to Hardt and Negri's critique of globalization (Balsamo 1996; Parisi 2004a). This new generation constitutes a departure from earlier Deleuzian feminist emphasis on immanence and becomings, but displays strong affinity with the radicalism, the creativity and hands-on approach of the second feminist wave. The micro-political feminists emphasize the role techno-sciences can play as tools by which to attack advanced capitalism.

A striking example of this political climate is the analysis of the labour and economic politics of the globalized world, as exemplified by those who do not fit into the ruling neo-liberal minority and thus compose the new digital proletariat. A significant case is provided by the workers in call centres which cater for the information society by processing phone enquiries from selected locations miles away from the caller's home. Denounced strongly by Arundhati Roy (2001) these 'call centres' or data outsourcing agencies are a multi-billion-dollar industry which has attracted a great deal of critical attention both in mainstream (e.g. Luke Harding 2001) and in alternative media. Workers in these centres answer queries on a wide range of subjects ranging from car rentals, credit card enquiries to plane tickets and operating instructions of digital or other equipment. The heart of this business is never to let the caller as much as suspect that his or her call is being processed in Delhi. Thus the students have to learn to speak English with the appropriate and expected accents – mostly British or American; they need to read the local newspapers to be up to date on small items of news and, of course, they need to erase their own identity and change names, in order to 'pass'. This kind of labour presents a number of features that are reminiscent of the old exploitative conditions of the working class, but also innovate on them.

The Raqs Media Collective (2003) in a series of visual installations has commented on the specific form of simulation that is embodied in these call centres, namely the erasure of their remoteness from the caller's home. They cite the example of a woman known on the phone line as Sandra, but whose real name in her own home in Delhi is Sunita. In her work replying to phone enquiries, Sunita simulates Sandra, who is supposed to live in Minneapolis, USA and knows all about the product or firm she is representing. This strategy is not mere impersonation, for there is no visual or physical contact between the parties involved. Nor can it be seen as a form of identification, as the worker need not feel or experience herself as being from a different culture/nation in order to fulfil her contractual obligations. It is more like a logistical issue: working in a call centre is about carefully orchestrated simulation. As such, it requires a radical 'Othering' of oneself, or a mild form of schizophrenia, which is not a masquerade, in the ironical sense of self-exploration, but reification of the worker's own life-world. Not unlike characters in a chat room, the call-centre worker performs her labour market persona in such a way as to emerge from the process neither wiser nor enriched (especially considering that workers in these call centres are paid one tenth the wage of their Western counterparts) but rather firmly located as 'the emerging digital proletariat that underpins the new world economy' (Raqs Media Collective 2003: 85). Another significant example of the same phenomenon is the extensive reliance of the computer games industry on testplayers drawn from mostly male youths in former Eastern Europe. Playing computer games up to fifteen hours a day at a time – in an industry that operates continuously, twenty-four hours a day, seven days a week – for wages of about 130 US dollars a month, these digital workers have invented the virtual sweatshop (see Thompson 2005: 17).

It is this kind of materially embodied and embedded performance that challenges the limits of the linguistic framework of interpretation of global gender politics. The cultural cross-dressing performed by call-centre digital proletarians is neither the creative mimesis of strategic repetitions (Irigaray 1977), nor is it the destabilizing effect of queer identity politics (Butler 1991). It is just today's variation on the theme of bodily exploitation, which fits into the global marketing of both material commodities and Western life-styles, cultures and accents. Hardt and Negri (2000) stress the immaterial and affective nature of this labour force which trades phonetic skills, linguistic ability and proper accents services, as well as requiring attention, concentration and great care. It is in this sense that I critique the exclusively linguistic reference to mimesis and not in the superficial mode that Butler wrongfully attributes to my work (Butler 2004a). This tour de force by the digital workers of the new global economy rests on an acute and explicit awareness of one's location in space and time and yet it functions through border crossings, nomadic shifts and paths of deterritorialization. The allegedly ethereal nature of cyberspace and the flow of mobility it sustains are fashioned by the material labour of women and men from areas of the world that are thought to be peripheral. The collapse of the binary opposition of centre–periphery introduces, as I argued in chapter 1, a new fluctuating continuum between discrete spaces in the global economy. This space of fluctuation is racialized and sexualized to a very high degree and it is exploited accordingly.

In *Metamorphoses* I argued that the difference between the winners and the losers of the present economic world order is that the winners only put their money on the line, while the losers risk their bodies. In terms of bodily materialism, the perverse logic of advanced capitalism offers a number of significant power differentials as well. Let's take the dominant subject-position of the cyborg: it simultaneously evokes an abstract image or spectral commodification (think of Schwarzenegger's metallized body) and a very embodied, concrete and actualized one. The latter refers to the digital proletariat: mostly anonymous, underpaid exploited bodies of labourers, usually ethnic, natives or immigrant, which fuel the technological revolution. Their anonymity means they coincide with their exploited bodies, which paradoxically end up making them invisible in the perverse economy of media culture. The dominant subject position, however, consists in reaching high definitions of identity or singularity by over-exposure, that is to say in gaining access to visibility, albeit of the spectral kind. Gender and ethnicity play a central role in regulating access to visibility with high definitions of identity, as opposed to the invisible anonymity of those who are marginalized. In other words, power today is a matter of selection and control, entitlement and access: it is bio-power, centred on the body in its material and immaterial manifestations. It engenders a system of integrated and all-encompassing surveillance which postulates potential, virtual enemies everywhere, also and especially within the by now exploded boundaries of the subject.

Vandana Shiva's plea for biodiversity in global culture focuses on a different facet of the same problem and criticizes the practice of patenting bio-technological products, which she labels 'bio-piracy' (Shiva 1997). Shiva connects this practice to European empire-building over the last 500 years and sees a continuum between them and the policies of the WTO and the World Bank. Moreover, in a very interesting Foucauldian shift, Shiva links bio-piracy to the individualistic philosophies of Locke, Hume and other 'fathers' of liberalism. Shiva argues that their theoretical works both reflect and legitimate capitalist appropriation of the world's resources and the eviction of others. These theories are still operational in contemporary practices such as intellectual property rights and the policies of the World Trade Organization and the GATT apparatus. What specifically marks the present historical era, argues Shiva, is the fact that the target of capitalist looting has shifted from the former colonies to the 'new frontiers', or the 'natural resources' represented by human genetics in general, and women's reproductive powers in particular. Capital is the generative power of living matter and the resilient vitality of 'Life'. The self-generative power of living matter is both denied and enhanced by patenting and branding for the sake of corporate profit. *Bios/zoe*, as actualized in seeds and cells, is cash.

In Shiva's assessment, 'bio-piracy', as the ultimate colonization of the interior of living organisms, destroys biodiversity, endangering the many species that used to live on this planet. Mary Midgley commented ironi-cally on the immorality of this disregard for biodiversity:

> If humans need wood, trees must be replanted, but they should always be the trees that will supply this need most quickly and economically. There is no reason to conserve existing species, and certainly none to aim at diversity as such. And after all there are a lot of kinds of trees about. So, what could possibly be wrong with universal monocultured eucalyptus? (Midgley 1996: 123)

It also threatens cultural diversity by depleting the capital of human knowledge through the devalorization of local knowledge systems and world-views. On top of legitimating theft, these practices also devalue indigenous forms of knowledge, cultural and legal systems. Eurocentric models of scientific rationality and technological development damage human diversity. The patent system legalizes bio-piracy, spreads mono-cultures and homogenization in both nature and social systems. The strat-egy of resistance proposed by Shiva is vintage eco-feminism, which I will analyse in more detail in the next chapter.

In a significant divergence of opinion with Vandana Shiva, Franklin, Lury and Stacey (2000) analyse the 'seed' not as the site of resistance, but rather as one of the agents of the global economy. As a privatized icon for commercialized biodiversity the seed connects the old universalist idea of 'nature' to the financial reality of global culture. Just as the humans have their Genome project, plants have their Heritage Seed catalogue, which patents a number of seeds. They are advertised as organic, home-grown, but also ancient and as such the repository of old lore and cultural authenticity. This holistic ethos guarantees both the perpetuation of the species and the preservation of culture. The female body as a whole is the seed which corporate capitalism wants to patent and eventually clone, according to the paradox of a new global compound of nature/culture that is naturalized and commercialized simultaneously. Practising the feminist politics of location, Franklin *et aliae* differentiate this financial and cultural mystique of seeds from their political usage in the work of Shiva as a form of resistance to the appropriation by industry. In both cases, however, the seed conveys the notion of purity of the lineage and of direct genetic inheritance. It is therefore the opposite of the discourse and the practice of hybridity and mixity in genetic engineering and more espe-cially in transgenic species experiments.

Franklin, Lury and Stacey (2000) are on the side of postmodernism and hence of philosophical post-humanism when they point out the ambiguity of the notion of cultural diversity in the era of globalization. Diversity, even in the form of indigenous or local knowledge systems, has become a highly valuable and marketable commodity. In its commercialized form it has increased the uniformity of consumers' habits, while sponsoring the proliferation of 'local' differences or micro-diversities. The global market is fuelled by 'differences' because the 'local' is a political space constructed by the global flows of capital (Hardt and Negri 2000). Because the proliferation of local differences for the sake of marketability is one of the features of the global economy, globalization functions through the incorporation of otherness. Therefore, one must beware of taking any claim to cultural identity and difference at face value. All identities are in process and consequently are inherently contradictory. They are best approached in an open-ended and contested manner, in keeping with the cognitive and figural 'style' of philosophical nomadism (Braidotti 2002).

The point of consensus between Franklin, Lury and Stacey and Shiva is the resistance against the celebration of '*bios*' by a system that persists in its conventional bio-centrism and hierarchical thinking. The only aim of capital is to expand, to spread into new territories, such as the cells, women's reproductive body and the very generative forces of the earth. Both Franklin and Shiva agree that Life as *zoe* somewhat escapes total entrapment in this regime. They differ, however, on strategies. Shiva's analysis does not rest on poststructuralist philosophies of power as a non-dialectical web of relations. She assumes instead a dialectical opposition between centre and periphery and thus functions within a dualistic frame of reference. This is the shortcoming of Shiva's position: it is not correct to say that the process of capitalist expansion is moving into new and previously uncharted territories. It is rather the case that it actively creates potential new territories for the sake of profit.

This distinction is not merely academic: in my (post-Foucauldian) frame of reference, it cannot be assumed that an object of bio-political interest – for instance, seeds, cells or women's reproductive powers – is an externally constituted 'other' which gets invested or taken over by the powers-that-be. The residual humanism of Foucault's notion of 'bio-power' is displaced by the emergence of vital *bios* and *zoe* as major forces in shaping contemporary social spaces. They create an unexpected form of contiguity between material processes of constitution of areas or objects of interest, like the 'cell', or the 'seed' and processes of subjectivation. In other words, it is not that 'life' is being vampirized by bio-technology but rather that, as a result of bio-technological material and discursive practices, 'life as *bios/zoe*' produces ever-growing new areas of activity and intervention. 'Life' has emerged as the subject, and not as the object of political processes. A non-human, inhuman or post-human subject, but a subject nonetheless. Hence the importance of analysing the category of 'life' – as *bios* and *zoe* – to see who is constructing it and for what purpose, who has access to it and for what aim. If it is the case that the production of certain categories, such as seeds or cells, or human embryos, is coextensive with its commercial exploitation, the task of social critics is both to recognize and to contest the formation of these categories, so as to disrupt their social status.

Post-humanism and the limits of liberal individualism

Vandana Shiva's critique of European humanism concerns its limitations, not its substance. A non-Western humanist herself, Shiva shrewdly points out the credibility gap between pretensions or aspirations and real accomplishments and calls for a less self-congratulatory assessment of the European humanist ideal. Pointing out the complicity between Western enlightened humanism on the one hand and colonial conquest and exploitation on the other, Shiva issues a strong word of warning. Shiva's call for a more inclusive sense of humanism is analogous to the position taken by the black feminist theorist Patricia Hill Collins. Collins (1991) proposes a very affirmative brand of standpoint theory, which she links directly to the tradition of *Ubuntu*, or African humanism. The Afrocentric context shifts the terms of reference and hence of definition of this notion, linking it to the Black theological tradition and to African-American spirituality. This tradition offers a political culture of resistance as well as creative alternatives for the formulation of the identity of oppressed groups. Supported by a dialogical system and informed by the notion of care as a collective responsibility for one's community, Afrocentric humanism is a resource for all that want to resist the attrition and devastation of technological abuses.

Vandana Shiva compares unfavourably the individualism of Western traditions to the more communitarian spirit of non-Western traditions of knowledge, where the free exchange of information is as widely practised as communally held properties. The argument against Eurocentrism consequently supports a non-profit approach. This supports a neo-humanist argument against the commercialization of living organisms as 'biotechnological products'. This is a double violence, which not only reifies living organisms into objects of commercial consumption, but also denies their self-organizing and self-reproducing capacities.

Shiva's neo-humanism is shared by a number of contemporary social critics working within race, post-colonial or non-Western perspectives. I would like to set this position, as a sort of travelling companion, alongside the anti- or post-humanism of cultural and social critics that address the same issues within a Western-situated perspective. The point of this cartographic move, which aligns theoretically diverse positions along the same axis, is to facilitate the transposition of the respective political affects that activate them. I do like putting the 'active' back into 'activism'.[1] This transposition is like a musical variation that leaps across scales and compositions to find a pitch or a sharable level of intensity. What matters to my thought is the synchronization of the different elements, their affective dimension, the affinity, not the political or theoretical correctness.

[1] With thanks to Judy Butler for this warm formulation of my work.

Thus, in her criticism of the exploitative logic of Western techno-sciences from within, Donna Haraway – one of the figureheads of feminist post-humanism – stresses a number of crucial features. The first is power as a dynamic web of interconnections or hybrid contaminations, as a principle of radical non-purity. The second is the refusal to fall into the pitfall of the classical nature/culture divide: there is no natural *telos* or order, as distinct from technological mediation. In order to restructure our collective relationship to the new nature/culture compound of contemporary techno-sciences, Haraway calls for a renewed kinship system, radicalized by concretely affectionate ties to the non-human 'others'. Haraway argues that the subject–object, nature–culture divides are linked to patriarchal, Oedipal familial narratives. Against them, she mobilizes an enlarged sense of community, based on empathy, accountability and recognition. Moreover, she extends these prerogatives to non-human agents or subjects, such as animals, plants, cells, bacteria and the earth as a whole.

This position has important implications for gender politics and becoming-woman. In the era of techno-bodies, the maternal body not only reproduces the future, but also carries the burden of inscribing futurity within the regime of high-tech commodification which runs today's market economies. This means that the maternal feminine in the double mode of the reproductive machine integrated into the electronic circuitry on the one hand, and as an array of resisting bodies on the other, is a multi-layered site. To express this in Deleuzian terms, it translates simultaneously the despotic face of the majority and the pathetic face of the struggling minorities. In any case, it is in the contaminated, traumatized body of this kind of maternal feminine as key to the future that post-industrial culture fights the battle for its survival. The challenge is how to incorporate the maternal feminine, in order the better to metabolize her offspring. In reaction to this paradox of the simultaneous de- and re-territorialization of woman's body in relation to the institution of femininity, of nature in relation to the bio-technological apparatus and of 'life' with reference to the globalized cash nexus, the question of ethics arises. Which ethical criteria can we apply, in order to tell the difference between progressive and regressive forms of re-embodiment or territorialization? In chapters 4 and 5 I will propose an ethics of sustainable transformations as the answer. For now, I wish to proceed with the cartography.

Let me stress another crucial feature of this discussion. In the historical era of *bios* and *zoe* as political subjects, it is methodologically unsound and ethically impossible to separate categorically the different axes of difference. Genderization, racialization and naturalization are, in the grand philosophical tradition, the three structural axes of Otherness. They need to be connected transversally in a series of nomadic lines of interconnection in order to produce a valid cartography of contemporary power relations. Thus, the pathetic and despotic face of femininity, in the historical era of advanced technologies, bears a privileged link to white-ness as a term that signifies Sameness and thus indexes access to power and to the structural advantages that being white entails (Braidotti 2002). The convergence between the new media and information technologies and bio-technologies propels a spectral economy that trades with equal nonchalance on corporate brands of gender, queer, multicultural, genetic and posthuman diversity. This results in a planetary circulation of global icons such as the white goddess princess Diana or the black athlete Michael Jordan, the ubiquitous panda bear, the cosmic dolphin or the blue icon of the planet earth (Bryld and Lykke 1999). They become commodities deprived of liberatory potential, and are all the more profitable for it (Gilroy 2000). The circulation of such iconic commodities, albeit non-human ones, within the spectral economy of global transmission supports the global market of Sameness. It is a case of quantitative pluralism, as opposed to qualitative multiplicity (Braidotti 2002), in an economy of the eternal return that saturates the social space with an overflow of images and representations.

A philosophical approach based on neo-materialist vitalism is the most effective way to address these contradictions and work towards a mat-erialist culture of critical affirmation. Radical immanence and sustainable ethics are a strategy to free ourselves from the binary affective scheme of euphoria-melancholia and disintoxicate ourselves from the fumes of the prosthetic promises of perfectibility that neo-liberal technologies are selling us. I would like to face instead the specific complexities of our embodied subjectivity in the age of *zoe*-power. 'We' humans are definitely in *this* together, and we are not alone. Just how crowded the nomadic spaces of transposition actually are, will become apparent in the next section.

BECOMING-OTHER: TRANSPOSING RACIALIZED DIFFERENCE

In the previous section I have argued that the political economy of global capitalism consists in multiplying and distributing differences for the sake of profit. It produces ever-shifting waves of genderization and sexuali-zation, racialization and naturalization of multiple 'others'. It has thus effectively disrupted the traditional dialectical relationship between the empirical referents of Otherness – women, natives and animal or earth others – and the processes of discursive formation of genderization/racialization/naturalization. Once this dialectical bond is unhinged, advanced capitalism looks like a system that promotes feminism without women, racism without races, natural laws without nature, reproduction without sex, sexuality without genders, multiculturalism without ending racism, economic growth without development, and cash flow without money. Late capitalism also produces fat-free ice creams and alcohol-free beer next to genetically modified health food, companion species along-side computer viruses, new animal and human immunity breakdowns and deficiencies, and the increased longevity of these who inhabit the advanced world. Welcome to capitalism as schizophrenia!

Multiple diasporic spaces

This section concentrates on the cartography of the processes of racializa-tion in this new world disorder. In the historical era of generalized nomad-ism, the figuration of the diaspora has gained the largest consensus in expressing the paradox of uprooting and regrounding which is at the heart of the global political economy of today. As Lorde points out: 'By the year 2000 the 20 largest cities in the world will have one thing in common: none of them will be in Europe, none in the United States.' (quoted in Mohanty et al. 1991: 1). The main frame of reference is a trans-national cultural space of transitions and flows, which expresses 'the overlapping and non-linear contact zones between natures and cultures: border, travel, creolization, transculturation, hybridity and diaspora' (Clifford 1994: 303). In her seminal work on the cartographies of diasporic social spaces, Avtar Brah (1996) argues that they are sites of transition and exchange of people, information, cultures, commodities and capital. The diaspora affects as much the roots of indigenous people as the routes of the itinerant subjects in the post-colonial world order.

Greek in origin, Jewish in connotations, the term 'diaspora' provides a non-normative description of the uprooting and dispersal of a great many populations: the Armenian, Turkish, Palestinian, Cuban, Greek, Chinese, Hungarian and Chilean, to name but a few. Clifford comments: 'In the late twentieth century, all or most communities have diasporic dimen-sions (moments, tactics, practices, articulations). Some are more diasporic than others' (Clifford 1994: 310), Robin Cohen (1997) subjects Clifford's notion of 'travelling cultures' to detailed analysis. While resisting the metaphorization of diasporic subject positions as some icon of postmod-ernity, Cohen inscribes them at the heart of the historical condition of globalization. The diasporic subject position is not only negative, but also productive of two-way processes of cultural signification, especially in terms of anti-nationalism. Cohen comments: 'Diasporas are positioned somewhere between nation-states and "travelling cultures"' (Cohen 1997: 135). Avtar Brah confirms that diasporic space is made of relationality and that it inscribes 'a homing desire while simultaneously critiquing dis-courses of fixed origins' (Brah 1996: 193).

The global diaspora has enormous implications for a world economy linked by a thick web of transnational flows of capital and labour. Such a system is marked by internal processes of migration implying mobil-ity, flexibility or precariousness of work conditions, transience and impermanent settlements. Last but not least, globalization is about the deterritorialization of social identity that challenges the hegemony of nation-states and their claim to exclusive citizenship (Cohen 1997). This proliferation of ethnic and racialized differences produces the stratification of layers of multiple control in a political economy of 'scattered hegemonies' (Grewal and Kaplan 1994). This is a system of centreless but constant surveillance and manipulation, which pitches the centre against the many peripheries in a complex logic that operates not only between the geopolitical blocks, but also within them. It also makes for a rather fashionable market for 'diversity', which commodifies different ethnicities and races under the general cover of 'world music', 'fusion cuisine' and 'black looks' (hooks 1990). The political economy of the circulation of goods is visual, in the spectral sense of endlessly recycling logos and iconic images that clone themselves and seem to lead their own life, such as Che Guevara and Angela Davis T-shirts, United Colours of Benetton (Franklin, Lury and Stacey 2000) and the global swoosh of Nike (Klein 1999).

The 'disposable' bodies of women, youths and others who are racialized or marked off by age and marginality come to be inscribed with particularly ruthless violence in this regime of power. They experience dispossession of their embodied and embedded selves, in a political economy of repeated and structurally enforced eviction (Sassen 1996). This again brings out the schizophrenic character of advanced capitalism, namely the paradox of high levels of mobility of capital flows in some sectors of the economic elites but also high levels of centralization and great immobility for most of the population. As Vandana Shiva (1993) points out, within globalization we must distinguish between different modes of mobility: 'One group is mobile on a world scale, with no country, no home, but the whole world as its property, the other has lost even the mobility within rootedness, lives in refugee camps, resettlement colonies and reserves' (Mies and Shiva 1993: 98).

Translated into the language of philosophical nomadism, global migration is a molar line of segmentation or reterritorialization that controls access to different forms of mobility and immobility. The global city and the refugee camps are not dialectical or moral opposites: they are two sides of the same global coin. They express the schizoid political economy of our times. The point of nomadic subjectivity is to identify a line of flight, that is to say a creative alternative space of becoming that would fall not between the mobile/immobile, the resident/the foreigner, but within these categories. The point is neither to dismiss nor to glorify the status of marginal, alien others, but to find a more accurate, complex location for a transformation of the terms of this political interaction.

Massive concentrations of infrastructures exist alongside complex, worldwide dissemination of goods. The technologically driven advanced culture that prides itself on being called the 'information society' is in reality a concrete, material infrastructure that is concentrated on the sedentary global city. Sassen defines global economies as: 'the location of transnational spaces within national territories' (Sassen 1994: xiii). Sassen quarrels with the state of current scholarship which tends to exclude from accounts of the global economies the heterogeneous aspects, especially the significant and highly effective presence of migrant cultures within the urban space of the global cities. The result is the exclusion 'from the account of the place-boundedness of significant components of the global information economy' (Sassen 1994: 7), namely the immigrant cultures of contemporary cities. Immigration and ethnicity, instead of being constituted as different areas of scholarship, should be studied as new forms of racialization of the labour market (Sassen 1996: 21). Sassen wants to reintegrate these racialized elements at the heart of the analysis of global economic culture, as localized instances 'of the internationalization of capital as a fundamental aspect of globalization' (1996: 21).

Given the fluid, internally contradictory and cannibalistic nature of advanced capitalism, the social and cultural critic needs to make innovations in the very tools of analysis. A trans-disciplinary approach that cuts across the established methods and conventions of many disciplines is best suited to the task of providing an adequate cartography of the shifting lines of racialization of the global labour market. This process cannot be kept separate from the genderization and sexualization of the same market. This is the line taken by Zillah Eisenstein (1998) in her critique of globalization. She argues that this is a system which contains structural inequalities that legitimate exploitative and brutal power-relations, especially for women and girls. Eisenstein explores ways of enlarging the practice of democracy in the global era, so as to respect diversity, while embracing issues such as community, responsibility and the principle of non-profit. The link between individualism and consumer culture is emphasized, and through her critical reading of the role of the media, Eisenstein demolishes the myth of consumer society as open, free and democratic. Quoting Benjamin Barber, she describes such myths as: 'a universalized culture of videology, infotainment and Holly-world' (Eisenstein 1998: 105).

The critique of this social imaginary which amalgamates citizenship with consumerism and sells cheap promises of human liberation through endless consumption is central to Eisenstein's politics. In opposition to it, she stresses the continuing patterns of both racial and sexist oppression and the important role they play in structuring the global economy. The disadvantaged position of girls and women from developing countries, as well as from ethnic minorities within the developed countries, is especially crucial. It allows Eisenstein to proclaim that: 'global capital thrives because of a racial-patriarchal division of labour . . . that disproportionately locates women and girls, especially those of colour, in low-wage assembly and information jobs and in sexual ghettos elsewhere in the market. Meanwhile, women are still expected to continue rearing children and performing familial labour' (Eisenstein 1998: 134). Developing forms of resistance against such a universal pattern of domination is a top political priority. Poststructuralist feminism has met this challenge by analysing the complex inextricable links and interrelations between gender, ethnicity and processes of racialization within the shifting horizons of global capital flow (Alexander and Mohanty 1997).

The critical legal studies scholar Kim Crenshaw has coined the term 'intersectionality' to describe the methodological approach that defines difference as a bundle of simultaneous but distinct axes of subjectivation and analyses them interactively. This is an attempt to encompass the multiple grounds of identity in a discussion about power-relations. It is also in keeping with the poststructuralist insights about the multi-layered structure of identity within each singular subject. Crenshaw stresses that since Foucault, the non-unitary structure of the subject, far from eroding the grounds for possible political alliances, constitutes an opportunity to create more coalitions with multiple forces. Crenshaw is also very careful to point out that intersectionality is not a new theory, but rather 'a provisional concept linking contemporary politics with postmodern theory' (Crenshaw 1989: 180). This means that all axes of differentiation – racialization, sexualization and naturalization – are internally differentiated in a complex manner. They also zigzag in and out of one another, triggering all kinds of combinations. The point is that the process, the movement and the trajectories of these lines of becoming deserve more attention than any of the specific identity formations they give rise to. The flows matter more than steady roots. Let me explore this further in the next section.

RELOCATING BLACKNESS

Bios-diversity

Transpositions induced by the convergence of bio- and information technologies have been especially strong in the area of anti-racism and gender. The new politics of *bios/zoe* and the acknowledgement of the methodological limitations of social constructivism have affected the scholarship in these areas. Historically, the emancipatory struggles against slavery and colonialism rebuked biological determinism through the analysis of the social construction of racialized and ethnicized 'others'. All this is shifting under the impact of the current technological revolution. For instance, Wilson (1998) has rejected the historical ties that bind feminism to a sort of compulsory anti-essentialism. The assumption that biological discourse is intrinsically regressive and politically reactionary is one of

the least useful aspects of the Marxist legacy. Contemporary developments in genetics, molecular biology, neurology and artificial intelligence
force us to reconsider the material foundations of the embodied subject.
This cannot fail to influence social and political activism. In chapter 1 I
showed how conservative thinkers like Fukuyama take this opportunity
to attack the entire tradition of social constructionism in order to reintro-
duce hierarchical differences supported by his own definition of the
genetic code. DNA-based social discrimination differs only in name from
other historical forms of naturalized exclusion. In opposition to this, let
us see how progressive anti-racist thinkers react to the challenges induced
by the new *bios/zoe*-power.

In a clean sweep from the social constructivist past, the philosopher
Lucius Outlaw makes a powerful case for racialized biodiversity (1996).
This provocative move is intended as a criticism of the essentialized uses
to which notions of ethnicity and race are currently put in debates on
social philosophy. Outlaw is fully aware of the strategic uses of essentialist
claims of a 'black' experience or a 'black history', but does not state a
counter-claim to an essential radical difference. Arguing that the grounds
for such radical claims cannot be sustained, and loath to reinvent a tradition out of the suffering of the black community, Outlaw looks elsewhere
for alternative foundations for black subjectivity.

He starts by rejecting identity politics altogether and then recommends
that we turn instead to the classical principles of Enlightenment democracy and belief in reason, argument and public discussions. Quoting
Appiah, he suggests that we replace dangerous notions such as 'race' and
'ethnicity' with more useful terms of reference, such as 'communities of
meaning'. However, in a move that goes beyond these stated beliefs in
liberal individualism, Outlaw strikes a blow for an enlightened notion of
human biodiversity as the basis for anti-racist politics and thinking.
He argues that 'for important reasons we should understand races and
ethnicities as natural: that is, as particular types of bio-social collectivities
that develop or evolve, as do all things in the natural world, but in
ways that are characteristically human' (Outlaw 1996: 12). What is
characteristically human, of course, are the social, ethical and political
capacities for dialogue, exchange and peaceful settlement of differences.
The human is a political animal, as Aristotle argued millennia ago.
Politikon Zoon is the actual term he uses and if we process this idea with
the neo-materialist vitalist approach I associate with nomadic subjectivity,
the following happens – 'Life', as the flow of transformations and becomings, takes a specific form in the case of humans. Claire Colebrook (2000a)
puts it admirably in stating that the human becoming – or actualization
of life forces – is sexually embodied, historically located and politically
related. Sexualization, time-and-space locations and webs of interrelations
are constitutive of the human subjects and not external to them. Outlaw's
thought moves in the same direction and sides resolutely with *bios/zoe*.

Instead of relinquishing these coordinates within a diffuse network of socially constructed and historically implemented effects of subjectification, as Foucault suggests, Outlaw recommends the opposite road. Racialization and ethnicization are crucial mechanisms by which humans are constituted and construct their social realities. Outlaw argues that the issue of 'Life' needs to be addressed in its specificity and, with it, questions of genetic differences. To prevent the new forms of stratification recommended by the right-wing proponents of a genetic hierarchy, Outlaw takes great care to steer the discussion in the direction of respect for human rights.

The respect for biodiversity, which has been accepted as a ruling principle for the management of the environment and of other species, should also be applied to human beings. Echoing Shiva, Outlaw argues that racism depletes the pool of human diversity, denies its variety and wealth and is therefore conducive to a global impoverishment of the human species. The respect for biodiversity is put in the service of anti-racist activism. This is a treacherous path to tread and it is one which Outlaw finds very well suited to philosophy defined as the activity of 'figuring out the means and rules for surviving, stabilizing living and perpetuating the biological and cultural reproduction of the society through successive generations, in certain spaces (both natural and built), in and through time' (1996: 13). An ethical concern for the future is combined with a strong sense of accountability to provide a radical shift of perspective that points beyond the canon of social constructivist thinking.

Outlaw's call for human biodiversity reasserts the positivity of a notion of race that is deprived of essentialist attributes and recognized in its singularity. This approach breaks from some of the dogmas of social constructivism and helps us focus on the singularity of biodiversity as a social concept. This is a radical political strategy that unveils the privileges of the majority, the hegemonic dominant subject position. Notions like whiteness, masculinity and health are implied in the everyday understanding of what constitutes the norm, in the sense of 'normative' and 'normal'. The political economy of invisibility means that the only notion of 'race' that our culture has produced, is in the mode of a minority. Race is synonymous with inferiority, or pejorative difference. Outlaw's strategy is to introduce a dose of pure positivity into the notion of 'race', so as to disengage it from this pernicious and murderous logic.

Rethinking the positivity of race means delinking the practice of racialization from its dialectical dependence on dualistic thinking. Outlaw argues a similar case, in human biodiversity. I see this as a powerful form of becoming-minoritarian of racial privilege, according to the affirmative ethics of nomadic subjectivity, and an attempt to set the former minorities into an affirmative process of becoming, or self-affirmation. It is an empowering, albeit risky, strategy.

Global hybridity

A similar approach is proposed by Paul Gilroy in his recent work on the current bio-technological revolution. In a Deleuzian mode of nomadic or transversal lines of becoming, Gilroy enquires to what extent the trans- species commerce, which is central to contemporary genetic engineering, will affect the understanding of racial differences and the social practice of race relations. Again, it is clear that 'we' are in *this* together, but the point is to agree on who 'we' actually are. Gilroy provides a balancing act in tracking the shifting boundaries between the 'genomic orthodoxy' (Gilroy 2000: 21) of the centre and the relocation of pejorative racialized categories from the margins. Stressing the schizoid, non-linear and irra- tional nature of these shifts, Gilroy focuses on the cultural anxieties and hence the social discrimination which are created 'not by the ruthless enforcement of stable racial categories but from a disturbing inability to maintain them' (Gilroy 2000: 22).

Gilroy's cartography of the reconfigurations of racialized identities in the age when *bios*/*zoe*-power is saturated by technological relations bears strong affinity to my own project of relocating sexual difference, embodi- ment and accountability in contemporary culture. He argues that, in an analogy with 'feminism without women', contemporary racialization processes do not imply a notion of race and hence have become estranged from 'the scales respectively associated with political economy and epi- dermalization' (Gilroy 2000: 47). Gilroy's analysis of the racialized politi- cal economy of *bios* and *zoe* focuses on the global repackaging and commercial consumption of black physicality in the global marketing campaigns of Nike and other corporations, with Michael Jordan as the global icon. Gilroy singles out the explosion of black youth culture in the MTV-mode, represented by the streetwise black rappers from the ghetto. African-American people have effectively become the hyper-racialized hybrids that express both the 'ultramodern and the ultraprimitive aspects of global culture' (Gilroy 2000: 347).

This process of consumption of black masculine looks in 'corporate multiculturalism' is compounded by the emergence of a new class of black entrepreneurs and leaders, represented by Spike Lee and Colin Powell. They are the emblems of a black middle class that has become integral to the working of the global economy. The black, middle-class bodies of women like Condoleeza Rice or Naomi Campbell enjoy the same privil- ege of high profiles combined with extreme visibility. Next to them, the planetary images of AIDS-afflicted African people, yet again, embody the anonymous marginalization of human frailty at its most intense, i.e. most mortal, level.

Gilroy's work places combined emphasis on colonialism and fascism, racism and anti-Semitism, showing their continuity without falling into facile analogies, but rather fully respecting their historical specificity. The continuity between these aspects of European history lies at the heart of Gilroy's case for the coextensivity of European discourses of modernization and racialized discourses and practices. Gilroy stresses the murderous charge that 'difference' has assumed in European history, and hence also the coextensivity of terror, murder and violence with lofty ideals of scientific rationality, national identity and Europe's self-appointed role as 'civilizing influence' in the world. The critique of the power of institutionalized discourses in the human and social sciences owes a lot to feminist epistemologies and critiques of science as frameworks, which analyse the complicity of rationality with domination and terror.

On this point, in spite of his Deleuzian undertones, Gilroy strikes a neo-humanist note. He considers colonialism and fascism as a betrayal of the European ideal of the Enlightenment, which he is determined to defend, holding Europeans accountable for their ethical and political failings. Racism splits common humanity and disengages whites from any ethical sensibility, reducing them to an infra-human moral status. It also reduces non-whites to a subhuman ontological status that exposes them to murderous violence. Taking a strong stand against the return of fundamentalist appeals to ethnic differences by a variety of white, black, Serbian, Rwandan, Texan and other nationalists, Gilroy denounces these 'microfascisms' as the epidemics of our globalized times. He locates the site of the ethical transformation in the critique of each nationalistic category, not in the assertion of any dominant one. He sets diasporic mobility and transcultural interconnections up against the forces of nationalism. This is a theory of mixture, hybridity and cosmopolitanism that is resolutely non-racial. Against the enduring power of nation-states, Gilroy posits instead the affirmative politics of transversal movements, such as antislavery, feminism, Médecins sans Frontières and the like. Gilroy refers to this ideal as 'planetary humanism', defined as a 'postracial and postanthropological version of what it means to be human' (Gilroy 2000: 15) in the age of bio-politics and genetic power.

Gilroy's cosmopolitan neo-humanism is a strategic post-racial and inclusive neo-universalism, similar to that proposed by Vandana Shiva. It suggests the possibility of a 'distinctive ecology of belonging' (Gilroy 2000: 55) which would recompose the relationship between self, territory, individuality and society through multiple connections. Planetary humanism marks a social and also symbolic recomposition of one's relationship to space, time and community. It turns hybridity into an eco-philosophical notion. The challenge is not to return to fixed identities, clear boundaries and an allegedly pure past but rather to grab the opportunities offered by the cultural intermixture already available within our own post-industrial ethno/gender landscapes, so as to create yet unknown possibilities for bonding and community-building. I will return to this in chapter 4.

Avtar Brah (1996) stresses the importance of understanding and accounting for the intimate web of interconnections between race, gender, class and ethnicity, in order to refine our understanding of the insidious workings of racism in the age of global hybridity. The latter refers to the workings and the cultural logic of advanced capitalism as a difference engine, which both multiplies and capitalizes on the quantitative pluralities it produces. Differences proliferate for the sake of commodification and, ultimately, profit. This cannot fail to affect identities as well as commodities. Brah defines diasporic identities as 'processes of multi-locationality across geographical, cultural and psychic boundaries' (Brah 1996: 194). These are multiplied by the new information technologies, which complicate the relationship between the local and the global.

This complex articulation of multiple differences between and within diasporic subjects marked by multiple locality creates both methodological and ethical problems. Methodologically, Brah adopts the feminist politics of location as a strategic mapping of the multiple layers of identity and newly emerging ethnicities. This approach includes border-crossings and non-unitary identities, the latter sustaining the former. Accounting for these non-linear and complex differences is a challenge for the social critic. Ethically, this vision establishes the relation to multiple others at the core of subjectivity. A non-dialectical and hence not mutually exclusive relationship is established between self and other. Subjects constituted in and by multiplicity, however, are marked by contradictions. This makes them especially open and opposed to fixed, essential identities and to the power of dominant categories, even that of race itself. This emphasis on complexity and relationality, which facilitates cross-border connections and alliances among differently located constituencies, is a political position. Brah, like Gilroy, de-essentializes blackness and connects it to other social variables, but only for the purpose of re-grounding anti-racist politics on the more effective principle of hybrid multi-locations.

Rhizomic politics

A multiply located, non-unitary subject position and a rhizomic politics of relations is also recommended by the Deleuzian philosopher Edouard Glissant. He develops an effective rhizomatic poetics and politics, taking as his point of reference the historical experience and the specific location of Africans and West Indians caught in the transatlantic slave trade. Glissant foregrounds the importance of memory and the productivity of mixity as the centrepieces of his theory of Relation. He argues that even an experience as devastating as slavery produces specific forms of knowledge and subjectivization that transcend the burden of the negative.

There are several important features at stake in Glissant's remarkable position; the first is the primacy of the Relation over any of its terms, including the negative ones. A relation functions through the middle, the 'milieu' (more on this in the next chapter). People who are culturally and ethnically positioned in the middle – like the Caribbeans or West Indians – have a head start in understanding the crucial importance of the relation. They also have, however, a historical legacy of destruction and violence, which is hard to transcend in that it includes both the erasure of the original culture and the forceful absorption of the colonizing culture. In response to this ethical and political challenge, Glissant actively theorizes the becoming-minoritarian or becoming-rhizomatic of blacks, creoles, descendants of slaves and colonized peoples. This is described as a spiritual but also logistical shift in the structure of the subject in the direction of openness towards both self and other.

Glissant's position includes a sharp critique of the West, which is based on the ontology of Sameness or the rule of One. This includes a dualistic relationship to the rest of the human race. There exists a dominant mode of nomadism in Western culture – in the form of epic journeys of discovery, which find their historical apogee in colonialism. The power of Sameness in the west is best described in terms of monolinguism, or the illusion of a single cultural and linguistic root. Glissant, in a very Deleuzian mode, plays the rhizome against the root and advocates global poly-linguism. This includes the deconstruction of the hubris of European master cultures and the arrogance with which they consider their languages as the voice of humanity. This universalistic pretence is one of the mechanisms supporting colonialism. It also entails the reappraisal of minor languages, dialects and hybrids, in a phenomenon that Glissant describes as creolization: 'Poets from the Caribbean, the Maghreb and other parts of Africa are not moving toward that elsewhere that is the aim of projectile movement, nor are they returning toward a Centre. They create their works in metropolitan regions, where their peoples have made a sudden appearance' (Glissant 1997: 31). Glissant offers a striking example of the poetics of relation in his analysis of how, in the Caribbean colonized territories, the French *colons* spoke their own homegrown dialects – Norman or Breton – rather than the high and noble language of the French nation. It is this bastardized language that mingles with that of the local population, creating a crossover between two distinct but analogous forms of linguistic non-purity. Creolization, therefore, cuts both ways and it differs from the master *langue* in its very structures. The thought of relation as a form of philosophical nomadism stresses the importance of the middle, in this mode of non-origin, non-purity and not-Oneness. Glissant defines this productive multiplicity as 'echoes of the world' – modes of resonance of the great vitality of human biodiversity at both the biological and the cultural level. They reconnect us to the living chaos of the world as living matter in transformation, a hybrid, dynamic resilient *bios/zoe* force of global creolization. Glissant captures this vitality and honours it as a poetics or an ethics of rhizomatic interconnections.

Contrary to what some ungenerous critics suggested (Gedalof 1996, 2000; Boer 1996; Felski 1997; Pels 1999), my nomadic subject pursues the same critique of power as black and post-colonial theories, not in spite but because of the fact that it is located somewhere else. Philosophical nomadism addresses in both a critical and creative manner the role of the former 'centre' in redefining power relations. Margins and centre shift and destabilize each other in parallel, albeit dissymmetrical, movements. My position is equally resistant to the identification of the centre as inertia and self-perpetuation and to the aporetic repetition of Sameness. The challenge is to destabilize dogmatic, hegemonic, exclusionary power structures at the very heart of the identity structures of the dominant subject through rhizomic interventions. If we are to move beyond the sociology of travel and the breast-beating of critical thinkers crushed by white guilt, we need to enact a vision of the subject that encompasses changes in the deep structures. The point is not just mere deconstruction, but the relocation of identities on new grounds that account for multiple belongings, i.e. a non-unitary vision of a subject. This subject actively yearns for and constructs itself in complex and internally contradictory social relations. To account for these we need to look at the internal forms of movement that privilege processes rather than essences and transformations, rather than counter-claims to identity. The sociological variables (gender, class, race and ethnicity, age, health) need to be supplemented by a theory of the subject that calls into question the inner fibres of the self. These include the desire, the ability and the courage to sustain multiple belongings in a context which celebrates and rewards Sameness and one-way thinking. In chapters 4 and 5 I will address this challenge further, which is an ethical as well as a political enterprise. It is my contribution, as a European nomadic subject moving across the variegated landscape of whiteness, to a debate which black, anti-racist, post-colonial and other critical thinkers have put on the map.

RELOCATING WHITENESS

For a post-nationalist European Union

The shift in the structural position of the 'others' cannot leave unaltered the position of the 'same'. I consequently want to look at the changing position of Europe in a globalized world. My argument proceeds in two phases: firstly, I will argue that the new context of the European Union, defined as a post-nationalist project, provides the ground for a significant relocation of whiteness by introducing a disjunction between traditional European cultural identities and the notion of a new European citizenship (Balibar 2001). Secondly, in so far as it unsettles molar European identity, I will argue that the European

Union marks a process of becoming-minor of the masterful European subject.

The 'new' European Union is a multi-layered and contested social space. As a major player within the global economy, the EU is positioned simultaneously as the main ally and the main alternative to American hegemony. It can consequently be seen as the contemporary variation on the theme of a self-appointed centre which universalizes its own reading of 'civilization'. It also constitutes, however, a solid social democratic and hence relatively progressive project that not only counteracts the United States on a number of key issues (privacy laws, genetically modified food, women's and gay rights), but also makes a deliberate attempt to distance itself from Europe's former role as imperial centre. The post-nationalist or 'becoming-minoritarian' idea of Europe raises potentially explosive issues of entitlement and cultural diversity. The renewed emphasis on the unification process has made 'difference' more divisive and contested than ever, according to the paradox of simultaneous globalization and fragmentation, which is characteristic of late postmodernity. The disintegration of the Soviet Union and the ethnic wars that followed have resurrected the ghost of pejorative differences and show once again Europeans' inability to live with their own diversity. In such a context, post-nationalism is a political project and an open challenge.

Yet, the founding fathers of the European Union, in the aftermath of fascism, after the Second World War, defended the post-nationalistic definition of European identity and the flexible forms of citizenship it may entail. Albert Hirschman's autobiographical accounts (Hirschman 1995; 1994) are very illuminating on this score, as is the history of his own sister, Ursula Hirschmann (1993), a pioneer of the European Union, married to Altiero Spinelli, the first European commissioner (Spinelli 1992, 1988).

The European Union also aimed at streamlining the reconstruction of Europe's war-torn economy, in opposition to the Soviet-dominated countries of the East, and thus it was a major pawn in Cold War politics. Fundamentally, however, the European unification process was the price that member states were made to pay for their belligerence and for the Holocaust. In this respect, the project of the European Union is negatively linked to Jewishness. The positive link to Jewish tradition is through the notion of trans-European cosmopolitanism and the idea of the diaspora. Diasporic Jewish subjects embody a brand of cosmopolitanism which configures a supra-national type of subjectivity. Ursula Hirschmann argued that the Jewish citizen, like the European Federalist, represents an enlightened, anti-nationalist subject-position, which does not define his or her country merely by topological or territorial concerns. This expressed a non-nationalistic sense of Europeanness, which is at home in the diaspora.

Neither Hirschmann nor I are intent on metaphorizing the figure of the Jew, or erecting it into a ready-made icon of homelessness and rootlessness. We are perfectly aware of the huge human and historical price that Jewish citizens had to pay for their homeless condition. This is not about metaphors, but rather about alternative genealogies and locations. Hannah Arendt's work on the pariahs, or the stateless people who do not have the right to have any rights, is extremely significant here. Arendt's account of the genesis of an enlightened European polity alongside the perpetual barbarism of xenophobia, anti-Semitism and racism attributes to the diasporic Jew a positive role by introducing from the eighteenth century a much-needed dose of cosmopolitanism in the provincial European mindset (Arendt 1968). By necessity and by his or her own inspiration, the Jewish citizen becomes the signifier of cross-national mobility and multiple allegiances. In Arendt's philosophy the cosmopolitan Jew is the mark of emancipated and highly evolved moral and political behaviour and an antidote to the rampant nationalism that she witnessed during her life. After the Eichmann trial, Arendt (1963) extended this criticism to the state of Israel itself. Arendt's political model of flexible citizenship is one of the reasons for the reappraisal of her work by feminist political theorists like Benhabib (1996), in an attempt to avoid the universalizing tendency of cosmopolitanism, exemplified by Nussbaum. The Jewish diasporic cosmopolitan subject stands for a flexible model of accountable and responsible citizenship that allows for multiple modes of belonging. This is of great inspiration for a new European civil and political space.

Critiquing Eurocentrism from within

The post-nationalist process of European unification involves the critique of the self-appointed missionary role of Europe as the alleged centre of the world. It promotes a re-grounding of this false universalism into a more situated, local perspective. Feminist epistemologists and post-colonial critics have produced some of the most significant critiques of the false universalism of the European subject of knowledge: science as white man's burden. As a project of becoming-minoritarian, the European Union has to do with the rejection of the false universalism that historically has made Europe into the home of nationalism, colonialism and fascism. This is an attempt to come to terms with the paradoxes and internal contradictions of our own historical predicament as 'post-Europe Europeans', much as gender theory has had to deal with the fragments, the deconstruction and reconstruction of the 'post-Woman women' in the feminist process of transformation from dominant Woman to nomadic women-in-becoming (Braidotti 2002).

The European Union project has to do with the sobering experience of taking stock of our specific location and, following the feminist politics of location, adopting embedded and embodied perspectives. It is about turning our collective memory to the service of a new political and ethical project, which is forward-looking and not nostalgic. Daniel Cohn-Bendit recently stated that if we want to make this European business work, we really must start from the assumption that Europe is the specific periphery where we live and that we must take responsibility for it (1995). Imagining anything else would be a repetition of that flight into abstraction for which our culture is (in)famous: at best, it may procure us the benefits of escapism; at worst, the luxury of guilt. We have to start from where we are. We need both political strategies and imaginary figurations that are adequate to our historicity.

This is, however, only one side of the paradoxical coin of European deconstruction; the other side, simultaneously true and yet absolutely contradictory, is the danger of recreating a sovereign centre through the new European Union. That the two be simultaneously the case again demonstrates the schizoid logic of the global world, marked by the simultaneous occurrence of opposite effects. It also makes European identity into one of the most contested areas of political and social philosophy at the moment. The reactive tendency towards a sovereign sense of the Union is also known as the 'Fortress Europe' syndrome, which has been extensively criticized by feminists and anti-racists such as Helma Lutz, Nira Yuval-Davis and Anne Phoenix (Lutz et al. 1996), Avtar Brah (1993), Yuval-Davis and Floya Anthias (Yuval-Davis 1997; Yuval-Davis and Anthias 1989), and Philomena Essed (1991). They warn us against the danger of replacing the former Eurocentrism with a new 'Europ-ism', i.e. the belief in an ethnically pure and self-defining Europe. The question of ethnic purity is, of course, the germ of Eurofascism. It entails not only a forcibly instilled form of amnesia – the omission of colonialism as the structural 'other' that defines European identity. It also supports a solipsistic fantasy of immunity from contamination that denies the importance of all kinds of others.

In response to this danger, the post-nationalist project of the European Union offers new perspectives for the strategic relocation of whiteness. Whiteness is a contaminated colour and progressive European social theory has historically not engaged with it. Centuries of explicit white supremacist discourses in colonialism, fascism and now the 'clash of civilizations' make it difficult to approach this issue because in European culture explicit theories of white supremacy have been formulated in the language of science, along biologically and culturally deterministic lines (Griffin and Braidotti 2002). Critical studies of whiteness proliferate, however, in the aftermath of post-colonial and black studies in the United States, Canada and Australia.

Feminist critics like Frankenberg (1994a; 1994b) and Brodkin Sacks (1994), for instance, have analysed extensively the phenomenon known as the 'whitening' of Euro-immigrants, especially Jews and Italians, in their English-speaking host countries. Cultural identity being relational, external and retrospective, this whitening process takes place in the confrontation with other, native and usually black, peoples. Cornel West also analyses the interdependence of the categories of Blackness and Whiteness and their link to the diaspora of European colonists, immigrants and exiles, which runs throughout the last two centuries. European immigrants to the United States tended to conceive of themselves in regional or linguistic terms, as 'Sicilians', 'Lithuanians', 'Slavs', etc. West comments: 'They had to learn that they were "White", principally by adopting American discourse of positively-valued Whiteness and negatively-charged Blackness' (West 1990: 29). The extent to which this kind of 'whitened' identity is as illusory as it is racist can be seen by how divided the diasporic Euro-immigrant communities actually are, all in their respective ghettos, and locked in mutual suspicion of each other. But all are equally 'whitened' by the gaze of the colonizer.

Michael Walzer (1992) has argued that multiculturalism is the foundational political myth in the United States, whereas cultural homogeneity is central to the tales of European nationalism. Historical evidence argues against such an idea: waves of migrations from the East and the South make a mockery of any claim to ethnic or cultural homogeneity in Europe, while the centuries-old presence of Jewish and Muslim citizens challenges the identification of Europe with Christianity. Historical accuracy, however, can hardly be taken as the primary function of political myths. Thus, the idea of a fundamental cultural homogeneity as the binding factor of the different European countries, across their great linguistic diversity, is central to the recent European Constitutional Charter. It outlines the defining traits of European culture in: humanism, or the respect for human rights; rationalism and the faith in scientific progress and secularism; or the separation of church from state. These are all Enlightenment-based ideals that fail to account for the less glorious, and considerably more murderous, aspects of European history.

This appeal to a largely invented notion of cultural homogeneity is at the heart of contemporary ethnocentrism and racism. It results in reterritorializing the European subject on culturally essentialist foundations. This creates new challenges for anti-racist politics, which is caught between the return of this master narrative of identity on the one hand and the forces of global hybridization on the other. Anti-racist op-positional forces are very active within Europe: black activists raise issues of entitlement and access to multicultural citizenship and challenge any assumption of monoculturalism: can one be European and black or Muslim (Gilroy 1987)? What is the legal status of the multiple forms of cultural belonging for second- and third-generation Muslim migrants born and raised in contemporary Europe? Avtar Brah stresses the perpetuation of colonial habits of framing the 'others' within Europe and wonders: 'what is the likely impact of the Single European Market upon women and other groups discursively represented as minorities?' (Brah 1996).

I would situate European anti-racist relocations of whiteness in this perspective and grab the opportunity offered by the process of the European Union to develop specific racialized locations, and hence historically embedded memories and accountability, for anti-racist whites. Any fantasy of cultural homogeneity and lily-white European ethnic purity is shattered by a process that aims at grounding identities, deflating their universal imposture and holding them to account for their history. This strategy of making identities immanent, instead of upholding transcendental universals, marks the 'becoming-minoritarian' of Europe. Specific strategies are needed to critique whiteness within Europe, because this category creates serious methodological, as well as political, problems. In his analysis of the representation of whiteness as an ethnic category in mainstream films, Richard Dyer (1997) defines it as 'an emptiness, absence, denial or even a kind of death'. Being the norm, it is invisible, as if natural, inevitable or the ordinary way to do things (Ware 1992). The source of the representational power of white is the propensity to be everything and nothing, whereas black, of course, is always marked off as *a* colour. The effect of this structured invisibility and of the process of naturalization of whiteness is that it masks itself off into a 'colourless multicolouredness'. White contains all other colours.

The vacuous nature of dominant power formations has been analysed by Foucault as the Panopticon; the void that lies at the heart of the system and which defines the contour of both social and symbolic visibility. Deleuze and Guattari also comment on the fact that any dominant notion such as masculinity or race has no positive definition. The prerogative of being dominant means that a concept gets defined oppositionally, by casting outwards upon others the mark of oppression or marginalization. The centre is dead and void; there is no becoming there. The action is at the city gates, where nomadic tribes of world-travelled polyglots are taking a short break. Virginia Woolf had already commented on this aspect of the logic of domination when she asserted that what matters is not so much that He, the male, should be superior, so long as She, the Other, be clearly defined as inferior. There is no dominant concept other than as a term to index and police access and participation to entitlements and powers. Thus, the invisibility of the dominant concepts is also the expression of their insubstantiality, which makes them all the more effective in their murderous intentions against the many others on whose structural exclusion they rest their powers.

The immediate consequence of this process of naturalization or invisibility is not only political, but also methodological, namely that whiteness is very difficult to analyse critically. Dyer states that: 'whiteness falls apart in your hands as soon as you begin'. It tends to break down into subcategories of whiteness: Irishness, Italianness, Jewishness, etc. It follows therefore that non-whites have a much clearer perception of whiteness than whites. Just think of bell hooks's important work on whiteness as terror and as death-giving force (1992) and Toni Morrison's pioneer work on the structural function of blackness in literature (1992).

The lesson I want to draw from this is that whiteness needs to be de-linked from its dialectics of power and forced to confront itself. Its location needs to shift from the logic of opposition and domination, to a higher level of self-reflexivity. By learning to view their subject position as racialized white people, we can work towards anti-racist forms of whiteness, or at least anti-racist strategies to rework whiteness. This is the idea of a post-nationalist Europe as the site of becoming-minoritarian, which Étienne Balibar (2001) expresses in terms of Europe as borderland. The common anti-racist political strategy in this regard is to support the claim of European identity as an open and multi-layered project, not as a fixed or given essence, which can be turned into a space of critical resistance. To rework whiteness in the era of postmodernity we need firstly to situate it in the geo-historical space of Europe and within the political project of the European Union. This amounts to de-essentializing it, historicizing it and de-mystifying its allegedly 'natural' locations. The next step, following the method of the feminist politics of location, is to analyse it critically, to revisit it by successive deconstructive repetitions that aim at emptying out the different layers of this complex identity, excavating it till it opens out.

The challenge consists in trying to relocate white European identity, so as to undo its hegemonic tendencies. I refer to this kind of identity as 'nomadic'. Being a nomadic European subject means to be in transit within different identity-formations, but sufficiently anchored to a historical position to accept responsibility for it. Dispelling the privilege of invisibility that was conferred on Europe as an alleged centre of the world and assuming full responsibility for the partial perspective of its own location can open up a minoritarian European space. This conscious retreat from the imperialist fantasy can also be described as the effort to 'provincialize Europe' (Chakrabarty 2000). Nietzsche (1994) argued in the nineteenth century that many Europeans no longer feel at home in Europe. Many would want to argue that those who do not identify with Europe as a centre today are ideally suited to the task of reframing Europe as a post-nationalist space.

The non-unitary vision of the subject represented in the figuration of nomadic subjectivity has proved at best controversial, at times polemical and always provocative. The most sophisticated theoretical attack against philosophical nomadism is provided by Spivak's criticism of poststructuralist (1988, revised in Spivak 1999) philosophy's concern for the crisis of the subject as one of its tools of domination and control. European philosophy perpetuates its hegemony – paradoxically – in and through the discourse of its alleged 'crisis' (see chapter 1). Spivak takes Foucault and Deleuze to task over what she describes as their contradictory relationship to heterogeneity and alterity. Spivak accuses them of conflating two meanings of the term 'representation': 'speaking for', as in politics, and 're-presenting', as in art or philosophy. This confusion allows Foucault and Deleuze conveniently to dismiss the question of their own power. This results in reinstating an implicit, all-knowing subject, who is allegedly transparent by refusing to speak 'on behalf' of the oppressed. This universalistic stance is for Spivak typical of the Eurocentric subject and instrumental to his or her power. Foucault and Deleuze perpetuate this model of subjectivity by failing to situate their own discursive stance. They consequently perpetuate the invisibility of the oppressed and occupy the white privileged position of the hegemonic radicals.

I beg to differ from Spivak's assessment. The charge of vampiristic or consumerist consumption of others is an ill-informed way of approaching the issue, in that it ignores the rigorous anti-humanistic, cartographic and materialistic roots of poststructuralism. It specifically rests on a misreading of what is involved in the poststructuralist critique of representation and on what is at stake in the task of redefining alternative subject-positions. Spivak attempts to rescue Derrida, whom she credits with far more self-reflexivity and political integrity than she is prepared to grant to Foucault and Deleuze. The grounds for this preferential treatment are highly debatable. Nomadic thinking challenges the semiotic approach that is crucial to the 'linguistic turn' and also to deconstruction. Both Deleuze and Foucault engage in a critical dialogue with it and work towards an alternative model of political and ethical practice. It seems paradoxical that thinkers who are committed to an analytics of contemporary subject-positions get accused of actually having caused the events which they account for; as if they were single-handedly responsible for, or even profiting from, the accounts they offer as cartographies. Naming the networks of power-relations in late postmodernity, however, is not as simple as metaphorizing and therefore consuming them. In my view there is no vampiristic approach towards 'otherness' on the part of the poststructuralists. Moreover, I find that approach compatible with the emerging subjectivities of the former 'others' of Western reason. Late postmodernity has seen the proliferation of many and potentially contradictory discourses and practices of difference, which have dislocated the classical axis of distinction between Self or Same/Other or Different. The point of coalition between different critical voices and the poststructuralists is the process of elaborating the spaces in-between self and other, which means the practice of the Relation. They stress the need to elaborate forms of social and political implementation of non-pejorative and non-dualistic notions of 'others'.

This is what I referred to (Braidotti 2002) as the process of becoming-minoritarian of both the Majority – the Same, or the dominant subject position – and of His (the gender is no coincidence) Minorities, or Others. The process of becoming-minoritarian/woman/animal/insect/imperceptible can be contiguous, but in so far as there is a structural dissymmetry in the starting positions of the Same and of His Others, their lines or paths of becoming are discontinuous. Some becomings operate a much-needed dislodgement of dominant subject-positions (masculinity, hetero-sexuality, whiteness, Eurocentrism in the imperialist mode). Others mark instead the conditions for the affirmation of new subject-positions and thus lay the foundations for possible futures. The difference between the two lines is not a matter of relativism, but of major power dissymmetry and thus of structural differences. Philosophical nomadism allows us to think of these differences in embodied and embedded terms and to index them on an ethical scale based on empowerment. The relationship between these two sequences is not progressive, or successive, but is rather a matter of ethical and political forces. Becoming-minoritarian traces lines of evolution that actualize the ethical substance of a subject which, as we shall see in chapter 4, is defined with Spinoza as a complex dynamic entity bent upon the expression of his or her *conatus*.

A similar line is run by Robert Young (1990) in his analysis of the anti-imperialist politics of the poststructuralist philosophers. Stressing their explicit involvement with French anticolonial politics and especially the Algerian war of independence, Young traces a direct equivalence between the critique of humanism proposed by Foucault, Deleuze, Derrida and others, and their critique of European imperialism down to and including fascism and the events of the Second World War. The poststructuralist rejection of logocentrism implies the in-depth critique of Eurocentrism and, with it, the Hegelian dialectical vision of the Subject and of his role in History. The rejection of this totalizing way of conceiving the role of the unitary subject is the defining feature of poststructuralist philosophy. The 'ontological imperialism' (Young 1990: 13) of European thought and its connection with world-domination is the main target of the poststruc-turalists. It establishes a conceptual line of continuity with post-colonial theories. This does not mean that the two 'post's' 'are the same, but rather that their respective differences can be highlighted against a common historical and theoretical background' (Appiah 1991).

On this point, both bell hooks and Stuart Hall have in fact warned of the cheap trick that consists in 'saving' the marginal others from the destabilizing impact of postmodernism in general and poststructuralist philosophies in particular. In 'Postmodern blackness' bell hooks strongly objects to the way in which blacks and other 'others' are not entitled to deconstructive approaches to identity. It is as if they should be stuck with the burden of 'authentic' experience, empirical 'reality' and real-life socio-economic 'conditions', thus leaving the task of theorizing to others. hooks (1990: 23) argues that 'Racism is perpetuated when blackness is associated solely with concrete, gut-level experience, conceived as either opposing or having no connection to abstract thinking and the production of critical theory'. It is rather the case that postmodern blackness is infinitely more dangerous to racism, in so far as it exposes the white arrogance which consists in automatically assimilating the marginal 'others' to 'the view from below'.

The task of bringing into adequate representation the sort of new mixtures that contemporary subjects have become is at the heart of poststructuralist philosophies and hence of philosophical nomadism. The aim here is to provide a materially based practice of conceptual representation of the subjects in-becoming within the fast-shifting social landscape of post-industrial societies. The process of drawing cartographies of the present is central to social theory and cultural studies, in both feminist and mainstream theories. The great advantage of a poststructuralist approach is that it allows for a radical critique of 'representational' thinking and the kind of metaphorization processes it implies. Priority is given to the quest for new figurations that account for processes of changes and transformation, that is to say in-between-ness and flows. The aim is not to validate or sacralize the authenticity of experience, but rather to develop politically empowering methods of deconstructing identities, so as to enable a radical shift of perspective within the subject and to lay the foundations for new interconnections and alliances. bell hooks put it succinctly (hooks 1990: 27): 'Radical postmodernism calls attention to those shared sensibilities which cross the boundaries of class, gender, race, etc. that could be fertile ground for the construction of empathy – ties that would promote recognition of common commitments, and serve as a base for solidarity and coalition.'

The point of the matter for poststructuralist thought is that, whether we like it or not, displacement is a central feature of the postmodern era (Probyn 1990). Contemporary post-industrial societies function by flows of cash and data (Dahrendorf 1990) and are organized along multiple axes of mobility of people and commodities (Cresswell 1997). Mouffe (1994) and Laclau (1995) analyse the political economy of contemporary post-industrial societies in terms of vast and collectively renegotiated processes of hybridization. The loss of unitary subjectivity, be it in post-communist, post-industrial or post-colonial societies, is such as to require a return of the political in the sense of resistance and democratic confrontations.

Theoretically, my position on philosophical nomadism is quite the opposite of the metaphorization processes that Clifford rightly criticizes as 'pseudouniversal cosmopolitan bravado' (1994: 312). It is rather a situated and highly politicized attempt to rethink the subject in terms of his or her embodied singularity, which addresses specifically, but not exclusively, those who choose to make themselves accountable for their 'centre', in a world structured by multiple and dynamic centres of power. Shifts, mutations and processes of change are a key feature of our particular historical period. Social critics therefore need to be situated in their approach to the analysis of the new subject positions which have become available in post-industrial times. The differences in degrees, types, kinds and modes of mobility and – even more significantly – of non-mobility need to be mapped out with precision and sensitivity. The aim of this affirmative and non-aporetic deconstruction is to undo the structures of phallo-logocentric power, as Irigaray would phrase it, or the voice of the Majority, as Deleuze would put it, and to subvert it. The becoming-minoritarian, or becoming-nomadic is the pattern of subversion that is open to both the empirical members of the majority (the 'same') and to those of the minority (the 'others'). Both need to relinquish their ties, but they do so in dissymmetrical ways. Cartographic accuracy is made necessary by the fact that nomadism is precisely not a universal metaphor, but rather a generic term of indexation for qualitatively different degrees of access and entitlement to power. Grounded, historicized accounts for the multiply positioned subjects of postmodernity are needed for people who are situated in one of the many poly-located centres that weave together the global economy. Power is the key issue, and mobility is a term that indexes access to it. As such, power-relations are internally contradictory. The politics of location and the politically invested cartographies they produce are the main tools – in a conceptual as well as political sense of the term. Producing a cartography is a way of embedding critical practice in a specific situated perspective, avoiding universalistic generalizations and grounding it so as to make it accountable.

On flexible citizenship and multiple belongings[2]

This post-nationalistic sense of diasporic, hybrid and nomadic identity can be translated into the political notion of flexible citizenship, in the framework of the 'new' European Union. 'Flexible forms of citizenship' would allow for all 'others', all kinds of hybrid citizens, to acquire legal status in what would otherwise deserve the label of 'Fortress Europe'. A double de-linking could be implemented so as to disengage citizenship from nationality and national identity (i.e. not space-bound) and from permanence, so that it could be extended to temporary residence (i.e. not time-bound). This allows for complex allegiances and multiple forms of cultural belongings. Dismantling the us/them binary, it replaces a fixed notion of European citizenship with a functionally differentiated network of affiliations and loyalties. For the citizens of the member states of the European Union this leads to the disconnection of the three elements of citizenship, nationality and national identity. These effects boil down to one central idea: the end of pure and steady identities, or in other words, creolization and hybridization producing a multicultural minoritarian Europe, within which 'new' Europeans can take their place alongside others.

[2] This term has gained widespread acceptance; I first read it in Aihwa Ong's work on Chinese migrants (Ong 1993).

According to Ulrich Preuss, a European notion of citizenship so disengaged from national foundations lays the ground for a new kind of civil
society, beyond the boundaries of any single nation-state. Because such a
notion of 'alienage' (Preuss 1996: 551) would become an integral part of
citizenship in the European Union, Preuss argues that all European citizens would end up being 'privileged foreigners'. In other words, they
would function together without reference to a centralized and homogeneous sphere of political power (Preuss 1996: 280). Potentially, this
notion of citizenship could therefore lead to a new concept of politics,
which would no longer be bound to the nation-state. It is one of the possible forms of subjects we could become.

This possibility has also generated a reaction of panic at the potential
loss of a 'strong' European identity by conservative forces that uphold the
power of nation-states. The project of European unification has in fact
triggered a wave of nostalgic political reactions on the issue of migration
and citizenship, which are simultaneously anti-European and racist. The
short term effect of this wave is nationalistic paranoia and xenophobic
fears, which also enact a fragmentation of larger national identities into
regional or localized sub-identities. It is indeed the case, as Benhabib points
out (1999), that the redefinition of European boundaries and a relative fluidity about European identity coincide with the resurgence of micro-national-
isms at all levels in Europe today. According to the schizoid workings of
globalization or advanced capitalism, the unification of Europe coexists
with the closing down of its borders; the coming of a common European
citizenship and a common currency with increasing internal fragmentation
and regionalism; a new, allegedly post-nationalist identity has to coexist
with the return of xenophobia, racism and anti-Semitism. The law of
excluded middle does not hold in postmodernity: one thing and its opposite
can simultaneously be the case.

A clear sign of this power-ridden reaction in defence of a hard-core
European identity is the crisis of the universal value attributed to secularism in European culture. Recent measures taken by EU member states
such as France to outlaw the public display of religious allegiances, especially wearing the headscarf by Muslim women, are clear indications of
the fear. This reaction is myopic in forgetting, not only that secularism is
not yet a consensual factor in Europe, it is also no longer a reliable ground
for European identity. Given the extent to which second-generation
Muslim migrants and post-colonial subjects embrace religion as a defence
of an ethnic identity which is under attack, it follows that an automatic
and unreflective brand of normative secularism runs the risk of becoming
complicitous with xenophobia and racism (Connolly 1999). The crisis of
secularism is especially poignant for feminists – in that the separation of
church from state and the universality of human rights are foundational
values for the European women's movements. Elisabeth Badinter (2003)
has provided a contemporary example of how normative this position can

become by castigating any attempt to question the secular tradition of French feminism. This is a problematic political position in so far as it fails to acknowledge the historical specificity of the situation. The decline of secularism is a reaction against and hence it is historically situated within the horizon of globalization, not outside it. Even a conservative social thinker like Samuel Huntington (1996) acknowledges that the crisis of secularism is related to the specific conditions of post-colonial migration and global mobility of the workforce. It is a contemporary problem, which unfortunately reactivates some bad memories for Western feminists: it is as if we relived our own struggle against the powers of the Christian church, through the contemporary situation of Muslim women in Europe. This is understandable, but it is not, however, an accurate cartography. We need to position the practices of secularism, in both the West and the East, in their respective historical and geopolitical locations. A failure to recognize this historical specificity runs the risk of bringing European feminism close to that 'cultural racism' that Stuart Hall and black migrant women so eloquently denounce. Identities are problematic at all times, but especially when they are under threat.

In her recent work on European citizenship, Benhabib (2002) interrogates critically the disjunction between the concepts of nation, the state and cultural identity. A self-professed Kantian cosmopolitan, Benhabib argues forcefully that 'democratic citizenship can be exercised across national boundaries and in transnational contexts' (Benhabib 2002: 183). Solidly grounded in her theory of communicative ethics, Benhabib stipulates 'norms of universal respect and egalitarian reciprocity as guiding principles of human interaction' (Benhabib 2002: 11). She is especially keen to demonstrate that the distinction between national minority and ethnic group does very little 'to determine whether an identity/difference-driven movement is democratic, liberal, inclusive and universalist' (Benhabib 2002: 65). For Benhabib the European Union is a good example of the new modes of non-nationalist citizenship which have become available in the new world order. She praises, for instance, the medieval European tradition of city-based asylum rights as partial forms of alternative citizenship and as a way of elaborating new rules of 'glocal' democracy within a multicultural horizon.

Within the specific location of Europe, important work has been done to analyse the ongoing process of the European Union both as a player in the global economy and as an attempt to move beyond the traditional grounds on which European nationalism has prospered, namely essentialized identities. One interesting cluster of work on the new European citizenship has emerged specifically in Southern Europe as part of the critique of globalization. It is organized around journals such as *Multitudes* in France, *Posse* in Italy and *Archipelago* in Spain. Some of it refers back to the philosophy of non-unitary subjectivity and the notion of politics as mediation, which Balibar (2002) has been developing, as well as work on migration and citizenship (Moulier Boutang 1986). A sizeable part of it, however, is generated as an extension of Hardt and Negri's best-selling *Empire*. This school of thought combines a monistic Spinozist political economy with a post-Marxian brand of materialist analysis of labour conditions under advanced capitalism (Virno 1994; 2001). It views Europe as a potential space of becoming and thus has profound affinity with my project. Negri's work, however, especially his theory of the revolutionary multitude as the motor of world resistance, remains, even after all these years, over-enthusiastic. Although Hardt and Negri theorize capitalism as schizophrenia, they fail, in my eyes, to practice what they preach. Their vision of the allegedly ongoing revolutionary process, which they express in a euphoric and at times hyperbolical language, contradicts the conceptual premises of their thought. The process of becoming-revolutionary, as Deleuze teaches in a more ascetic tone, is just that: a process, a practice, an art, an experiment. There is no overarching meta-narrative of one global multitude in Deleuze's philosophy of radical immanence, as there is in Hardt and Negri's totalizing neo-Marxist narrative.

This meta-narrative of labour also has problematic consequences for their vision of Europe, which is taken *de facto* as the space of the alternative to globalization and global capitalism. This normative injunction expresses a wish I share, namely that of steering the incipient and struggling European Union in the direction of more political power, self-determination and opposition to American belligerence. Hardt and Negri's zealous belief that this is the revolutionary option sanctioned by history and the will of the multitude is, however, unconvincing. This belief assumes that someone – the multitude – is actually in charge of the course of history and that its collective voice merges with the prophetic desire of the intellectuals. I find a deep-seated Marxian hard core in Hardt and Negri's philosophy of power, which flatly contradicts their poststructuralist allegiance, making a mockery of their claim to honour multiplicity and complexity. On key issues they openly disagree with Deleuze's philosophical nomadology; for instance, on the concept of the virtual, which they assimilate to the material process of labour and hence to the endeavours of the multitude. There is also a clear divergence on politics, which they reinscribe in a world-historical mass movement of insurrection. They differ also on the subject of philosophy, which they subject to an instrumental use in terms of classical Marxist praxis, thus losing the emphasis on technologies of the self, or the humble and patient creation of new concepts. Ultimately, they share less with poststructuralism than with Marxism, less with Deleuze than with Laclau and Mouffe. Such clear-cut certainties beg too many questions and are thus ultimately unsatisfactory.

The idea of 'national identity', a subtler theoretical perspective, inspired by Homi Bhabha (1990; 1994) or Edward Said (1978), reveals that common ideas of 'nation' are to a large extent imaginary tales. They uphold

Eurocentric power and project a reassuring but nonetheless illusory unity over the fragmented and often incoherent regional and linguistic differences that make up the European nation-states. Moreover, a feminist perspective enriches this insight by showing to what extent the legitimating tales of nationhood in the West have been constructed over the bodies of women, as well as in the crucible of imperial and colonial masculinity.

The fact that these allegedly universal or all-encompassing ideas of 'nation' or 'national identity' are flawed and internally incoherent does not make them any less effective, nor does it prevent them from exercising hegemonic power. But the awareness of the instability and lack of coherence of fundamental categories, such as national identity, far from resulting in passive resignation to sovereign power, leads to renewed efforts to ground political resistance in the specific paradoxes of our historical condition. Considering the complex structure of the globalized world, political activism must also be multi-layered and as internally differentiated as the world it moves in. One-way revolutionary roads will not help in the maze of the globally mediated world. Equally untenable is the opposite political position: the belief in the natural foundations and consequently the fixed nature of any system of values, meanings or beliefs. What sustains political engagement is a qualitative shift of perspective, a yearning for resistance and empowerment. This is primarily an ethical affect.

THE QUEST FOR A NEW GLOBAL ETHICS

What can be the ethical import of the process of multiple belongings and becoming nomadic or minoritarian, in which affects take centre stage? Becoming-political is part of this same process, which involves a radical repositioning or internal transformation on the part of subjects who want to become-minoritarian in a productive and affirmative manner. In chapters 4 and 5 I shall outline this internal landscape in detail; for the moment, let me just illustrate the case, for instance the move towards a post-nationalist European identity. It is clear that this shift requires changes that are neither simple nor self-evident. They mobilize the affectivity of the subjects involved and can be seen as a process of transformation of negative into positive passions. Fear, anxiety and nostalgia are clear examples of the negative emotions involved in the project of detaching ourselves from familiar and cherished forms of identity. To achieve a post-nationalist sense of European identity requires the disidentification from established, nation-bound references. Such an enterprise involves a sense of loss of cherished habits of thought and representation, and thus it is not free of pain. No process of consciousness-raising ever is.

The beneficial side-effects of this process are unquestionable and in some way they compensate for the pain of loss. Thus, the critical relocation of whiteness can produce an affirmative, situated form of anti-racist European subject-position. In a more Spinozist vein, it also produces a more adequate cartography of our real-life condition, free of delusions of grandeur. This mature and sobering experience is similar to the cathartic eye-opening or moral awakening of Greek tragedies. It is an enriching and positive experience; nonetheless, pain is an integral part of it. Migrants, exiles, refugees have first-hand experience of the extent to which the process of disidentification from familiar identities is linked to the pain of loss and uprooting. Diasporic subjects of all kinds express the same sense of wound, as we saw in the earlier sections of this chapter. Multilocality is the affirmative translation of this negative sense of loss. Following Glissant, the becoming-nomadic marks the process of positive transformation of the pain of loss into the active production of multiple forms of belonging and complex allegiances. What is lost, in the sense of fixed origins, is gained in an increased desire to belong, in a multiple rhizomic manner which transcends the classical bilateralism of binary identity formations.

The qualitative leap through pain, across the mournful landscapes of nostalgic yearning, is the gesture of active creation of affirmative ways of belonging. It is a fundamental reconfiguration of our way of being in the world, which acknowledges the pain of loss, but moves further. Ultimately, it is a practice of freedom. That is the defining moment for the process of becoming-ethical: the move across and beyond pain, loss and negative passions. Taking suffering into account is the starting point, the real aim of the process, however, is the quest for ways of overcoming the stultifying effects of passivity, brought about by pain. The internal disarray, fracture and pain are the conditions of possibility for ethical transformation. Clearly, this is an antithesis of the Kantian moral imperative to avoid pain, or to view pain as the obstacle to moral behaviour. Nomadic ethics is not about the avoidance of pain, but rather about transcending the resignation and passivity that ensue from being hurt, lost and dispossessed. One has to become-ethical, as opposed to just applying moral rules and protocols as a form of self-protection. Transformations express the affirmative power of Life as the vitalism of '*bios/zoe*', which is the opposite of morality as a form of life insurance. I will develop this further in chapters 4 and 5.

The awakening of ethical and political consciousness through the pain of loss has been acknowledged by Edgar Morin (1987). He describes his 'becoming-European' as a double affect: the first concerns the disappointment with the unfulfilled promises of Marxism, which has been Morin's first political engagement and passion. The second is compassion for the uneasy, struggling and marginal position of post-war Europe, squashed between the United States and the Soviet Union. The pain of this awareness that Europe was unloved and a castaway, 'une pauvre vieille petite chose' 'a poor old thing', (Morin 1987: 23), results in a new kind of bonding, and a renewed sense of care and accountability. The sobering experience – the humble and productive recognition of loss, limitations and shortcomings – has to do with self-representations. Established mental habits, images and terminology railroad us back towards established ways of thinking about ourselves. Traditional modes of representation are legal forms of addiction. To change them is not unlike undertaking a disintoxication cure. A great deal of courage and creativity is needed to develop forms of representation that do justice to the complexities of the kind of subjects we have already become. We already live and inhabit social reality in ways that surpass tradition: we move about, in the flow of current social transformations, in hybrid, multi-cultural, polyglot, post-identity spaces of becoming (Braidotti 2002). We fail, however, to bring them into adequate representation. There is a shortage on the part of our social imaginary, a deficit of representational power, which underscores the political timidity of the European unification process. Some of this difficulty is contingent and may be linked to the lack of a European public space, as Habermas suggests (1992); or the lack of visionary leadership among politicians, as Meny put it (2000). In any case, European issues fail to trigger our imagination and make us dream (Passerini 1998).

The real issue, however, is conceptual: how do we develop a new post-nationalist European social imaginary, through the pain of disidentification and loss? Given that identifications constitute an inner scaffolding that supports one's sense of identity, how do changes of this magnitude take place? Shifting an imaginary is not like casting away a used garment, but more like shedding an old skin. It actually, happens often enough at the molecular level, but at the social level, it is a painful experience. Part of the answer lies in the formulation of the question: 'we' are in *this* together. This is a collective activity, a group project that connects active conscious and desiring citizens. It points towards a virtual destination, post-nationalist Europe, but it is not utopian. As a project it is historically grounded, socially embedded and already partly actualized in the joint endeavour, i.e. the community, of those who are actively working towards it. If this is at all utopian, it is only in the sense of the positive affects that are mobilized in the process: the necessary dose of imagination, dreamlike vision and bonding, without which no social project can take off.

Feminism is a great example of this kind of transformative political project: feminists are those subjects who have taken their critical distance from the dominant social institutions of femininity and masculinity, relating them to other crucial variables, such as ethnicity, race and class. Feminist theory has addressed the issue of the imaginary, through the emphasis it had placed both on identification as a factor in identity formation, and on disidentification as a strategic support of consciousness-raising. It has done so, however, mostly within a psychoanalytic frame of reference, with emphasis on the imaginary as the process of linguistic mediation. This refers to a system of representation by which a subject gets captured or captivated by a ruling social and cultural formation: legal addictions to certain identities, images and terminologies, as I said in the prologue. These are governed and 'beamed down', both for Althusser and for Lacan, by a symbolic system represented by the Phallic Law. The interaction or mediation between the self and these imaginary institutions provides the motor for the process of becoming-subject. Needless to say, for Lacan this process labours under the burden of negativity, in the sense of lack, mourning and melancholia. This Hegelian legacy reduces the subject to a process of being-subjected-to, i.e. the negative sense of power as *potestas*.

The poststructuralist generation, starting with Foucault, challenges both the negativity and the static nature of the Lacanian master code on which all forms of mediation are supposed to hinge. The binary opposition of Self to society is too narrow to account for the complex workings of power in our culture. A thick and highly dynamic web of power effects is the factor through which self and society are mutually shaped by one another. The choreography of constraints and entitlements, controls and desire is the hard core of power. This core is void of any substantial essence and is a force, or an activity – a verb, not a noun. Power as positive or *potentia* is crucial in forming the subject as an entity enmeshed in a network of interrelated social and discursive effects. Bio-power, or power over living matter, is a good example of it. For Foucault, the system of mediation is not merely linguistic, but also material.

The 'imaginary' refers to a set of socially mediated practices which function as the anchoring point, albeit unstable and contingent, for identifications and therefore for identity-formation. These practices act like interactive structures where desire as a subjective yearning and agency in a broader socio-political sense are mutually shaped by one another. Neither 'pure' imagination – locked in its classical opposition to reason – nor fantasy in the Freudian sense, the imaginary marks a space of transitions and transactions. Nomadic, it flows like symbolic glue between the social and the self, the outside and the subject; the material and the ethereal. It flows, but it is sticky: it catches on as it goes. It possesses fluidity, but it distinctly lacks transparency. The term 'desire' connotes the subject's own investment – or enmeshment – in this sticky network of interrelated social and discursive effects, which constitutes the social field as a libidinal – or affective – landscape, as well as a normative – or disciplinary – framework.

The material embedding of imaginary formations, through embodiment and changing historical conditions, became a point of discussion among feminists and other critical theorists. Towards the 1990s the consensus of opinion shifted away from the Lacanian vision of the unconscious as a linguistic structure ruled by the laws of metaphor and metonymy. The concept of memory that Lacan renders through his vision of the unconscious is that of an essential 'black-box' that allegedly records the central data flow of psychic life. That is a very one-directional and

rather despotic notion of how unconscious memories work, which testi-
fies to Lacan's psychic essentialism and to a static vision of psychic life.
The notion that the unconscious is historical and social and hence contingent emerges as the bone of contention between Lacan and Irigaray. Irigaray's concept of strategic mimesis and the sensible transcendental subject
provides the tools for implementing changes at the in-depth level of the
self. The idea that the symbolic is porous to historical transformations and
hence mutable is compatible with Deleuze's emphasis on creative collective evolution and on the subject as empirical transcendental. I shall
return to this question in chapter 4. The imaginary continues to be of relevance, providing the leverage we need to implement changes in the
social realm, as well as in the depths of the subject. Irigaray's specular
regime of visualization of the imaginary, as a double-looking concave
mirror, is significant as a strategic tool that helps the female feminist subjects to navigate out of the murky waters of the Phallic symbolic. Nomadic
subjectivity, however, needs to go further.

Deleuze's imaginary is not postulated along linguistic lines at all – it
is like a prism or a fractal that disintegrates the unity of vision into
bundles of multi-directional perceptive tools. Deleuze relies on Spinoza's
idea of 'collective imaginings' (Gatens and Lloyd 1999), to elucidate this
crucial idea: that the imaginary is ultimately an image of thought. That is
to say, it is a habit that captures and blocks the many potential alternative
ways we may be able to think about our environment and ourselves.
Collectively, we can empower some of these alternative becomings. This
process is collective and affective: it is driven by a desire for change
that is sustained by some, if not many. The European post-nationalist
identity is such a project: political at heart, it has a strong ethical pull made
of convictions, vision and desire. It does require labour-intensive efforts
on the part of all and thus is risky. As a project, it also requires active
participation and enjoyment: a new virtual love that targets less what we
are, more what we are capable of becoming. This liberatory potential
is directly proportional to the desire and collective affects it mobilizes.
The recognition of Europe as a post-nationalist entity is the premise for the
creation of a sense of accountability for the specific margin of the planet that
Europeans occupy. The becoming-minoritarian of Europe enacts this reconfiguration as an active experiment with different ways of inhabiting this
social space.

Far from being the prelude to a neo-universalistic stance, or its dialectical pluralistic counterpart, the relativistic acceptance of all and any locations, the project of the becoming-minoritarian of Europe is an ethical
transformation by a former centre that chooses the path of immanent
changes. Through the pain of loss and disenchantment, just as 'post-
Woman women' have moved towards a redefinition of their 'being-
gendered-in-the-world', 'post-Europe Europeans' may be able to find
enough self-respect and grown-up love for themselves to be able to seize

this historical chance to become, at last, just what we can be: Europeans, *à peine, et de justesse* ('just Europeans and not without difficulty').

Nomadic activism

Nomadic political subjects are already enacting, in a multicultural European social space, specific forms of activism and of social participation which are innovative and distinctly post-nationalist. A significant case is that of cross-border activism by women in former Yugoslavia. The project is called 'Trans-Europeanness' and in 2002 it assembled a caravan of itinerant militant feminists who travelled in a sort of pilgrimage through the sites and the territories of the Yugoslav war atrocities. The written and visual documents that followed this itinerant project are very telling (Deschaumes and Slapsak 2002), as they mark the persistent presence of the IDP's (internally displaced people) throughout the territory of that ancient multicultural and intra-religious culture which was Yugoslavia. The insanity of extremist nationalism and the atrocities it entailed are exposed by the proliferation of internal borders among the different portions of that once unified country.

As the spokeswoman for the caravan writes as they cross the border between Macedonia and Kosovo: 'We move off without knowing what we have just passed through: a checkpoint in a country at war? A border in a country at peace? A non-border between two non-countries? An emerging border between two emerging countries? (. . .) We've just passed through . . . we don't know what' (Deschaumes 2002: 236). This kind of contemporary nomadic activism combines two features that are crucial to my project of nomadic subjectivity: the sharpened sense of territoriality under the impact of the European Union and hence the notion of border-crossings. It also actualizes a productive form of activism, as an embodied political practice. The account of this pilgrimage, across the sites of massive killings, rapes and looting, makes for an instructive read. The subjects involved are in mourning, yet determined to work through their grief, their own sense of bereavement and pain. In confronting one another, they also evoke the spectre of their own nationalistic emotions, the resentment and xenophobic gut-feelings. The ethical process of transmutation of negative into positive passions could not find a better illustration: working through the suffering, these subjects enact gratuitous forms of joyful affirmation of more productive affects. Bearing witness, receiving and containing the pain of others, just being there – are the basic gestures of life – affirming bonding, not *in spite of*, but *across* the wounds and pain.

Just how novel and creative this kind of nomadic activism is, can be assessed by comparing it to the political paradigm of 'exit', proposed by Albert Hirschman (1993) as a political practice opposed to 'voice'. 'Voice' stands for the activity of actively denouncing a situation with the intent of achieving some improvement. 'Exit', on the other hand, indicates the act of leaving altogether, of walking away from a given situation and thus giving up on it. When practised on a massive scale, 'exit' can lead to the deterioration of the state of an organization; when practised more selectively, however, it can improve its performance. The two activities differ: exit is solitary and silent, voice is collective and loud, but they can reinforce each other, as evidenced by the events that led to the fall of the Berlin Wall. The mass emigration of citizens from the former German Democratic Republic is a political gesture of 'exit' and the million citizens who stayed and voiced their dissent contributed to the same process through a diametrically opposed tactic.

However effective the exit–voice scheme may be, it begs the fundamental question of what political affect or desire motivates the subject of such deep transformations. By contrast, the 'Trans-European' women's caravan as a significant case of nomadic activism provides a more embedded and embodied form of ethical accountability.

Another obvious point of comparison is Zygmunt Bauman's notion of the pilgrim as the postmodern ethical subject. This project, as I argued in chapter 1, aims to reconstitute ethical agency on the ruins of the modernist hope of combining the autonomy of rational individuals with the heteronomy of choices, i.e. how to make people choose what is best for them. Bauman proposes a hierarchy of subject-positions, with the pilgrim or vagabond at the top, as free movers across the social space, without fixed routes, itinerary or schedule. As a figuration of gratuitous being-there, the pilgrim has a saintly dimension: he or she just passes through, moving in an episodic manner, inhabiting the planet as a temporary visitor, treading gently as she goes. The nomad is discarded by Bauman because he is not free from teleological design but follows set routes and familiar paths. The bottom of the ethical scale is occupied by the tourist, who cruises along like a bad shopper, looking for bargains and taking no responsibility for his or her actions. As the prototypical post-industrial hyper-consumer, the tourist collects sensations and souvenirs.

The problem with Bauman's ethical project is that it disregards the multiple differences that constitute any categories and thus fails to situate them. The tourist, for instance, has been taken by John Urry (1990) as the prototypical 'flâneur', free from the constraints of paid labour, devoted to the gratuitous exercise of leisure. Far from being exploitative and rapacious, the tourist gazes upon the world with admiration and joy. MacCannell's (1992) study of tourism also stresses the quest for authenticity of this subject-position, which brings it closer to the pilgrim. Bauman's pilgrim lacks a politics of location and thus constitutes a weak proposition. In their critique, Jokinen and Veijola (1997) point out the flaws in Bauman's thought by injecting sexual difference and ethnicity into this rather abstract picture. Thus, the vagabond doubles up as the homeless drunk and the tourist as the sex-tourist. A wave of counter-figurations emerges: the *flâneur* turns into the obnoxious paparazzo, whereas on the horizon of postmodernity more telling figurations of mobility emerge: the au pair girl; the mail-order bride; the illegal immigrant; the cross-border prostitute; and even the babysitter. These are figures of displacement, which retain as anchoring points spatio-temporal coordinates in terms of gender, sexual identity, race, class, and age. Bauman does not pay enough attention to situated perspectives and thus ends up over-generalizing his important case.

Figurations are not mere metaphors, but rather markers of more concretely situated historical positions. A figuration is the expression of one's specific positioning in both space and time. It marks certain territorial or geopolitical coordinates, but it also points out one's sense of genealogy or of historical inscription. Figurations deterritorialize and destabilize the certainties of the subject and allow for a proliferation of situated or 'micro' narratives of self and others. As often is the case, artists and activists respond more promptly to the call for more creativity than professional academics do. Thus, Ursula Biemann investigates 'the logic of particular human economic circuits in a changed world order: the female teleservice industries in India, illegal refugee boats entering the Mediterranean Sea, the European industrial prison complex, the smuggling paths across the Spanish–Moroccan border. These sites and non-sites speak of a re-articulation of the relations between social and territorial conditions' (Biemann 2003: 22). This results in a spatialized reading of history which traces the routes of new mobile forms of subjectivity amidst the politics of global mobility. It produces an alternative relational geography which assumes as its starting position the diasporic identity of a multi-located subject and attempts to articulate it across the many variables that compose it. Technologies such as satellite surveillance (Parks 2003) and reconnaissance and border-patrolling video and electronic devices play a central role in Biemann's embodied and embedded new geography of power-relations.

Two concrete projects illustrate this strategy of multiple border-crossings: one is an art project called 'Frontera Sur RRUT – Europe's Southern border in real remote and virtual time'. It concerns the implications created by the enlargement of the European Union in the Spanish–Moroccan enclave of Ceuta and Melilla, which happens to be physically located on the African continent. The project explores both the continuation of a colonial legacy of the European occupation of North Africa, and the transformation of the southern borders in order to uphold the new European identity. Again, concludes Biemann, 'Europe defines itself by its outermost edge', which in this case is signified by large shopping malls, symbols of both the wealth and the value system of the European Union (Biemann 2003: 90).

The real function of such a border is to ensure control over the mobility of population and goods, and thus it acquires its function by being crossed.

This art project provides a very detailed logbook of the various types of border-crossings that occur in such a liminal but central space. This in turn depicts a geography of embodied crossings which includes the routes of container ships, the night boat rides taken by aspiring migrants, the itinerant paths of workers who pick vegetables for the EU markets, without forgetting the domestic workers, the smugglers, the sex workers and 'the Moroccans who peel imported shrimps for Dutch companies in Tangiers' (Biemann 2003: 90). This cartography draws a micro-geography of power-relations that are simultaneously local and global. They rely for their transnational effects on very advanced technologies for the control of human mobility, which encompass radar and satellite technologies, video and infrared cameras in order to ensure the safe flow of mobility of the population. Intrinsic to this world-view is the concomitance of the legal and illegal aspects of the economic world order: transiting, entering, smuggling go hand in hand for local inhabitants, tourists, military personnel, traders and others. To reduce some of these hastily to an 'illegal economy' is a failure to see the deep complicity and mutual implication of many of these lucrative activities. They all practice the cartography of struggle, by different means. On the side of the legal economies, these transit areas are used mostly to process components and products meant for the European markets.

The second significant art project that Ursula Biemann draws our attention to is the 'Solid sea project' by the art collective Multiplicity. This addresses the Mediterranean sea as an impenetrable block of neo-colonial economic relations, a non-transparent surface inhabited by tourists, immigrants, refugees, military staff. It is an insurmountable stretch of water, hypercontrolled by both advanced technology and the official navies of the EU member states. A solid space, strictly regulated into the forms of crossings it allows. Oil rig technicians, cruise-ship tourists, sailors, clandestine immigrants, fishermen, smugglers, military personnel all define their own paths across this solid surface. The art project traces the different routes of the various modes of crossings of this solid space, through a rationalized accounts of ports, military patrol routes, the itineraries of tobacco and other smugglers and also the complexities of the intricate system of cables and telecommunication networks that allows for this system to function. Translated into my language, this materially embedded geography is a politically invested cartography of *bios / zoe* power relations in a technologically linked global world.

CONCLUSION

Advanced capitalism and its globalized economy is a machine that spins off and multiplies differences for the sake of their commodification and profit. As such, it engenders, propels and contains simultaneously opposite effects: degrees of gender equality with growing segregation of the sexes; gender trouble on the one hand and polarized sexual difference on the other. Similarly, a global multiculturalism does not guarantee the end of racist class stratification, nor does cultural diversity protect us from growing racism. The post-nationalist project of the European Union does not put an end to nationalistic feelings and in some way even accelerates them. Gilroy sums this situation up in terms of: 'the untidy workings of creolised, synchretised, hybridised and impure cultural forms that were once rooted in the complicity of rationalised terror and racialised reason' (Gilroy 1996: 23).

This proliferation of multiple identities also challenges the equation of culture with the idea of belonging to a common identity. It relocates culture instead in multiple locations, routes and movements. To disengage 'culture' from 'identity' so as to render it as a process that has its own specific workings amounts to emphasizing the processes of transition and border-crossings, embodied genealogies and imaginary homelands, which are definitional of the non-unitary subject.

The transpositions also result in the deconstruction of the key concepts of European theoretical and political discourse and the Enlightenment-based rule of reason, such as subjectivity, individualism, equality. Their deconstruction, however, does not result in their disappearance but rather, as Foucault teaches us, in their discursive proliferation, under the guise of 'multiculturalism', 'post-coloniality' and other claims to counter-subjectivity.

Furthermore, identities are commodified and exchanged globally, in a world that is no longer organized along the dialectical axis of centre–periphery. Given that diasporic identities and transnational flows of people, goods and ideas are constitutive of globalization, the question is how to account for this proliferating multiplicity of hybrid subject positions. Comparing diasporas raises ethical questions about the methods of laying alongside each other different forms of traumatic dispersal.

Faced with a proliferation of such discourses and social practices of nomadism, how can we tell the proactive from the regressive ones? The counter-method starts from the politics of locations. This is both a strategy and a method based on politically informed cartographies of one's position, starting not from gender alone, but from a bundle of interrelated social relations. The practice of the politics of location rests on notions like experience, situatedness, accountability and transversal alliances (Braidotti 2002). This politics of locations is best served by a non-unitary vision of the subject that stresses nomadic complexity and open-endedness. As Haraway puts it:

> Location is not a listing of adjectives or assigning of labels such as race, sex and class. Location is not the concrete to the abstract of decontextu-alization. Location is the always partial, always finite, always fraught

play of foreground and background, text and context, that constitutes critical enquiry. Above all, location is not self-evident or transparent. Location is also partial in the sense of being for some worlds and not others. (Haraway 1997: 37)

The politics of location is both materialist and immanent and it provides the grounding for political accountability. As a method, it combines issues of self-reflexivity and accountability with ways of enlarging scientific objectivity. It involves dialogical confrontations with others, in a mixture of affectivity/involvement and objectivity/distance, which needs to be balanced in a critical manner. Such a methodology can only be transdisciplinary and thus scientifically impure.

The cartographies presented in this chapter argue forcefully for a new vision of the subject to sustain the critical work of accounting for the present and also to provide the moral barometer to steer an ethical course. This is a non-unitary subject position that yearns for becoming-minoritarian. The times and modes of this becoming are contingent on the specific locations of the subjects involved. The politics of location establish ethical boundaries. A new brand of non-Western neo-humanism is emerging from the debris of Western Enlightenment's unfulfilled promises and broken hopes. Simultaneously, different brands of post-humanism are at work within advanced Western societies, under the impact of technological and social forces that target Life (as *bios* and *zoe*) as their subject. Faced with these proliferating discourses, it is not a question of establishing new methodological or political hierarchies of values, so as to apportion respective merits and deficits. It is not a matter of mutually incompatible systems and options, but rather of grounding the different ethical values concretely, historically and geopolitically, so as to be able to account for them. These situated cartographies provide the material dialogical exchanges within the horizon of diversity and not under the empire of Sameness.

The material presented in this chapter shows that in a globally linked world, 'we' are indeed in *this* together. But this pan-human factor need not result in new universalizing master-narratives, or the eternal return of Kantian moral universalism. The polylingual voices of the multi-located subjects of the global nomadic, diasporic, hybrid diversity are producing concretely grounded micro-narratives that call for a joyful kind of dissonance. For ethical discourse to sing the same tune some extra effort is needed.

The intersecting cartographies demonstrate my two main arguments. Firstly, that a non-unitary vision of the subject is the necessary precondition for the creation of more adequate accounts of our location. Secondly, that far from resulting in moral relativism, non-unitary subject positions engender alternative systems of values and specific forms of accountability. The key to understanding both these arguments lies in the definition of 'non-unitary'. Nomadic subjects are not quantitative pluralities, but rather qualitative multiplicities. The former is merely a multiple of One – multiplied across an extended space. This is the political economy of global capitalism as a system that generates differences for the purpose of commodifying them. Qualitative multiplicities, however, pertain to an altogether different logic. They express changes not of scale, but of intensity, force, or *potentia* (positive power of expression), which trace patterns of becoming.

This complicates the picture: non-unitary subject defined as a qualitative multiplicity is not only extended in space, but also in time. Let us take an example from the anti-racist question: 'can one be Black, or Muslim, and European?'; or the feminist one: 'can one be black, or lesbian and a feminist?' These questions rest on the assumption that political discourse implies a vision of the subject as a unified identity. Thus, to be 'European' is postulated on an implicit identity that excludes blacks and Muslims. To be a feminist assumes an identity that excludes blacks and lesbians, and so on. If we approach this political problem within the nomadic subject as a qualitative or intensive, not quantitative or extensive, entity, however, steady identities are rejected as the implicit or explicit assumption for any subject position. Difference emerges accordingly in all its positivity, having abandoned the dialectical frame. Internal differentiations in *potentia*, or the productive power to act, become a crucial factor. Intensities or forces are best expressed in degrees or variations and accounted for in terms of time, not only of space.

The point of these multiple intensive variables is that they constitute what the material consciousness is made of. This is a temporal, not a spatial phenomenon. It is absolutely the case that one is not a muslim on Tuesday and a european on Wednesday, or a woman on Monday, black on Sunday and Lesbian on Thursday afternoons. These variables coexist in time. They also intersect, coincide or clash; they are seldom synchronized. The point is that one's consciousness of oneself does not always coincide with all these variables *all* the time. One may, for a period of time, coincide with some categories, but seldom with them all. Consciousness is a rather narrow exercise, which brings entities into focus by selecting and hence excluding. Synchronization is the key to consciousness-raising in so far as consciousness is the ability to self-represent and narrate one's relation-ship to the variables that structure one's location in the social space: woman/adult/white/human/lesbian/healthy/urbanized/English-speaking.

Synchronization frames the experience of constituting a subject position. This synchronization occurs in relation to the requirements and expectations of society (*potestas*) as well as one's own intensity (*potentia*). By definition, such synchronizing exercises can only be temporary and occur in random patterns. To track the different modes of synchronization so as to bring them into adequate conceptual representation is the task of philosophy, on which I elaborate in chapter 4. This is not about the confirmation of steady identities, or the claim to counter-identities, but about the creation of alternative thinkable and shareable subject positions. These entail accountability for ethical values and collective bonding, so that the internal complexities can be sustained and expressed. Consciousness is about co-synchronicity: shared time zones, shared memories and shareable time-lines of projects. That is the subject of the next chapter.

3

Transplants: Transposing Nature

Domestic cows no longer belong to the domain of herbivores . . . but there seems to be no real basis (no grounds) on which to regard feeding sheep to cattle as shocking when multimedia is the name of the game and computer viruses might be alive.

Marilyn Strathern, *After Nature*

If we are to conceive of Man as separate from nature, then Man does not exist.

Michael Hardt and Antonio Negri, *Empire*

Aaaaarrrgggggggghhhhhhhhhhhhhzzzzzzzzzzzzzzwwwwwwwww

Diamanda Galas, *Vena Cava*

INTRODUCTION: BECOMING-ANIMAL

The third axis of transposition or becoming-other concerns the naturalized or 'earth' others. In the previous chapter I have argued for the need to rethink the embodied structure of contemporary subjectivity in terms of the convergence of biotechnologies and information technologies and the proliferation of commodified differences which they engender. The biological and the informational bodies converge into a new subject compound, which is nomadic and hence not unitary, hybrid and hence impure, and denaturalized through technological mediation and hence post-humanist.

The political economy of contemporary embodied subjects can be rendered through the notion of radical immanence in philosophical nomadism. The regime of *bios/zoe*-power processed by the new technologies constructs the body as a multi-layered material entity that is situated at the intersection of biological, genetic, social, cultural and endless other levels of codes of information. We should think of contemporary techno-bodies as highly complex machines: they are sensors; integrated sites of information networks; vectors of multiple information systems: cardio-vascular, respiratory, acoustic, tactile, olfactory, hormonal, psychic, emotional, erotic, etc. The body is also a living recording device actualized by a highly personalized and enfleshed memory-system, which is capable of storing and retrieving essential and vital information at such high speed that it ends up looking 'instinctual'. Fundamentally prone to pleasure, the embodied entity remembers in the sense of being able to recollect and to repeat its experiences. The body is not only multi-functional, but also multi-expressive: it speaks through temperature, motion, speed, emotions, excitement, fluids, and sounds and a variety of rhythms. Not even the most diehard social constructivist today can deny the vitalistic materialism of the kind of bodies our culture has constructed with and for us. The point about bodies is, of course, that they are not all human, either.

Whereas the dislocation of the status and location of sexualized and racialized differences can be accommodated into the critique of advanced capitalism, as they are integral to it, the transposition of nature poses a number of conceptual, methodological and practical complications linked to the critique of anthropocentrism. This is due to the pragmatic fact that, as embodied and embedded entities, we are all part of nature, even though philosophy continues to claim transcendental grounds for human consciousness. As a brand of 'enchanted materialism', philosophical nomadism contests the arrogance of anthropocentrism and strikes an alliance with the productive force of *zoe* – or life in its inhuman aspects. Nomadic philosophies also challenge the new perverse dualism that is surreptitiously introduced 'when nature is unhumanized and mankind is artificialized', as Keith Ansell-Pearson so aptly put it (Ansell-Pearson 1997b: 161).

Thus, affinity for *zoe* is a good starting point for what may constitute the last act of the critique of dominant subject positions, namely the return of animal, or earth life in all its potency. The breakdown of species distinction (human/non-human) and the explosion of *zoe*-power, therefore, shifts the grounds of the problem of the breakdown of categories of individuation (gender and sexuality; ethnicity and race). This introduces the issue of becoming into a planetary or worldwide dimension, the earth being not one element among others, but rather that which brings them all together. In this chapter I will consequently explore the relevance of nomadic philosophy for political ecology.

Our post-human historical conditions are ripe with contradictions. If people in war-torn lands like Afghanistan are reduced to eating grass in order to survive (Nessman 2002), the former herbivore bovine animals of the United Kingdom and parts of the European Union have turned carnivore. Our agricultural bio-technological sector has taken an unexpected cannibalistic turn by fattening cows, sheep and chickens on animal feed. This is not the least of the paradoxes confronting the critical thinker and the aware citizen these days. Animals (mice, sheep, goats, cattle, pigs, rabbits, birds, poultry and cats) are bred in industrial farming, locked up in battery-cage production units reminiscent of torture chambers. Paradoxically, however, because they are an integral part of the bio-technological industrial complex, more animals enjoy peculiar privileges. Thus, livestock in the European Union receives a subsidy to the tune of 803 US dollars per cow. Which is not so remarkable, when compared to the 1,057 US dollars that are granted to each American cow and 2,555 US dollars given to each cow in Japan. These figures look quite different when compared to the Gross National Income *per capita* in countries like Ethiopia (120 US dollars), Bangladesh (360 US dollars), Angola (660 US dollars) or Honduras (920 US dollars) (Brabeck 2003).

Animals provide living material for scientific experiments. They are manipulated, mistreated, tortured and genetically recombined in ways that are productive for our bio-technological agriculture, the cosmetics industry, drugs and pharmaceutical industries, and other sectors of the economy. The monitoring group GeneWatch puts their numbers at half a million a year; other animals, like pigs, are genetically modified to produce organs for humans in xeno-transplantation experiments (Vidal 2002). The category of 'class' is accordingly linked to that of tradable disposable bodies of all categories and species, in a global mode of post-human exploitation. Animals are also sold as exotic commodities and constitute the third largest illegal trade in the world today, after drugs and arms but ahead of women. Brazil provides the majority of the imports, stolen from the fast-disappearing Amazon forest; the Mariatee butterfly, the Amazon turtle, the black tamarin (a tiny primate smaller than the palm of a hand) and the pink river dolphin are the most sought-after items with prices ranging from 4,000 to 70,000 US dollars. RENCTAS, the Portuguese acronym for the National Network to Fight Traffic in Wild Animals estimates the industry to be worth $15 billion a year (Faiola 2001–2).

Cloning animals is now an established practice: Oncomouse and Dolly the Sheep are already part of history; the first cloned horse was born in Italy on 28 May 2003. It took more than 800 embryos and 9 would-be surrogate mother mares to produce just one foal (Anon. 2003). These developments are in keeping with the complex and dynamic logic of contemporary genetics. They confront us in ways that cannot be ade-quately described as dialectical opposites, but are better rendered as non-linear transpositions. Globalization means the commercialization of planet earth in all its forms, through a series of interrelated modes of appropria-tion. According to Haraway these are: the techno-military proliferation of micro-conflicts on a global scale; the hyper-capitalist accumulation of wealth; the turning of the ecosystem into a planetary apparatus of production and the global infotainment apparatus of the new multimedia environment.

As I argued in the previous chapter, the new techno-cultural context writes hybridity into our social and symbolic sphere and as such it challenges all notions of purity. Mixity and intercontaminations are the norm and they go against the grain of the European master-narrative of rational progress. Two pillars of Enlightenment thought get transposed in the process: the first and foremost is the categorical and self-congratulatory distinction between human and non-human. The second, albeit interrelated, is the issue of reproduction, human filiations and hence the kinship system.

Whereas mainstream culture reacts to these innovations with a mixture of euphoria and panic, over-optimism and nostalgia, I want to strike a more productive note, both affectively and conceptually. The mutual contaminations and crossbreeding that mark our historical era are also breeding grounds for rich new alliances.

Against anthropocentrism

The becoming-animal axis of transformation entails the displacement of anthropocentrism and the recognition of trans-species solidarity on the basis of our being environmentally based, that is to say: embodied, embedded and in symbiosis. This organic or corporeal brand of materialism lays the foundations for a system of ethical values where 'life' stands central. This ethics will form the focus of the next two chapters. 'Life', far from being codified as the exclusive property or the unalienable right of one species – the human – over all others or of being sacralized as a pre-established given, however, is posited as process, interactive and open-ended. *Bios/zoe* as generative vitality is a major transversal force that cuts across and reconnects previously segregated domains. This transposition follows the perverse logic of a system of bio-power that has made the gene-centred world-view into its driving force. Bio-centred egalitarianism is, for me, such a materialist, secular, precise and unsentimental response to a transversal, trans-species structural connection of those whose bodies are 'disposable' in the logic of advanced capitalism.

Post-anthropocentrism is therefore on the agenda, in so far as advanced technologies have displaced the notion of a single, common standard and contradicted the humanistic dictum that 'Man is the measure of all things'. At the height of the Cold War George Orwell ironically turned this around by having one of his characters state: 'all animals are equal, but some are more equal than others'. At the dawn of the third millennium, in a world caught in indefinite warfare, such metaphorical grandeur rings rather hollow. Bio-centred egalitarianism rather suggests the opposite: no animal is more equal than any other, because they are all equally inscribed in a logic of exchange that makes them disposable and hence negotiable. All other distinctions are erased. This is not relativism, but the politics of location, that is to say a cartography of embedded and embodied positions on the map of *bios/zoe* power.

However, we must not let the unfamiliarity of the situation detract from its creative potential. For example, reproduction, which is by now technologically assisted to a very large extent, provides the experimental grounds for unique forms of experimentation. These are integral to bio-technological capital, but this does not prevent them from offering potential new forms of social relations and kinship. If the cyborg is our political ontology, as Haraway recommends, then we had better adjust our internal and external watches to the multiple time zones we inhabit. For instance, cloning as a non-linear form of reproduction is a new technique, practised on a regular basis since the mid-1990s, whereas sexual intercourse is an established practice, which has been around for 500 million years, but we are not to let this small time factor interfere with our desire to experiment. It is only a matter of time.

In the universe that I inhabit as a post-industrial subject of so-called advanced capitalism, there is more familiarity, i.e. more to share in the way of embodied and embedded locations, between female humans and the cloned sheep Dolly, or oncomouse and other genetically engineered members of the former animal kingdom, than with humanistic ideals of the uniqueness of my species. Similarly, my situated position as a female of the species makes me structurally serviceable and thus closer to the organisms that are willing or unwilling providers of organs or cells as spare parts than to any notion of the inviolability and integrity of the human species. My historical and geopolitical position is such that I see a close link between the epidemic of anorexia–bulimia, i.e. the spasmodic waves of expansion and shrinking of the body-weight in the population of the opulent classes of the world, and the thinning out and wilful depletion of the world's reserves of biodiversity in seeds, grains, plants and water supplies. I recognize the fact that the status of embodied humans who become 'collateral damage' in high-tech wars that hit them from the sky with 'intelligent bombs' dropped by computer-driven, unmanned flying objects is closer to that of the animals at Sarajevo zoo who were forcibly freed as a result of NATO bombing and roamed the streets – terrorized and terrifying till they succumbed to friendly fire – than it is to the Geneva convention definition of 'casualties of war'. I want to think from within the awareness that the market prices of exotic birds and quasi extinct animals are comparable, often to the advantage of the plumed species, to that of the disposable bodies of women, children and others in the global sex trade and industry.

I would like to acknowledge therefore a transversal structural link in the position of these embodied non-human subjects that were previously known as the 'others' of the humanistic subject. Contemporary popular culture, especially cinema and visual culture, supports this transversal interconnection by offering a spectacular and significant set of variations on the theme of monstrous or alien others in the shape of trans-species hybrids, extraterrestrial recombined mutants, contaminating viruses, malignant bacteria and other 'horrors' (Braidotti 2002). The gothic elements of this cyber imaginary are as striking as they are predictable. Most of these alien others embody the characteristics of anomaly, abnormality and pejorative difference which have historically been the prerogative of the classical others of Man. The revival of misogynist and racist representation is played out nowadays on the disposable bodies of the technologically recombined organisms.

Donna Haraway proposes that we start rethinking this historical condition in a more pragmatic and positive manner from the figuration of oncomouse as the first patented animal in the world, a transgenic organism created for the purposes of research. The oncomouse is the techno-body *par excellence*: it has been created for the purpose of profit-making trafficking between the laboratories and the market place, and thus navigates between patenting offices and the research benches. Genetically modified mice are the most expensive animals in the world and there are about 2,000–3,000 different kinds of GM mice available at present. A breeding trio of males of the TG 2576 series (born to contract Alzheimer's) is worth up to a million dollars. Which is not much, considering that the potential market for the Alzheimer's cure could be worth 150 billion dollars (Meek 2000).

Haraway wants to establish and emphasize a sense of kinship and connection with this transgenic animal. Calling her 'my sibling . . . male or female, s/he is my sister' (1997: 79), Haraway stresses also the extent to which oncomouse is both a victim and a scapegoat, a Christ-like figure that sacrifices herself in order to find the cure for breast cancer and thus save the lives of many women: a mammal rescuing other mammals. Because the oncomouse breaks the purity of lineage, she is also a spectral figure: the never dead that pollutes the natural order simply by being manufactured and not born. S/he is, in my terms, a cyber-teratological apparatus that scrambles the established codes and thus destabilizes the subject.

This implicated or non-innocent way to approach the oncomouse is symptomatic of Haraway's project that contains a cognitive, as well as an ethical, angle. It is about thinking across established categories, such as nature/culture; born/man-made; but also about criticizing commodity fetishism and the so-called market economy in its corporate and global phase. The ethical part of the project concerns the creation of a new kinship system: a new social nexus and new forms of social connection with these techno-others. What kinds of bonds can be established and how can they be sustained? Here the notion of the 'patent', which was so crucial to Shiva's analysis of globalization, returns with a vengeance. Haraway, however, is closer to Franklin and Stacey in stressing the productive potential of patents. They challenge established categories of ownership in the name of that very mixity and impurity which technological culture is now capable of producing. Both kinship and ownership need to be redefined in such a way as to rethink links of affectivity and responsibility for these newly patented creatures – they are our offspring, much as Frankenstein is Mary Shelley's 'hideous progeny'.

In this framework, Haraway draws an analogy between oncomouse and Irigaray's 'hysteria', or matrix – it is the site of procreation, or the womb-passage. Western science answers the masculine fantasy of self-birth through rational acquisition – the mind replacing the womb as the site of creation. While natural offspring are being replaced by corporate brands and manufactured and patented bio-products, the ethical imperative to bind to them and be accountable for their well-being remains as strong as ever. We just need new genealogies, alternative theoretical and legal representations of the new kinship system, and adequate narratives to live up to this challenge.

The minimum requirement is that the dualism human–animal has to be relinquished, in favour of a more dynamic notion of relation or relationality. In her recent work on 'Companion Species' (2003), Donna Haraway draws a direct line between the early figurations of the cyborg and of oncomouse on the one hand, and of companion species like dogs on the other. They mark the shifting boundaries of very affective and dynamic kinship relations. For Haraway this needs to be redefined in the context of a techno-scientific world that has replaced the traditional natural order with a nature–culture compound. An epistemological question therefore generates a new ethical dimension. Accordingly, the human–animal relation needs to be lifted out of the Oedipal and infantilizing narrative within which it has historically been confined. The most dominant spin-off of this narrative is the sentimental discourse about dogs' devotion and unconditional loyalty, which Haraway argues against with all her mighty passion. As a nature–culture compound, a dog – not unlike other products of techno-science – is a radical other, albeit a significant other. We need to devise a symbolic kinship system that matches its complexity. This is not a reference to the literary bestiary as an established genre, with its own grammar and a metaphorical reference to animals like letters in an alternative alphabet (Braidotti 2002). Something less sophisticated and more material is occurring in the contemporary, processes of becoming-animal, which has nothing to do with metaphors of animality. Nor does it proceed as an argument by analogy. It is rather the case that it requires a shift of the ontological grounds of embodiment. Arguing that humans are 'scent blind', Barbara Noske comments:

Not many people have seriously tried to imagine what it must be like to perceive and conceive the world in terms of 'olfactory images' (such as dogs must do) or 'tactile images' (as horses do to a large extent), or 'acoustic pictures' (as dolphins and whales must do). . . . We humans are heavily biased towards the visual . . . But for a dog scenting is believing. (1989: 158)

A nomadic post-anthropocentric philosophy displaces the primacy of the visual. The process of becoming-animal is connected to an expansion or creation of new sensorial and perceptive capacities or powers, which alter or stretch what a body can actually do. Nomadic thought actualizes different potentials in and of a body. In so doing, it is again attuned to our historical condition: for example, the superior olfactory capacity of dogs has been recognized in contemporary technological research. Smell has functioned as a potent indicator of well-being since antiquity. Nowadays it is being turned into a diagnostic tool and highly sophisticated 'electronic noses' are designed for diagnoses in medicine, as well as hygiene-control in the food industry. Spectrometers are chemical sensing computer systems that match patterns of smells by picking up chemical signatures. This technology is based on the model of dogs, whose sensorial perception is vastly superior to that of humans (Witchalls 2003).

Writers who explore the vitality of the living world, such as Virginia Woolf, share this shift of perspective in favour of the non-human. In *Flush*, Woolf writes:

The human nose is practically non-existent. The greatest poets in the world have smelt nothing but roses on the one hand and dung on the other. The infinite gradations that lie between are unrecorded. Yet it was in the world of smell that Flush most lived. Love was chiefly smell; music and architecture, law, politics and science were smell. (1993: 138)

Animal imagery was an important part of Woolf's language and the key to the many *dramatis personae* she invented in both her public and private writings, to convey aspects of her relationships which were either too intimate or too playful for her to acknowledge in any other form (Lee 1996).

Although Woolf's sexual timidity is notorious, as is her self-censorship on such matters, this is combined 'with a powerful, intense sensuality, an erotic susceptibility to people and landscape, language and atmosphere and a highly charged physical life' (Lee 1996: 332). Animals, and dogs especially, were a vehicle for her to express the private, intimate side of life. Also in her correspondence and diaries animal language and play function as an amorous code for her and Leonard or an emotional one with her siblings: it was a way of expressing desires, passions and pleasures. Dogs' imagery was especially important: in 1926 Vita Sackville-West gave Virginia a red cocker spaniel capped Pinka, which became the model for the main canine character in her short novel *Flush*. The unruly behaviour of dogs allowed for a break with the Victorian conventions of proper behaviour, especially in terms of physical sensations, which Virginia relished. Dogs are not only messy, but also openly sexual. They unleash a reservoir of images for sexual explicitness and even aggression, as well as unbridled freedom: they are a vehicle for *zoe*.

The structural link between women, 'native others' and animals has a dense and complex unity; women and 'others' personify the animal–human continuity, while men embody its discontinuity. In my language, the former are structurally closer to *zoe*, men to *bios*. The structural link between women and *zoe* is also a matter of sharing a second-class status, as shown by the relative marginalization of animal life (*zoe*) in relation to discursive life (*bios*). Evolutionary theory supports this by attributing human development to white male skills, while women and 'others' are considered mere objects of exchange. Similarly, motherhood has traditionally been considered as an automatic biological process, while fatherhood is seen as a social and cultural institution that rules over and governs biological relations. According to socio-biology and to contemporary testosterone-driven evolutionary psychology, males are existential entrepreneurs competing on a free market for reproductive success to accumulate the means of (re)production through which they increase their genetic capital. Women are the passive partners in this firm.

Considering all these associative links, the question then becomes: how can we respect animals' otherness? How can we address this issue in its immanent and material specificity, without falling into the worn-out rhetoric of human dignity defined as the denial of our shared animality? How can we disengage this discussion from the platitudes and the nostalgia that marks the discussion of 'animal rights', also and especially in neo-liberal political discourse (Fukuyama 2002)? My answer is by stepping beyond anthropocentrism and trying to look at the world from a dramatically different perspective, which does not assume a passive nature and a consciousness that must be by definition human.

Noske makes this into an issue of social justice. She sees the history of animal–human interaction as a continuum of exploitation that goes back to the historical origins of agriculture and hence the dawn of civilization. Scientific descriptions and classifications of animals since antiquity have stressed their industrial applications and their technological capacities, approaching them as natural labourers or natural-born industrial slaves.

Capitalist exploitation intensifies the trend by maximizing the output of animal-driven profit in a 'rational' system of commercialization, with the help of science. The essence of the scientific input is to speed up the cycles of physiological production and reproduction by animals so as to increase their profitability. In this respect, genetic engineering is the logical outcome of a long-standing historical process of manipulation.

The basic form of alienation suffered by animals, according to Noske, has to do with their being disconnected from their habitat and having their eco-sphere redesigned and manipulated by technologies. Owned by large companies and forced to work endless hours the bodies of animals are played out within the bio-technological spheres and have become automated and alienated from their environmental surroundings and from other animals. Thus, all of European agro-business today is bio-technologically driven, while the bulk of the agricultural labour force is composed by poorly paid migrant workers. The global counterpart of this system is the situation that Vandana Shiva describes, namely that the developing world is reduced to forcible patterns of monocultures that deplete and upset local eco-systems, uprooting social habits and structures, with disastrous consequences for both the environment and the human habitat.

Scientific research both intensifies and pursues this form of exploitation: millions of animals annually are involved in experiments for military, security or medical purposes. This works on a moral paradox, 'that of a presumed compatibility of animals and human, and at the same time the negation of this compatibility' (Noske 1989: 37). It follows that for Noske the ethical challenge is to adopt a non-exploitative, inter-subjective attitude to animals, moving beyond the principles of greed and profit. This implies also a critique of the social sciences and of social philosophy in terms of their anthropocentrism and their rhetorical reference to the plight of animals. She makes an exception for Marx and Engels, who stressed the unity of human, social and natural progress, inscribing the status of the natural environment at the heart of the programme for social progress. By contrast, genetics and molecular biology appear as reductive and deterministic.

In my own language, the same point needs to be made about the ethics of becoming-animal as of those of becoming-woman, namely it requires a qualitative shift of perspective. This is made all the more difficult, but also more necessary, by the extent to which advanced capitalism has already erased the classical metaphysical distinctions between humans and animals on at least three grounds: firstly, in their commercial values as objects of exchange for the sake of profit; secondly, in terms of genetic engineering and the circulation of cellular and other matter among different species; thirdly, in the timid attempts to include animals in the logic of 'human' rights. I shall turn to this next.

Beyond Animal Rights

A critique of human arrogance as an epistemological and moral assumption is explicitly stated in mainstream discussions about animal rights, as it is in most environmental thinking. Within the tradition of liberal feminism, for instance, Mary Midgley (1996) argues that, since the Enlightenment, social contract theory has privileged the human, to the detriment of all non-human agents such as animals and plants. She warns us that social contract thinking must not be taken as the ultimate guide, but only as a provisional tool to protect basic forms of liberty, to be alerted and updated whenever necessary.

In this vein, Midgley is careful to point out the very destructive side of that individualism which lies at the heart of contract thinking and which entails selfishness and individualistic ideologies leading to moral cowardice. She also acknowledges that the opposite approach, the organic model, has been discredited through association with tyranny. Midgley argues that the new environmental consciousness may lift the taboo on organic ways of thinking. 'It may even become possible for our species to admit that it is not really some supernatural variety of Lego, but a kind of animal. This ought to make it easier to admit that we are not self-contained and self-sufficient, either as a species or as individuals, but live naturally in deep mutual dependence' (1996: 9–10).

In keeping with the classical liberal tradition that she espouses, Midgley warns us not to take any models for granted but to keep a healthy dose of scepticism. Unfortunately, scepticism becomes only the pretext to a series of digs against the postmodernist treatment of ethics. Yet Midgley agrees that the notion of liberal individualism has always been biased in favour of men and is a masculine ideal, which entails not only the exclusion of many others, but also a very deceptive picture of what counts as independence and autonomy: 'the supposed independence of the male was a lie, which concealed its parasitic dependence on the love and the service of non-autonomous females. A false universal' (1996: 76).

Species politics, on the other hand, has militated in favour of anthropocentrism since Greek antiquity. Midgley does not like the term 'anthropocentrism' and prefers 'human chauvinism; narrowness of sympathy, comparable to national, or race or gender-chauvinism. It could also be called exclusive humanism, as opposed to the hospitable, friendly, inclusive kind' (1996: 105). Because of this critical approach to human chauvinism, Midgley defends the end of 'anthropolatry' and calls for more respect and priority to be given to the interests of other species and life-forms: less ego, both individually and collectively.

The question is not the Kantian one, 'can animals think?', but rather the empathic one: 'can they suffer?' Because they clearly do, concludes Midgley, we need new concepts, new world-views and whole new relations to the non-human world. While attacking the inertia of habits, Midgley also defends human rationality not as a hegemonic monoculture, but rather as a form of resistance to it, in terms of moral pluralism. I sympathize with Midgley's critique of anthropocentrism, although this unitary vision of subjectivity traces a cartography of our historical situation and a vision of the world, which I cannot recognize: I live at the tail end of bio-power, that is to say amidst the relentless consumption of all that lives. I am committed to starting from there, not from a nostalgic reinvention of an all-inclusive holistic ideal. I want to think from here and now, from Dolly my sister and oncomouse as my totemic divinity; from missing seeds and dying species. But also, simultaneously and without contradiction, from the staggering, unexpected and relentlessly generative ways in which life, as *bios* and as *zoe*, is fighting back. This is the kind of materialism that makes me an anti-humanist at heart.

Even less satisfactory is the moral rationalism of the animal rights advocate Peter Singer. Singer's utilitarian position consists in anthropomorphizing animals, by extending to them the principle of equality or equal rights. His philosophical stance is the becoming-human of animals. However admirable in intention, his position is self-contradictory. In philosophical nomadism, no qualitative becoming can be generated by or at the centre, or in a dominant position. Man is a dead static core of ego-indexed negativity. To introduce animal and earth others into this category is not exactly doing them a favour. I object to the humanization of this debate on the grounds of bio-centred egalitarianism. We need to move beyond anthropocentrism altogether, rather than to extend humanism to the formerly exploited others. Humanism in this context is only the prelude to possessive individualism and the extension of individual rights to non-human actors. As such it also leads to commercialization and commodification, as Vandana Shiva forcefully argues.

Moreover, the logic of 'rights' had already been called into question by feminists and other critical philosophers on several scores: for instance, Luce Irigaray (1977) on the grounds of its uncritical imitation of masculine prerogatives and modes of behaviour; or Patricia Williams (1991) on the grounds of race and ethnicity. Within French poststructuralism, Jean-François Lyotard (1988) referred to some historical responsibilities – like the holocaust of the Jews, Roma, communist resistance fighters and gay people of Europe – as a 'differend': something for which there is no possible settlement or compensation. Gilroy (2000) has argued against the culture of claims and legal compensation. In the light of these critical objections, I am extremely reluctant to take up the logic of rights to address as complex an issue as that of our destruction of *our* environment.

The point about 'animal rights' is that, by attempting to redress the moral and legal balance in favour of animals, it humanizes them. This is problematic on two scores, firstly it confirms the binary distinction human/animal by extending one category – the human – to cover the other. Secondly, it denies the specificity of animals altogether. The point is to see the inter-*relation* human/animal as constitutive of the identity of *each*. It is therefore a relation, a transformative or symbiotic relationship that hybridizes, shifts and alters the 'nature' of each one. This challenges the liberal individualism that is implicit in animal rights and foregrounds the ethics and politics of the Relation, i.e. the middle grounds or the 'milieu' of the human/non-human continuum.

Anthropocentrism breeds a kind of solidarity between the human dwellers of this planet, currently traumatized by technology, and their animal others. They share a fundamental anxiety about the future. The humanization of these others is the inevitable outcome of the realization that 'we' are in *this* together. The 'we' in question is all the more problematic at a historical time when the very category of the 'human' has become de-territorialized and challenged. In fact, it has imploded under the strain of the *bios/zoe*-powers that act upon it. At such a time of deep epistemological, ethical and political crises of values in human societies, extending the privileges of the human to other categories can hardly be considered as a generous or a particularly productive move. Anthropocentrism thus imposed breeds nostalgia and paranoia.

Josephine Donovan (1996) argues against the moral rationalism of Peter Singer, saying that cultural feminism can provide a more viable theoretical basis for animal ethics, by including the emotions more effectively. She stresses that two approaches are dominant in animal rights right now: that of natural rights and that of utilitarianism. The natural rights discourse rests on Locke's argument that animals have the same unalienable rights as humans; this in turn refuses the Kantian assumption of the unique rational structure of 'Man'. In this perspective, 'species-ism' is criticized and is held analogous to sexism or racism in privileging humans, males and whites over all others. So animal ethics is a matter of justice, not of kindness: principles of individual rights and of rational choice are upheld and extended to animals. Utilitarianism, on the other hand, makes more room for the emotions, asking the question of whether animals can suffer. It assumes that the common condition that unites humans with animals is sensibility and the capacity to feel pain and pleasure. This is a different kind of principle of equality and it is on this basis that equal rights and prerogatives can be posited. Donovan argues, however, that this utilitarian approach is rather hypocritical and in its practical applications it relapses into the mode of manipulative mastery that is not unlike that of medical experimenters and scientific managers. The 'mathematization of the world' is but the prelude to its ruthless exploitation. Hence the need for a corrective influence by feminism, defined as the movement which: 'articulated a critique of the atomistic individualism and rationalism of the liberal tradition. They did so by proposing a vision that emphasized collectivity, emotional bonding and an organic (or holistic) concept of life' (Donovan 1996: 40). The structural analogy between women and animals works here in favour of a general theory of male domination of both women and of the natural environment, which is in keeping with the tenets of eco-feminism – to which I shall return shortly.

This argument respects complex interrelations and is thus more helpful. It stresses that the barriers between the species have always been racialized and genderized. This brings to the fore the multi-layered dimension of such a system of oppression where overlapping variables trace transversal connections among sexual, social, racial and species inequalities, all of which profit the same patriarchal system.

Carol Adams's (1990) analysis of the sexual politics of meat works in this framework: she argues that female/animal and other bodies are sexualized so as to be made more available and hence more disposable. Species hierarchy is reinstated in sexism – where non-human bodies are rendered female or feminized in the pejorative sense of the term. It also works in racism, where animalizing discourses are used about oppressed, disenfranchised or marginal peoples. These overlapping variables stress the interdependent nature of structural inequalities. Adams concludes that this points to a 'sex-species' system which tends to remain unacknowledged and uncriticized even in the framework of animal rights activism. Specific gender analysis is therefore needed in order to address this problem adequately. Adams proposes a new deal between animal rights, feminist politics and the philosophy of rights, so as to reclaim the full range of our embodied practices and emotions.

The ethics of bio-centred egalitarianism

I described (Braidotti 2002) *zoe* as the affirmative power of life, as a vector of transformation, a conveyor or a carrier that enacts in-depth transformations. As such, it actualizes a set of both social and symbolic interactions that inscribe the human–animal bond, also known as bio-centred egalitarianism, at the heart of our concerns. The notion of the Relation is central to this discussion. Ecological theories and practice Reflect an idea of interconnectedness that is quite relevant, in spite of its holistic connotations. Relations and interactions within philosophical nomadism are posited along the more materialist lines of becoming as deep transformations of self and society. I thus want to resist the sacralization of 'life' while addressing the issue of limits and values in terms of thresholds of sustainability. I propose such a position as a possible alliance with moral and social philosophers from other theoretical traditions.

'Life' is a slippery concept, especially animal or insect life in the vitalist mode of *zoe*; it is far too often assimilated to the abject in the sense of the monstrous object of horror (Kristeva 1980; Creed 1993). It is thus represented as the unassimilated, the unpresentable, the unrepresented and even the unthinkable. Philosophical nomadism allows us to think of it as an integral part of ourselves and as such not as an alien other. To think this way, I reconfigure the subject as embodied materiality: the analogy between woman, animal, mother and earth is as relevant for the poststructuralists as it is for eco-feminism. Contrary to the latter, however, I do not adopt the method of identification of women with animals, the logic of rights and claims, or the political strategy of holism. I prefer another approach that starts with asserting the primacy of life as production, or *zoe* as generative power. I then want to activate *zoe* also through sexual difference, or the 'matter' that is produced in the maternal/material feminine as a virtual path of becoming which leads outwards, outside the human. This aims to point a way out of the meta-physical quagmire of classical femininity and patriarchally ordained motherhood and to transpose it. This is a metamorphosis in the sense of a shift of location and an active site of transformation of a minority into a 'becoming-minoritarian'. An integral part of this process is to confront and go through those unrepresentable, unthinkable and abject elements of the very embodiment that is being activated and transformed. *Zoe* needs to be put centre stage. Although, for the purposes of my ethical project, the human still gets preferential treatment, I consider this a matter of habit, not of values.

Bio-centred egalitarianism is a philosophy of affirmative becoming, which activates a nomadic subject into sustainable processes of transfor-mation. The political and theoretical values I want to defend in relation to this include the principle of *non-profit*, which means a stand against individualism and exploitation, in favour of self-expression and commu-nally held property rights over both biological and cultural artefacts. This calls for the respect for *diversity*, in both its biological and cultural dimen-sion, as well as a firm commitment to collective ownership and open access to technological 'products'. Equally important is the radical imma-nence of this vision of the materially embedded subject and the process of becoming that characterizes it.

The human body, and especially the female body, is both *bios* and *zoe* and as such it is a highly contested social and physical sphere. *Zoe* is not value-free or neutral, but a highly sexualized, racialized and 'species-fied' concept. The change of scale from the macro- to the micro-processes in itself is no guarantee of a qualitative shift. Thus, the issue of power does not miraculously evaporate in this admittedly momentous transition – it merely shifts its ground. Relentlessly vital, *zoe* is endowed with endurance and resilience – qualities that I will discuss more extensively in the next chapter. *Zoe* carries on regardless: it is radically immanent. Consciousness attempts to contain it, but actually lives in fear of it. Such a life force is experienced as threatening by a mind that fears the loss of control. This is the dominant view of consciousness as feeding on negative passions: a clearing house of the kind of neuroses (such as narcissism and paranoia) that are rewarded in the socialized civilized West. Civilization and its discontents extol their pound of flesh as the price to pay for not being a pack of werewolves howling, mating and killing in the moonlight. Thus, the self is politics by another name and the dominant vision of the self we have institutionalized in the West, that of liberal individualism, serves the purpose of a vampire-like economic system based on stock and exchange, common standards and unjust distribution, accumulation and profit. In opposition to this, I propose a nomadic view of the subject, composed by multiple internal and social differences. Consciousness gets redefined as an affirmative function in the sense of synchronizing complex differences and allowing them to coexist. Ethics is transposed into bio-centred egalitarianism.

The strength of animals is that they are immanent in their territories and environmentally bound: insects and animals mark their territory acoustically, olfactorily, by their own sign system. Hence the slight obscenity of the sentimental version in the familiar culture of pets and domesticated 'four-legged friends'. This culture constitutes the epitome of humanism: pets are those Oedipalized entities we sleep and watch television with. Donna Haraway moves a step beyond the Oedipal configuration by proposing a new kinship system that includes 'companion species' alongside other siblings and relatives. In philosophical nomadism, on the other hand, this proximity is returned to the territorial materialist foundations from whence it came. *Zoe* rules through a trans-species and transgenic interconnection, or rather a chain of connections which can best be described as an ecological philosophy of non-unitary, embodied subjects.

An ethical approach based on post-humanist values, or on bio-centred egalitarianism critiques individualism and attempts to think the interconnection of human and non-human agents. My position aims at rethinking the ethical and political implications of a non-unitary subject. This involves negotiating the tension between complexities on the one hand and a sustained commitment to social justice and emancipatory politics on the other. This balancing act takes us to another dimension of this epistemological but also ethical shift away from anthropocentrism. To argue for the recognition of animal 'otherness' breaks many an established taboo, not the least of which is the established expectation of reciprocity. The latter can almost be considered as the trademark of liberal individualism and its idea of moral responsibility: reciprocal respect is a foundational principle. In opposition to this, a biocentric ethics of sustainable relations posits a different expectation: that of an approach to the other which assumes the impossibility of mutual recognition – for instance between humans and animals – and replaces it with a relation of mutual specification. This raises a number of ethical issues, which I will address in the next two chapters.

BECOMING-WORLD: MERGING WITH THE ENVIRONMENT

Eco-feminisms and their discontent

Late postmodernity is the era when '*bios/zoe*' meets and merges with '*techne*'. This awareness can be considered as constitutive of the coalition known as 'eco-feminism', which is anything but a monolithic position. Eco-feminism, working within a tradition of socialist or of standpoint theory (Harding 1986) or of moral philosophy, has generally approached the issues of bio-technologies by attaching it firmly to the experience of real-life women. Karen Warren offers a relevant working definition of the field: 'Ecofeminism is an umbrella term which captures a variety of multicultural perspectives on the nature of the connection within social systems of domination between those humans in subdominant or subordinate positions, particularly women, and the domination of nonhuman nature' (1994: 1). As such, it is committed to the elimination of gender bias wherever it occurs and the development of analyses that are not gender-biased. It includes a critique of anthropocentrism in the name of ecological awareness, the recognition of multicultural perspectives and the critique of imperialism and ethnocentrism. Eco-feminism consequently refers to a variety of positions and is as diverse as the feminism from which it gains its strength. Nonetheless, some central assumptions have acquired axiomatic value. For instance, Mies and Shiva (1993), in what counts as a manifesto of eco-feminism, take consciously and deliberately the risk of universalizing their commitment to global justice. They create transnational links between their respective positions as a Northern and a Southern feminist activist committed to addressing the kernel of the eco-feminist agenda: 'The inherent inequalities in world structures which permit the North to dominate the South, men to dominate women, and the frenetic plunder of even more resources for ever more unequally distributed economic gain to dominate nature' (1993: 2). Eco-feminism raises the issue of the structural interconnection between the domination of women, natives and the domination of nature. This leads to a critique of patriarchal power in two specific forms: firstly the idea of progress, modernization and development and, secondly, the dominant notions of science and technology. Both of them involve epistemic and physical violence over the structural 'others' and are related to the European Enlightenment ideal of 'reason'. This is a world-view which equates mastery with rational scientific control over 'others'; as such, conclude Mies and Shiva, it militates against the respect for the diversity of living matter and of human cultures. As an alternative, they call for a new holistic approach that combines cosmology with anthropology and feminist spirituality to assert the need for loving respect for diversity in both its human and non-human forms. This emphasis on loving and caring also implies a concept of freedom and of understanding which Shiva in particular opposes to Western standards of rationality and of progress built upon the rational control of the natural order. Instead of the emphasis on emancipation from the realm of natural necessity, Shiva pleads for a form of emancipation that occurs within that realm and in harmony with it. From this shift of perspective there follows also a critique of the ideal of equality as the emulation of masculine modes of behaviour, the rejection of the model of development that is built upon this ideal, and the critique of globalization as a worldwide form of market domination.

Although such a radical dismissal of the Enlightenment ideals brings them close to a poststructuralist position, Mies and Shiva take great care to distance themselves from anything that is even remotely related to 'post'-modernism/colonialism/feminism. They rather dismiss it all as being relativistic in that it questions universal ideas, and hence it compromises the applicability of 'universal human rights'. Although they share with the poststructuralist generation the critique of the homogenization of cultures as the effect of advanced capitalism, they see it as a retreat into relativism and hence into apolitical resignation. In my brand of philosophical nomadism, however, relativism of either the cultural or the cognitive kind is not at all implied as an assumption or as a consequence: it simply does not apply. What does follow from nomadic views of subjectivity and the rejection of the unitarian Enlightenment-based vision of the subject is rather a robust type of sustainable ethics, or an embedded and embodied form of accountability. I will develop this form of ethics in the next chapter.

For Mies and Shiva, on the contrary, the rejection of relativism – wrongly attributed to the postmodernist front – leads to the reassertion of the need for new basic universal rights in the sense of interconnectedness among humans, on a worldwide scale. Too much emphasis on diversity for its own sake can be dangerous for this project. They focus therefore on the quest for basic needs, that is to say a concrete brand of universalism. They set this in opposition to the abstract universalism of the Eurocentric Enlightenment ideals. Thus, universal needs are amalgamated to universal rights and they cover as much basic and concrete necessities (food, shelter, health, safety) as higher cultural needs (education, identity, dignity, knowledge, affection, joy and care). These constitute the material regrounding of the claim to universal values.

Significantly, Mies and Shiva stress the importance of life-sustaining spirituality in this struggle for new concrete forms of universality: a reverence for the sacredness of life, of deeply seated respect for all that lives, which is opposed to Western rationality and to the West's investment in science and technology. In a holistic perspective, they call for the 're-enchantment of the world' (1993: 18), or for healing the Earth and that which has been so cruelly disconnected. This spiritual brand of immanence reflects the concrete needs as well as the cultural traditions of grassroots women's groups in the areas currently being marginalized and exploited by the globalization process in the developing world.

A more secular approach is proposed by Bina Agarwal (1992), who pleads for a more materialist type of analysis and a more pragmatic political approach based on the gendered division of roles in labour. Bina Agarwal's brand of 'feminist environmentalism', as a social constructivist notion, stresses the role of customs, laws and social structures in determining women's relationship to their environment. This approach raises broader issues about the management of gender relations in society and thus locates the issue of sustainable societies in the heart of the transformative project of feminist politics. Support for the critiques elaborated by women from the developing world for UN-based ideas of development emerged throughout the 1970s from several quarters. Marxist feminists (Mies and Shiva 1993) provided a critique of consumerism that pleads for radical changes in spending habits, with intense social programmes of recycling and the aim to put an end to over-consumption. 'Social-minded eco-feminists' stressed the need for a different kind of economic planning that would start from the assumption that the historical phase of economic growth is over. Because women are the main consumers, this would imply a different use of female resources, both financial and human.

Strong opposition to eco-feminism has come – perhaps not surprisingly – from mainstream moral philosophers, working within a universalist framework, who reject the factual or empirical bases of eco-feminist knowledge and thus reject their moral claims as 'unrecognizable' (Gruen 1994: 121). The moral case of eco-feminism rests on the critique of objectivity, autonomy and distance as main criteria of moral reasoning. Abstract universalist claims are rejected, in favour of the recognition of diversity. Greater value is given to interdependence and compassion as ways of bridging the differences of positions and contexts. It includes 'material' and non-human elements and objects as sources of moral obligations and as cognitive agents.

The criteria for eco-feminist moral epistemology are firstly a commitment to communities that goes beyond classical communitarianism and has a richer understanding of what an enlarged community could be. The very terms of constitution of a community are questioned and not merely the web of interests that hold them together. Communities of choice get the priority, especially those based on friendship or affinity. An even higher moral priority is given to 'oppositional communities' which challenge dominant ways of thinking and being in the world and provide resistance to sexist, racist, heterosexist and speciesist biases. Oppositional communities tend to ask uncomfortable theoretical questions, for instance, of what constitutes a situated self. They also privilege a self-reflexive approach that questions the legitimacy of dominant cultural definitions.

In keeping with the epistemological tradition of standpoint feminism, a second main criterion for the ecofeminist moral philosophy is, according to Gruen, that of experience both as a central component of knowledge-production and as a non-transparent notion, which does not grant direct or immediate access to 'facts'. Central to the category of experience is therefore the idea of situatedness, which is presented by Gruen as a sort of epistemological humility, or the assumption that we cannot immediately comprehend everything. An eco-feminist moral epistemology therefore 'results from the recognition of the inter-dependent nature of science and society, reason and the emotion, facts and values, and the complex ecological crises that the planet now faces' (1994: 134).

The strong moral claim made by eco-feminism is very significant and very relevant to the case I would like to make for sustainable ethics, so let me venture a few words of commentary. The first one concerns the distinction between morality and ethics (see chapter 1). Morality is the set of norms and normative conventions that are operational in a given social context; it deals with the negative or restricted sense of power as *potestas*. Ethics, on the other hand, is the inquiry about the role, position and relationship that subjects entertain to alterity. Neo-Nietzschean in inspiration, the post-structuralist generation has worked extensively on ethics and has inscribed it at the centre of its vision of power. The second remark follows from this: the moral claims of eco-feminism are undeniable, but however steadfast and lucid Gruen's defence of the eco-feminist case may be, it begs the question. What is omitted is precisely the disruptive, epistemologically radical and politically transgressive potential of an ethical position. In an excess of zeal, Gruen equates the moral eco-feminist claims to a 'feminist empiricist' position, that is to say a form of homologation on mainstream modes of thought. This constitutes in my eyes a serious reduction of the critical and innovative potential of the different eco-feminist positions. It leaves all issues of power basically unaltered. To support my case, let me turn to a more radical branch of eco-feminism, which stresses the subversive force of the critique of the dominant subject.

Deep ecology and the holistic legacy of Spinoza

The philosophical implications of sustainability have been raised by all environmental thinkers. Of special interest is the case of 'deep ecology', also known as the 'Gaia' hypothesis, which considers the whole earth as a single organism in a holistic manner. Arne Naess (1977) argues that deep ecology stretches the limits of anthropocentrism by stressing how the moral domain is open to all organisms. Arne Naess also joins forces with the social-minded eco-feminists and calls into question some of the wider issues around respect for nature, such as consumerism and materialism, thus developing a critique of technocratic reason. Naess, however, pursues this critique of the subject much further. This has implications for her vision of the self, whose realization is defined in terms other than those dictated by the laws of the market – hence the emphasis on spirituality and self-realization. It also redefines the environment itself, which is awarded a sense of 'biocentric equality'. Because there are no boundaries and everything is interrelated to hurt nature is ultimately to hurt ourselves. The approach at the heart of deep ecology anthropomorphizes the earth environment and thus extends to it the same rights and forms of respect as to humans.

It is in the framework of this holistic approach that references to Spinoza's monism are made. His idea of the unity of mind and soul supports the ecofeminist belief that all that lives is holy and the greatest respect is due to it. This idolatry of the natural order is attributed to Spinoza's vision of God and the unity between man and nature. Deep ecology is therefore a spiritually charged brand of ecosophy that stresses the harmony and coincidence between the human and the ecological habitat and proposes a sort of ultimate synthesis of the two. Spinozist ethics are so crucial to my case for sustainability, that I will devote a great deal of time to a detailed discussion of this issue in chapter 4. Contrary to Naess, however, I will refer less to Hegel and more to Deleuze's and Lloyd's reinterpretations of Spinoza's idea of the unity of substance, and thus his critique of mind–body dualism.

The excessive degree of anthropomorphism in Naess's thought seems problematic to me. It provides a cosmological basis for the unity of 'Spaceship Earth' and has the capacity to connect in holistic bond terrestrial and extraterrestrial concerns. This universalistic sweep is based on the analysis of the impending catastrophe: the environmental crisis and the global warming issue, not to speak of the exploration and the militarization of space, reduce all of humanity to a comparable degree of vulnerability; 'we' are really in *this* together. The problem with this position is that in spite of and in flagrant contradiction to its explicitly stated aims, deep ecology promotes full-scale humanization of the environment. This strikes me as a regressive move, reminiscent of the Romantic phases of European culture. There is something sentimental about it, which translates into a lack of rigour in the way in which the contradictions of the case are addressed. According to Val Plumwood (1993; 2002), Naess's deep ecology does not question the structures of possessive egoism and self-interest, but merely expands them to include non-human interests. What we end up with, therefore, is a quantitative expansion of liberal individualism, but individualism nonetheless. The human dimension here equates with the most classical anthropocentrism.

In the same vein, Cheney (1994) argues that the ecosophy implicit in deep ecology provides a sort of 'bio-spherical egalitarianism': the unity of cosmos and humanity's place in the wider scheme of things. The reference to Spinoza means that the universe is one being and all of its parts are expressions of the same substance, namely God. This holistic approach according to Cheney conceals the subversive potential of 'biospherical egalitarianism', namely the fact that it entails the end of the security of modernism, the decline of anthropocentricity and the proliferation of postmodern differences. In other words, the subtext of deep ecology is a strategy of containment aimed at damming up the effects of fragmentation and loss of certainty. Ultimately it ends up 'subsuming difference within a totalising vision or salvation project' (Cheney 1994: 164). Deep ecology consequently displays the moral arrogance that consists in granting to non-humans the same moral rights as to humans. The current ecological crisis, on the other hand, rather calls for a deeper capacity for caring and for an extension of the moral community to the non-human world.

A similar turn towards deep ecology has been taken by Luce Irigaray in her more recent work. Irigaray's *corpus* is distinctly split into an earlier and a later phase. The former is a philosophy of complexity and of difference as not-One; the latter is a return to the metaphysics of two in a very heterosexual frame of reference. In the earlier phase, nature was melted in the nature–culture continuum and the elemental relocation of the subject, which is at the heart of Irigaray's new cosmology. In the later phase, Irigaray explicitly addresses the issue of the environment in relation to Eastern religions and spiritual traditions (Irigaray 1997). This produces a rather reductive effect, lacking subtlety and complexity. The discrepancy between Irigaray's treatment of sexual difference and of other differences, such as ethnicity or race, has been critically commented upon by younger feminists (Deutscher 2003). I find Irigaray's treatment of the environment similarly unsatisfactory.

As Ynestra King put it:

> The piece of the pie that women have only begun to sample as a result of the feminist movement is rotten and carcinogenic, and surely our feminist theory and politics must take account of this however much we yearn for the opportunities within this society that have been denied to us. What is the point of partaking equally in a system that is killing us all? (1989: 115)

I fully share this concern and have enormous sympathy for all the 'what's the point?' and 'so what?' questions. I am, however, dissatisfied with the monological and linear certainties professed by eco-feminists and environmental activists alike. I remain equally unconvinced by the holism of their position and by their essentialist methods. Instead, I recommend that we draw this position somewhat closer to the critiques of globalization that I have mentioned in the previous chapter, so as to decentre the Western bias and obtain a more balanced perspective on the ecological catastrophe that we are confronted with.

In my nomadic perspective, moreover, a Spinozist–Deleuzian ethics actualizes a non-unitary and post-individualistic vision of the subject.

It also promotes 'freedom through the understanding of our bondage', which exemplifies critical theory as an empowering gesture, that is to say a form of self-reflexivity in terms of the politics of locations and accountability. It can also be described as a way of taking responsibility while avoiding taking over, because it is a rejection of the violent appropriation of the discourse of others, constituting a responsible form of anti-foundationalism. Moreover, it is a secular and anti-dogmatic approach that seeks to establish dialogues with social and natural scientists and does not preach only to the converted. Last but not least, it is pragmatic and committed to a variety of possible approaches. Neither monolithic nor unilinear, it also expresses a generous attitude that acts out of love for the world and in a spirit of engagement towards making a positive difference. It is a non-prescriptive mode gesture aiming at a possible alliance with other kindred spirits. This is in tune with the politics of affinity and the strategy of coalitions which I favour in the context of postmodernity.

Having bracketed off the explicitly religious dimension of the eco-feminist debate, I do not wish either to dismiss it or to minimize its spiritual implications. I have chosen to address them in a style that is empathic, though resiliently secular, in keeping with the philosophical tradition of materialism that I have elected as my genealogy. One of the effects of this discursive choice is greater priority to the issue of ethics in terms of accountability, self-reflexivity and an enlarged sense of responsibility. In the next chapter I will address them directly. Let me start here by outlining the many points of transversal alliance between eco-feminism and other groups.

The ethics of care revisited

Eco-feminists stress the distinctly ethical dimension of women as 'caretakers' with a special link to the natural environment (Vandana Shiva 1988). This line of thought stresses women's privileged bond with their territory and in some respects posits them as natural managers. It is rather essentialist in its structures and it gives to the issue deep spiritual resonance. In a different vein, Val Plumwood (1993) tries to adapt the Gilligan-inspired (1982) 'ethics of care' to women's relationship to their natural environment, again stressing all the untapped human resources that women can still offer. By focusing on the theoretical and political link between the domination of nature and that of women, Plumwood critiques instrumental rationalism while defending a relational account of the self as an ethical subject.

In a broader spectrum, Joan Tronto (1993) provides a significant definition of care and of its role in supporting the pursuit of democracy and freedom as well as providing a bridge between morality and politics:

We suggest that caring be viewed as a species activity that includes everything that we do to maintain, continue and repair our 'world' so that we can live in it as well as possible. That world includes our bodies, our selves, and our environment, all of which we seek to interweave in a complex, life-sustaining web. Caring thus consists of the sum total of practices by which we take care of ourselves, others and the natural world. (Tronto 1993: 103)

Care is the key to social accountability and responsible citizenship. This constitutes a break from the reduction of 'care' to the private realm reserved for women, as something 'below' politics. Contrary to these traditional views, Tronto argues that: 'care is a complex process that ultimately reflects structures of power, economic order, the separation of public and private life, and our notions of autonomy and equality' (1995: 12). Arguing that fair and equal access to care should be a prerequisite for any democracy worthy of its name, Tronto makes a strong claim for a more moral approach to politics in such a way as to respect the interconnectedness of individuals with others. Care thus involves competence in the moral but also professional or technical sense of the term and responsiveness on the part of those who are being cared for. For Tronto care is a political ideal, which goes beyond the confines of discussions about morality. Care entails qualities of attentiveness, responsibility, competence and responsiveness that can help construct better citizens, as well as making better moral agents. Care allows for neither neutrality nor distance and calls for self-reflection and constant reappraisals of one's condition. In my language: care is a situated and accountable practice. Tronto's approach constitutes a moral variation on standpoint feminist theory. She reappraises qualities or virtues traditionally coded as 'feminine', not by attaching them more firmly to female specificity, but by showing their relevance for broader issues and for society at large.

Relying completely on a liberal vision of the subject as a moral agent, Tronto cannot, however, answer the very riddle she poses herself: why should people care? How can one make them care? And what do we do with those who do not care at all? Issues of power raise their ugly head again and apart from stressing the fact that 'We are in this together', the 'ethics of care' argument cannot answer the issue of constructing – in my language – subjects who actively desire to care. We cannot adequately account for the construction of desiring subjects of an alternative, more 'caring' kind, by remaining within the liberal definition of the individual. Interconnectedness and the argument that 'we' are all in *this* together, are best served by a nomadic, non-unitary vision of the subject which has dissolved the boundaries of bourgeois individualism and redefined itself as a collective, multi-layered yet singular entity. Approached from this angle, the ethics of sustainability are compatible with the ethics of care – all other differences notwithstanding.

Selma Sevenhuijsen's work on the ethics of care as a key to social agency and effective citizenship is very relevant to this discussion (1998). In her perspective, care is extended from the domain of moral theory of emotions into a fully-fledged political theory. Caring values include democratic values such as responsiveness, responsibility, respect for alterity and diversity, and peaceful resolution of conflicts. More poststructuralist in her approach, Sevenhuijsen draws a powerful transversal connection between the language of rights, social justice, autonomy, equality and power, while arguing for feminist theory to take a firmer ethical stance or rather, to adopt a meta-ethical reflection on its own political and other judgements. This prompts the notions of 'judging with care', where the notion of judgement refers to ethical evaluations of human actions in a way that both respects individuality and diversity and also the radical alterity of human subjects. Firmly based on the case of motherhood as the laboratory for a political philosophy of care, Sevenhuijsen is also open to the influence of postmodernist critiques of essentialism. She is careful to point out that one does not need master narratives in order to support ethical judgements. Like Bauman, Sevenhuijsen sees the postmodern condition as a form of liberation of ethics from modernist morality and its repertoire of autonomy and individualism. By stressing the gendered modes of alterity that are embodied in caring motherhood, Sevenhuijsen focuses her analysis on the axis: gender, power, care and ethics. This is presented as constituting 'a neo-republican idea of active citizenship' (Sevenhuijsen 1998: 14). This postmodern form of humanism stresses the interdependence of self and others, acknowledges contingency and values responsibility.

Digital caring

There are many fruitful grounds for an alliance between bio-centred egalitarianism and the ethics of care as a micro-political practice. An emblematic example of the relevance of this new mode of interaction to the fast-shifting landscapes of transposing differences, which I am mapping out in this book, is the new electronically mediated ethics of care. For instance, digital burial places that were created on the internet for all the expired Tamagochis – the electronic pets that keep infants and young children busy the world over by beeping incessantly when in need of care. The idea of actually burying – albeit in digital form – the Tamagochi which did not survive shows both compassion and a need for rituals. This position contrasts with the cynical reading of the Tamagochi phenomenon by Žižek (1999), who, working within the philosophy of Lack and the Phallic Law, interprets it in the most negative manner possible, as a sadistic training for murder and neglect. Electronic pets testify to the dignified status reached by these interactive technologies and the kinds of relationships they engender. These new 'necronauts' are true archaeologists of the present. Cyberpunk icon Bruce Sterling's 'Dead media project' went one step further and honoured with a decent burial the technologies that were either badly designed, never mass-produced, or simply ceased to work. The exhibits – real funerary monuments to the machines that were – could be consulted online. Sterling argued:

> There are thousands of people who are paid to invent new media and publicize new media. But there is no one whose job it is to describe media that don't work anymore and have collapsed in humiliating, money-losing ways. But this job needs to be done. Otherwise, commercial pressures can lead to a grave misunderstanding of the true nature and behaviour of technology.

Thus, collectors of 'fossil media' like old cameras and typewriters or my beloved LP records acknowledge how vulnerable and mortal technology can be, and act accordingly. In this regard, my own fond memory goes to the Morse Code, which expired recently after decades and two world wars of honourable service: may it rest in peace. This capacity to develop caring relationships towards inanimate, inorganic, functional, fictional and electronically interactive 'others' reveals a number of features that I consider worth stressing.

Firstly, the human 'other' is overestimated as a standard-bearer for ethical behaviour. There is no epistemological, affective or moral reason why one would develop ethical forms of interaction only towards human or anthropomorphic 'others'. Animals, machines and earth 'others' can be equal partners in an ethical exchange. In fact, in the area generally known as 'environmental ethics', the point is made that ethics begins with a responsible and accountable interaction with one's 'natural' habitat. Secondly, technological artefacts are powerful mediators for affectivity and desire. Tamagochis and Pokemons, as well as more advanced fictional figures from the twilight zone known as 'virtual reality', are no less likely to make a profound impact upon the affective structures of the subject than any traditional literary or cinematic character, or indeed any living human or companion species. They act as points of support for what psychoanalysis deemed as the process of 'transference'. I have nomadically redefined them as 'attractors' or affective magnets that connect the self to the social, and vice versa in a complex feedback mechanism. They ultimately constitute means of affective movement, flows or fluxes that allow for projections, interaction and encounter with a network of 'others'. In that sense, all 'others' – anthropomorphic or not – are equal.

Some may be more equal than others, but this difference is not a qualitative one in terms of species or categories of beings. This hierarchical disposition would inevitably re-establish the habits of thought of humanism and thus locate 'Man' (male/white/Christian/heterosexual/ speaking a 'world' language/owning property/entitled to citizenship) at the centre of the spectrum. As I am committed to displacing this hegemonic formation and thus replace 'Man' with a multiplicity of compounds or clustered entities in the nomadic mode, I would posit the line of demarcation not between species or categorical divides, but rather at the molecular level of the forces, passions, intensities or affectivity that get invested in them. In other words, it is the typology of affects, or the ethology of forces, that makes all the difference. As Haraway puts its wittily: 'One can hardly invoke that individual and his stripped-down, body-phobic societies to object to the liveliness of mice, microbes, narrative figures, lab machines, and various chimerical collectives of humans and non-humans.' (Haraway 1997: 284). I shall discuss this more fully in the next chapter.

Thirdly, the capacity to develop significant degrees of attachment to inorganic, technological or anthropomorphic 'others' is the characteristic of younger generations which have lived through powerful processes of transition. These are to be taken more seriously and neutrally than they commonly are in contemporary social and cultural critiques. In keeping with the deep-seated 'technophobia' of so much dominant morality, in fact, emotional attachment to technological 'others' or to virtual beings tends to be classified as a minor perversion, or an infantile and regressive stage. The reasons for this are never made explicit, but rather pertain to the 'common-sense' set of values that is the result of centuries of humanistic *ethos*. They need reviewing.

What I am calling into question is less the value and dignity of this *ethos*, than its reliance on a hegemonic vision of the subject: Man. There is no reason why an *ethos* of respect and affectivity should be the exclusive entitlement of such a subject. Giving a decent burial to the many electronically deceased Tamagochis, just like lovingly collecting the many technological items that have gone out of fashion, stock or production, can be a perfect manifestation of a caring ethics, or at least of an *ethos* that would begin to disengage itself from the limitations of humanistic anthropocentrism.

This is connected to the broader issue of developing more conceptual creativity in dealing with these questions: we need to create figurations that do justice to the paradoxes and complexities of the day. For instance, our technologically mediated world offers a framework for some significant relocations of human caring. Thus, the pregnant body becomes the site of some inspiring 'met(r)amorphoses' (Lichtenberg-Ettinger 1992; Braidotti 2002). It can be read as a host environment, with the foetus as a positive parasite. It can also be seen as a mindless, *zoe*-driven proliferation of cells aiming at their own self-perpetuation. The foetus is neither self nor other, but a generative in-between. As such it constitutes a vital nexus, like that of any animal, virus or parasite, to its environment or territory. Becoming is a zoological, biological and geological event, which feeds upon multiple territories. As in the case of the placenta (Rouch 1987) we are faced here with figurations of the self/other interaction that do not follow the Hegelian dialectical model. They therefore move beyond the exercise of normative reason and of rational violence that, according to Jessica Benjamin (1988), is the key to the constitution of subjectivity.

These maternal-feminine, anti-essentialist yet vitalistic figurations rather suggest a model of porosity, fluidity, multiple interconnections and symbolic interrelation, a transversal subjectivity. They are figurations for hybrid interrelation. Viral politics requires sustainable ethics to negotiate with the generative powers of *zoe*, this life in 'me' which does not bear my name and does not even fully qualify as human. All the more so in the historical context of technology-driven post-industrialism where life is being commodified by a very commercial-minded bio-scientific industry and affiliated research. A more generalized becoming-ethical is on the way.

BECOMING-ETHICAL: AN ECO-PHILOSOPHY OF MULTIPLE BELONGINGS

Chaosmosis: beyond holism

The ecological crisis for Guattari and Deleuze is something more than a problem of the environment; it aims at producing a virtual ecology. It includes social, political, ethical and aesthetic dimensions as well. To address it adequately, we need a qualitative leap of our ethical liberty so as to reconstitute ethics, politics and a new processual aesthetics. The method is to create transversal links between the categories, while facing the 'ethical vertigo' that is the sign of change. Intellectuals should devote themselves to creating conditions for the implementation of transversality. The fundamental political desire is for an individual and collective reappropriation of the production of subjectivity, along the lines of 'ontological heterogenesis', chaosmic desegregation of the different categories. We need actively to desire to reinvent subjectivity as a set of mutant values and to draw our pleasure from that, not from the static contemplation of the perpetuation of the regime of the Same. Chaosmos is the universe of reference for becomings in the sense of the unfolding of virtualities, or mutant values.

The work of Francisco Varela is of the greatest importance in redesigning this type of environmentally bound, post-anthropocentric and anti-Cartesian ethics of co-determination between self and other. The notion of co-dependence replaces that of recognition, much as the ethics of sustainability replaces the moral philosophy of rights. Within the frame of bio-centred egalitarianism, the co-dependence of different species not only challenges liberal humanism, but also reiterates the importance of grounded, situated and very specific and hence accountable perspectives.

This amounts to accepting a strong sense of limits in the kind of ethical relations we can engage in – and also in those we are able to sustain.

Shiva, resting on a distinction proposed by Maturana and Varela (1972), distinguishes between on the one hand 'autopoietic systems', which are mostly biological organisms, self-organizing and capable of self-renewal, and, on the other hand, 'allopoietic systems'. The latter are mostly technical artefacts that need input from the outside in order to function. In the mechanistic world order imposed by the Western idea of science, argues Shiva, the former is often coined as 'chaos', whereas the latter enjoys the privilege of 'order': one is organic, the other machinic. According to Shiva, the autopoietic systems are dynamic structures which, being endogenously driven, constitute the sheer essence of health and ecological stability for living systems. They are structurally opposed to genetic engineering and the mechanistic way of life. This has particular relevance to the status of women and the technological takeover of the maternal function in biotechnologies and human genetic engineering. The theft of the regenerative powers of women may well be the last act in this ultimate colonization of living organisms by predatory Western science.

Felix Guattari, in his analysis of the 'collective existential mutations' (1995: 2) currently taking place, also refers to the same distinction between autopoietic and allopoietic systems as Vandana Shiva does. Guattari's use of the distinction (autopoietic/allopoietic), however, goes further than Shiva's. He relates it firstly to the quest for redefinitions of subjectivity, which he considers the main challenge for contemporary philosophy. Secondly, he extends the principle of autopoiesis, which for Varela as for Shiva is reserved for the biological organisms, to cover also the machines or technological ones. Another name for chaosmosis is autopoietic subjectivation: 'poiesis', in other words, refers to the process of re-singularized universes of subjectivation, or self-styling.

Guattari's machinic autopoiesis establishes a qualitative link between organic matter and technological or machinic artifacts 'and even the incorporeal machines of language, theory and aesthetic creation' (Guattari 1995: 93). This results in a radical redefinition of the generative power of 'Life'. The failure to recognize the autopoietic nature of machines helps the hegemony of scientific reductionism in Western thought. Machines have their own temporality and develop through 'generations': they contain their own virtuality and futurity. Consequently, they entertain their own forms of alterity not only towards humans, but also among themselves. Whereas organic structures are inhabited by the desire for eternity, machines are driven by the desire for abolition. Through this shift of perspective, Guattari moves beyond the distinction proposed by Varela and proposes a transversal definition of the technological elements as 'others', or 'a more collective machinism without delimited unity, whose autonomy accommodates diverse mediums of alterity' (1995: 42).

Heterogeneity is the key idea in this non-human model of enunciation that constitutes the specific enunciative consistency of machines.

As for Deleuze, the problem then becomes how to relate these collective approaches to processes of subjectivation. Guattari defines the collective as a transversalist notion 'the sense of a multiplicity that deploys itself as much beyond the individual, on the side of the *socius*, as before the person, on the side of preverbal intensities, indicating a logic of affects rather than a logic of delimited sets' (1995: 9). Whether subjectivity becomes individualized or collectivized depends on the historical contexts. The paradox of subjectivation and individualization raises the question of how to reconcile the need to redefine subjectivity nomadically yet in an accountable manner, against the forces that tend to reterritorialize it, or essentialize it. The answer to these paradoxes, according to Guattari, is a 'transversalist conception of subjectivity' that cuts across and therefore recombines these opposite trends. As a schizo-analyst, Guattari stresses the 'non-human' parts of human subjectivity, which is not an anti-humanist position but merely the acknowledgement that subjectivity does not and need not coincide with either the notion of the individual or that of person. It is rather the case that these are historical manifestations of the subject. This leads us to a very dynamic vision of the subject as a self-organizing or 'autopoietic system', which is Guattari's aesthetic and political paradigm.

Autopoiesis is the maintenance of a machinic system, through the mediation of potential energy into organized and distributed matter. Disparate orders of magnitude are thus brought into communication, to create the metastability which is the precondition of individuation. The system achieves stability while avoiding closure: it engenders self-organization with high levels of creativity or autonomy from the flow of forces. Ansell-Pearson puts it as follows:

> An autopoietic machine is one which continuously generates and specifies its own organization through its operation as a system of production of its own components. . . . An autopoietic machine is defined not in terms of the components or their static relations, but by the particular network of processes (relations) of production. The relations of production of components are given only as processes; if the processes 'stop', then the relations vanish. Therefore machines require regeneration by the components they produce. (1997b: 140–1)

This autopoietic system accounts both for living organisms, humans as self-organizing systems, and also the inorganic matter, challenging the prejudice that only humans can manufacture a living and self-organizing system. Although Maturana and Varela's dualistic scheme opposes the inert to the living and is thus more oppositional than nomadic, it has proved of great inspirational force in rethinking the 'life' force of inorganic matter.

The bio-centred egalitarianism I want to defend pursues the same project of coming to terms with the generative power of non-human and non organic entities. This line is pursued with great lucidity by Keith Ansell-Pearson, who starts from the assumption that the bio-technical revolution of today entails a redefinition of evolution in a distinctly less anthropocentric manner than most would expect. In his critique of the rhetoric of bio-technological vitalism (1997b) Ansell-Pearson warns us against the pernicious fantasy of a re-naturalized evolution led by bio-technological capitalism. He sees this as one of the master narratives of neo-liberalism and as a serious error in the assessment of our historical condition. The paranoid mode of presentation of a totalizing techno-future perpetuates the split between 'Life' and the human, pitching one against the other and expressing the fear of loss of mastery by the latter. The point is to rethink evolution in a non-deterministic but also a non-anthropocentric manner. In a response to the divinely ordained evolutionary teleology of Teilhard de Chardin (1959), the emphasis falls instead on the quest for a more adequate understanding of the topology and the ethology of forces involved in chaosmosis defined as the radical immanence of life as a complex system. Central to this non-essentialist vision of vitalism is the idea of affinity among different forces, in a set of connective disjunctions which are not a synthesis, but a recomposition. Basing his argument on Guattari's concept of 'chaosmosis', Ansell-Pearson wants to think the vital autonomy of evolution in terms of the specific enunciative practices of machinic phylogenesis. Machinic autopoiesis means that the machine is a site of becoming, or the threshold to many possible worlds. We humans therefore need to review our schemes of representation of the machinic processes.

This combination of flow or movement and self-organizing systems is at the heart of the high-tech brand of neo-organicism we are experiencing in contemporary computational culture. Katherine Hayles's work on embodiment is part of this movement, which she aptly calls 'the posthuman' life of codes and computing systems. How to reconcile bodily spaces and experiences with the possibilities afforded by the new computational technologies is at the heart of what Hayles describes as 'humanistic informatics'. Similarly, autopoiesis is processual creativity, which I would locate in an enlarged ontology of gratuitousness, or non-profit. The subjects' fundamental aspiration is neither to 'make sense', that is to say to emit meaningful utterances within a signifying system, nor is it about conforming to ideal models of behaviour. The subject merely aims at self-completion, that is to say at achieving singularity: it is an enduring, affective entity capable of affecting and of being affected by a multiplicity of others. As subject-in-becoming, she or he is a vector of subjectivation. Subjectivity for Guattari is 'pathetic' in the sense of empathic, affective, multiply mediated and complex. Like Deleuze, Guattari investigates the paradox of this affectivity which is constantly evacuated from discourse although, or maybe because, it is that which makes it possible in the first instance.

To understand such a subject we need to approach it through his or her three fundamental ecologies: that of the environment, that of the *socius*, and that of the psyche. And more importantly, we need to create transversal lines through all three of them. It is crucial to see the interconnections among the greenhouse effect, the status of women, racism and xenophobia, and frantic consumerism. We must not stop at any fragmented portions of these realities, but rather trace transversal interconnections among them. The subject is a plane of consistency that includes 'territorialized existential territories' and 'deterritorialized incorporeal universes' (1995: 26). Under phallogocentrism this complexity is misread and reduced to a logic of discourse where Capital becomes the referent for labour, the Signifier for semiotic expression, and Being the great principle of reduction of that very ontological polyvocality which Guattari locates at the heart of the matter of subjectivity.

Psychoanalytic theory is of no great assistance, being equally subjected to the rule of the signifier. Freudian metapsychology, moreover, opposes two antagonistic drives, of life and death, complexity and chaos. By contrast, the idea of chaosmosis establishes a common background, which is not indifferentiation, but the vital energy of virtual ways and modes of becoming: of positive alterity as complexity.

Guattari proposes an analysis of complexity in four dimensions: instead of the libido, the notion of material and semiotic fluxes of energy. Instead of the realm of the linguistic signifier, the concrete and abstract machinic entities (or phylums); instead of the unconscious, virtual universes of value; and in place of the self, finite existential territories. Again, the point of such a distinction is to create transversal connections across the lines in a creative process of transversality.

The choice of multiplicity, against such a reduction, is for Guattari an ethical choice (1995: 29): 'There is an ethical choice in favour of the richness of the possible, an ethics and politics of the virtual that decorporealizes and deterritorializes contingency, linear causality and the pressure of circumstances and significations which besiege us. It is a choice for processuality, irreversibility and resingularisation.' Guattari stresses that our world is incapable of absorbing the techno-mutations that are currently shaking it. As the terms of reference break down one by one, a vertiginous race towards radical renewal is the only positive alternative: 'An ecology of the virtual is just as pressing as ecologies of the visible world' (1995: 91).

How to deal with this ontological intensity in a secular and creative manner is the challenge. Guattari expresses it in terms of registers of coexistence and crystallization of intensity. It is literally a question of synchronizing the ontological intensity with machinic arrangements of the structure of affectivity that would allow it to resonate freely. This refers to the parallelism of mind and body defended by Spinoza, to which I will return in the next chapter.

How to reconstitute the subject? By empowering processes of becoming, in the chaosmic deterritorializations within it. This includes high levels of intensity and a state of flux or oscillation between the 'no longer' and the 'not yet', i.e. between a proliferation of possibilities and a degree zero of self-presence. This is akin to a schizoid state. Not only is it the case that the existence of chaosmic stases is not the privilege of psychopathology, but without it there would be no creativity of any kind.

This qualitative step forward is necessary if we want subjectivity to escape the regime of self-withdrawal, the infantilization through the media and the denial of alterity that are the traits of our historical era. 'Virtual ecology' aims at engendering the conditions for the creation and the development of unprecedented formations of subjectivity. It is a generalized ecology, also known as ecosophy, which aims at crossing transversally the multiple layers of the subject, from interiority to exteriority and everything in between. These are Deleuze's becomings defined as nuclei of differentiation and singularization.

Luciana Parisi (2004b) suggests that Guattari's scheme of the three ecologies provides an answer to the question of the transversal interconnections among these lines of subjectivation. His answer is a mixed semiotics that combines the virtual (indeterminate) and the actual domains. The non-semiotic codes (the DNA or all genetic material) intersect with semiotic a-signification, which is a complex assemblage of affects, embodied practices and other performances that include but are not confined to the linguistic.

Parisi argues that a similar case is made quite powerfully by the new epistemology of Margulis and Sagan (1995), through the concept of endosymbiosis, which, like autopoiesis, indicates a creative form of evolution. It defines the vitality of matter as an ecology of differentiation, which means that the genetic material is exposed to processes of becoming. This questions any ontological foundation for difference while avoiding social constructivism. The assumption of Spinozist monism underscores this project and defines nature/culture as a continuum that evolves through variations or differentiations. Deleuze and Guattari theorize them in terms of transversal assemblages.

The punch line of this dense argument is twofold: the first point is that difference emerges as pure production of becoming-molecular and that the transitions or stratifications are internal to the single process of formation or of assemblage. They are intensive or affective variations that produce semiotic and a-semiotic practices. This is not just about dismissing semiotics or the linguistic turn, but rather an attempt at using it more rigorously, within the domains of its strict application (Massumi 2002). It is also important to connect it transversally to other discourses. The second key point is that primacy is given to the Relation over the terms. Parisi expresses this in Guattari's language as 'schizogenesis' – or the affective being of the middle, the interconnection, the Relation. This is the space–time where the differentiation occurs and with it the modifications. As we shall see in the next chapter, these variations in intensity are also expressed in the concept of the Body-without-Organs or the incorporeal. The emphasis falls on the micropolitics of relations, as a post-humanist ethics that traces transversal connections among material and symbolic, concrete and discursive lines or forces. Transversality actualizes bio-centred egalitarianism as an ethics and also as a method to account for both material and immaterial forms of labour subjectivity in the age of *bios/zoe*-power, which trades in all that lives and breeds. An ethics based on the primacy of the Relation, of interdependence, values *zoe* in itself.

FOR THE LOVE OF ZOE

Philosophical nomadism is a *bios/zoe*-politics. Monistic and thus opposed to the nature–culture divide, it offers both a geophilosophy, or an ecosophy, a topology of affects, and an ethics. The earth being the framework for all activities and becomings, Deleuze stresses the immanence, the diversity and the multiplicity of what the earth-body can do. The 'milieu' is, as the term suggests, a middle ground for modes of relation that offer to nomadic subjects a micro-political ecology and ethics of interconnections. Central to this vision is the notion of the productive nature of the transversal interconnections that sustain the subject as a *bios/zoe*-centred entity.

Ethics is related to the physics and the biology of bodies. That means that it deals with the question of what exactly a body can do and how much it can take. This is the issue that I code as 'sustainability': how much a body can take in pleasure or enhancement of its potentials, as in pain or impoverishment of its *potentia* (or *conatus*). This implies also an equation between ethical virtue, empowerment, joy and the understanding. To represent adequately to oneself one's own *potentia* amounts to understanding it. Such an act of understanding, however, is not the mere cognitive acquisition of certain ideas. It rather coincides with a bodily process, an activity that enacts or embodies what is good for the subject, the actualization of his or her *potentia*.

What attracts me to the biological egalitarianism of *zoe* is the part of me that has long become disenchanted with and disengaged from the anthropocentrism that is built into humanistic thought, even in what is left of the political Left and feminism with it. That in me which no longer identifies with the dominant categories of subjectivity, but which is not yet completely out of the cage of identity, runs with *zoe*. This rebellious

component of my subject-position, which is disidentified from phallogocentric premises, is related to my feminist consciousness of what it means
to be an embodied female. As such, I am a she-wolf, a breeder that multiplies cells in all directions; I am an incubator and a carrier of vital and
lethal viruses. I am mother-earth, the generator of the future. In the political economy of phallogocentrism and of anthropocentric humanism,
which predicates the sovereignty of Sameness in a falsely universalistic
mode, my sex fell on the side of 'Otherness', understood as pejorative
difference, or as being-worth-less-than. The becoming-animal/becoming-
world speaks to my feminist self, partly because my gender, historically
speaking, never quite made it into full humanity, so my allegiance to that
category is at best negotiable and never to be taken for granted.

This is neither an essentialist statement, nor one of semiotic constructivism. It is rather the materialist acknowledgement of a historical location: a starting position of asymmetrical power differentials. This location
is not only geopolitical, but also genealogical and time-bound. It marks a
sedimented multi-layering of genetic coding, cultural meanings and representations that position me in the spatio-temporal coordinates of a
socio-symbolic entity commonly known as 'woman'. In other words, a
bond of sympathy, empathy or affinity exists among the many and multi-
layered 'others' of the former phallogocentric empire: women, natives,
natural, infantilized and criminalized 'others'. As Lefanu (1988) pointed
out in her analysis of science-fiction texts written by women, many of
them show explicitly this kind of bonding between women and various
brands of monstrous or alien others, allied in their struggle against
a common colonizer. Far closer to *zoe* than *bios* in the materiality of bodies
that are vulnerable and deviant, feminist-minded women have shown
a propensity to go as far as possible in subverting the sovereignty of
the Same.

My position as a non-unitary, nomadic feminist and accountable subject
facilitates this bond of both empathy and responsibility towards non-
human others. The recognition of a sexualized and racialized axis that
tends to define certain subjects as 'non-human' and hence as more mortal
in the sense of being ontologically inferior, is facilitated by a non-unitary
vision of the subject, not at all hindered by it. Furthermore, I would argue
that the real hindrance in this discussion – that is to say a position that
generates both cognitive and moral obstacles – comes from the classical
humanistic *hubris* which declares 'Man' as the measure of *all* things, oblivious to the sexism and the ethnocentrism of such a position. This is why
I want to reclaim my *zoe*-philic location and enlist it in support of the
project of undoing anthropocentrism and its spin-off, androcentrism. I
want to unfasten their joint reliance on the phallic signifier, i.e. the political
economy of Sameness and of its specular, binary and constitutive 'Others'.
I want to run with the she-wolves against the gravitational pull of the
humanization and hence the commodification of all that lives. And I want

to celebrate instead not so much the mystery of nature – a sentimental notion dear to deep ecology which sounds unconvincing to my agnostic ears – but rather the immense generative power, the intelligence and artistry of the non-human, of *zoe* as generative force. I want to be able to think and represent positively those organic and inorganic 'others' and the specific kind of vitality they express.

Loyal to the method and the political practice of locations, however, I also want to situate this discussion in terms of more general, geopolitical power-relations within advanced societies. From this angle animals and humans are close in that they are being exploited as commercial objects of exchange, as well as experimental sites for science. In this respect, bio-centred egalitarianism joins forces with many other social and ethical movements that call for limitations to be placed on this ruthless exploitation of all that lives. In so far as I partake of the dominant, molar position of white, educated women, I want to praise bio-centred egalitarianism as a way of equalizing what is at stake for human and non-human participants in the project of social sustainability. 'We' are in *this* together, but we are not all the same. Dolly the Sheep and I share a structural proximity in terms of our inscription in genetic engineering, but this cannot be adequately accounted for within the logic of rights. I therefore want to defend the qualitative process of becoming-animal as a creative transformation that stresses the productivity of bio-power in terms of *zoe*, or generative, non-logocentric life: a micro-politics of affective becomings.

Transversal subjects

In this and the previous chapter I have traced a cartography of the transpositions that are taking place in the axes of sexualization, racialization and naturalization of Otherness. I have relocated them towards productive forms of becoming. The three case studies support the idea that a non-unitary, nomadic vision of the subject is the *sine qua non*, that is to say the prerequisite for ethical agency and political accountability of contemporary subjects. The three axes of becoming actually amount to a set of deeply interrelated phenomena. They highlight the extent to which, in the age of *bios/zoe*-power, transversal interconnections make it impossible on the cognitive plane and irresponsible on the ethical level actually to uphold categorical distinctions between human and other-than-human subject positions. Read alongside the knotted problems that surround gender and ethnicity politics and human reproduction, the status of animals and the plight of the environment show clearly the structural analogies that connect them, both politically and theoretically.

The punch line, however, is ethical: how far can we push this redefinition of the embodied selves, i.e. how much can our bodies take?

In order even to begin to grapple with our contemporary rendition of Spinoza's question, however, we first need to draw as detailed a cartography as possible of what is happening between our 'selves' and our 'bodies'.

The three intersecting transpositions relocate the bodies of subjects previously defined as 'others' within the shifting horizons of globalization. The former 'others', unhinged from the metaphysical frame of reference that used to contain them, enter a schizoid or non-linear logic of motion. This produces femininity without women, racialization without races and naturalization without nature. This process enacts a number of dematerializations or transpositions of embodied and embedded entities, which are both a dislocation (negative) and a new departure (productive). Embodiment, far from being a foundation, has rematerialized the others as both the threshold of multiple becoming and as the site for 'disposable bodies'. Because such processes are structurally connected to technologies in the context of *bios/zoe*-power, they mark the paradox of simultaneous takeover or consumption and recomposition or reinvention of 'others'.

'Disposable bodies' refer to the negative impact of these transpositions. They refer to sets of organs disengaged from organic unity, consistency or integrity: a collection of organs that are up for grabs. See the case of women's bodies farmed for their ova, the nurturing capacities of their uterus, their generative powers, as Shiva points out. See how the bodies of animals, just like black or native bodies, are 'farmed' for their productive, reproductive and generative powers; for sexual services in the global sex trade; for spare parts in the organ transplant industries. Think of the martyrized body of oncomouse, the farming ground for the new genetic revolution and manufacturer of spare parts for other species; think of trans-species organ transplants.

Fortunately, however, those who are empirically marked as 'disposable bodies' do not fully coincide with the mark of pejorative difference that is cast upon them. Their being a minority, a marginal or peripheral entity, also provides the grounds for their becoming also the active subjects of processes of transformation and active empowerment. In the intricate web of power (as *potestas*) relations, in the age of control over Life (as in *bios* and *zoe*), active affirmation of alternative subject-positions (as *potentia*) will always strike back. The transversal subject-positions of the 'others' are not likely to give in to uncritical and mindless homologation into values, norms and modes of behaviour that are modelled on the social genetic imaginary and on the commercialization of life in its imperial mode.

In other words, the dislocations and re-assemblages of intersecting subject positions are not only negative expressions of devalued otherness. As active processes of becoming, they also express strong and affirmative recomposed subjectivities of those who were previously labelled as 'others': women, ethnic or indigenous racialized others, animals and environmental issue have developed a voice, a style and a relevance of their own. How to do justice to them remains the responsibility of and a challenge to the social and cultural critics. The most effective way to proceed with these challenges is by constructing transversal alliances across disciplines and discursive communities, across geopolitical locations and different genealogies and traditions. In the age of transpositions, we need to move towards a trans-political style of activism.

The process of becoming does not amount to a reversal of this dialectical scheme which would turn the former 'others' into the Same, but rather a radical disruption of this scheme altogether. 'Becoming minoritarian' is the code name for overturning the dialectical logic that legitimates a central norm through hierarchically organized binary oppositions. You do not have to be an empirical minority in order to become minoritarian, but that position is a great starting point and a privileged epistemological and political vantage point. In itself, however, it is not enough. A further step in the process is necessary, a sort of leap of consciousness. Even women have to become-woman in the sense of disengaging themselves from the Phallic signifier. What the process of becoming stands for is this qualitative shift of perspective.

Now let me apply this qualitative criterion to the three cases I discussed in this and the previous chapter. Becoming-minoritarian (becoming woman/animal/molecular) marks a shift from the dominant subject-position, but nevertheless remains tied to it. These becomings-minoritarian unfold from the minorities and aim at a shift of consciousness, but they are like Benjamin's angel of history: always looking backward slightly, even as they advance towards the future. The becomings-minoritarian draw their strength from a consciousness that comes from experience, usually the experience of an exclusion or a marginalization, but they do not stop there. It is important to see the limitations of the knowledge that comes from experience and not to be confined to its authority. This sacralization of experiential knowledge is one of the greatest problems affecting identity politics. In their political implications, the processes of becoming-minoritarian can result in progressive positions. There is a becoming-woman, for instance, which refers to established counter-ideologies and theoretical frameworks, and emancipatory ideals and practices. Not only is there nothing wrong with emancipatory or egalitarian politics and the struggle to win the same rights as the subjects who count as the standardized norm, but it is also the case that such a position is urgent and necessary. The context of the new global world order is in fact marked by such a swelling tide of structural injustices that the repair work of egalitarian politics is more necessary than ever.

My point is that one should simply not stop there. Given the complexity and paradoxes of our times, there cannot be only one political frontline or precise strategy. Multiple positions are needed instead. This statement contains an inbuilt critique of egalitarian or emancipatory politics, in so far as it questions the desirability of that very norm which is being pursued in the logic of rights and the pursuit of equality (Irigaray 1987a). It need not be an indictment of this logic, however. Nomadic politics is a complex and multi-layered approach that does not pursue right lines or straight paths, but combines even potentially contradictory positions in a zigzag-ging pattern of mixed strategies. The ultimate political aim of this strategy is twofold: firstly to create both concepts and values that break from the established norm and do not reproduce it. Secondly, to produce dynamic transversal interaction or movement among the heterogeneous and diverse sites and strategies. Conceptual and ethical creativity is the key term here.

In the case of the becoming-woman/animal, which are classical cases of minoritarian or oppositional politics, it can be argued that such a posi-tion incurs a rather high risk of colluding with the strategies of advanced capitalism, in so far as this system can be described as a force that deter-ritorializes, plurifies and complexifies for the purpose of profit. The great vampire incorporates and displaces all that lives in a series of successive waves of consumption. Poststructuralist philosophers have therefore argued time and again that the only way to resist is to work from within this system, for the purpose of enacting forms of resistance. Processes of becoming are such forms of resistance, in that they aim at empowerment and the enhancement of what subjects can do (their *potentia*) for the sake of non-profit. This non-rapacious production of empowering and affirma-tive differences is a qualitative change of gears within the system of advanced capitalism. Becoming woman/animal/etc. trace the same pat-terns as minority formations, but disrupt them and qualitatively shift their aims and forces.

What looks from one angle therefore as a potential threat of contamina-tion of the minorities by the dominant norm or standard, from another appears instead as active resistance and innovation. This is not relativism, but the politics of location. What keeps the danger of homologation or vampiristic absorption at bay is the strategy of inserting motion, accelera-tion and hence disruption within the processes of successive de- and reterritorialization which are induced by the flows of capital. This dynamic process of motion ensures that the processes keep on going and never stop. In the mode of emancipatory politics this means that they do not stop at the mere assertion of counter-identities, but rather go further and push towards qualitatively stronger de-territorializations. Even identity politics and feminist strategic essentialism can open paths of becoming, so long as they do not stop at the mere reassertions of identities they taught us to despise.

Becoming-world

At this stage it is important to see the difference between the minoritarian becomings and the third case I examined, namely the becoming-world or merging with the environment, or the earth. This does not fit in with this pattern because it is a pure form of becoming, which is immanent to all the others: it is planetary. It is the only form of becoming which is not minoritarian,[1] but qualitatively at a distance from the standard or norm of the dominant subject-position or majority. As such it has the power to deterritorialize the majority and its main categories and classifications. The becoming-imperceptible is the most forceful expression of this positive or qualitative shift or deterritorialization. It concerns the movement of the totality of all that lives, of that great animal/machine that is the cosmos itself. It concerns the planet as a whole. In this sense the becoming-imperceptible traces a general eco-philosophy of becoming that produces positive interconnections on a planetary scale. My phrase 'we are in *this* together' accurately sums up the global dimension of the problems we are facing when we take the power-relations around *bios/zoe* as the defining feature of our historicity. How to think accurately about the complex singularity of the subject at the same time as the generic materiality of this earthily embedded, 'glocalized' and universal subject is the question I address in chapter 5.

One of the consequences here concerns the limitations of liberal individualism as a point of reference for the discussion of the proliferation of discourses about *bios/zoe*. An emphasis on the unitary subject of possessive individualism is of hindrance, rather than assistance, in addressing the complexities of our post-human condition. Two core objections have emerged to it: one targets its deep-seated anthropocentrism, the other its universalism. The post-humanism of social and cultural critics working within a Western perspective can be set alongside the form of neo-humanism, shared by a number of contemporary social critics working within racial, post-colonial or non-Western perspectives. It is neither a question of flattening out structural differences, nor of drawing facile analogies, but rather of practising the politics of location. Bio-centred post-humanism and non-Western neo-humanism can be travelling companions along productive axes of transposition. This transposition is like a musical variation that leaps across scales and compositions to find a pitch or a shareable level of intensity. What matters to my thought is the affective dimension, the affinity, not the political or theoretical correctness.

Anti-individualistic nomadic politics is a critique of the centre from the centre. It assumes a multiplicity of centres in a world of scattered

[1] I am grateful to Paul Patton for clarifying this point at the Seminar on Political Ontology held at the Erasmus University in Rotterdam, 10–12 June 2002.

hegemonies (Grewal and Kaplan, 1994). The cartographic reading of the present points to a post-humanist system in which the human has been subsumed into global networks of control and commodification which have taken 'Life' and living matter as target. The political economy of euphoria and gloom of advanced capitalism inscribes us in a state of constant crisis. The crisis of human rights, of human life, of the environment or of human survival is on the agenda. The generic figure of the human is in trouble. Donna Haraway puts is as follows: 'our authenticity is warranted by a database for the human genome. The molecular database is held in an informational database as legally branded intellectual property in a national laboratory with the mandate to make the text publicly available for the progress of science and the advancement of industry. This is Man the taxonomic type become Man the brand' (1997: 74). This standard is posited in a universal mode as *Man*, but this pseudo-universal has been widely criticized (Lloyd 1985) precisely because of its partiality. Universal *Man*, in fact, is implicitly assumed to be masculine, white, urbanized, speaking a standard language, heterosexually inscribed in a reproductive unit and a full citizen of a recognized polity. Massumi refers to this phenomenon as 'Ex-Man', 'a genetic matrix embedded in the materiality of the human' (1998: 60), and as such undergoing significant mutations: 'species integrity is lost in a bio-chemical mode expressing the mutability of human matter' (1998: 60).

To this end, I do not think that the reference or the return to a universal is inevitable or even necessary. On the contrary, I want to argue for a more specific and grounded sense of singular subjectivities that are collectively bound and outward-oriented. In other words, 'we' need a redefinition of that subject position and consequently some input from philosophies that attempt to struggle with this question. We need to revisit the notion of 'pan-humanity' from within a non-unitary understanding of the subject. Two contemporary contributions come to mind here: Irigaray's idea of the 'sensible transcendental' and Deleuze's 'empirical transcendental' (Braidotti 2002).

Deleuze's notion of 'anybody' in the sense of '*tout le monde*' is also extremely relevant because it refers to concretely embodied singularities that are structurally connected. What this singular, but collectively bound subject may look like is the question that I will address in the next two chapters. An important reason for needing a new grounded, embodied and embedded subject has to do with the second half of that crucial sentence: 'we' are in *this* together. What *this* refers to is the cartography as a cluster of interconnected problems that touches the structure of subjectivity and the very possibility of the future as a sustainable option. 'We' are in *this* together, in fact, enlarges the sense of collectively bound subjectivity to non-human agents, from our genetic neighbours the animals, to the earth as a biosphere as a whole. 'We', therefore, is a non-anthropocentric construct, which refers to a commonly shared territory or habitat (*this*).

How to do justice to this relatively simple yet highly problematic reality requires a shift of perspective. As Haraway suggests, we need to work towards 'a new techno-scientific democracy' (1997: 95). *This* is indeed a totality, finite and confined. The implications of this fact are multiple and they concern the issue of the limits of social constructivism with which I opened this chapter. Because of the kind of complexities 'we' are facing, we need to review methodologies that have tended to underplay the role of biological or genetic factors. This calls for a new set of alliances of a more transversal and transdisciplinary nature, with different communities of scholars and activists. I propose the idea of 'sustainability' as the rallying point.

What 'sustainability' stands for, therefore, is a regrounding of the subject in a materially embedded sense of responsibility and ethical accountability for the environments she or he inhabits. What is at stake is the very possibility of the future, of duration or continuity. Becomings are the sustainable shifts or changes undergone by nomadic subjects in their active resistance against being subsumed in the commodification of their own diversity. Becomings are unprogrammed as mutations, disruptions, and points of resistance. Their time frame is always the future anterior, that is to say a linkage across present, and past in the act of constructing and actualizing possible futures. I shall return to this issue in the next chapter.

In disagreement with other feminist theorists, especially in the field of science studies, I maintain that the subject – in the non-unitary, processual but accountable form I defend in my philosophical nomadism – is a crucial term of reference in this project. I want to keep an equal distance from both the humanistic assumptions of the unitary subject and the extreme forms of epistemologically driven post-humanism which dismiss the need for a subject altogether. This is where my dialogue with Donna Haraway reaches some point of genuine disagreement. It is not the case that the subject's transcendent nature needs to result in either disembodied abstractions or in universalistic pretensions. On the contrary, I want to argue that a great deal of Continental philosophy in the second half of the twentieth century has attempted to rethink the embodied, materialist foundations of the subject in a non-essentialist yet accountable manner.

As a consequence, I would enlist, rather than dismiss, the contribution that philosophical materialism and especially nomadism can make to this debate. It is not the case that only social studies of science, or feminist cultural studies, can offer useful tools of analysis for the complex phenomena and cluster of problems surrounding the techno-bodies of advanced capitalism. Philosophical investigations of alternative ways of accounting for the embedded and embodied nature of the subject are indeed relevant and generous allies in the ongoing efforts to develop an approach to subjectivity worthy of the complexities of our age. One needs at least *some* subject position: this need not be either unitary, or exclusively anthropocentric, but it must be the site for political and ethical accountability.

CONCLUSION: OF SYNCHRONICITY

This book is driven by the desire to reconstitute discursive communities and set up dialogues among players, actors and subjects who do not talk enough to one another. I am saddened and concerned by the lack of transversal dialogues among intellectual and political communities that should be structural allies. One of the points I want to stress through my analysis of processes of becoming woman/other/animal/world is that in the present context these transpositions run the risk of creating new segregations of discursive practices. I wonder why scholarship on globalization tends to ignore feminist theory. I am puzzled by the extent of a mirror game that multiculturalism and multimedia research seem to be playing with each other: new digital media scholarship does not take on the question of ethnicity or race, while race discourse remains mostly unchallenged in its technophobia.

One of the major axes of discursive segregation I have explicitly addressed in the last two chapters is the continuing drift that exists, in both mainstream and feminist cultures, between science studies on the one hand and philosophies of the subject on the other. The missing links of this dialogue are manifold and they converge on a collision course upon the theme of 'post-humanism'. If such a theme is to strike a note of resonance and relevance in both communities, however, it needs more detailed analyses than have been offered so far. Science studies need to address their resistance to theories of the subject, and to notions such as embodiment and affectivity. Philosophies of the subject, on the other hand, have to confront their mistrust and mis-cognition of bio-sciences.

Transversal connections require middle grounds, or modes of relation, which in turn demand an ethics of interrelations. This requirement is not only ethical, but also pragmatic. I have tried to show that each discursive field currently being transposed in the era of *bios/zoe* engenders its own specific modes of activism and political resistance. Seeking for transversal interconnections among them is a worthy practice for the left in the third millennium. Sustainable nomadic ethics and the forms of political practice it gives rise to precisely because it assumes a non-unitary and transversal subject also requires transversal discursive practices. This includes extensive rhizomatic alliances: a concrete practice of cross-disciplinary discussions needs to be adopted, with transposable notions moving about, if sustainable ethical behaviour is to come into effect. We need to connect more systematically different discursive communities, such as feminists, environmentalists, anti-racists, pacifists, anti-nationalistic and antimilitaristic concerns with philosophical discussions about the new forms of subjectivity.

We need to think the spaces in-between and their interconnections, without stopping at any one centralized concept: a nomadic style of thinking which is open to encounters with others – other systems of thought or thinking environment. The urgency of constituting these transversal alliances needs to be stressed as one of the pre-conditions for the quest for sustainable standards. In order to strike such alliances as discursive and dialogical links, it is important to go beyond the quest for consensus at all costs. I even think – contrary to Habermas – that alliances need to be struck precisely on the understanding that no common agreement can be reached on matters of content. What can be agreed upon is the need for a common project, for an aim (not for common starting premises), for an *ethos*, not a universal ethics (Hans Kung 1998).

There is a clear parallelism between the three areas that I have transposed in this and the previous chapter. I am, however, wary of easy analogies between the different transposed fields and wish instead for a more comparative and dynamic transversal analysis of the transposed axes of subjectivity, in keeping with a materialist approach and a self-reflexive account of positionality, or the politics of location. Another danger I want to avoid is that culture of claims that Gilroy also criticizes: the absolutist claim to exclusive status as the most oppressed, in a hierarchy of 'new' subject positions that would reward the most oppressed. Last, but not least, I appreciate intersectional modes of analysis of gender, race and class, but do insist on linking them to a philosophical reading of the non-unitary structure of subjects. The nomadic subject encompasses, revisits and is transversally connected to the multiple axes of transposition I have been analysing. How it is connected is a matter of timing.

The approach I want to defend in connecting the different lines of transposition is one of synchronization. The synchronicity among the different claims or variables is not flat equivalence, superficial comparison, easy parallelism or hierarchy of oppressions, but a way of operationalizing the politics of location. It provides a missing link between binary opposites and criticizes the excesses of identity politics. To synchronize the different moments and claims to subject-position is a balancing act, linked to the quest for thresholds of sustainability. What does the synchronization exercise involve? It involves living within the multiple and internally differentiated time zones that compose our embedded and embodied selves in advanced capitalism. Given that this system makes us live in a constant state of jet lag or temporal disruption (more of this in the next chapter), synchronization is a major political issue. We need to negotiate with different axes of power. On the side of power as *potestas* or negative force, the subject has to get synchronized with the public representations that are made of its multiple axes of location: gender or sexuality, ethnicity, physicality. The construction of these representations is always outward-looking or external and hence collective; interactive and driven by memory or genealogical. A crucial navigational tool to sustain this process of synchronization is consciousness-raising, which is neither the coincidence of self with conscious representations, nor flat identity politics as an exercise in self-naming and counter-claims. Consciousness is the search engine that makes certain categories emerge some of the time and hence selects them at what appears as a random pattern, which is a web of intersecting lines, made by different speeds and rhythms of intensity. It is rather a completely different system: temporary, non-linear and aiming at finding a sustainable pitch of shared intensity, neither synthesis nor harmony. Time is the crucial factor here.

This project is not about the creation of new identities as much as the construction of thinkable and shareable subject-positions in terms of accountability, ethical values and collective bonds, so that the internal multiplicity can be sustained and expressed. As I argued in the last chapter, consciousness is con-synchronicity. This synchronicity not only mimes and sustains the mind–body parallelism of Spinoza and the quest for adequate figurations, but it also undoes and repairs the dissonance of the historical times, which is the trademark of advanced capitalism. It creates the internal conditions for sustaining an affirmative present.

One of the many positive side-effects of feminist theory is that one gets used to time loops, or a permanent state of jet lag. A feminist critical position assumes the dislocation of the linearity of time and hence the necessity to inhabit different and even potentially contradictory time zones at the same time: a sort of trip through chrono-topia. Feminists have developed crucial critiques of ideologies, revisions of the symbolic, and a vast array of counter-models and paradigms to configure the shifts of subjectivity actually in progress in our globalized world. Those who were still hoping to use such immense creativity to correct the mistakes of the patriarchal order soon realized they would run out of time before they could attain their goal. One of the possible figurations of oppression is being systematically behind: living in one time zone behind the times – like reading yesterday's paper. It is not so much being second-best as being minus-one.

To give a concrete example from my own politics of location, I speak as a privileged twenty-first-century subject in a cutting-edge university setting, engaged in critical theory. The point is that 'I' is not only 'there' and not even 'that'. I am not-One, because I am socio-symbolically signified as a woman, but also because I claim back my not-Oneness as a feminist location. So there is a part of me that is only too well aware of the persisting patterns of marginalization and exclusion of women in the world today. Were I to put this awareness aside, I would make a functional subject of advanced capitalism and a worthy one, being myself an institutional manager of female emancipation. Yet I will not. Choosing to resist this monological reduction, I acknowledge the multiplication of my possible locations, which are not only spatial but also temporal. My memories splinter and proliferate accordingly, bringing in data that may or may not relate directly to my lived experience but are integral to my consciousness. Whenever I fail to forget the continuing patterns of marginalization of women and others, I simply 'forget to forget', which does not mean that I fall into a stupor, but rather that I am zigzagging across different time sequences. Forgetting to forget the imperative of one-way time travel, I inhabit my critical consciousness as a time machine that allows me to travel across different realities, or spatio-temporal coordinates. Being a critical female subject, inscribed asymmetrically into the power relations of advanced capitalism, splits me temporarily. Attempting to reconcile the pieces would be madness: better to settle into the everyday schizophrenia of late postmodernity, also known as early global techno-culture. I call this a form of active resistance, understood as a strategy to deal with the schizophrenia that is typical of our times.

Schizophrenia means the co-occurrence of internally contradictory and even incompatible trends and time zones. And the status of women and of minorities is a powerful indicator of these. These are historical times that see the return of the most primitive forms of naturalization of the status of women, ethnic and earth 'others', alongside high-technological celebration about the death of the naturalized order. Geopolitical wars are being justified in the light of the backward status of women in non-Christian cultures. More than ever, sexual difference is exacerbated and polarized. Gender roles and stereotypes, far from being effaced, are strengthened in the new world order, as is violence against women. Hence, the status of women and others is both central to and paradoxically multiplied across the social and political agenda. In such a context, the feminist awareness of internal discrepancies, or differences within the subject, becomes a good viewpoint. Feminist reappropriations of feminine specificity strike a dissonant note in this framework, to mark forms of political resistance: a multiplicity of possible strategies, internally contradictory, paradoxical and non-linear. They may not be one united party, but a kind of a kaleidoscope of potentially contradictory and therefore highly subversive strategies.

The orthodox Deleuzian clones will object that this claim to specificity is a way of blocking nomadic subjectivization. In response I would say that I do not understand why feminist appropriations of feminine specificity as a moment in a process should be set in opposition to nomadic becomings. I do not see the necessity for such a belligerent logic of mutual opposition and elimination. These are, after all, processes and their ethical indexing depends on the affective forces that they express and are expressive of. Moreover, I am neither a dutiful nor an Oedipalized daughter, but very much a child of my schizoid times. I believe we need visions and practices of complex and multiple differences as an antidote to the fortifying of unitary identities which is happening through the global world order these days: a resurgence of many specular forms of fundamentalism. While fundamentalism is about claiming as authentic an identity others taught you to despise, feminism is about suspending belief in all authentic identities. We need a web-like approach, a zigzagging pattern that cuts across the paradoxes, the asymmetrical locations and the revival of brutal power relations that underscore them, because not one linear or progressive political line can account for them all. If power relations are not linear, nor is resistance. Synchronizing the discordant time zones is as good as a strategy gets on the micropolitical lines of flights.

While resisting the new master-narratives of neo-liberalism and the new social genetic imaginary, in my cartography of the multiple and intersecting transpositions, I have sought both a micro-politics of becoming and an ethics. Considering that advanced capitalism is a system that constructs and proliferates differences for the sake of commercialized profit, I want to work towards a system of ethical coding for differences that are productive, as opposed to those that perpetuate established systems of exclusion and marginalization. One issue that especially concerns me is the philosophical status of the subject. I would not want the change in scale from macro- to micro-political subject formations, which is one of the advantages of nomadic subjectivity, to intersect with the emergence of life, as in *bios/zoe*, to produce a cheap parallelism. Overemphasis on vitality and generative powers runs the risk of wiping out all other power differentials and structural inequalities that still persist and even increase under the impact of globalization. Cartographies of power-relations need to be kept high on the agenda.

My concern is, as always, to make sure that dissymmetry and hence power differences are not levelled out. The times and modes of women's and other marginal groups can be respected while we engage in the process of negotiation and of constructive dialogue with the technocratic cultures of our days. The bare fact of human embodiment, of that corporeal materiality which is definitional of the subject, remains central. Embodiment, however, has to be thought of in the nomadic mode of a sexualized, racialized and enfleshed complexity, not as a unity. However technologically mediated and in spite of electronic fantasies, we are still mortal (not-forever), enfleshed (not-immaterial), made of language (interactive) and hence of alterity (interconnective). At both the organic and the symbolic level we are made of the encounter of different cells and genetic codes (principle of not-One). The raw materiality of life and death, which I refer to as the *bios/zoe* principle, is staring us in the face, requiring urgent new forms of configuration. The very thinkability of *zoe*, its relentless and in some ways careless generative powers, is the heart of the matter. *Zoe* has a monstrously strong capacity for becoming and for upsetting established categorical distinctions of thought. Given this *potentia* and the technological means we have at our disposal all sorts of alternative worlds have become possible.

Before we can get there, however, we need to elaborate narratives that match the complexity of our age and resist both the lure of euphoria and the temptation of nostalgic regression. The issue of how far we can push the ongoing changes and what we can collectively hope for needs to be grounded in a more inclusive and materialist analysis of how much 'we' can take of *this*. In this cartography of risks and challenges, I want to stress the fact that the only changes worthy of serious consideration on the ethical plane are not those that reproduce quantitative pluralities, but rather that far rarer phenomenon which induces a qualitative multiplicity. This is why we need a theory of the subject, which is what I will turn to next.

4

Transits: Transposing the Subject

We leave a great blank here, which must be taken to indicate that the space is filled to repletion.

Virginia Woolf quoted in Lee, *Virginia Woolf*

You have the individuality of a day, a season, a year, *a life* . . . , a climate, a wind, a fog, a swarm, a pack. . . . A cloud of locusts carried in by the wind at 5 in the evening; a vampire who goes out at night, a werewolf at full moon. . . . It is the entire assemblage in its individuated aggregate that is a haecceity . . .

Deleuze and Guattari, *A Thousand Plateaus*

To write is to do other than announce oneself as an enclosed individual. . . . To write, . . . is to write to a stranger, to a friend. . . . Friendship is always a political act, for it unites citizens into a polis, a (political) community. . . . It is the difference between me and my friend that allows meaning. And it is meaning, the meaningfulness of the world, that is consciousness.

Kathy Acker, *Bodies of Work*

AFFECTS

At the end of the previous chapter I concluded that the three cases I presented were in fact variations on one and the same theme of transpositions: they illustrate the paradoxes and complexities of the saturation of *bios*/*zoe* with technological power effects. This structural transversal connection is important for a radical revision of the subject along axes of multiplicity and hence of further complexity. The new global situation engendered by techno-science requires a robust new theory of the subject as a multi-layered entity that is not unitary and still capable of ethical and political accountability. In the last part of this study I want to explore and ground this seemingly simple claim and address more directly the ethical roots of philosophical nomadism. A nomadic reappraisal of Spinoza is necessary in order to rethink the totality of the subjects and of their environment in a manner that undoes dualism and allows for a series of productive transversal connections. The chapter therefore moves from eco-philosophical concerns right into the structure of nomadic sustainable subjectivity.

Philosophical nomadism is a creative process. Becoming nomadic is neither the swinging of the pendulum of dialectical opposition, nor is it the unfolding of an essence in a teleologically ordained process leading to the establishment of a supervising agency – be it the ego, the self or the bourgeois liberal definition of the individual. Nomadic becomings are rather the affirmation of the unalterably positive structure of difference, meant as a multiple and complex process of transformation, a flux of multiple becomings, the play of complexity, or the principle of not-One. Accordingly, the thinking subject is not the expression of in-depth interiority, nor is it the enactment of transcendental models of reflexive consciousness. According to Gatens and Lloyd (1999) this nomadic becoming is an ethology, that is to say a process of expression, composition, selection, and incorporation of forces aimed at positive transformation of the subject. As such it is also crucial to the project of a creative redefinition of philosophical reason as imagination and affectivity.

Becoming has to do with emptying out the self, opening it out to possible encounters with the 'outside'. Virginia Woolf's 'stream of consciousness' is a good starting point, in that the artist's 'eye' captures the outside world by making itself receptive to the totality of an assemblage of elements, in an almost geographical or cartographic manner, like the shade of the light at dusk, or the curve of the wind. In those moments of floating awareness when rational control releases its hold, 'Life' rushes on towards the sensorial/perceptive apparatus with exceptional vigour. This onrush of data, information, affectivity, is the relational bond that simultaneously propels the self out of the black hole of its atomized isolation and disperses it into a myriad of bits and pieces of data imprinting or impressions. It also, however, confirms the singularity of that particular entity which both receives and recomposes itself around the onrush of data and affects.

One needs to be able to sustain the impact with the onrushing affectivity, to 'hold' it, without being completely overwhelmed by it. But 'holding' it or capturing it does not occur on the paranoid or rapacious model of a dominant, dialectically driven consciousness. It rather takes the form of a sustainable model of an affective, depersonalized, highly receptive subject which quite simply is not one, not there, not that. The singularity of this nomadic, floating subjectivity rests on the spatio-temporal coordinates that make it possible for him or her to coincide with nothing more than the degrees, levels, expansion and extension of the head-on rush of the 'outside' inwards. What is mobilized is one's capacity to feel, sense, process and sustain the impact with the complex materiality of the outside.

A seemingly absent-minded floating attention or a fluid sensibility that is porous to the outside and which our culture has coded as 'feminine' are central to the process.

The processes and flows of becoming, and the heightened states of perception and receptivity which they both assume and engender, have a great deal in common with the painter's experience. It is pure creativity, or an aesthetic mode of absolute immersion of one's sensibility in the field of forces – music, colour, light, speed, temperature, intensity – which one is attempting to capture. Deleuze argues that painters make visible forces that previously were not, much as composers make us hear sounds that were unheard of. Similarly, philosophers can make thinkable concepts that did not exist before. It comes down to a question of style, but style here is no mere rhetorical device, it is rather a set of material coordinates that, assembled and composed in a sustainable and enduring manner, allow for the expression of the affectivity and the forces involved. They thus trigger the process of becoming.

Spinoza revisited

Spinoza is the landscape within which Deleuze and Guattari draw their philosophical nomadism. It is however quite a different approach to Spinoza from the holistic one that dominates the thinking of deep ecology (see previous chapter). The nomadic Spinoza is related to the 'enchanted materialism' of the French school of philosophy.

Spinoza is one of the sacred monsters of the history of philosophy and a thinker whose rigour, complexity and uncompromising passion have generated the most diverse reactions. The central problem of his philosophy is to distinguish between different orders of truth claims through the rigorous use of reasoned arguments. This mixture of methodological rigour and radical content attracts Deleuze. Contrary to the Anglo-American thinkers for whom it is axiomatic that ideas are interesting only in so far as they achieve requisite standards of logical consistency and truth, the French reception of Spinozist philosophy stresses simultaneously its corporeal and materialistic aspects. The Anglo-American emphasis on Spinozist rationalism is openly contested by the radical French reading of Spinoza's ethics as a politics of resistance. Christopher Norris (1991) argues that references to Spinoza have been quite current in French philosophy since the 1960s, when, under the influence of Louis Althusser, new emphasis was placed on Spinoza's 'metaphysical materialism' in opposition to the more rigid school of scientific materialism of orthodox Marxist philosophies. Norris concludes that not only is it the case that Spinoza is a source of inspiration for poststructuralist critical theory, but also for a critique of fundamentalist beliefs in the authority of holy texts of all kinds. Last, but not least, Spinoza's ethics implies a strong aesthetic component in that he rejects the view that fictions are removed from or antithetical to reason and truth.

Antonio Negri (1981) defends Spinoza's materialist metaphysics as a new political ontology. Spinozist materialism is immanent and dynamic and it locates the imagination and shared desires at the heart of the self. All passions are external and collective in that they engage others or, in Negri's terminology, 'the multitude' as a collective social subject which finds its highest juridical form in a democracy. The problem of the production and constitution of a democratic regime is central to an ethics of collective passions. Drawing the distinction between power as *potestas*, in the sense of a centralized, mediating, transcendental force of command, and *potentia* as a more local, immediate and actual force of constitution of resistance, Negri gives a Marxist interpretation of Spinoza's ethics. In this reading, Spinoza advocates republican and democratic *potentia* against the dogmatic and autocratic *potestas*, on the model of the opposition between the power of capitalist relations of production and the proletarian production of liberation. Hence the revolutionary aspect of Spinoza's philosophy, which singles out the gap between the metaphysical structure of the subject as the agent of freedom and the order of capitalist production.

This basic conceptual structure is still at work in Negri's recent work with Hardt on globalization and the prospects of global revolution, which I commented on in chapter 2. Deleuze, loyal to Spinoza, stresses the need for a link between historical processes and the flows of becoming, thus emphasizing their interdependence, whereas Negri pushes the tension between the two to the extreme. The experiments in resistance by the multitude are conceptualized in terms of becomings and they are qualitatively different from historical processes, though they become actualized historically. In other words, Deleuze argues that we need both the historical dimension and the event as becoming and rejects the suggestion that any collective or singular identity may be in charge of the process. The multitude, therefore, is not the same as Deleuze's complex singularities.

The key notion is the parallelism between the order of ideas or rational thought and the order of the real world, also known as radical monism. Spinoza argues that truth has its own necessity and that human freedom consists in the will to accept it. 'Freedom' is what comes from acknowledging truths in accordance with reason and nature alike. Norris stresses that Deleuze is attracted to this double structure of Spinoza's work: on the one hand the logical rigour, on the other the passionate commitment to freedom. His is a practical philosophy, while Spinoza also accomplishes the task of philosophy *sub specie aeternitatis*. Knowledge is the most powerful affect for Spinoza in that it ensures the adequate understanding of one's embodied self. Pursuing this line, Edwin Curley stresses the materialism of Spinoza's philosophy: the idea that constitutes the actual being of my mind must be an idea of something actually existing. That idea is the body, a highly complex organism that differs from the simpler bodies whose identity is secured by mere reference to motion and rest. Following Spinozist vitalism and the unity of substance, human freedom is defined as the capacity to express and explore the subject's ability to affect and be affected, i.e. his or her interactive capacity. This is not a neutral move, because affects are evaluated in terms of the degree and kind of forces that constitute them. Primary among them is the distinction between active and reactive, positive and negative forces.

Affectivity is understood as intrinsically positive: it is the force that aims at fulfilling the subject's capacity for interaction and freedom. It is Spinoza's *conatus*, or the notion of *potentia* as the affirmative aspect of power. It is joyful and pleasure-prone and it is immanent in that it coincides with the terms and modes of its expression. This means concretely that ethical behaviour confirms, facilitates and enhances the subject's *potentia*, as the capacity to express his or her freedom. The positivity of this desire to express one's innermost and constitutive freedom can be termed as *conatus, potentia* or becoming. It is conducive to ethical behaviour only if the subject is capable of making it last and endure, thus allowing it to sustain its own impetus. Unethical behaviour achieves the opposite: it denies, hinders and diminishes that impetus, or is unable to sustain it. This introduces a temporal dimension into the discussion that leads to the very conditions of the possibility of the future – to futurity as such. For an ethics of sustainability, the expression of positive affects is that which makes the subject last or endure: it is like a source of long-term rechargeable energy at the affective core of subjectivity.

Nomadic subjectivity is defined in terms of processes of becoming. This is a general trait, provided we do not take this as a direct representative model. The becoming minoritarian/woman/anima/insect/imperceptible do not represent a metaphorical stand-in for empirical or qualitative subjects: women, animals, insects, technologies (and their alleged claims to 'equal rights'). The flows of becoming rather mark a qualitative process of structural shifts in the parameters and the boundaries of subjectivity. This shift entails an ethical dimension, in so far as it makes the subjects into transversal and interconnecting entities, defined in terms of common propensities. They are intelligent matter, activated by shared affectivity.

As Lloyd puts it, Spinozist ideas are 'perspectival' (Lloyd 1994: 22) in that they rest upon the interconnectedness of mind and body. This means that fragmentary or inadequate ideas are the norm, and the quest for adequate ideas the ideal. Spinozist self-knowledge is mediated through bodily awareness and must share in its inadequacy. Clearly, bodies are not passive entities, but contain their own forces and seek for connection with them. The synchronization with these forces is the source of consciousness and hence self-knowledge: it is a matter of physics as of affectivity. The perspectival awareness means that the limits of my body are the limits of my awareness. The crucial factor concerns the borderlines, or lines of demarcation, between my and other external bodies. This line is guaranteed but also policed by affectivity, which consequently emerges from the physics of bodies. In other words, the embodied subject's sense of self depends on not being isolated from the environment, in so far as this subject is defined by the body's capacity either to impede or to enhance its own power to interact with others.

Whereas the body cannot exist in isolation from its surrounding totality, the mind is capable of thinking itself as an autonomous substance. This is also its weakness, however, because in so far as consciousness fails to understand its interconnectedness, the mind fails to understand also its own loves and hates and its interrelation to its habits, hence failing to understand itself. Genevieve Lloyd sums it up aptly: 'Cartesian selves are ambiguously located between the individuality of substancehood and the universality of reason. Spinozist selves rejoin nature through the individuality of bodies construed as uniquely differentiated parts of nature. Spinoza takes seriously the inclusion of minds, no less than bodies, in the totality of nature' (Lloyd 1994: 3). The degree of affinity or difference that bodies are capable of experiencing and expressing defines their inner nature. This is not a predetermined essence, but rather is the result of a process, an itinerary, a path of development. This is a deeply socialized process. Human nature is the play of similarity and differences under the impact of social forces that are constructed by relations of power among human beings. As Genevieve Lloyd argues, the *conatus* of each subject can be enriched by good forms of social organization, which support the collective pursuit of reason and adequate understanding. It can also be diminished, of course, by adverse systems. Spinoza's writings on politics are based on the relation between freedom and the ethical faculty of discerning good from evil. A strong social dimension exists, in the Spinozist vision of the subjects: their minds reflect the specialization process. This means that power is a key issue for Spinoza as it acts upon the body. Gatens and Lloyd (1999) argue that Spinoza's philosophy of the subject has profound political implications in that it allows connecting the idea of 'autonomous individual selfhood with ideals of community, without thereby collapsing hard-won individuality into an all-encompassing pre-existing collective identity' (Gatens and Lloyd 1999: 2). Spinozist ethics move beyond morality and redefine responsibility as a commonly shared sensibility.

Quoting extensively Étienne Balibar's idea of 'trans-individuality', Gatens and Lloyd stress the collective yet highly singular notion of responsibility in Spinoza's work: by virtue of being interconnected to other human and non-human actors, we share in responsibility even for deeds we have not done ourselves. Here the reference to Hannah Arendt is crucial: the reason for our responsibility is our membership in a group which no voluntary act of ours can dissolve, in so far as we acquire it simply by virtue of being born into a community. For Spinoza, human beings belong to a complex multiplicity of potentially conflicting communities, so that their sociability is inherent and it entails affective and emotional bonds. The temporal dimension is again crucial: a location is a spatial but also a temporal site, because it involves a commonly shared memory and sense of the past that continue to affect the present and will carry on into the future. Understanding this is the key both to citizenship and to the forms of ethical agency that it empowers.

Because each human is defined by his or her *conatus*, by connectibility and hence sociability, the social and political dimensions are built into the subject. It is like an inbuilt human capacity, which means that there is no rupture between the personal and the political: the common bond of human imagination and understanding ties each individual into a larger whole. The aim of good government is to preserve these rights and to enhance them, whereas bad governments repress them or limit them. This is an ethological approach to citizenship. Culture and politics are the storage of rules and suggestions for how to enhance the *potentia* of each and everyone, thus developing the powers of an idea of reason that also includes affectivity.

Clearly, the Spinozist–Deleuzian ethics of nomadic subjectivity neither denies nor degrades the process of subjectivation. It merely relocates it away from liberal individualism in an external, collective, activity-oriented vision of the subject. Hegel's criticism of Spinoza concentrates on his alleged neglect of individuality. This has cast a long shadow over the reception of the notion of desire as *conatus* and of its implicit positivity. For Hegel a desire-driven subject that aims at his or her fulfilment is at best a reservoir of irrepressible spontaneity and at worst a pool of narcissism. Neither is in fact the case. Spinoza's ethics cannot be dissociated from his politics: the vitality of the *conatus* is community-bound and so socio-political factors are an integral part of the structure of subjectivity. They provide a frame of support (a 'house' as Deleuze put it) as well as forms of containment for the subject's desire. Socio-political mechanisms (*potestas*) mark, police, sustain and repress the subject's inner freedom, defined as *potentia* or as *conatus*. This highly specific definition of freedom clashes with the mainstream ideas on this matter, especially in liberal political philosophy (Patton 2000). As such it has important repercussions for the discussion on moral philosophy and on ethics.

As Norris (1991) argues, Spinoza offers a powerful alternative to Hegel in dispensing with the transcendental subject as locus of truth that emerges in the fullness of time through the progress of Spirit in its world-historical march towards absolute reason, Christianity and the Prussian nation-state. Spinoza's notion of freedom requires instead the suspension of all outside guarantees and even of the promise of the final resolution of contradictions by a unitary or reunited self. By equating freedom with the understanding of the causal necessity of our bondage, which is both of the order of reason and of the order of the world, the transcendental subject is dislocated: 'It is precisely in so far as we lack this knowledge, in the measure that our concepts are defective, inadequate or "confused" that we strive after a false (imaginary) notion of the self-caused, autonomous, free-willing agent' (Norris 1991: 44). The social imaginary in question here is collectively produced and actualized, not according to a linguistic model of representation, but in a materialist fashion as I explained in chapter 2. This imposes a vision of the subject as fully immersed in relations of power, but ethically compelled to strive after freedom in the form of adequate understanding. According to Norris this position strikes a middle ground between the idealist indifference to the realities of lived experience and the empiricist refusal to break with that experience in the name of a more rigorously theorized knowledge. Thus, far from producing alternatively an excess of spontaneity or a pitfall of relativism, this view of the desiring subject increases the range and span of interconnections and hence of ethical agency. The commonly held social imaginary of virtue is the binding element here. The point about collective responsibility is that it calls for recognition, acknowledgement and understanding: this is the only ethical freedom we dispose of.

BODIES-IN-TIME: TEMPORALITY AND ENDURANCE

The monistic unity of the subject is also posited in terms of time. A subject is a genealogical entity, possessing his or her own counter-memory, which in turn is an expression of degrees of affectivity and interconnectedness. Viewed spatially, the poststructuralist subject may appear as fragmented and disunited; on a temporal scale, however, its unity is that of a continuing power to synchronize its recollections. This creates a continuity of disconnected fragments: a discontinuous sense of time, which falls under Nietzsche's genealogical sense of the Dionysiac as opposed to the Apollonian. It provides the grounds for unity in an otherwise dispersed self. Deleuze borrows from the ancient Greeks the useful distinction between the molar sense of linear, recorded time (*chronos*) and the molecular sense of cyclical, discontinuous time (*aion*). The former is related to being/the molar/the masculine, the latter to becoming/the molecular/ the feminine.

A post-humanist and post-anthropocentric philosophy gives time a more central place in the structuring of the subject. Deleuze's 'nomadology' as a philosophy of immanence rests on the idea of memory as a principle of containment and actualization of a subject's resources, understood environmentally, affectively and cognitively. A subject thus constituted inhabits a time that is the active tense of continuous 'becoming'. Deleuze defines the latter with reference to Bergson's concept of 'duration', thus proposing the notion of the subject as an entity that lasts, that is to say that endures sustainable changes and transformation and enacts them around him or herself in a community or collectivity. The notion of 'endurance' is disengaged from the metaphysical tradition that associates it with the idea of essence, i.e. of permanence. Deleuze invests 'endurance' with spatio-temporal force, or mobility. For him it is a form of transcendental empiricism. Deleuze and Guattari turn to Spinoza to find philosophical foundations for a vitalistic yet anti-essentialist brand of immanence that bypasses liberal individualism and dislocates the anthropocentric bias of communitarianism. We need to rethink continuities and totalities, but without reference to a humanistic or holistic world-views. As Lloyd (1996) puts it, this subject's mind is 'part of nature' and therefore embedded and embodied, that is to say immanent and dynamic. It is structurally interactive and thus also ethically accountable.

This emphasis on recomposing modes of synchronizing the heterogeneous and fragmented time-sequence is especially important if one considers the political economy of time in advanced capitalism. This comes down to the imperative: 'I shop, therefore I am'. This consumerist injunction saturates the social space with commodities, which results in immobility and sedentary accumulation. To translate this into a temporal mode: capitalist saturation of our social space by consumerism steals the present away from us; it deprives us of time, while offering all sorts of technological gadgets that promise to save us time. It is a system that arrests the flows of becoming, freezes the rhizomic propensity for multiple connections and expropriates nomadic intensities through quantitative build-ups of the acquired commodities.

It produces immobility in the sense of a stasis due to accumulation of toxins in the mode of commodities. It is also a suspension of active desire, in favour of the addictive pursuit of commodified non-necessities. As Massumi (1998) points out, the commodity circulates like a never-dead object of desire within the spectral economy of advanced capitalism. As such, it contracts the space/time continuum of the humanistic world order: it simultaneously embodies the promise of enjoyment and its perennial deferral. The deferred fulfilment, or simultaneous arousal and frustration of desire, means that the commodity embodies futurity, as time stored (future used) or time saved (a productivity enhancer). It follows that commodities become coextensive with the inner space of subjectivity, as well as the outer space of the market and of social relations. This cycle of presence–absence of fulfilment lies at the heart of the affects induced by this system, namely a manic-depressive cycle of frenzy and fear, euphoria and paranoia. It induces addictive habits of consumption that enslave us and keep us coming back for more. Deleuze and Guattari's (1980) critique of capitalism as schizophrenia analyses the specific temporality of this perverse political economy of induced addiction to commodities. It becomes necessary to develop an ethical and political stance to create forms of resistance that make qualitative distinctions between degrees of involvement with this schizoid political economy.

The fast turnover of available commodities and the acceleration they induce results, in fact, in our being in a state of constant jet lag: we are structurally always behind the times and getting synchronized is a real challenge. A clear example of this perverse logic that condemns us never to be up to date is the succession of gadgets and of 'next generation' technological commodities that age and become obsolete at an impossible speed. In chapter 3 I commented ironically on how my generation of the Baby Boomers owns a mini-museum of dead media in our very homes through the accumulation of technologies we have known in our times: from the transistor radio to the hand-held computers of today, we have consumed and have been survived by a staggering array of technological 'others'.

The same logic of titillation without ever reaching fulfilment is at the heart of contemporary popular culture, which under the cover of 'Holly-world' and 'info-tainment' keeps us waiting for the next sequel or instalment of *Harry Potter*, or *Lord of the Rings*, not to speak of movies that are conceptualized as sequels, such as the *Star Wars* series. These are legalized but forceful forms of mild addiction. Being kept hanging on is not only addictive, it is also intrinsically frustrating. Susan Kappeler (1987) defines this mixture of dependency and dissatisfaction in terms of the pornography of representation. It is pornographic because it titillates without providing fulfilment, inducing dependency without taking responsibility for it. It constitutes power in the most restrictive (*potestas*) sense of the term. In nomadic language, it induces negative passions, such as resentment, frustration, envy and bitterness: 'gimme more', could be its motto.

In terms of time, this logic suspends the present in a series of deferrals and delegations to a future that is measured in terms of commodified pleasures. It is against this static absence of desire in the actual *here and now* that Deleuze and Guattari posit processes of becoming as the antidote and introduce flows of empowering desire that mobilize the subject and thus destabilize the sedentary gravitational pull of addictive and coercive consumption. Resistance takes place from within. Eugene Holland (1999) introduces an analytical distinction between the market economy as an axiomatic system and capitalism as a historical event that captures and arrests the manifold potentials of a 'free' market. In exactly the same spirit I want to separate sexualized, racialized and naturalized difference defined as a multiplicity system (and not as a mere quantitative proliferation) from the production of profit-oriented 'differences' in the political economy of globalized capitalism. What gets rescued through these categorical distinctions is the window of opportunity through which the seeds of hope can spread. Hope for change and transformations for mobility and becomings are the key to ethics.

To bring about an empowering present, however, is a project and a process which requires the reorganization of the entire time structure of subjectivity. To resist the dominant post-industrial modes of subjectivation requires the synchronization of heterogeneous elements. This entails the transformation of passive reactions on our part into active desire. The conditions of possibility for such an ethical position of productivity rely on a consciousness that is not bound by resentment or any other reactive emotions indexed on the ego. The process of becoming-active of consciousness requires a memory that is freed from fear and other negative traces. As such it is capable of forgetting the hurt, envy and resentment and opening up spaces in which to activate a productive force. This active force of repetition or remembrance constitutes both a present free of negative passions and also the possibility of the future. Ansell-Pearson (1997a; 1999) has commented on the apparent paradox involved in the fact that only forgetting (the negative) fully expresses the absolute force of memory, or *potentia*, which is power to repeat beyond negativity. It is repetition itself – positive memory – that constitutes the opening of time and engenders the possibility of a horizon of hope, a productive consciousness that yearns for a future.

Longing for activity, for positivity, amounts to yearning for a qualitative better future which will help us break the chain of addictive repetition-without-difference which lies at the heart of the theft of the present induced by advanced capitalism. This shift of coordinates is a gesture of transcendence in the sense of radical immanence: it plunges us into the unprogrammed-for and hence the unheard-of, the unthought-of, or the obscene in the sense of the off-set. To desire a vibrant, affirmative and empowering present is to live in intensity and thus to unfold possible futures. This is what goes under the name of 'becoming-imperceptible': the eruption of events that construct sustainable futures. This intensive shift of gears marks a new political ontology, but it takes the form of a radical ethics of sustainability.

Bodies-in-time are embodied and embedded entities fully immersed in webs of complex interaction, negotiation and transformation with and through other entities. Subjectivity is a process that aims at flows of interconnections and mutual impact. Affectivity is the key term here and it plays a structural function in the nomadic vision of subjectivity, related to the inbuilt temporality of the subject and thus to what is commonly known as 'memory'.

The issue of time has emerged in the critical discussion between Deleuze, feminist and anti-racist or critical theorists as a major dividing line (Braidotti 2002). For Deleuze the molar, streamlined and linear historical time, as implied, for instance, in emancipatory politics, is both unavoidable and confining. The more effective time-span, however, is the cyclical, dynamic and molecular time of becoming. In other words, to paraphrase Deleuze, at the level of chronos feminists, anti-racists and human rights activists, at this point in history, are legitimate in pursuing 'molar' positions, claiming identity-centred redefinition of their political subjectivity. In this respect, they cannot easily become 'molecular'. Perhaps they cannot even afford to undertake a full-scale deconstruction of their sex-specific identity. Their engagement with linear historical time, however, must neither replace nor encompass the relationship to the discontinuous time of becoming (*aion*). All political movements must simply avoid one-way streets, dialectical reversals of ego-indexed claims to single strategies or monolithic value-systems. Here the key-terms are complexity, multiplicity and heteroglossia. A systematic quest for hybridity in political activity is preferable to centralized and closed systems (Braidotti 1991, 1994, 2002).

In Irigaray's work, for instance, the asymmetry between the sexes stretches all the way to the most fundamental structures of being, including space and time. The constitutive dissymmetry turns into a strategic redefinition of the terms of their dialectical interaction and envisages the genderization of time and space as well as of memory and history. Irigaray calls for women's sense of their own genealogies, based on a bond of grateful recognition of the maternal feminine as the site of origin. Kristeva (1981), on the other hand, brings the two-tiered level of time to bear on the distinction between the longer, linear model of history and the more discontinuous timing of personal genealogy and unconscious desire. Kristeva codes this distinction historically: the equality or Enlightenment-minded emancipatory or modernist women's movement fits in with the linear historical time. Sexual-difference feminism and post-colonial theories, however, are more attuned to the discontinuous and cyclical time of postmodernity. Although this association of female subjectivity with certain moments of historical consciousness has been criticized for its Eurocentrism (Spivak 1989), it still is useful in a discussion about the temporal structure of subjectivity.

Stuart Hall (1996) has also taught us that modernity is represented by what he calls the 'supplementary character of its temporality', which is defined as follows: 'Hybridity, syncretism, multidimensional temporalities, the double inscription of colonial and metropolitan times, the two-way cultural traffic characteristic of the contact zones of the cities of the "colonized" long before they have become the characteristic tropes of the cities of the "colonizing"' (Hall 1996: 251). The supplementary character of time becomes the temporal dimension of the world order that emerges from colonialism and in some ways perpetuates it, with the difference, noted before, that the 'constitutive others' of modernity shift location and refuse to fulfil the task of alternatively settling for the aporias of the in-between or reasserting the dominion of Sameness. Stuart Hall also points out that the ever-shifting nature of both the postmodern temporality and the multiple subject-positions it engenders, spreads a generalized anti-foundationalism. This requires materialist and accountable analyses of these new subject-positions, as I argued in chapter 2.

Of joy and positive passions

What is, then, this subject in becoming? It is a slice of living, sensible matter activated by a fundamental drive to life: a *potentia* (rather than a *potestas*) – neither by the will of God, nor by the secret encryption of the genetic code – and yet this subject is embedded in the corporeal material-ity of the self. The enfleshed intensive or nomadic subject is rather a transversal entity: a folding-in of external influences and a simultaneous unfolding-outwards of affects. A mobile unit in space and time and there-fore an enfleshed kind of memory, this subject is not only in process, but is also capable of lasting through sets of discontinuous variations, while remaining extraordinarily faithful to itself.

This idea of the 'faithfulness' of the subject is important and it builds on the rejection of liberal individualism. This may appear counter-intui-tive to the Anglo-American readers and require of them an effort of the imagination. Allow me to plead for the short-term benefits that will flow, however, from this stretching exercise, and for the dividends it will return in terms of added understanding. This 'faithfulness to oneself', conse-quently, is not to be understood in the mode of the psychological or sen-timental attachment to a personal 'identity' that often is little more than a social security number and a set of photo albums. Nor is it the mark of authenticity of a self ('me, myself and I') that is a clearing house for nar-cissism and paranoia – the great pillars on which Western identity predi-cates itself. It is rather the faithfulness of mutual sets of interdependence and interconnections, that is to say sets of relations and encounters. It is a play of complexity that encompasses all levels of one's multi-layered subjectivity, binding the cognitive to the emotional, the intellectual to the affective, and connecting them all to a socially embedded ethics of sustain-ability. Thus, the faithfulness that is at stake in nomadic ethics coincides with the awareness of one's condition of interaction with others, that is to say one's capacity to affect and to be affected. Translated into a tem-poral scale, this is the faithfulness of duration, the expression of one's continuing attachment to certain dynamic spatio-temporal coordinates.

In a philosophy of temporally inscribed radical immanence, subjects differ. But they differ along materially embedded coordinates, because they come in different mileage, temperatures and beats. One can and does change gears and move across these coordinates, but cannot claim all of them, all of the time. The latitudinal and longitudinal forces that structure the subject have limits of sustainability. By latitudinal forces Deleuze means the affects a subject is capable of, following the degrees of intensity or potency: how intensely they run. By longitude is meant the span of extension: how far they can go. Sustainability is about how much of it a subject can take.

In other words, sustainable subjectivity reinscribes the singularity of the self, while challenging the anthropocentrism of Western philosophies' understanding of the subject, and of the attributes usually reserved for 'agency'. This sense of limits is extremely important to ensure productive synchronizations and prevent nihilistic self-destruction. To be active, intensive, or nomadic, does not mean that one is limitless. That would be the kind of delirious expression of megalomania that you find in the new master narratives of the cyber-culture of today, ready and willing to 'dissolve the bodily self into the matrix'. On the contrary, to make sense of this intensive, materially embedded vision of the subject, we need a sustainability threshold or frame. The containment of the intensities or enfleshed passions, so as to ensure their duration, is a crucial prerequisite to allow them to do their job, which consists in shooting through the humanistic frame of the subject, exploding it outwards. The dosage of the threshold of intensity is both crucial and inherent to the process of becoming, in so far as the subject is embodied and hence set in a spatio-temporal frame.

What is this threshold of sustainability, then, and how does it get fixed? A radically immanent intensive body is an assemblage of forces, or flows, intensities and passions that solidify in space, and consolidate in time, within the singular configuration commonly known as an 'individual' self. This intensive and dynamic entity – it is worth stressing it again – does not coincide with the enumeration of inner rationalist laws, nor is it merely the unfolding of genetic data and information. It is rather a portion of forces that is stable enough to sustain and to undergo constant, though non-destructive, fluxes of transformation. D. W. Smith argues that there are three essential questions about immanent ethics: 'How is a mode of existence determined? How are modes of existence to be evaluated? What are the conditions for the creation of new modes of existence?' (Smith 1998: 259). On all three scores, it is the body's degrees and levels of affectivity that determined the modes of differentiation. Joyful or positive passions and the transcendence of reactive affects are the desirable mode. The emphasis on 'existence' implies a commitment to duration and conversely a rejection of self-destruction. Positivity is built into this programme through the idea of thresholds of sustainability. Thus, an ethically empowering option increases one's *potentia* and creates joyful energy in the process. The conditions which can encourage such a quest are not only historical; they all concern processes of self-transformation or self-fashioning in the direction of affirming positivity. Because all subjects share in this common nature, there is a common ground on which to negotiate the interests and the eventual conflicts.

It is important to see in fact that this fundamentally positive vision of the ethical subject does not deny conflicts, tension or even violent disagreements between different subjects. Again, the legacy of Hegel's critique of Spinoza is still looming large here. It is simply not the case that the positivity of desire cancels or denies the tensions of conflicting interests. It merely displaces the grounds on which the negotiations take place. The Kantian imperative of not doing to others what you would not want done to you is not rejected as much as enlarged. In terms of the ethics of *conatus*, in fact, the harm that you do to others is immediately reflected in the harm you do to yourself, in terms of loss of *potentia*, positivity, self-awareness and inner freedom.

This move away from the Kantian vision of an ethics that obliges people, and especially women, natives and others, to act morally in the name of a transcendent standard or a universal moral rule is not a simple one, as I indicated in chapter 1. I defend it as a forceful answer to the complexities of our historical situation: it is a move towards radical immanence against all Platonistic and classical humanistic denials of embodiment, *mater* and the flesh. What is at risk, however, in nomadic ethics is the notion of containment of the other.[1] This is expressed by a number of moral thinkers in the Continental tradition, such as Jessica Benjamin (1988) in her radicalization of Irigaray's horizontal transcendence; Lyotard in the 'differend' (1983) and his notion of the 'unattuned'; and Butler (2004b) in her emphasis on 'precarious life'. They stress that moral reasoning locates the constitution of subjectivity in the interrelation to others, which is a form of exposure, availability and vulnerability. This recognition entails the necessity of containing the other, the suffering and the enjoyment of others in the expression of the intensity of our affective streams. An embodied and connecting containment as a moral category could emerge from this, over and against the hierarchical forms of containment implied by Kantian forms of universal morality.

This objection is predictable and that it is connected to the issue of the boundaries, limits and costs of an expressive and dynamic vision of nomadic subjectivity is similar to the point about the assessment of ethical costs in the ethics of sustainability. I will address this more directly in the next chapter. For now, suffice it to say that the nomadic view of ethics takes place within a monistic ontology that sees subjects as modes of individuation within a common flow of *zoe*. Consequently there is no self-other distinction in the traditional mode, but variations of intensities, assemblages set by affinities and complex synchronizations. In chapter 3 I argued that bio-centred egalitarianism breaks the expectation of mutual reciprocity that is central to liberal individualism. Accepting the impossibility of mutual recognition and replacing it with mutual specification and mutual co-dependence is what is at stake in a nomadic ethics of sustainability. This is against both the moral philosophy of rights and Levinas's tradition of making the anthropocentric Other into the privileged site and inescapable horizon of otherness.

If the point of ethics is to explore how much a body can do, in the pursuit of active modes of empowerment through experimentation, how do we know when we have gone too far? How does one know if one has reached the threshold of sustainability?

This is where the non-individualistic vision of the subject as embodied and hence affective and interrelational, but also fundamentally social, is of major importance. Your body will thus tell you if and when you have

[1] I am grateful to Harry Kunneman for these insights, developed in private conversations.

reached a threshold or a limit. The warning can take the form of falling ill, feeling sick, or it can take other somatic manifestations, like fear, anxiety or a sense of insecurity. Whereas the semiotic-linguistic frame of psychoanalysis reduces these manifestations to symptoms awaiting diagnosis, I see them as corporeal warning signals or boundary markers that express a clear message: 'too much!'. One of the reasons why Deleuze and Guattari are so interested in studying self-destructive or pathological modes of behaviour, such as schizophrenia, masochism, anorexia, various forms of addiction, and the black hole of murderous violence, is precisely in order to explore their function as markers of thresholds. I shall discuss this in the next chapter. This assumes a qualitative distinction between, on the one hand, the desire that propels the subject's expression of his or her *conatus*, which in a neo-Spinozist perspective is implicitly positive in that it expresses the essential best of the subject, and on the other hand the constraints imposed by society. The specific, contextually determined conditions are the forms in which the desire is actualized or actually expressed.

Advanced capitalism is a system that tends constantly to stretch its limits and plays with the idea of over-reaching itself, moving towards 'timeless time' (Castells 1996). How shall I put it? All planes are always overbooked, and this is a fitting metaphor for the political economy of profit and its saturation of our social space. In so far as the subject is under constant pressure to function and find points of stability within the ever-shifting limits or boundaries, capitalism is a system that actively generates schizophrenia in the sense of enhancing the value of unfixed meanings: an unlimited semiosis without fixed referents (Holland 1999). This makes the question of negotiating thresholds of sustainability all the more urgent. If the boundaries are forever being stretched and hence blurred, however, perspectival shifts are necessary in order to keep up and account for the process and thus identify points of resistance. Schizophrenia is a molecular mode of undoing the molar aggregates of the commodification system, of inducing flows into them. This avoids the consolidation and the over-codification (constant control) that are characteristic of the majority, but in return it runs the danger of fluidity to the point of self-destruction. How to find a point of balance is an ethical question.

This historical context makes it difficult to detect the thresholds of sustainability, or markers of the limits. If your body will not make it manifest or if you choose to ignore the message that this is 'too much!', others are likely to send out significant warning signals. Just think, for instance, of the famous heart shot in the overdose scene of Quentin Tarantino's film *Pulp Fiction* as a graphic representation of unsustainability, or of being over the top. The directness of the bodily or the enfleshed reactions is worth stressing. In the case of impending heart-failure due to overdose – as in all extreme situations – something raw and immediate about one's bodily situation comes to the fore. Following the nomadic revisitation of Spinoza, these events should get extracted from the category of 'extreme cases' and become relocated instead as the mainstream experience, that is to say the standard-setting event.

The subject lies at the intersection with external, relational forces. It is about assemblages. Encountering them is almost a matter for geography, because it is a question of orientations, points of entry and exit, a constant unfolding. In this field of transformative forces, sustainability is a very concrete social and ethical practice – not the abstract economic ideal that development and social-planning specialists often reduce it to. It is a concrete concept about the embodied and embedded nature of the subject. The sensibility to and availability for changes or transformation are directly proportional to the subject's ability to sustain the shifts without cracking. The border, the framing or containing practices are crucial to the whole operation; one which aims at affirmative and not nihilistic processes of becoming. In other words, joyful-becoming as *potentia*, or a radical force of empowerment.

Lloyd (1994, 1996) explains how such a vitalistic and positive vision of the subject is linked to an ethics of passion that aims at joy and not at destruction. She carefully points out the difficulties involved in approaching Spinoza's concept of ethics as 'the collective powers and affinities of bodies' (Lloyd 1996: 23). She stresses the advantages of approaching these potencies of embodied subjects in terms of the ethology proposed by Deleuze, in so far as it challenges the centrality of the notion of the individual to an ethical sense of values or to a socially well-functioning system.

It is the case that the composition of the forces that propel the subject, the rhythm, speed and sequencing of the affects as well as the selection of the constitutive elements are the key processes. It is the orchestrated repetition and reoccurrence of these changes that marks the steps in the process of becoming-intensive. In other words, the actualization of a field of forces is the effect of an adequate dosage, while it is also simultaneously the prerequisite for sustaining those same forces. This is because the subject is an affective entity, a *conatus* defined as a 'striving' without an agent in control of it. This founding desire is a life force that intersects with all that moves and exists. Far from being the case that the individual possesses or controls such a force, it is rather the case that being a subject consists in partaking in such a striving.

The notion of the individual is enlarged to enclose a structural sense of interconnection between the singular self and the environment or totality in which it is embodied and embedded. Lloyd defines this interconnectiveness not as a synthesis, but rather as a series of 'nested embeddings of individuals' (Lloyd 1994: 12). According to this enlarged sense of the individual, an inward-looking understanding of the individual self is not only an error, but also a cognitive and an ethical misjudgement. The inward-looking individual fails to see the interconnection as part and

parcel of his or her nature, and is thus inhabited by an inadequate understanding of him or herself. The truth of self lies in its interrelations to
others in a rhizomic manner that defies dualistic modes of opposition.
Reaching out for an adequate representation of oneself includes the
process of clearing up the confusion concerning one's true nature as an
affective, interconnected entity. Ultimately this implies understanding the
bodily structure of the self. Because of this bodily nature, the process of
self-consciousness is forever ongoing and therefore incomplete, or partial.
This partiality is built into Spinoza's understanding of the subject.

Bodily entities, in fact, are not passive, but rather dynamic and sensitive
forces forever in motion which 'form unities only through fragile synchronization of forces' (Lloyd 1994: 23). This fragility concerns mostly the pitch
of the synchronization efforts, the lines of demarcation between the different bodily boundaries, the borders that are the thresholds of encounter and
connection with other forces, the standard term for which is 'limits'.
Because of his monistic understanding of the subject, Spinoza sees bodily
limits as the limits of our awareness as well, which means that his theory
of affectivity is connected to the physics of motion. Another word for
Spinoza's *conatus* is therefore self-preservation, not in the liberal individualistic sense of the term, but rather as the actualization of one's essence, that
is to say of one's ontological drive to become. This is not an automatic nor
an intrinsically harmonious process, in so far as it involves interconnection
with other forces and consequently also conflicts and clashes. Negotiations
have to occur as stepping-stones to sustainable flows of becoming. The
bodily self's interaction with his or her environment can either increase or
decrease that body's *conatus* or *potentia*. The mind as a sensor that prompts
understanding can assist by helping to discern and choose those forces that
increase its power of acting and its activity in both physical and mental
terms. A higher form of self-knowledge by understanding the nature of
one's affectivity is the key to a Spinozist ethics of empowerment. It includes
a more adequate understanding of the interconnections between the self
and a multitude of other forces, and it thus undermines the liberal individual understanding of the subject. It also implies, however, the body's
ability to comprehend and physically to sustain a greater number of
complex interconnections, and to deal with complexity without being
overburdened. Thus, only an appreciation of complexity and of increasing
degrees of complexity can guarantee the freedom of the mind in the awareness of its true, affective and dynamic nature.

In thinking the unity of body and mind, sustainable ethics stresses the
power (*potentia*) of affects (*affectus*). Starting from the assumption that the
property of substance is to express itself, the term 'expression' implies
'dynamic articulation' (Lloyd 1996: 31) and not merely passive reflection:
'Affectus refers to the passage from one state to another in the affected
body – the increase or decrease in its powers of acting' (Lloyd 1996: 72).
This 'power of acting' – which is in fact a flow of transpositions – is

expressed by Spinoza in terms of achieving freedom through an adequate understanding of our passions and consequently of our bondage. Coming into possession of freedom requires the understanding of affects or passions by a mind that is always already embodied. The desire to reach an adequate understanding of one's *potentia* is the human being's fundamental desire or *conatus*. An error of judgement is a form of misunderstanding (the true nature of the subject) that results in a decrease in the power, positivity and activity of the subject. By extension: reason is affective, embodied, dynamic – understanding the passions is our way of experiencing them – and making them work in our favour. In this respect Spinoza argues that desires arise from our passions. Because of this, they can never be excessive, given that affectivity is the power that activates our body and makes it want to act. The human being's inbuilt tendency is towards joy and self-expression, not towards implosion. This fundamental positivity is the key to Deleuze's attachment to Spinoza.

Lloyd argues that Spinoza's treatment of the mind as part of nature is a source of inspiration for contemporary ethics. Spinozist monism acts: 'As a basis for developing a broader concept of ethology, a study of relations of individual and collective and being affected' (Lloyd 1996: 18). Clearly, it is a very non-moralistic understanding of ethics which focuses on the subject's powers to act and to express their dynamic and positive essence. An ethology stresses the field of composition of forces and affects, speed and transformation. In this perspective, ethics is the pursuit of self-preservation, which assumes the dissolution of the self: what is good is what increases our power of acting and that is what we must strive for. This results not in egotism, but in mutually embedded nests of shared interests. Lloyd calls this 'a collaborative morality' (Lloyd 1996: 74). Because the starting point for Spinoza is not the isolated individual, but complex and mutually dependent co-realities, the self–other interaction also follows a different model. To be an individual means to be open to being affected by and through others, thus undergoing transformations in such a way as to be able to sustain them and make them work towards growth. The distinction activity/passivity is far more important than that between self and other, good and bad. What binds the two is the idea of interconnection and affectivity as the defining features of the subject. An ethical life pursues that which enhances and strengthens the subject without reference to transcendental values but rather in the awareness of one's interconnection with others.

Lloyd and Deleuze can be synthesized into the concept of a sustainable, non-unitary, perspectival self that aims at endurance. Endurance has a temporal dimension. It has to do with lasting in time, hence duration and self-perpetuation (traces of Bergson, here). But it also has a spatial side to do with the space of the body as an enfleshed field of actualization of passions or forces. It evolves affectivity and joy (traces of Spinoza), as in the capacity for being affected by these forces to the point of pain or extreme pleasure (which amounts to the same thing). It may require putting up with and tolerating hardship and physical pain. It also entails the effort to move beyond it, to construct affirmative interaction. Apart from providing the key to an aetiology of forces, endurance is also an ethical principle of affirmation of the positivity of the intensive subject, or in other words its joyful affirmation as *potentia*. The subject is a spatio-temporal compound that frames the boundaries of processes of becoming. This works by transforming negative into positive passions through the power of an understanding that is no longer indexed upon a phallogo-centric set of standards, but is rather nomadic and affective.

This turning of the tide of negativity is the transformative process of achieving freedom of understanding, through the awareness of our limits, of our bondage. This results in the freedom to affirm one's essence as joy, through encounters and minglings with other bodies, entities, beings and forces. Ethics means faithfulness to this *potentia*, or the desire to become.

Becoming is an intransitive process: it is not about becoming anything in particular. Inter-relations occur on the basis of affinity, in a pragmatic mode of random attraction. It is life on the edge, but not over it. It is not deprived of violence, but deeply compassionate. It is an ethical and political sensibility that begins with the recognition of one's limitations as the necessary counterpart of one's forces or intensive encounters with multiple others. It has to do with the adequacy of one's intensity to the modes and time of its enactment. It can only be empirically embodied and embedded, because it is interrelational and collective.

MEMORY AND THE IMAGINATION

Crucial to a Spinozist–Deleuzian understanding of the subject as an integrated unity of affectivity and reason is the notion of inbuilt temporality. Lloyd argues that the mind and body can act as synchronized entities is owing to the body's capacity to recollect sensations, traces and experiences even after their immediate activity has subsided. Memory is the key term here. Moreover, the embodied subject is also marked by the capacity to discern similarities and differences between diverse experiences, traces and sensations. The imagination here is the necessary counterpart of affectivity. Lloyd (1996) points out that, as a result of the deeply social nature of subjects, who find their fulfilment in social reality and coexistence with others, both affectivity and imaginings acquire a special importance. The faculty of the imagination plays a role also in making it possible for the subject to discern and gain access to the contingent realities of social existence and how ordinary experience is constructed.

Gatens and Lloyd point to the intrinsically socialized version of the human mind that is at work in Spinoza's philosophy. Although the imagination can be dangerous because it runs amok with affectivity and dreams or fictions, it is also the binding force that makes it possible for human reason to draw connections and establish links. This endows it with a force that then gets channelled towards the faculty of human understanding, though it never fully coincides with it. As Christopher Norris points out (1991), Spinoza gives ample space to the imagination, but also recognizes it as a source of misrecognition or delusion, in a manner that Norris judges analogous to the concept of 'ideology' or the 'imaginary' in Althusser and Lacan. It is an uncritical mode of thought which is not completely devoid of truth in so far as it gives access to everyday experience, but it presents this truth in an imaginary form *as if* it were the truth. This capacity to *do as if* is crucial to the Spinozist vision of the subject as an affective and rational entity. This profound ambivalence which structures the subject lies at the heart of his or her strength and hence also of his or her weakness. The imagination consequently marks a temporary lack of critical judgement that results from the restrictions that are placed upon the faculty of rational thought. The function of theoretical reason, on the other hand, is to think through these limits by a critique that elucidates their nature, eliminates their incoherence and produces adequate ideas.

The 'imagination', or 'savage anomaly' (Negri 1981), coincides with the socially binding force of collectively shared political passions. The logic of associative social relations lies at the heart of both the ethics of affectivity and the constitution of social and political forms of democratic power, which would take the collectivity – or 'multitude' – as its subject. The imagination thus cuts two ways. On the negative side, it makes way to ever expanding webs of associations and interconnections. Anyone familiar with the history of philosophy will know the sort of ethical and epistemological problems that the notion of the imagination has created since the seventeenth century. Feminist philosophers have also highlighted the highly genderized nature of the troublesome notion of the imagination (Lloyd 1985; Bordo 1986). The volatility of this idea makes it prone to being disciplined and subjected to a number of strategies of containment, which constitute an integral part of scientific rationality.

On the positive side, on the other hand, the imagination makes the embodied self capable of understanding itself as *conatus* and acting on its desire to grow and increase its degrees of activity. This means that no intervention by the will is necessary for Spinoza, as for Deleuze, in order to justify volitional activity or choice. The radical materialism of this vision of the subject makes for a parallelism between mental and bodily activity. Being an affective entity means essentially being interconnected with all that lives and thus to be engulfed in affects, emotions and passions. None of these are implicitly clear and thus require the intervention of reason to become more understandable. Understanding this interdependence, however, is the prerequisite for ethical life. Ethics means understanding our sharing in a common nature with others, yet remaining concerned for individuals around us and thus being able to transcend our self-interest in the concern for those who are similar to us. The under-standing of this interconnection is a source of joy and empowerment.

The role of the imagination, the dense materiality of images and of the process of imaging itself, has received a very distinctive treatment within philosophical nomadism. This idea has also become more charged politi-cally as a result of the power of global media and of the ongoing informa-tion and communication technologies, as I discussed in chapter 2.

An ethics of sustainability rests on the twin concepts of temporality and endurance, that is to say a nomadic understanding of memory. Remembering is about repetition or the retrieval of information. In the human subject, that information is stored throughout the physical and experiential density of the embodied self and not only in the 'black box' of the psyche. In this respect, Deleuze's distinction between a 'majority' and a 'minority' memory is useful in illuminating the paradoxes and the riches of repetition as the engine of identity and coherence of the self.

The notion of a minoritarian memory is crucial to Deleuze's process of becoming. The phallogocentric subject, representing the majority of white, heterosexual, property-owning males, holds a large data bank of central-ized knowledge. He holds the keys to the central memory of the system and has reduced to the rank of a-signifying practices the alternative or subjugated memories of the many others: women, natives, animals have no history.

Théâtre de Complicité's play *Mnemonic* illustrates this principle per-fectly. It is a nomadic disquisition on memory and the imagination, which guides the audience through an elating trip across both *chronos* and *aion*. Linear time and circular genealogies cut across each other in a Bergsonian continuous present that is a space of active creation. Théâtre de Complicité argues: 'We can think of memory as a pattern, a map. But not a stable neatly printed ordnance-survey map, but one that is constantly changing and developing. . . . Remembering is essentially not only an act of retrieval but a creative thing, it happens in the moment, it's an act . . . of the imagi-nation' (1999: 4). The specific temporality of genetics and evolution zigzags in and out of human history, with its baggage of blood, sweat and tears. All these different cycles are embedded in specific territories or spaces, which the characters in the drama inhabit, visit and cross in their quest for their own origins. All the protagonists are displaced people, the result of contemporary European history's spasmodic changes and displace-ments: migrant, exiles, refugees, diasporic entities without a fixed home. Their quest for either belonging or origins is set in the context of the rampant regional nationalism of the European Union today. The bone of contention becomes the discovery of the 'Ice Man', or ' the Man from Similaun', the 5,200-year-old corpse that was found on 19 September 1991 in the Alps, in Similaun on the border between Italy and Austria. This 'first European' literally embodies a frozen slab of history. He was a nomadic traveller who fled to the high mountains in the vain attempt to escape the pursuit of his enemies who had destroyed his community. Already a refugee, this 'first European' was a stateless, homeless, vulnerable being seeking in vain for a safe haven. In the beginning there is always and already displacement, loss, persecution and homelessness. Fortunately, time is a dynamic entity and nothing is ever played out for good. Thus, the past is always ahead of those who have a flair for minoritarian becomings.

On the issue of memory, the critical dialogue with psychoanalytic theory is crucial. Freud's early psychoanalytic insights had caught a glimpse of two crucial notions. Firstly, that processes of remembrance extend well beyond the rational control of consciousness. In fact, consciousness is merely the tip of the iceberg of a far more complex set of resonances, echo and data processing which we commonly call 'memory'. Consciousness is the co-synchronicity of different time sequences.

Secondly, Freud argued that these processes of remembrance are enfleshed, because they encompass the embodied self as a whole and therefore rest on somatic layers that call for a specific form of (psycho)analysis. According to Deleuze and Guattari, however, Freud immediately closed the door that he had half-opened, by reindexing this vitalist and time-bound definition of the subject onto the necessity to conform to dominant socio-cultural expectations and normal norms about civilized, adult, human behaviour.

Lacan, through his 'return to Freud', operated a sort of kidnapping of the subject from the bodily or somatic grounds of Freudian psychoanalysis. This has the advantage of radicalizing the politics of psychoanalysis by attacking conventional morality and expectations about bourgeois propriety. It also lifts the taboo that Freud had imposed on politics. Lacanian psychoanalysis inscribes the politics of subjectivity at the heart of its concerns and aims at attacking the humanistic assumptions about the 'individual', replacing them with the creative contradictions of split subjectivity. By launching his war cry 'where the ego was, the id shall be', Lacan radicalizes psychoanalysis and attempts to turn it into a philosophy of subversion of the subject, against the political conformism and the reformist impact of American-dominated 'ego-psychology'. This ambitious project, however, has the disadvantage of introducing into the conceptual framework of the psychoanalytic subject a heavier dose of Hegelian dialectics than before. This manifests itself through the idea of desire as lack and the role of negativity in the constitution of consciousness, which emerge as major points of disagreement between Lacan and Deleuze (Braidotti 2002).

Deleuze's becomings contain a critique of dialectical time. Thus the Bergsonian continuous present is set in opposition to the tyranny of the past – in the history of philosophy, for instance, but also in the psychoanalytic notion of remembrance, repetition and the retrieval of repressed psychic material. Deleuze disengages memory from its indexation on a fixed identity; predicated upon a majority-subject. The memory of the logocentric or 'molar' subject is a huge data bank of centralized information, which is relayed through every aspect of his activities. The majority subject holds the key to the central memory of the system, thus reducing 'others' to an insignificant or rather 'a-signifying' role. The memories of the minorities nonetheless engender empowering differences. In reaction to this centralized, monolithic memory, Deleuze activates a minority-memory, which is a power of remembrance without *a priori* propositional attachment to the centralized data bank. This intensive, zigzagging, cyclical and messy type of remembering does not even aim at retrieving information in a linear manner. It simply intuitively endures; it also functions as a deterritorializing agency that dislodges the subject from a unified and centralized location. It disconnects the subject from his or her identification with logocentric consciousness and it shifts the emphasis from being to becoming. The minoritarian memory propels the process of becoming by liberating something akin to Foucault's 'counter-memory': a faculty that, instead of retrieving in a linear order specifically catalogued memories, functions instead as a deterritorializing agency which dislodges the subject from his or her sense of unified and consolidated identity. It destabilizes identity by opening up spaces where virtual possibilities can be actualized. It is a sort of empowerment of all that was not programmed within the dominant memory. Minoritarian memory bears a close link to the idea of a traumatic event. A trauma is by definition an event that shatters the boundaries of the subject and blurs his or her sense of identity. Traumas cancel and even suppress the actual content of memories. As memory is the data bank of one's identity, the struggle to remember or retrieve the embodied experiences that are too painful for immediate recollection is formidable. It also makes for no less formidable narratives.

Reassembling the pieces shattered by the traumatic event is especially painful, as testified by Primo Levi and other concentration camp survivors, but also by rape victims and others. The effect of the trauma is to flatten time out into a generalized sense of numbness that traces an oppressively linear eternal and unsustainable 'now'. The tyranny of this linearity functions like a black hole into which possible futures implode and disappear. Extreme situations of totalitarian domination or oppression strip the subject of any added complexity and reduce him or her to a brutally oversimplified chunk of meat, 'bare life' (see Agamben (1998) on concentration-camps) forced to conform to whichever negative label makes him or her infra-human (see Gilroy (1993) on the effects of slavery), less-than, less human than and consequently considerably more mortal than the dominant subjects.

Glissant, however, stresses the deep generative powers of memory as a political project. The struggle to remember, to repossess a historical or genealogical memory, is a struggle against this sort of reductivism, this shortcut through human complexities. Feminism argues that active remembrance is the overcoming of the traces of violence, which are enforced with lethal regularity by oppressive regimes the world over. It is an act of creation that mobilizes the imagination, not only the lived experience.

Remembering in the nomadic mode requires composition, selection and dosage; the careful layout of empowering conditions that allow for the actualizations of affirmative forces. Like a choreography of flows or intensities that require adequate framing in order to be composed into a form, intensive memories activate empathy and cohesion between their constitutive elements. Nomadic remembering is like a constant quest for temporary moments when a balance can be sustained, before the forces dissolve again and move on. And on it goes, never equal to itself, but faithful enough to itself to endure, and to pass on.

Of course, the question of the 'lived temporality' of the subject has wider implications. There is a genetic, even evolutionary side to it: the specific information contained in the organic layer of the individual is crucial to the unfolding of one's life-span, and the vicissitudes of one's organic existence. Deleuze refers to this question, in a sort of zigzagging dialogue with Saint-Hilaire and Darwin, in terms of the 'animality' of the self, his or her *zoe*-driven vitality. That is to say, the substratum of the radical immanence of the self which is a life has its own built-in biological clock: its duration is limited and only partially negotiable. The inner beat of life is portioned off and partitioned carefully. The 'I' that inhabits the specific portion of space and time within which it moves is not the owner of that life: she or he is renting it, on a time-base. My life is only a time-share.

Memory is fluid and flowing; it opens up unexpected or virtual possibilities. It is also transgressive in that it works against the programmes of the dominant memory system. This continuous memory is, however, not necessarily or inevitably linked to 'real' experience. In what I consider to be one of the more radical conceptual attacks on the authority of 'experience' and the extent to which the appeal to experience both confirms and perpetuates the belief in steady and unitary identities, Deleuze rather links memory to the imagination.

The imagination plays a crucial role in enabling the whole process of becoming-minoritarian and hence of conceptual creativity and ethical empowerment. The imaginative, affective force of remembrance – that which returns and is remembered or repeated – is the propelling force in this idea of becoming-intensive. When you remember in the intensive or minority-mode, you open up spaces of movement and of de-territorialization which actualize virtual possibilities which had been frozen in the image of the past. Opening up these virtual spaces is a creative effort. When you remember to become what you are – a subject-in-becoming – you actually reinvent yourself on the basis of what you hope you could become with a little help from your friends.

It is crucial in fact to see to what an extent processes of becoming are collective, intersubjective and not individual or isolated. 'Others' are the integral element of one's successive becomings. Again, my quarrel here is with any notion of the subject that would imply an ethics of individual responsibility in the liberal model. A Deleuzian approach would rather favour the destitution of the sovereign subject altogether and consequently the overcoming of the dualism Self/Other, Sameness/Difference which that vision of the subject engenders. Subjects are fields of forces that aim at duration and joyful self-realization and which, in order to fulfil them, need to negotiate their way across the pitfalls of negativity that phallogocentric culture is going to throw in the way of the fulfilment of their intrinsic positivity.

Remembering in this nomadic mode is the active reinvention of a self that is joyfully discontinuous, as opposed to being mournfully consistent, as programmed by phallogocentric culture. It destabilizes the sanctity of the past and the authority of experience. The tense that best expresses the power of the imagination is the future perfect: 'I will have been free'. Quoting Virginia Woolf, Deleuze also says: 'it will have been a childhood, though not necessarily my childhood'. Shifting away from the reassuring platitudes of the past to the openings hinted at by the future perfect: this is the tense of a virtual sense of potential. Memories need the imagination to empower the actualization of virtual possibilities in the subject. They allow the subject to differ from oneself as much as possible while remaining faithful to oneself, or in other words: enduring.

Thus a Deleuzian feminism seeks not to pursue Hegelian or Lacanian identities, based on the need for a phallogocentric position, however equal or unequal. Rather, if such a feminism is to be articulated as a mode of becoming, then it is to do so through a becoming as breathing gender, as shifting pressure points, as molecular transformations of gender itself. What takes place, then, is a radical challenge to any notion of a self that plays itself out in a matrix of having and lacking Self and Other as psychoanalytic or transcendental categories. Becoming is a personalized overthrowing of the internal simulacra of the self. This kind of imaginative recollection of the self is about repetition, but it is less about forgetting to forget (Freud's definition of the neurotic symptoms), than about retaking, as in refilming a sequence. The imaginative force of this operation is central to a vitalist, yet anti-essentialist theory of desire, and also to a new concept and practice of ethics.

Desire is the propelling and compelling force that is attracted to self-affirmation or the transformation of negative into positive passions. This is a desire not to preserve, but to change a deep yearning for transformation or a process of affirmation. To enact the different steps of this process of becoming, one has to work on the conceptual coordinates. These are not elaborated by voluntaristic self-naming, but rather through processes of careful revisitations and retakes, or patterns of repetition. Empathy and

compassion are key features of this nomadic yearning for in-depth transformation. The space of becoming is a space of affinity and correlation of
elements, among compatible and mutually attractive forces and the constitutive elements of the process. Proximity or intellectual sympathy is
both a topological and qualitative notion; both geography or meteorology
and ethical temperature. It is an affective framing for the becoming of
subjects as sensible or intelligent matter. The affectivity of the imagination is the motor for these encounters and of the conceptual creativity
they trigger off. It is a transformative force that propels multiple,
heterogeneous 'becomings' of the subject.

ON STYLE: BY MEMORY/BY HEART

The notion of 'figurations', the quest for an adequate style, as opposed to
'metaphors', emerges as crucial to Deleuze's use of the imagination as a
concept. Figurations are forms of literal expression which represent that
which the system had declared off-limits. There are situated practices that
require the awareness of the limitations as well as the specificity of one's
locations. They illuminate all the aspects of one's subjectivity that the phallogocentric regime does not want us to become. This kind of philosophical
creativity operates a shift of paradigm towards a positive appraisal of differences, deviances or anomalies, not as an end in themselves but as steps
in a process of recomposition of the coordinates of subjectivity in techno-
culture. This post-humanistic acceptance of hybridization and the inter-
mingling of the biological with the cultural, the physical with the
technological is neither nihilistic nor decadent. Nor is it a romantic valori-
zation of otherness *per se*. It is rather an attempt to disengage the process of
becoming from the classical topos of the dichotomy self–other and the
notion of 'difference' from its hegemonic and negative implications. It aims
at finding accurate cartographies of the changes that are occurring in post-
industrial cultures. It is a way of mapping the metamorphoses.

There are some important methodological implications in this vision
of the role and function of Memory and its complicity with the Imagination. What exactly is involved in 'working from memory' when one is
writing commentaries on the history of philosophy or on other theoretical
texts? The most notorious statement to this effect concerns Deleuze's two-
volume study of cinema, in which he states that he did not watch again
any of the movies he was to discuss. He just wrote from memory, from
the first time he saw them, which in some cases occurred years before.
Most of his literary citations, however, bear the same style: they are rarely
verbatim repetitions of the original texts. Nor are they 'close textual readings', following the dominant mode of teaching philosophy in the
academic world today, where the repetition of 'his master's voice' is the
name of the game. 'Faithfulness' here equates flat repetition.

Writing from memory involves a number of precise steps. Firstly, it means that one is exempted from checking against the original, at least during the process of writing the actual commentary. This expresses the conviction that the 'truth' of a text is somehow never really 'written'. Neither is it contained within the signifying space of the book, nor is it about the authority of a proper noun, a signature, a tradition, a canon, let alone the prestige of a discipline. Deleuze's critique of the power of philosophy as a majority discourse shines through this disregard for the authoritativeness of citation. Deleuze advocates a kind of accuracy of an altogether different kind. The 'truth' of a text resides rather in the kind of outward-bound interconnections or relations that it enables, provokes, engenders and sustains. Thus, a text is a relay point between different moments in space and time, as well as different levels, degrees, forms and configurations of the thinking process. Thinking, like breathing, is not held in the mould of linearity, or the confines of the printed page. The linguistic signifier is merely one of the points in a chain of effects, not its centre or its endgame.

Secondly, and as a consequence of the above, 'working from memory' implies respecting the specific, non-linear temporality of this intensive process of thinking. The notion of 'duration' is of crucial importance here. The active, minoritarian or nomadic memory triggers molecular becomings and thus works towards affirmation. In order to do so, however, it constantly reconnects to the virtual totality of a continuously recomposing block of past and present moments. It is yet another synchronization exercise. Moments in time coincide in the 'here and now' of actualizing, making concrete steps towards, processes of heightened intensity or becoming.

What does this Bergsonian concept mean, when applied to the reading of theoretical, social and cultural texts and the practice of commentary and citation? It means that one starts working from what is left over, what remains, what has somehow caught and stuck around, the drags and the sediments of the reading and the cognitive process. It would be a mistake to think of the latter as a superficial, associative approach. This position assumes that 'depth' has to do with detailed reproduction of the text's intentions, meanings and conceptual structures. I find this fetishism of depth, textual interiority and close readings very claustrophobic. Like Deleuze, I find no sense in the passive mimetic game of commenting on commentaries and see no reason for it, other than the inertia of habit. Equally striking is the weight of Oedipal tradition and the empire of the phallogocentric symbolic upon this habit of faithful textual commentaries.

I prefer to think of this way of relating to memory in terms of transpositions, that is to say as creative and highly generative interconnections which mix and match, mingle and multiply possibilities of expansion and growth among different units or entities. Transpositions require precision in terms of the coordinates of the encounters, but also a high charge of imaginative force. It may appear as random association to the naked eye, but in fact it is a specific and accurate topology of forces of attraction, which find their own modes of selection, combination and recomposition. Musical scores function by transpositions, much as the transmission of genetic information: they proceed by leaps and bounds, but this movement is neither anarchic nor chaotic (see the prologue). The coherence of this system is the result of the affinity and empathy that allowed for the preliminary selection to be made in the first place, resulting in the storage of the data in or as memory. Similar processes of selection are at work in the effort of combining and recomposing after the mixing has occurred. The image of the musical 'refrain' which one cannot get out of one's head is very illuminating here: it exemplifies the powers of a force of remembrance that does not depend on the will, but is not anarchic or romantically spontaneous either. There is no spontaneity at work here, but rather a careful dosage of forces, a process of selective affinities.

Nomadic methodology is of a different kind: it works from minoritarian, positive and productive memory. What matters is the structure of the affective forces that make it perceivable to the viewer. Precepts, affects and concepts are the key elements of the complex, yet somewhat elementary materialism that Deleuze applies also to the task of textual commentaries, working them 'from memory'. The model for this is the quick glance of the painter that captures the 'essence' of a landscape or the precise quality of the light upon it, in a fleeting moment and which is wrongly rendered in terms of 'insight'. It has nothing whatsoever to do with interiority, however, nor with inscrutable depths. It is rather related to external forces, their irresistible energy and mobility. Just like travellers can capture the 'essential lines' of landscape or of a place in the speed of crossing it, this is not superficiality, but a way of framing the longitudinal and latitudinal forces that structure a certain spatio-temporal 'moment'.

These multi-layered levels of affectivity are the building blocks for creative transpositions, which compose a plane of actualization of relations, that is to say points of contact between self and surroundings. They are the mark of immanent, embodied and embedded relations. Capturing such forces is not dependent upon the supervising control of a conscious subject who centralizes and ordains the information according to a hierarchy of sensorial and cognitive data.

Far from being superficial, moments like that – when the self is emptied out, dissolving into rawer and more elementary sensations – mark heightened levels of awareness and receptivity. In spiritual practices like meditation or disciplines like the martial arts what is labelled as concentration is represented by 'eyes wide shut' and deep vacuum. You look through reality to focus elsewhere. In fact, you are focusing on the ever-receding horizon of else-whereness itself – that is, infinity, an intransitive gaze that marks the intensive state of becoming. What looks like absent-mindedness on closer scrutiny reveals itself to be a qualitative leap towards a more focused, more precise, more accurate perception of one's own *potentia*, which is one's capacity to 'take in' the world, to encounter it, to go towards it. Zen Buddhism is based on this seemingly simple, yet highly complex principle. It is about respecting a creative void without forcefully imposing upon it a form that corresponds to the author's own intentions or desires. The form or the discursive event rather emerges from the creative encounter of the doer and the deed, or from the active process of becoming. The Zen archers who shoot their arrows with their eyes shut become the emblem for what I would describe as an ethical ideal: the 'becoming-imperceptible'. This amounts to turning the self into the threshold of gratuitous (principle of non-profit), aimless (principle of mobility or flow) acts through which the vital energy that is *bios/zoe* gets expressed in all its ruthless splendour.

If the activity of thinking is represented along these lines, it then follows that the more self-reflexive *a posteriori* process of theorizing this activity requires skills other than the ones that are usually praised, rewarded and perpetuated in academic circles. Notably, the key habit of 'faithfulness to the text' and of citation as repetition of the author's intended meaning, gets displaced. Instead, what comes to the fore is the creative capacity that consists in being able to render the more striking lines, forces or affective charges of any given text or author. To do so, what one needs to be loyal to is neither the spurious depth of the text, nor the author's latent or manifest intentionality, and even less the sovereignty of the Phallic Master. Loyalty is instead owed to what a text can do, what it has done, how it has impacted upon one according to the affective coordinates I outlined above. This requires memory, defined as an eco-philosophical notion, as the ability to retrace one's steps, like reading the wolf's imprints on the snow, finding the traces, but obviously not in the semiotic-linguistic limited sense of the term.

Accounting backwards for the affective impact of various items or data upon oneself is the process of remembering. In Bergson as in Deleuze it has as much to do with the imagination, that is to say creative reworking, as with the passive repetition of chronologically prior, recorded and hence retrievable experiences. Memory is ongoing and forward-looking precisely because it is a singular yet complex subject that is always already in motion and in process. This memory has to do with the capacity to endure, to 'hold' it in the sense of not cracking under the strain while perpetuating itself in time. Duration and endurance are also ethical categories concerned with sustainability, not just an aesthetic one.

Unfoldings

Applied to the activity of thinking, or of academic writing and citation, this means that a thought or an idea rests on an affective substratum which remains unthought at the heart of thinking in that it makes it possible and sustains it in the first place. This affective substratum can only be represented to oneself and to academic or theoretical language as being prior. Prior and always already out of reach. This priority, however, is an optical illusion, as it is a side-effect of the process of remembering in the continuous present mode. Following this intensive mode of representing subjectivity, the essential affective charge or substratum can only be rendered as originary, prior and unreachable or lost. This, however, is in itself a construction, a piece of creative imagining.

In other words, a 'prior' affective substratum is given as the anchoring point for complex and multiple processes of becoming, of encountering the outside as an onrush of data, precepts and sensations. In fact this moment takes place in the present, in the act of creation of active interconnections, commonly known as remembering. This process is more analogous to the use of colour in painting, however, than to psychoanalytic notions of fantasy or repression. The indexation of the process of becoming-subject upon a temporal axis has the curious effect of creating spatial dividing lines between a 'before' and an 'after'. For psychoanalysis, the dividing line marks the entry into the symbolic, with the corollary of the acquisition of language. This coincides with the loss of the mother's body and the foreclosure of the origin.

Both Irigaray and Deleuze take their distance from the psychoanalytic theory of the symbolic. They prefer to highlight the materiality of the enfleshed subject, and thus criticize the disembodied manner in which Lacan deals with the subject's inscription into the symbolic order. Their position also stresses the primacy of the prediscursive or the affective substratum in the life of the subject. This affectivity, this overwhelming vitality expresses the subject's propensity for life, as in *zoe* and in *bios*. As such, it founds the process of becoming in a vision of time as a continuous present.

For Deleuze especially, this emphasis on affectivity warrants his critique of the 'hidden' image of thought at work within philosophy. The 'image of thought' is the key note, the organizing principle that infuses the choice, composition and constitution of certain forces, which then become one with the subject. The best example of this is the notion of 'reason' in its hegemonic mode, as coinciding with truth, justice, order and a sense of measure. More than a concept, 'reason' can be seen to function therefore as a container, which implies a cluster of sub-notions as part of its capital. This clustered, associative web of nested meanings constitutes the image of thought. It also sets the ethical temperature of a concept, its level of affirmation or denial of *potentia*, *conatus* or desire. This is the level of intensity, the degree of positivity and the speed of the interconnections it engenders. This ethology of forces is crucial as a criterion to organize and classify the validity of ideas. By extension, ideas are not to be classified in terms of 'true' or false' in relation to their propositional contents, but rather in view of the affects that sustain them and the image of thought they convey. A level of temperature, a shade of colour in them, which is not the same as the manifest content: it is the geological assemblage of a text. Behaving ethically in research means learning to sustain the intensity of positive transformations or processes of becoming and accept responsibility for the transversal and collective nature of scientific enunciations. This places the practice of acknowledgement at the top of the ethical agenda in scholarship.

Thus, there is nothing chronologically or historically more ancient about these 'prior' conditions: their priority is of the order of a logical necessity. In the linearity of language, however, this precondition can only be rendered as *a priori* forces, but they rather ought to be thought of as a rush of complex, simultaneous and potentially contradictory elements. For instance, 'reason' should be thought of as a carrier of normative and normalizing values and assumptions, a moralistic 'image of thought'. This resistance to the authority of the past feeds into the emphasis that Deleuze places on the concept of duration. This means that the rigid distinction between past, present and future is made to collapse and is replaced by the joyful coexistence of different time zones. A true catastrophe for *chronos*, and yet this kind of mild schizophrenia or collapse of constitutive divides is one of the social effects induced by the pace of change under advanced capitalism. Also known as the uprooting of traditional values and the erasure of fixed meanings, this unlimitedness is part and parcel of our historicity. As such, we are fully immersed in it.

By extension, linearity may well be an ideal in phallocentric cultures and as such be constantly promoted and ubiquitously praised; nonetheless it is both unachievable and undesirable. This is due to the dynamic nature of language, which is living matter: words grow, split and multiply, sprouting new roots or side branches and resonating with all kinds of echoes and musical variations. Like insects, they mutate and grow antennae or extra limbs and new organs without any apparent strains. They simply carry, perform and transform energy as a matter of fact. This dynamic and volatile structure makes words into vehicles that transfer, convey and transform forces or energetic pulses. As in *Alice in Wonderland*, words as living entities keep on running about with maddening purposelessness and will never sit still. Thus, paradoxically enough, the very linearity that the phallogocentric system celebrates as a law cannot be imposed easily on the polysemic structure of language. In some ways, linearity is unachievable, undesirable and fundamentally unattainable. So much so, that in order to enforce the cultural ideal of linearity, a concerted effort needs to be made, which mobilizes all the gravitational pull of *potestas*, the gravity of institutional inertia, or the might of the status quo. Linearity is the result of the constraining effects of power in its negative form, the bulldozing effects of *potestas*: it is an effect, which is neither in the nature of things nor in the structure of language.

Read that 'non-linearity' can be re-territorialised ...

It is important to stress that Deleuze's defence of the unnaturalness of linearity or the collapse of temporal boundaries is not a replica of the logic of advanced capitalism, but rather a firm reaction against it. In a world constituted by flows and mobility, political agency is best served by a subject that is attuned to his or her historicity and is in turn flowing and mobile. This is no blind *mimesis*, as the cynics are likely to insinuate, but rather a synchronization of inner with outer time. A Spinozist vision of the subject as desire for change, or *conatus*-driven, encourages this view of synchronizing the forces that structure and contain subjectivity. Such synchronicity clears the ground for the negotiations concerning shifts, boundary-markers and thresholds that compose the field of sustainability for this non-unitary subject.

Any reference to the authority of a central concept, image or the past itself is dropped; in fact this prior affectivity, or hidden image of thought, also known as the social unconscious, lies always already before you. It is the necessary sonar wave that propels the subject forward, but always on the rebound, always already a repetition without originals. It is Echo that makes Narcissus tick, yet in the classical myth Narcissus falls into the black hole of taking himself with deadly seriousness. He thus forgets that Echo is already a simulacrum of himself and gets captured in his own sterile self-adoration. Supposing instead that we let Echo loose, in a joyful cacophony of multiple resonances. Random refrains and patterns of rebounds will emerge in due course and in a given time. One simply has to stay alert and pursue them, like the wolf pursuing its track: it forms part of a community yet is slightly off-side. Going for the sake of going, yet following familiar and beaten tracks, not looking for anything in particular, maybe even humming a familiar tune that one cannot get out of one's head.

A subject bent upon enduring in space and time cannot be a subject that wants to pursue power (*potestas*) as self-aggrandizement. This subject is structurally not-One, dynamic and driven to empowerment (*potentia*): she or he is on the go, following tracks or sounds or lines which she or he may never have seen before, yet whose consistency is anything but coincidental. Random patterns and the mobility of flows and affects are the real motor of nomadic subjectivity. To describe these forces as 'hidden' is ironical at best, because they are self-evident and easily accessible, on the surface of things. The only difficulty is the process of learning how to sustain them: how to compose them in a manner that allows the subject to express the best of him- or herself, stretching to the limit, without snapping. Negotiating thresholds of sustainability is what is at stake in nomadic processes of becoming.

Deleuze works from memory in his commentaries so as to express his loyalty to this vision of memory, the imagination and the thinking process. In other words, he practises enormous creativity but also functions in close intimacy or complicity with the texts or authors he cites. It then follows that for Deleuze there cannot be such a thing as a negative citation: why waste energy on paranoid investments in the activity of thinking? Memory is structurally pleasure-prone: one has to make a much bigger effort actually to recollect unpleasant experiences. The same goes for unloved or unappreciated texts: why bother to revisit them? Confining them to oblivion is a more effective way to deal with them. What one is silent about, one could simply cannot be bothered with.

In his discussion on the history of philosophy, Deleuze describes the study of classical philosophical texts as a set of portrait-studies, of landscapes as well as faces. The notion of the face as a landscape of forces is a response to the phenomenological tradition, in Levinas and others, which makes the face of the other into the privileged frame of containment of an ethical relationship. Philosophical nomadism extends this commitment to accountability beyond the visual, the human and the privileged other, to encompass a web of power relations governed by variables such as gender, race, ethnicity, age and social class. These are coordinates that intersect and flow across materially embedded and embodied subjects (Griggers 1997) and allow him or her to interact creatively with others. Faces are global landscapes, with histories, materialities, genetic and genealogical time sequences. The cartographic practice that consists in accounting for one's politics of location turns into the more conceptual exercise of producing diagrams of fluid or process-oriented non-human, transversal subjectivities. The face-as-landscape is a diagram of floating but accountable locations, a sort of text, but of the non-linguistic kind; it is a frame of containment.

Just as in the case of music, what matters here is the effort to stretch the boundaries of classical representability, and of its signifying practices. Transpositions are creative shifts that engender interconnections of the non-linear kind. Deleuze's reference to creativity through painting is crucial here, as it points to a pre-linguistic level of perception and apprehension of creative flows. Painting is a visual technique of marking which does not coincide with semiotic signification and has rather more in common with tattooing than with 'writing'. It is in the sense of referring to raw, vitalistic forces of creativity that Deleuze argues that learning to think philosophically is an apprenticeship in landscape painting.

By tending to each detail and nuance attentively, the apprentice learns gradually to approach the use of colours. Concepts are to philosophy what colour is to painting. To learn how to approach them, however, one needs modesty, hard work and, ultimately, time. These are long-term endeavours. Moreover, the process of creativity or of becoming is impersonal in that it requires the complete concentration of the author (be it the philosopher, writer, painter or composer) upon the field or territory she or he is immersed in. What is at stake is not the manipulation of a set of linguistic or narrative conventions; not the cognitive penetration of an object or the appropriation of a theme, but rather the development or the ability to find orientation in a territory. Thinking here is the skill that consists in developing a compass of the cognitive, affective and ethical kind. It is an apprenticeship in the art of conceptual colouring. *Homo faber* is better suited for this task than good old *homo sapiens*. As for the *feminae* in the story, we all know what kind of compasses they have been capable of inventing for the purpose of moving as unscathed as possible through the minefields of phallogocentric territories.

An exercise in cartographic bearings and orientation requires concentration upon the outside. In turn this implies the abandonment of the humanistic vision of the self and of the centuries-old habits of inward-looking identity. Deleuze calls for an ascetic surrender of the self, of one's cherished but ultimately limited identity, and the opening up of one's perceptive apparatus into a complex of multiple connections, sensations, perceptions and imaginings. To create (music, colours, concepts) means to be able to render in a sustainable format this complexity of intense but impersonal affects, as well as being capable of sustaining the internally dissonant forces that structure these affects. The activity of thinking in this respect is closer to that of mindful breathing than it is to the exercise of the sterile protocols of institutional reason.

Whereas psychoanalytic theories of artistic creation play the theme of subjectivity back upon the holy Hegelian trinity of Lack, Law and Power of the Signifier, an intensive or nomadic approach stresses the productive, rather than the regressive, structure of these forces. Shedding the mental habit that consists in Oedipalizing the process of creation by indexing it indefinitely on an economy of guilt and unaffordable ontological debts, what I find in rhizomatics is an overcoming of the dialectics of negativity. Nomadic, rhizomic thinking offers simultaneously a point of exit from the linguistic-semiotic vicious circles of absence and negativity, and also an empowerment of affective and unconscious forces as active, expressive, productive. At the heart of nomadology is a positive reading of the human as a positive, pleasure-prone machine capable of all sorts of empowering forces. It is just a question of establishing the most positive possible connections and resonances.

A new philosophical concept – say an alternative view of subjectivity, or a new system of representation, a new sound or an alternative image – is a break with the old mental habits. It is an affect that breaks through the established frame, it illuminates a territory by providing orientation coordinates; it makes visible/thinkable/sayable/hearable forces, passions and affects which were not perceived before. Thus, the question of creation is ultimately technological: it is about how. It is also geological: it is about where and in which territory. Ultimately, it is ethical: it is about where to set the limits and how to sustain the processes of change without hurting self or other. The issue about creative intensity is how to endure it, sustaining the altered states and the heightened intensity that the processes of becoming inevitably entail. The ethics of sustainability is also an aesthetics of becoming. As Dorothea Olkowski rightly suggests (1999), the limits of a process of becoming have to do with the level and degree of power (*potentia*) that the embodied entity possesses. Given that the subject is propelled by the desire to express and actualize its *potentia*, the limits of its power are also the limits of its desire. The cry 'I can't any more' therefore becomes an ethical and energetic statement that marks the limit of my desire to be transformed by multiple forces, external flows and contacts. I come back to these issues in the next chapter.

Neo-asceticism

This intense positivity marks Deleuze's conceptual style, his refusal to engage in negative criticism for its own sake and to act instead from positive and empowering relationships to the texts and authors he engages with. Ethics here is closely linked to high intellectual understanding and the quality of one's intellect. This is the Nietzschean aspect of philosophical nomadology, which stresses that the ethical dimension is a combination of genius and of humbleness. The latter entails a sort of impersonality, which could be mistaken for a universalizing faculty, but is really just a cognitive brand of empathy, or intense affinity. It is the capacity for compassion, which combines the power of understanding with the force to endure in sympathy with a people, all of humanity or civilization. It is an extra-personal and a trans-personal capacity, which should be driven away from any universalism and grounded instead in the radical immanence of a sense of belonging to and being accountable for a community, a people, a territory.

Nietzsche put it ever so wittily: 'a good writer possesses not only his own mind, but also the mind of his friends' (Nietzsche 1994: 119). This ethical line of transversality also covers effectively the much-discussed 'role of the intellectuals' and also the discussion of 'philosophical style'. Deleuze's style is compassionate, empathic, yet also very dry and rigorous. He does stress the positive or joyful aspects of a philosopher's work, stressing the effects of their thought, much as a painter would comment on the quality of a landscape. There is something precise and distant, uncompromising and unsentimental about it. It is indeed an impersonal, ascetic style, as sharp as a cartographer's gaze, but as involved as a lover's. Bogue (1996) describes it as a quest for sobriety, or a distinct lack of enthusiasm, an essential and filtered-down intensity, austere yet intense. The style is a philosopher's conceptual persona, his metamorphic body: that which she or he is destined to become.

A very modest man himself, who kept an extremely low profile in the media, Deleuze carefully avoided the circus of self-promotional activities that marked intellectual life in the West at the end of the millennium. He explicitly criticized the intrusion of the media and its 'star-system' (see the case of the '*nouveaux* philosophers' like Bernard-Henri Lévy) into the work of research and study that should remain the philosopher's main task. Deleuze kept his low-status job at the University of Paris VIII to the end of his life and never enjoyed the benefits of fame and wealth, unlike so many of his peers. He notably steered clear of the transatlantic academic exchange market, a major cash nexus which established so many marginal French philosophers in top chairs in the United States, particularly in California.

The self-aggrandizing gestures that mark social, professional and institutional life are examples of the micro-instances of reactive or negative morality. In ethical terms, social institutions generate, instil and reward the reproduction of negative passions (narcissism and paranoia being the two pillars of social institutions) in their Oedipally subjugated participants. Deleuze's career kept a healthy distance from the inevitable cycles of competition that propel academic, institutional and social life. He surveyed them with the distance and the compassion of someone who simultaneously knows that this negativity affects him or her, too, but also knows that she or he has nothing at stake. It shows humility and the capacity, deliberately to resist the power games of *potestas* (negativity), as if he had no stake in it, as if he were already put off the (rat) race. This ability to disconnect from the paranoid-narcissistic self-nexus, so as to activate a more affirmative set of passions, enacts simultaneously an act of withdrawal (a minus) and of addition (a plus). The subject subtracts him or herself from the reactive affects by stepping out of the negativity circuit. By virtue of this she or he transcends negativity, thereby generating and making room for more affirmative forces.

This institutional practice engages both a vision of the self and a role for the intellectual which consists not in leading the opinions (*doxa*), deliberating on truth (judgement), or administering the protocols of intellectual life (*potestas*), but rather in creating and disseminating new concepts and ideas (*potentia*). It is not a matter of representing others, or speaking on their behalf, but rather about injecting doses of positivity into institutional and academic practice, so as to turn it into an instrument of production of the new. The link between reason and the imagination, theory and passion, is crucial to this project.

Something analogous to this ascetism is at work in Donna Haraway's choice of the figuration of the 'modest witness' to describe the activity of critical thinking. In keeping with her preference for situated and partial forms of knowledge, Haraway (1997) offers the notion of modesty as a form of accountability, open-ended dialogue and critical thinking that aims at witnessing, not at judging. She specifies that not only is a feminist notion of modesty not allergic to power, but also that it provides an enlarged definition of scientific objectivity as a local, partial and yet valuable achievement. 'The approach I am trying to work for', she states, 'is rigorously committed to testing and attesting. To engage in and understand that this is always an interpretative, engaged, contingent, fallible engagement. It is never a disengaged account' (Haraway 2000: 160). Self-consciously 'consumed by the project of materialized refiguration' (1997: 23), Haraway rethinks the position of the researcher and the critical thinker in terms of empathy and affinity. The 'modest witness' is neither detached not uncaring, but a border-crossing figure who attempts to recontextual-ize his or her own practice within fast-changing social horizons. Accepting the techno-present without falling victim to its brutality; yearning for knowledge and depth in a fast-moving infotainment-consuming culture; aspiring to social justice in a world of global inequalities are some of the ethical values embodied in Haraway's vision of the subject. Refusing hegemonic positions, while accounting for clear disparities in access and means, is a way of reformulating knowledge in a techno-scientific world. Modesty and a strong imagination are the key virtues.

A similar appeal to a secular brand of asceticism is made by Hardt and Negri in their bestselling treatise *Empire* (2000). Stressing the paradigmatic function of poverty as a counterpoint to the logic of the advanced trans-national economy, they offer a powerful figuration for it in the image of Saint Francis. This ascetic style of practising the art of philosophical think-ing is also linked to Deleuze's own idea of the social unconscious as an externally oriented, productive ethical system bent on affirmation and not on negativity, on joy and not on lack. Massumi (2002) pursues this ethical line when he calls for less arrogance and self-importance in the exercise of critical thinking in the humanities. Less competitive point-scoring and more affirmative methods would be welcome to palliate the conceptual and ethical poverty of cultural criticism. What we need to invent is both new concepts and connections among concepts. In opposi-tion to the psychoanalytic unconscious as the inward-looking entity that is dominated by the past and linguistically mediated, Deleuze stresses the extent to which unconscious forces are the flows of intensity that create feedback relations between self and reality. They propel and sustain the process of dissolution and recomposition of temporally finite moments or planes of subjectivity, until the next onrush, or shift, and the next wave. This combination of an unassuming, ascetic style of conceptual thinking and of the rejection of psychoanalytic theories results in renewed empha-sis on the notion of the affect. In opposition to the sentimentality of emo-tions, linked to the preservation of one's ego as a stable entity, the affect points to an impersonal, or rather, a transpersonal flow of intensities (Massumi 2002).

The notion of interrelationships and especially of friendship is very important here, both for Haraway, who positions herself as a feminist and a social activist, and for Deleuze, who has given ample space to his philo-sophical relationships: the extremely positive one with Felix Guattari on the one hand and the more fraught friendship with Michel Foucault on the other. In both cases, Deleuze's uncommon generosity towards these friends and partners is moving, as is his acknowledgement of all that he learned, or acquired by contamination, through them. This humble tone and serene recognition of mutual bonds is truly the opposite of the standards of virile 'friendship', or camaraderie, that are celebrated in patriarchal culture. Quite a different sensibility is at work in Deleuze's philosophical partnerships and a deep affectivity which in my opinion paves the way for materialist post-humanistic ethics.

Sexual difference revisited

Irigaray's emphasis on the 'enchanted materialism' of feminine morphology constitutes a parallel but dissonant project in relation to the nomadic anti-foundationalism of Deleuze. They both presuppose an ethics of affirmation and positive desire; they reverse the tide of dialectical negativity and interrupt the eternal return of the Same. They propose a horizontal and non-hierarchical model of transcendence as radical immanence. The ethics of sexual difference and the ethics of sustainable nomadic subjectivity are two faces of the same coin: that of an enfleshed, immanent subject-in-becoming, for whom life is embodied, embedded and eroticized. A parallel reading of Irigaray's ethics of sexual difference (and the notion of the sensible transcendental) and Deleuze's sustainable nomadic ethics (transcendental empiricism) can be mutually illuminating in so far as both practise philosophy as a conceptual art that involves both retrieval (memory) and creation (imagination). Irigaray's project centres on speaking the silence of women within the language of Man (defined as phallic spokesman). For Deleuze, the challenge is a matter of thinking processes, in-between transitions and heterogeneous becomings. Both posit subjectivity as the effect of a process, an itinerary that has no pre-appointed destination: virtual subjects in becoming.

This vision of theoretical thought has important consequences for the issue of universal values. Both Irigaray and Deleuze embody and embed the universal, according to the principle of carnal materialism. They also conceptualize the spatio-temporal space of the Relation, the interconnection among forces and entities. The universal therefore is located transversally, in the specific singularity of immanent interrelations among subjects collectively engaged in the expression and actualization of *potentia*. The intersubjective space is a laboratory of becoming.

Deleuze's anti-essentialist, high-tech vitalism echoes the ideas of Irigaray about the subject as a bodily human entity, sensitive flesh framed by the skin. Irigaray turns to non-Christian religions, notably Judaism in the philosophy of Levinas and Buddhist practices like yoga, in her more recent work to find suitable figurations of alterity. Levinas writes a defence of the caress as a mode of approaching the other: the erotic, respectful touching of the other's skin is the model for haptic gaze and the basis for an ethics of sexual difference. This respectful contemplation of the contained boundaries of an other's life – his skin-cloud, enfleshed existence – is also a response to the philosophy of excess in Bataille. In an effort to break beyond the enclosed space of the embodied self, Bataille theorizes both the inevitability of violence, and also the desirability of a transcendence that requires ontologically the consumption of an other's body. As the other's body is preferentially the body of the woman as 'other-of-the-same' – the specular, necessary and necessarily devalorized other – Bataille's theory of transcendence is also an apology of female sacrifice. Deleuze takes his distance from both Irigaray's sexual difference ethics and from Bataille's notion of transcendence. What he proposes instead is a radically immanent concept of the subject as dynamic becoming, where the bodily self is analysed according to the concrete forces or material variables that compose it and sustain it.

The model of alternative ethics proposed by radically immanent philosophies of nomadism implies a non-hierarchical idea of transcendence and a non-binary model of interrelation. This has implications for the notion of desire as *potentia*. Western culture clearly codes as 'feminine' that vitalistic, anti-essentialist power of affirmation, no matter who or where it happens to actualize itself. Of course the aim is not to affirm the feminine, but to open up fields of multiple becomings. It is nonetheless the case that the kind of style and sensibility that sustain this process are unequivocally closer to the feminine. Vitalism poses several problems to the critical thinker, because of its historical links to the organicist philosophy of European fascism. Erin Carlston (1998) argues that some elements of this fascist definition of vitalism are the mystical union of the soul with an inflated idea of Nature, a tendency to naturalistic romanticism in opposition to the brutality of industrial culture, a mistrust of the masses and a touch of aristocratic disdain and a true worship of free will in its anarchical mode. Carlston argues that both lesbianism and Jewishness became major icons of fascistic aesthetics, as symbols of degeneration.

On this as on other issues (for instance the specification of European identity), philosophical nomadism enacts the denazification of philosophy. Vitalism is too important a notion to let it freeze in its historical past as a decadent aesthetics. In order to think the anti-essentialist vitality of *zoe* in the era of advanced technologies, we need to think vitalist ideas. Nomadism de-fascisticizes them, de-misogynizes them and de-racistifies them, as it does to all the molar or sedentary formations of Western culture. The wrong answers given by fascism cannot obscure the relevance of some of the questions that were asked then and now. Vitalism is one such question and the time has come to rethink this notion in a very rigorous and up-to-date fashion.

What is at stake in sustainable ethics is not the feminine as codified in the phallogocentric code of the patriarchal imaginary, but rather the feminine as project, as movement of destabilization of identity and hence of becoming. I call this the 'virtual feminine' and I connect it to the social and symbolic project of redefinition of female subjectivity that is undertaken by feminism. This 'virtual' feminine is admirably evoked by Virginia Woolf, when she posits the hypothesis that Shakespeare had a little sister, an equally great poetess whose work never saw the light of official recognition. This figuration of symbolic absence and misery functions simultaneously for Woolf as a source of empowerment and inspiration. Her empirical existence lies in the past, yet she is as present as ever in the force of the memory and the imagination that evokes her. Moreover, the traces of her unrecognized work motivate and shape the other woman's writing and thus help shape her future. A transhistorical interconnection is drawn, a genealogical line that puts wings on Woolf's writing. This is a virtual feminine, akin to what Camilla Griggers describes as the process of becoming-woman: the actualization of potentials that are marginal to the mainstream. The becoming-woman/animal/machine/insect/imperceptible is the work of many writers who never published a line, of many silences that resonated loudly further down the historical lane. Call it memory, if you wish, but it concerns the recollection of what never was but might have been, could still be and therefore is ready to be activated. If it is still active here and now, in the continuous present of desire, than it will not have been in vain. Tuning into this requires synchronization. I return to this theme in chapter 5.

A common feature of nomadic feminists is that sexual difference is simply not a problem for them (Colebrook 2000a). This statement can be construed in several different ways and the lines of differentiation are quite significant. For instance, in what could be described as a classical exposition of Deleuzian feminism, Gatens and Lloyd (1999) argue that the political ontology of monism, which Deleuze adapts from Spinoza, offers some relevant opportunities for feminist theory. This mind–body parallelism, as opposed to Cartesian dualism, can be rendered in terms of simultaneous effects. These entail the embodiment of mind, much as the 'embrainment of matter';[2] there is only one substance: an intelligent flesh–mind–matter compound. This implies that bodily differences are both a banality and a cornerstone in the process of differentiation of variation.

The resonances between this feminist project and Deleuze's nomadism are many and many-fold. Lloyd argues that the parallelism between mind and body and the intrinsically affective or *conatus*-driven vision of the subject implies that different bodies have different degrees and levels of power and force of understanding. This has clear implications for sexual difference. Given that the mind is the actual idea of the body, sexual difference can reach into the mind as the mind is not independent of the body in which it is situated. If bodies are differently sexed, so are minds. Lloyd emphasizes the extent to which Spinoza recognizes that there are

[2] The expression was coined by John Marks.

distinctive powers and pleasures associated with different kinds of bodies, which then are enacted in different minds. Thus, a female body cannot fail to affect a female mind. Spinoza's mind is not neutral and this, according to Lloyd, has great potential for a feminist theory of female subjectivity that aims at avoiding the essentialist trap of a genuine female nature, while rejecting the idea of the neutrality of the mind. Although Spinoza accepts the traditional subordinate vision of women of his time, and thus excludes women from the polity, Lloyd is careful in pointing out the liberatory potential of Spinoza's monistic vision of the embodied nature of the mind. Its worth can be measured most effectively in comparison with the Cartesian dualistic vision of the mind–body dichotomy, which historically proved more damaging for women than his idea of the sexual neutrality of the mind. What a female nature is must consequently be determined in each case and cannot be spelled out *a priori*, because each embodied compound has its own specificity. This is because, from a neo-Spinozist perspective, embodied subjects get constituted by encountering other forces in patterns of affinity or of dissonance. This gives them very clear configurations which cannot be known in advance.

In a monistic perspective, difference need not be rendered in essentialist terms, be it biological, psychic or any other type. The fact that for Spinoza the body is intelligent matter and the mind is embodied sensibility has the advantage of bypassing the pitfalls of essentialism altogether. This offers a way out of the essentialism–constructivism impasse. Accordingly Lloyd, even more than Gatens, contemplates a non-psychoanalytic theory of sexual difference which rests on Spinoza's monism and reaches out for what I have called the 'enchanted materialism' of immanence.

Lloyd (1994) stresses the continuing relevance of sexual difference, against the theoretical illusions of an infinitely malleable, free-floating gender. Grounded and situated, sexual difference as a mode of embodied and embedded actualization of difference shapes the space–time continuum of nomadic subjectivity. Lloyd and Gatens explicitly take aim at the dualism of the sex-gender distinction, which posits a transcendent gender as the matrix that formats sex. By extension, they also expose the absurdity of any political project that would aim at 'undoing gender' (Butler 2004a). To undo gender would mean to unmake bodies, and much as this aspiration fits in with the consumeristic logic of advanced bio-capitalism, it makes very little sense politically. As Lloyd puts it:

> There is no sexless soul waiting to be extricated from socially imposed sex roles. But nor is there any authentic male or female identity, existing independently of social power.... with regard to sexual difference, there are no facts of the matter other than those produced through the shifting play of the powers and pleasures of socialized, embodied, sexed human beings. (Lloyd 1994: 168)

Thus, Lloyd argues that sexually differentiated bodies mark sexually differentiated spatio-temporal segments of subjectivity. In other words, sexual difference speaks through or is expressed in every cognitive, moral, political or other activity of the subject. Whereas Irigaray and with her the feminism of sexual difference attribute a (positive) normative value to this statement, Lloyd keeps it neutral. It is a factual statement: it is just the way things are. What does become important for both Lloyd and Gatens, however, is the extent to which this monistic vision of the subject, and its inbuilt assertion of sexual difference, allows for an enlargement of both the notion of moral agency and that of political subjectivity and more particularly of citizenship. In so far as all subjects partake of the same essence and are therefore part of nature, their common features can be located precisely in this shared capacity for affecting and for being affected. This transversality lays the grounds for a post-individualistic understanding of the subject and a radical redefinition of common humanity. The latter is an embedded and embodied collection of singularities that are endowed with common features: qualitative complexities, not quantitative pluralities.

If for Lloyd and Gatens sexual difference is not a problem in that it remains of great relevance, for Claire Colebrook it is no longer a problem, because the political and theoretical terms of the feminist debate have shifted since the days of high, or early, feminist poststructuralism. Colebrook (2000a) suggests that a younger feminist wave is looking at the question of sexual difference as not only or primarily a question that concerns the subject or the subject's body. She is very vocal in wanting to move beyond the phenomenological legacy of feminist theory and enlists Deleuze's philosophy in the attempt to bypass the quasi-transcendentalist mode of feminist theory. Colebrook stresses that for Irigaray sexual difference is clearly a metaphysical question, but in the foundational sense that it determines metaphysics as such. Sexual difference poses the question of the conditions of possibility for thought as a self-originating system of representation of itself as the ultimate presence. Thus, sexual difference produces subjectivity in general. The conceptual tool by which Irigaray shows up this peculiar logic is the notion of 'the sensible transcendental'. By showing that what is erased in the process of erecting the transcendental subject are the maternal grounds of origin, Irigaray simultaneously demystifies the vertical transcendence of the subject and calls for an alternative metaphysics. Irigaray's transcendental is sensible and grounded in the very particular fact that all human life is, for the time being, still 'of woman born' (Rich 1976).

According to Colebrook, Deleuze's emphasis on the productive and positive force of difference is troublesome for feminist theory in so far as it challenges the foundational value of sexual difference. For Irigaray, the metaphysical question of sexual difference is the horizon of feminist theory; for Grosz (1994b) it is its precondition; for Butler (1993) it is the limit of the discourse of embodiment; for Braidotti (2002) it is a negotiable, transversal, affective space. The advantage of a Deleuzian approach is that the emphasis shifts from the metaphysics to the ethics of sexual difference. Deleuze's brand of philosophical pragmatism questions whether sexual difference demands a metaphysics at all. This, for Colebrook, translates into a crucial question: 'is feminism a critical inhabitation of metaphysical closure, or the task of thinking a new metaphysics?' (Colebrook 2000a: 112). Following Deleuze's empiricism, Colebrook wants to shift the grounds of the debate away from metaphysical foundations to a philosophy of immanence that stresses the need to create new concepts. This creative gesture is a way of responding to the given, to experience, and is thus linked to the notion of the event. The creation of concepts is itself experience or experimentation. There is a double implication here: firstly that philosophy need not be seen as the master discourse or the unavoidable horizon of thought: artistic and scientific practices have their role to play as well. Secondly, given that ethical questions do not require a metaphysics, the feminist engagement with concepts need not be critical but can be inventive and creative. In other words, experimenting with thinking is what we all need to learn.

Colebrook struggles with the idea of what kind of problem sexual difference could be, if it were not defined as a question of truth, recognition, self-representation or radical anteriority. She does not come to a convincing conclusion, but this does not detract from the relevance of her project. In order to answer the question of sexual difference, one would simply have to redefine the function or status of philosophy altogether. This is a classical radical feminist statement, which situates Colebrook's third-wave feminism in a continuum with previous generations. Feminist theory does indeed challenge what we have come to recognize as thinking. Calling for an embodied philosophy of radical immanence marks the start of a bodily philosophy of relations. The body is for Colebrook an incorporeal complex assemblage of virtualities: 'The body is a relation to what is not itself, a movement or an activity from a point of difference to other points of difference. And so difference is neither an imposed scheme, nor a uniform substance, nor is difference the relation between already differentiated self-identical entities. What something is is given through the activity of differentiation' (Colebrook 2000b: 87). This is the basic meaning of the positivity of difference and it is linked to corporeality through the notion of virtual becomings. Loyal to her Deleuzian premises, Colebrook defines the ethics of sexual difference 'not as the telos of some universal law, but as the responsibility and recognition of the self-formation of the body' (Colebrook 2000b: 88). In other words, as the becoming of bodies occurs within a single substance, the question is no longer 'how are the sexes differentiated?', but rather 'how are different modalities of sexual differentiation due to the specificity of different bodies?' (Colebrook 2000b: 90). Once this question is raised, the whole issue of essentialism simply collapses.

If for Colebrook sexual difference is no longer a problem, for even younger Guattarian feminists like Luciana Parisi (2004a) it was never a problem. I briefly sketched Parisi's 'viral' brand of epistemology in chapter 3. Here I will concentrate on her position on sexual difference. Like many scholars emerging from the field of science studies, Parisi has no sympathy for or affinity with philosophies of the subject. She consequently embraces Deleuze's theory of radical immanence as a way of dismissing the subject altogether. A pragmatist, like all nomadic feminists, Parisi is committed to working out fully the implications of the current genetic revolution for the social and human sciences: 'if molecular biotechnology is already detaching femininity from the imperative of sexual reproduction and genetic sex then why would a notion of femininity be relevant to the body politics?' (Parisi 2004a: 81).

Parisi stresses the importance of the ontology of relations as the mode of differentiation between different assemblages of bodies. Bodies are traditionally predicated on organic and genetic determinants of sex. The impact of the new technologies prompts, however, new forms of inquiry at the molecular level, which question sexual difference. Parisi locates the fundamental shift in the collapse of Darwinian kinship models that come to be replaced by non-linear alternative genealogies:

> If we engage with the theory of endosymbiosis, autopoiesis and turbulent organization, modes of sex and reproduction (information transmission) are not predetermined by the economy of survival, sexual competition, selection of the fittest and passive adaptation. Modes of sex and reproduction are not subjected to a predetermined aim – such as genealogical filiation aimed at increasing progression and emancipation of humanity – but involve molecular differentiation across singular states of cellular organization. (Parisi 2004a: 80)

In other words, sexual difference functions at the molecular level of a-semiotic encodings, which defy representation and semiotic analysis. The crucial point for Parisi is the transversal nature of the codes involved in producing such micro-femininity: genetic and informational, economic and viral, cultural and bacterial. They cut across the artificial divide set by institutional divisions between the humanities and the hard sciences. The mixedness of the codes, the tools, and the schemes of analysis involved here is of the greatest importance: This is not a deconstruction of the sex–gender binarism but 'a schizogenetic constructivism of sex–gender on a nature–culture continuum' (Parisi 2004a: 80).

In a move that has become familiar in postmodern theory, Parisi reasserts the simple fact that femininity no longer coincides with real-life women's identity. Oblivious to the fact that Lacanian psychoanalysis asserted this about fifty years ago, Parisi links this insight to the current bio-technological revolution and dissolves the issue of identity accordingly. Getting rid of femininity in order to replace it with the schizoanalysis of the new dynamics of stratification and destratification of sex and reproduction is the key strategy, which Parisi borrows from vintage Deleuzian feminists like Grosz and Gatens. She also points to the incorporeal or potential becomings or capacity for assemblages as the key to the deterritorializations and to Spinozist ethics as the way to evaluate the micropolitics of becoming. Central to this project is the creative production of new affective modulations which allow for the repositioning of molecular femininities, beyond the critique of representation, in the production of micro-singularities via the potentials of the relation, the 'milieu' or middle. 'Towards a schizogenesis of sexual difference: towards the abstract construction of new modifications of sex and reproduction' (Parisi 2004b: 86), a new transversal subjectivity emerges, which takes 'others' as constitutive moments in the construction of a common plane of becoming.

TRANSPORTS: TRANSPOSING DESIRE

Throughout this argument for nomadic sustainable subjects of difference defined as production, the notion of desire has been quite prominent, both cognitively and affectively. Deleuze, the most philosophical of the post-structuralists, offers in his philosophy a fully-fledged concept of desire, with the corollary of the imagination, memory and joy. What does the positivity of desire really do for us? How does *potentia* really work? In what ways does it constitute the driving force behind the quest for sustainable ethics? In so far as desire bears a privileged link to the 'feminine', is there no desire without some sort of 'becoming-woman'?

Virginia Woolf's extensive *corpus* constitutes a perfect example of the process of becoming, and consequently of creativity, writing and desire. Woolf exemplifies not only the becoming woman/animal/world in the minoritarian mode, but also the process that is immanent to all others and hence more powerful (in the sense of *potentia*), namely the becoming-imperceptible. Woolf's 'stream-of-consciousness' style expresses with uncanny precision the seriality, as well as the radical immanence and the structural contingency, of the patterns of repetition by which differences occur.

In *The Waves*, for instance, Woolf captures the concrete multiplicity – as well as the shimmering intensity – of becoming. The sheer genius of Woolf rests in her ability to present her life as a gesture of passing through. She is the writer of multiple and intransitive becomings, in-between ages, sexes, elements, characters. Woolf's texts enact a flow of positions, a crossing of boundaries, an overflowing into a plenitude of affects where life is asserted to its highest degree. Woolf also provides Deleuze with a model for the 'plane of immanence', where different elements can encounter one another, producing those assemblages of forces without which there is no becoming. She expresses with stark intensity the pain involved in trying to synchronize the heterogeneity of life as *zoe*.

Pisters (1997) has noted that Woolf's *Orlando* reflects the dual structure of time: the linear one, comparable to Deleuze's *chronos* and the undifferentiated one, *aion*. Being and becoming confront each other in an unsteady balance. *Aion* is the 'pure empty form of time', free of content, which is shot through with vibrations of becoming. These assemblages are geographical and even meteorological because they organize space and time around them. The 'haecceity', or individuated aggregate, is the specific and highly contingent actualization of a field of forces stable enough and consolidated by their structural affinity, so as to be able to constitute a plane of immanence. The 'plane of immanence' is a layer of proliferation of differences; the moments of actualization of becoming are relational, external and collective. Woolf's prose expresses the vitalist interconnections that make the whole process of becoming into a concrete and actualized event. This process of composition and assemblage of forces is what desire is all about, as an ontological layer of affinity and sympathy between different enfleshed subjects.

Although Deleuze recognizes the extraordinary position of Woolf as a conveyor or relay point for this passionate process of becoming in both *Dialogues* (Deleuze and Parnet 1987) and *A Thousand Plateaus* (Deleuze and Guattari 1987) he is very careful to disengage Woolf's work from her being-a-woman, and even more from the 'écriture féminine' style made popular by sexual difference feminism since the 1980s. Woolf's language expresses the free indirect speech that is central to the nomadic vision of the subject as heterogeneous assemblage. Yet, something in what feminists of sexual difference like myself call the 'feminine libidinal economy' of excess without self-destruction and desire as plenitude without lack is central to the whole Deleuzian project of becoming. This is why he positions the 'becoming-woman' so prominently as a necessary moment of transition in his scheme of things, not only in his philosophy of the subject, but also in the related theories of aesthetics and art. Nonetheless, as I have argued at length elsewhere (Braidotti 1991, 2002), Deleuze cannot resolve his ambivalence towards it.

Desire, or the art of living intensely

Woolf's style and her flair for affirming positive passions provide not only a significant illustration of the functions of desire, but also for the project of an ethics of sustainability. Let me explain. Throughout Woolf's letters and diaries as well as in her fictional works, the figure of Vita Sackville-West – the real-life model for *Orlando* – looms large. What makes it particularly striking is the highly defined field of perception that she enacts and, in some ways, organizes. From their very first encounter in 1923, which was dutifully recorded in Woolf's diaries, through to the end of her life, Vita stands for a life force of mythical proportions. Clearly magnified through the lens of erotic desire, but stretching beyond the whimsical tricks of Eros, that cruel god, Vita endures in a field of her own which is one of perpetual becomings. Spatio-temporal coordinates gather around Vita, carried by her statuesque legs, the arch of her shoulders, the specific hue of her complexion: she organizes Virginia's cosmos around her. There is a specific quality of light around her, which is recorded and repeated in the diaries with mathematical precision. It has to do with the porpoise radiance and the lustre of pink and of pearls. There is an acceleration of life about Vita owing to the speed of desire, but also to the more bearable lightness of becoming. The space gets filled with warmth, with that shimmering intensity which we also find in her novels. There is a heightening of sensorial perception, the flowing of deep-seated affinity, of immense compassion, to the very end:

> Vita was here: and when she went, I began to feel the quality of the evening – how it was spring coming; a silver light; mixing with the early lamps; the cabs all rushing through the streets; I had a tremendous sense of life beginning; mixed with that emotion, which is the essence of my feeling, but escapes description. . . . I felt the spring beginning and Vita's life so full and flush; and all the doors opening; and this is I believe the moth shaking its wings in me. (Woolf, *Diary*, 16 February 1930; Woolf 1980: 287)

Virginia will remember these affects, and be able to retrieve their spatio-temporal coordinates throughout her life, even when the actual relationship with Vita has lost its brilliance. These spatio-temporal, geographical, historical and meteorological features are Vita, such as she exists on the plane of immanence where she and Virginia activate a process of becoming which goes beyond their psychological, amorous and sexual relationship. Something much more elemental, rawer, is at stake: desire draws its own ethnoscapes (Appadurai 1994).

The polymorphous vitalism of the Vita–Virginia encounter enacts the conditions for what we commonly would call desire. What I want to stress is the impersonal, or rather apersonal, nature of the interaction that is enacted in this encounter, however, and which makes it sustainable. There is a sort of geometry, a geology and a meteorology of forces that gather round the actors (V&V), but do not fully coincide with them. The reader can map out these forces, in an exercise that is an ethology of affects, or a cartography of their effects. First and foremost among these effects, the sheer pleasure, the joy, even the *jouissance*, which is but a sort of acceleration, a becoming-intense of existence: 'life so full & flush', as Woolf admirably puts it. Secondly, and in some ways more importantly, it produces writing: 'the moth shaking its wings' in Woolf's highly sensitive inner sensors. Becoming woman, animal and writing machine proceed at equal speed.

The best way to measure the intensity mobilized in this encounter and to assess the scale of its magnitude – and hence of the possible becomings it activates – is by turning to the literature itself: the letters and diaries as well as the fictional work. All of Virginia Woolf's relationships mixed work and play, life and writing, starting with Leonard himself. Vita with her looks, intensity and unconventional manners provided more fuel and of a higher quality than most. Which is not to say that the affects and the passions are functional to the production of written work. Desire is a non-profit mechanism and its contribution to meaningful production is simply the form it takes to express itself: desire is always the desire to express and to make things happen. As Elspeth Probyn puts it: 'desire here is no metaphor; it is a method of doing things, of getting places. Desire here is the mode of connection and communication between things, inevitably giving way to the literalness of things' (1996: 40).

Desire is, nonetheless, a surplus value that does ensue from the expression of affectivity and its successful encounter with other forces. It is a gift in some ways, but one that is disengaged from the political economy of exchanges regulated by phallocentrism. Virginia and Vita simply cannot help but write to, of and through each other: it is a case of addiction. Addiction to what? An addiction to 'Life', a seduction into 'Life'. To the adrenalin charge, the intensification of existence, the rush of energy that occurs in the spatio-temporal zone of their encounter. Sexuality is not the 'cause' or the driving force of this (these two women were only accidental lovers), but a mere consequence of some more fundamental shift of perspective that they operate for each other: *potentia* is activated.

Let us look at their correspondence. This is neither a biography nor a love-letter; it is the unfolding, with meticulous regularity, of the virtual layers of *potentia* contained in the encounter between Virginia and Vita. The actualization of multiple and virtual realities, possibilities such as they are perceived, recognized and amplified by that writer of genius that was Woolf. In her study of Woolf's correspondence, Catharina Stimpson (1988) argues that the epistolary genre is very specific and can best be defined as an in-between space, bringing the public and the private together. As such, they possess a fluid quality that allows the readers to catch a glimpse of the fleeting state of the writer's mind. Moreover, the letters are interactive exchanges that construct an intersubjective space with her (privileged) interlocutor. The space of the letters is an in-between, a third party that does not fully coincide with either Virginia or Vita. It rather frames the space of their relationship. Read with Deleuze, it is a space of becoming. Read with Irigaray, it is a space of mediation of the love between them. Read with Glissant, it is a poetics of relation. As a mediating factor, it organizes space and time, thus allowing each partner to take care of the relationship as a space of transition. Virginia and Vita 'write' one another into their life, and they also produce a relationship as a space of transition. They draw a space of flow and becoming through a set of 'epistolary performances' which are expressed in order to be shared in a communal, albeit volatile, communicative space. Today's equivalent would be e-mail exchanges.

Hermione Lee (1996) argues that in the relationship between Virginia and Vita 'more was asked (on both sides) than could be given' (Lee 1996: 485) and that in their intense interchange, they made each other up imaginatively. They cast each other in dramatic roles which fed their respective writing, whereby: 'Virginia was the will of the wisp, the invalid, the frail virgin, the "ragamuffin" or "scallywag", the puritan . . . Vita was the rich, supple, luxurious, high-coloured, glowing, dusky, fruity, fiery, whiny, passionate, striding, adventuring traveller, also dumb, dense, a "donkey". Virginia was the one with the head, Vita was the one with the legs' (Lee 1996: 485). These imaginary constructions were their route to intimacy. This is no metaphor, but rather a vital form of literalness: conceptual personae. The intense and deep affectivity that is expressed in these letters opens a space of freedom that allows simultaneously for experiments with different writing techniques and for depositing residual and complex emotions. These letters, as Stimpson argues,

> occupy a psychological and rhetorical middle space between what she wrote for herself and what she produced for a general audience. They are a brilliant, glittering encyclopaedia of the partially-said . . . the materials of a full autobiography of consciousness, a mediation between life and work. . . . They concern social worlds that she needed and wanted. They form an autobiography of the self with others, a citizen/ denizen of relationships. (Stimpson 1988: 130)

It is the link, the affinity, the bond of *potentia* and recognition between each of them as a complex multiplicity which results in setting the frame for the affirmation of the joyful potency of desire.

This is all the more remarkable if you consider that, in real life – the actual V&V were far from the life forces that they happened to become together. Virginia could hardly sustain, in her frail body and even more vulnerable psychic balance, the intensity of the forces that she registered, evoked and recorded: she lived on the crack. As for Vita, Virginia put her finger on it, with the disarming cruelty of her superior intelligence: 'The thing I call central transparency sometimes fails you there too.' And again: 'There's something that doesn't vibrate in you; it may be purposely – you don't let it: but I see it with other people as well as with me: something reserved, muted' (Letter of Vita to Harold, 20 November 1926; Nicolson 1992: 173).

That she hit the mark is testified by Vita's comments in her correspondence to her husband Harold Nicolson: 'Damn the woman! She has put her finger on it. There is something that . . . doesn't come alive . . . it makes everything I do (i.e.: write) a little unreal; it gives the effect of having been drawn from the outside. It is the thing which spoils me as a writer; destroys me as a poet . . . It is what spoils my human relationships too . . . (Letter of

Vita to Harold, 20 November 1926; Nicolson 1992: 173). But this fundamental opacity of Vita's soul is compensated and sustained by a feminine
magnificence about her: 'Vita very free & easy, always giving me great
pleasure to watch & recalling some image of a ship breasting a sea, nobly,
magnificently, with all sails spread & the gold sunlight on them' (Woolf,
Diary, 4 July 1927). A Deleuzian feminist reader could draw a cartography
of the affective forces that frame the encounters between Virginia and Vita,
such as they are reported in the diaries and the letters (literature and work
of remembrance) as well as in the fiction (literature and work of the imagination). Again, I want to stress the apersonal nature of the desire at work
here: it does not coincide at all with the individual biographies of the protagonists. On the contrary, it actively reinvents them as they rewrite each
other's lives, intervening energetically in its course. There is an enormous
investment of the memory and of the imagination at work in the space of
the encounter between V&V; something which mobilizes the roots of their
embodied genealogy, but transcends it: a becoming-other.

The most recurrent images that Woolf recollects from her geometrical-
geological appreciation of Vita are that of the porpoise, pink light, the
pearls; images of radiance and vitality which occur systematically throughout Woolf's writings. Vita produces a diagram that contains forces of the
utmost intensity: a quality of the light, coupled with a degree of intensity
that may alternatively generate desire or trigger an outburst of comic
laughter. Vita becomes a factor that introduces acceleration in the pulse
of life, the opening up of possibilities, like the fluttering of wings before
one takes the flight. Vita not merely represents, but actually enacts and
organizes physically as well as in writing the becoming-woman of Virginia Woolf. A becoming-woman, becoming-animal that has a distinctly
marine quality about it, so ubiquitous are the images of fluidity, flowing,
waves and sea animals. It does mark a fundamental moment in Woolf's
race against time, the 'becoming-imperceptible', which is the space where
she could finally write. Hence the importance of the non-profit space of
writing as a sort of launching pad, a legal addiction that brings on a much-
needed acceleration of life, something that propels the writer onwards
and forward. It is this 'push' that constructs simultaneously the field of
becoming and also the space for the corpus of writing. Accordingly, the
assemblage of forces that activate the becoming-Orlando of Vita requires
a careful phase of composition of forces that go through the becoming-
woman of Virginia and the becoming-lesbian of both Vita and Virginia,
but only in order to move on, to keep on becoming until that last recognition of the bond to Vita as an imperceptible and all-encompassing life
force. A pattern of de-territorialization takes place between them, which
runs parallel to and in and out of their respective and mutual existences,
but certainly does not stop there.

It will have been a joyful and towering passion, though not entirely
Virginia's or Vita's or my own, or yours. You cannot have your own 'plane

of immanence' (or of transcendence, for the phenomenologically minded) and still hold onto it. You can only share in the composition of one, in the company of others. One does not run with Woolf alone: women, even Virginia Woolf herself, must learn to run with other (s/he)-wolves. How much of it she could or could not take is the issue of sustainability, but such a question can never be settled in isolation. It is a matter for negotiations, dosages and adjustments that can only take place interactively. They mark the place of the encounter. 'Too much-ness' and hence the question of limits is as crucial in pleasure as it is in pain. Learning to dose and time it, is the alchemy of a successful relationship, which includes the successful outcome of the participants' respective lives and life-projects, as well as their mutual fulfilment. A whole world is always implicated when a plane of immanent becoming is composed. Two is quite a crowd, when one is a multiple, complex and depersonalized entity to begin with.

The real-life Vita recognizes this interdependence, much as she had acknowledged from the start her friend's superior literary genius. After reading Orlando, for which she is the model, she actually fails to cope with the shock: 'How could you hung so splendid a garment on so poor a peg? . . . Also, you have invented a new form of narcissism – I confess – I am in love with Orlando – this is a complication I had not foreseen' (Vita to Virginia, 11 October 1928 in DeSalvo and Leaska 1984: 305–6). The life that Virginia sees in her is something that Vita herself deeply aspires to. This is nothing to do with narcissistic delight – it is actually a sort of yearning on Vita's part for the potential that lies not so much in her, as in the encounter between herself and Virginia. It is simultaneously the slightly ashamed recognition of her own limitations: ('I'm not that good, really!'), and the grateful recognition of what she owes to her lover's passionate enhancement of the life that is in her ('Thank God you saw that in me!').

In other words, the relation between what in psychoanalysis is called the empirical level (the real-life Vita) and its symbolic representation (the leading character in *Orlando*) is no longer adequate to make sense of the intense transformation that takes place around the field of forces that is activated by Virginia and Vita. The empirical psychology of the two women has nothing to do with this; the psychoanalytic notion of identifications is equally inadequate to account for the magnitude of the exchange that takes place between these two high-powered subjects. This becoming is not about being faithful to the authority of past experience and the solidity of foundations. It is about inventing it together in the space that is framed by the encounter between the two of them out of the transitory flows of multiple and incoherent experiences of all kinds, speeds and intensity, spaces where transformation can occur. The life that flew between Vita and Virginia certainly was an intensified and accelerated space of becoming.

Life (*bios/zoe*) has no brand-name on it nor does it have a price-tag attached to it. It does not flow within the constraints of a phallogocentric scheme of signification that imposes its old narrative: desire as lack; alterity and/as negativity; the burden of Being that coincides with consciousness. None of this applies any longer. Psychoanalysis cannot do justice to these kinds of concrete and highly singular processes of becoming. We are better off seeing Virginia and Vita as a transversal block of becoming, a plane for the realization of forces that transcend them both and yet require their presence and affinity in order to become actualized. Forces that are concentrated, focused and activated in the space between them and aim at the fulfilment of their own *potentia*. These forces are the accelerations of pure becoming.

Three concepts are crucial here. The first concerns the irrelevance of the category 'same sex' to account for the complex and multiple affects, generated in the relation between two beings. Virginia and Vita may happen to be two morphological empirical embodied subjects, and yet the space of becoming that connects them is complex, multiple and multi-layered. A polymorphous and highly sexual text such as *Orlando* is the perfect manifesto for it. The homophobic assumption that same-sex relationships cause fusion and confusion in so far as they fail to establish sufficiently strong boundaries of alterity is flatly reflected by the experience of high-singularity and intense definition, which emerges from the encounter of Virginia with Vita. The fact that Virginia and Vita meet within this category of sexual 'sameness' encourages them to look beyond the delusional aspects of the identity ('women'), which they are alleged to share. This proliferation of differences between women and within each one of them is evident in the outcomes and the products of their relationship, be it in the literature which Virginia and Vita produced, or in the many social, cultural and political projects they were engaged in. These included marriages, motherhood and child-rearing, political activism, socializing, campaigning, publishing and working as a publisher, gardening and the pursuit of friendships, of pleasures and of hard work.

Virginia and Vita propose an ethical model where the play of sameness-difference is not modelled on the dialectics of masculinity and femininity; rather it is an active space of becoming, which is productive of new meanings and definitions. It is in this spirit that Irigaray praises the specific instance of feminine homosexuality as a moment of high symbolic significance in confirming a woman's sense of self-worth. This primary narcissism, this love of oneself as reflected in the eyes of another who is morphologically 'the same', is, according to the early Irigaray, a necessary precondition for the affirmation of a positive difference that repairs the symbolic damage suffered by women in a phallogocentric system. Colette put it just as sharply: 'le diamant se polit au diamant . . . la femme affine la femme' (Colette 1979: 82).[3]

---

[3] Translation: 'One diamond polishes another. It takes a woman to define another woman.'

This is no essentialism, but rather a molecular, transversal space of formation of collectively sustained micro-singularities.

The second remark is that the disappearance of firm boundaries between self and other, in the love encounter, in intense friendship, in the spiritual experience as in more everyday interpersonal connections, is the necessary premise to the enlargement of one's fields of perception and capacity to experience. In pleasure as in pain, in a secular, spiritual, erotic mode that combines at once elements from all these, the decentring and opening up of the individual ego coincides not only with communication with other fellow human beings, but also with a heightening of the intensity of such communication. This shows the advantages of a non-unitary vision of the subject. A depersonalization of the self, in a gesture of everyday transcendence of the ego, is a connecting force, a binding force that links the self to larger internal and external relations. An isolated vision of the individual is of hindrance to such a process, as Kathy Acker and Virginia Woolf knew all too well.

The third comment is that such sets of interconnections or encounters constitute a project, which requires active involvement and work. Desire is never a given, like a long shadow projected from the past: it is a forward-moving horizon that lies ahead and towards which one moves. Between the no longer and the not yet, desire traces the possible patterns of becoming. These intersect with and mobilize sexuality, but never stop there as they construct space and time and thus design possible worlds by allowing the unfolding of ever intensified affects. Desire sketches the conditions for the future by bringing into focus the present, through the unavoidable accident of an encounter, a flush, a sudden acceleration that mark a point of non-return. Call it falling in love, if you wish, but only if you can rescue the notion from the sentimental banality into which it has sunk in commercial culture. Moreover, if falling in love it is, it is disengaged from the human subject that is wrongly held responsible for the event. In an intensive encounter that mobilizes the sheer quality of the light and the shape of the landscape. Deleuze's remark on the grasshoppers flying in at five p.m. on the back of the evening wind also invokes non-human cosmic elements in the creation of a space of becoming. This indicates that desire designs a whole territory and thus cannot be restricted to the mere human *persona* that enacts it. We need a post-anthropocentric theory of both desire and love in order to do justice to the complexity of subjects of becoming.

Vita herself does justice to this process by accepting to become other than she is, engaging with great generosity with her own reflected image. Fulfilling the nomadic prophecy, she ends up becoming her conceptual persona: thus, she becomes a mere reader and not the main star of the process of becoming-Orlando. As she was an aristocrat and a much celebrated author in her own right, this displacement required some humility and flexibility on Vita's part, qualities in which we know that she was notoriously deficient. Yet she displays surprising skills of adaptation by letting her narcissism be gratified: 'I love myself as Orlando!', but simultaneously blown to smithereens, not only in the sense of 'I will never have been as fascinating and complex as Orlando', but also 'Orlando is the literary creation of a woman who is a much greater writer than I will ever be!'.

In the framework of an ethics of joyful affirmation, the dilemma is clear. One oscillates between positive and negative passions, gratification and resentment, gratitude and envy, as Melanie Klein would put it. Ultimately I find that Vita settles for the more ethical option because she transforms negative into positive passions and agrees to go along with the process of alchemical transformation of her own life and image, which Virginia has actualized. Vita, too, goes running with Woolves. A transcendence of negative into positive passions is needed here, a qualitative transformation of potentially destructive emotions such as competition, jealousy and envy. Without such an alchemical shift, no affect is sustainable. *Potentia* can endure only if it receives the feedback of positive and life-enhancing charges. And both Virginia and Vita want their passion to endure because it provides intensity and added meaning to their lives. It also does engender, in a non-profit manner, written work that will in turn endure.

Thus, it is Vita's shameful recognition of her failing, not the jubilant assertion of her triumph, that opens the gates through which flows the intensity that shapes the encounter between Virginia and Vita. The moment of negative passion (envy, resentment, feeling of dispossession) is the prelude to the ethical gesture that involves transcending the negativity and accepting the displacement of the self through the impact of an other that is so very close. This is a case of destitution of the ego, not of its triumphant apotheosis. This is also the ethical moment in their interaction, which rescued *Orlando* from being an act of cannibalistic consumption of the other and turns it into one of the greatest love stories of all times. Similarly, Virginia's self-effacement is crucial to the whole process of being able to sustain, provoke, record and return the life that is in Vita, amplified to the nth power. Such is the task of *potentia*, and such is the genius of Virginia Woolf's writing.

In other words, one's affirmation of the life that one is shot through with is materially embodied and embedded in the singularity that is one's enfleshed self. But this singular entity is collectively defined, interrelational and external: it is impersonal but highly singular because it is crossed over with all sorts of 'encounters' with others and with multiple cultural codes, bits and pieces of the sticky social imaginary which constitutes the subject by literally gluing it together, for a while at least. This is not an atomized individual, but a moment in a chain of being that passes on, goes through the instance of individuation but does not stop there; it moves on nomadically, by multiple becomings: *zoe* as relentless vitality.

In her interesting reading of Virginia Woolf's *Orlando*, Benhabib (1999) seems pleasantly surprised that in spite of all the flux and fluidity of Orlando's successive metamorphoses she or he does coalesce into some simple 'real' entity. Benhabib's surprise is directly proportional to the scepticism she shows towards non-unitary identities, which Benhabib sees as an 'unrealistic conception of identity' (1999: 357). Yet if, instead of conceptualizing fluid identities spatially, one also projects them temporally as moments of being (following Virginia Woolf), the coherence and the unity of the self appear as the result of repetition, of orchestrated returns. Virginia Woolf knows this not only intuitively, but also because her own psychopathology opens her eyes to the fragility of life. It also made it imperative for her to find some balance, some stability within the exhausting roller-coaster of her embodied fluctuating self. Relationships, especially her lifelong love for Vita, were simultaneously stimulants and stabilizers: points of impact that could cause internal catastrophes (strong passions, unfulfilled desires, jealousy, etc.), but also points of harmony that could engender the bliss of sustainable intensity.

Moments: spatio-temporal zones, chronotropes, fleeting and contingent. They are just enough, however, to get her through the day, through the next book, the second-last diary entry, the last letter to Vita. Just enough, till Virginia could take it no longer and decided to walk back into her liquid element: death by water. For someone who had made fluency and fluidity into more than a style, they were her mode of relation. This partiality, this fluid interactivity, is the stuff of which coherence can be made, if by coherence we do not mean the despotic solidity of a relationistic self, or the hierarchically ordained implementation of a moral agency. Coherence is a matter for *a posteriori*, external, relational and momentary synchronizations. One's ability to remember it and reconstruct is as a unified block is the necessary, albeit delusional expression of a yearning for a unity, a self-presence, which are not within the reach of the humans of today – if they ever were. Molar memory tricks us into believing that the self is a linear, self-present entity. A molecular nomadic countermemory knows, however, that this is not the case. Whereas Benhabib chooses to invest the yearning for unity while recognizing its delusional character, I choose to invest the nomadic genealogies of becoming. 'It will have been me' is the mode that best expresses the impersonality and yet also, paradoxically, the deep faithfulness of the self – a self that endures, that painfully and joyfully goes on.

That capacity to endure is collective, it is to be shared. It is held together by narratives, stories, exchanges, shared emotions and affects. It is neither equal to itself nor does it guarantee self-perpetuation. It is a moment in a process of becoming; as Virginia Woolf puts it: 'But when we sit together, close . . . we melt into each other with phrases. We are edged with mist. We make an unsubstantial territory' (1977: 11). In other words, we become other than what we were before we came close. 'I flutter I ripple. I stream like a plant in the river, flowing this way, flowing that way, but rooted, so that he may come to me' (1977: 69).

'I' is rooted, but 'I' flows.

CONCLUSION

What will the sceptic say at this point? Is it not the specific property and quality of the imagination to magnify reality, especially in situations that, as Virginia would put it, are 'not untinged with amorosity' (Woolf 1980: 51)? There is something extremely familiar and almost self-evident about these processes of transformation of the self through an other who triggers processes of metamorphosis of the self. That is precisely the point. This theory of radical immanence is very simple at heart and intuitively accessible (*pace* Banhabib). What happens is really a relocation of the function of the subject through the joining of memory and the imagination into propelling a vital force that aims at transformation. As a rigorous reader of Spinoza, Deleuze suggests a positive and equal relationship between reason and the imagination. Overthrowing the traditional hierarchy of intellectual and mental faculties, which had discriminated against the imaginative and the oneiric, he locates the *potentia* of affirmation firmly on the side of the imagination. In so doing, he produces a new theory of desire.

Deleuze speaks openly of the 'shame' of being human, in relation to Primo Levi and the issue of the Holocaust which marks the fundamental moral bankruptcy of European civilization. In this respect, Deleuze can be compared to Bauman in that he takes the Holocaust as a point of no return and is committed to elaborating an ethics that faces up to the complexities engendered by Europe's genocide. Like Bauman, Deleuze connects this ethical failure of European culture to the historical decline of an Enlightenment-inspired faith in humanism (see chapter 1). It is in response to this failure that he formulates an alternative ethics.

As Buchanan (2000) points out, shame cuts two ways. You can feel shameful about doing certain things. It may also be the case, however, that you feel too ashamed to do anything. It can be a negative passion, akin to resentment, paranoia and other internal black holes, or it can be an empowering passion, in that it motivates us to repair the failings or limitations in our human endeavours. Primo Levi's evaluation of the ethical bankruptcy of Europeans over the Nazi death camps sums up both senses of the global shame about being human. Deleuze places full emphasis on the active force of shame as a step towards an ethics of affirmation, which is for him transcendence of negativity. The sense of shame about being human encompasses not only the macro events of our culture, such as the Holocaust of the Jews, fascism, colonialism, the economic exploitation of the many by the few, but it applies just as easily to the micro instances of life on this planet. Deleuze both practised and preached an ascetic style that conceptually expresses his rejection of a morality of negative passions (guilt, envy, resentment and anger) and his commitment to positive passions (affirmation, desire, sympathy, connection). His asceticism takes the form of a critique of the thinker as the judge (or the priest) of reason and affirms instead the potency of creativity and interconnections.

As the case of Virginia and Vita shows, however, the ethical moment is not so much the ascetic withdrawal from the world of negativity, of *potestas* with its quick, short-term, hit-and-run successes. It rather rests in the act of transcending the negativity itself, transforming it into something positive. This transformation is only possible if one does not sit in judgement either upon oneself or upon others, but rather recognizes within oneself the difficulties involved in not giving into the paranoid–narcissistic self-nexus. In fact, it is only at the point of utter destitution of one's 'self' that the transformation of negativity can actually be undertaken.

This effort requires endurance – some pain and some time – but it also calls for creativity, in so far as one needs to provide precisely what one does not immediately dispose of: positive passions. They have to be created in a process of patient cultivation of and efforts towards the kind of interaction with others that is likely to generate productive ethical relations. A pragmatic, active approach is needed. The ethical life is not given; it is a project, as I will argue in the next chapter. The conditions that allow for this creation must be immanent and depend on external circumstances, and therefore on others. They also call for an internal disposition of self-irony, a non-tragic sense of one's failings. One has to think the unthinkable and imagine the unimaginable. In other words, one has to contemplate the unedifying spectacle of one's failings or shortcomings. Over and against centuries of established logocentric philosophy which compel us to fill the Lack by rationalistic overcompensation and in opposition to the ideology of melancholia, one then has to have the courage to sit on the verge of the abyss, look into it and let other forces come to the rescue. The best part of this exercise is when they inevitably do.

Affirmation, the result of a process of transformation of negative into positive passions, is essentially and intrinsically the expression of joy and positivity. This is constitutive of the *potentia* of the subject. Such potency, however, is a virtuality, which needs to be materialized in very concrete, embodied conditions of expression. Bringing about such movements or mass of affectivity is crucial to the process of becoming as actualization. Deleuze's becomings are not successive drifts into repetitions for their own sake. It is rather the unfolding multiplicities that aim at self-expression. It is a question of finite wholes, capable of enduring, or of sustaining their actualized form, for a certain amount of time. 'Finite wholes' are thresholds of sustainability: forces that manage to assemble and combine, for a while. They are collective becomings, which involve a selective sort of plurality. They assemble by relations of positivity or affinity with other forces and they insist or persist in becoming.

Instead of judgemental self-imposed distance there are transpositions, which I understand as the active effort to reconnect oneself to the web of social exchanges, after one has subtracted oneself from their more destructive interrelational effects. The ethical moment consists in overcoming the slight sense of shame, the ethical nausea that marks the recognition of the intrinsically negative structure of one's passions. In other words, the ethical act consists in relinquishing the paranoid–narcissistic ego and installing instead an open-ended, interrelational self.

This is related to the point about death, which I will raise in the next chapter. If it is the case that the subject's innermost desire is to disappear, then death cannot be a merely negative event. The ethical moment consists in reaffirming *potentia*, even through one's death, thus cultivating an empowering sense of interconnection. Becoming imperceptible means becoming one with a 'Nature'– a living environment – which never ceases to grow and flow. This amounts to declaring that eternity is not an option, but also that *zoe* as a relentlessly generative force is immortal.

Left to itself, the sense of shame about humanity can breed negative effects such as misanthropy, fear and anger. This would defeat the purpose of this materialist ethics by reinstating negative passions. It is the empowerment of the positive side that marks the ethical moment of transformation, the reversal of the negative dialectic and its eternal repetitions, the transcendence of one's starving ego. What matters most is the process by which the transformation takes place, which is neither painless nor self-evident. Desire is the driving force, as Jeanette Winterson put it. You must play on: you win, you play, you lose, you play, you play. Hence the importance of literature, the arts, theatre, music and film. They do not fulfil merely an illustrative function, but they are the privileged field of application for the kind of conceptual creativity that Deleuze would like to make operative also within philosophy. What is expressed as a result of this process is a force of affirmation, the potency of a joy that goes beyond the metaphysical divide of sexual or other forms of differentiation. And yet, the affirmation of that life force requires, as its inalienable and inevitable starting point, the process of becoming-woman. It requires it of Virginia and Vita, as it does of Deleuze and any of his readers.

The benefits of such a relation are elsewhere and of an altogether different nature than the terms that compose it. The desire and the flair for *potentia* is a way of stretching the subject to the outer boundaries of his or her capacity to endure, pushing them open so that they turn into thresholds of becoming. Another name for this process is in-depth transformations or metamorphoses. Being or not being able to take it, becoming speechless with it all, is the beginning of wisdom and of affirmation. What it expresses is the depth of interconnection that makes us into subjects.

Paradoxically, this requires also the recognition of the impersonality of the many forces that compose us. Sustaining them, so as to endure positive changes, is the key political and ethical concern of an era of transition like ours. Finding adequate representation for these processes is a challenge for all thinking beings. One that is best met not by critique, but by taking the risk of creativity. A risk that may involve the kind of cognitive and affective stutter that shatters all uncertainties and opens the doors of perception to multiple lines of unexpected possibilities. Changes of this magnitude mark qualitative shifts and internal forms of mobility. They can happen anytime, anywhere and whenever subjects become events, or assemblages. Then Virginia Woolf's moth flutters its wings and 'Life' rushes onto you with intensive, untimely and unending vitality.

5

Transcendence: Transposing Death

I meant to write about death, only life came breaking in as usual.
Virginia Woolf, *Diary*, 17 February 1922

And we can feel shame at being human in utterly trivial situations, too:
in the face of too great a vulgarization of thinking, in the face of TV
entertainment, of a ministerial speech, of 'jolly people' gossiping. This
is one of the most powerful incentives towards philosophy.
Gilles Deleuze, *Negotiations*

If a phoenix can arise from ashes, why should a book not nurture the
next generation of mice?
Stephen Jay Gould and Rosamond Wolff Purcell, *Crossing Over*

In this chapter, I will explore further the concept of sustainable ethics,
with reference to my project of nomadic subjectivity as eco-philosophy of
the subject. The urge that prompts this investigation is not only abstract,
but also very practical. Nomadic philosophy mobilizes one's affectivity
and enacts the desire for in-depth transformations in the status of the kind
of subjects we have become. Such in-depth changes, however, are at best
demanding and at worst painful processes. My political generation, that
of the baby-boomers, has had to come to terms with this harsh reality,
which put a check on the intense and often fatal impatience that characterizes those who yearn for change.

We lost so many of our members to dead-end experimentations of the
existential, political, sexual, narcotic, or technological kind. Although it is
true that we lost as many if not more of our members to the stultifying
inertia of the status quo – a sort of generalized 'Stepford wives' syndrome
– it is nonetheless the case that I have developed an acute awareness of
how painful, dangerous and difficult changes are.

This is not meant as a deterrent against them. On the contrary: the
political climate in the current social context has placed undue emphasis
on the risks involved in changes, playing *ad nauseam* the refrain about the

death of ideologies. Such a conservative reaction aims at disciplining the citizens and reducing their desire for the 'new' to docile and compulsive forms of consumerism. Nothing could be further removed from my project than this approach. I simply want to issue a cautionary note: processes of change and transformation are so important and ever so vital and necessary, that they have to be handled with care. The concept of ethical sustainability addresses these complex issues. We have to take pain into account not only as an obstacle to, but also as a major incentive for, an ethics of changes and transformations. This shift of ethical perspective rests on a vision of the knowing subject in terms of affectivity, interrelationality, territories, resources, locations and forces. In so doing, we shall take our final leave from the spatio-temporal continuum of classical humanism, though not necessarily from its ideals. Equally positively, distance is established from the reductions of social constructivism, which underplays the continuity of the nature–culture continuum and hence misconstrues the embodied foundations of the subject.

'How do you make people *want* to be free, generous, decent and caring?' is the perennial question at the core of both ethics and politics. Not rationality, but rather affectivity counts here; it is a question of 'wanting to', of desire. That implies that the crucial mechanism by which the subject operates is the expression of his or her innermost core that is affectivity and the capacity for interrelations. Nomadic ethics is political in the sense that it involves social relations; it addresses the issue of power as both *potestas* and *potentia* and it foregrounds the quest for interactive de-territorializations. This micro-political level is an embodied and embedded form of activism that contrasts with the return of overarching master narratives both on the Right (neo-liberalism and the genetic social imaginary) and on the Left (the revolutionary multitudes) of the political spectrum.

The nomadic ethico-political project focuses on becomings or transformations as a pragmatic philosophy that stresses the need to act, to experiment with different modes of constituting subjectivity and of relating to alterity. Which, in a philosophy of radical immanence, means different ways of inhabiting our corporeality. It is crucial to adopt a rigorous stance in order not to romanticize philosophical nomadism as an anarcho-revolutionary philosophy, but to keep in mind the ascetic style it cultivates, as I argued in chapter 4. Accordingly, nomadic politics is not about a master strategy, but rather about multiple micro-political modes of daily activism or interventions on the world.

Whatever gets you through the day

Sustainability or beyond social constructivism

In the age of bio-power and genetic engineering, of the Seattle anti-WTO movement, of 'new' wars of all kinds (including a mutant variant called 'humanitarian wars'), in the background of impending ecological disaster and with growing evidence for the extent of environmental degradation, the idea of 'sustainability' can be rightfully considered as mainstream. Having been accepted as a policy guideline or norm, however, 'sustainability' has predictably lost out in terms of both focus and incisiveness. Born as a critique of the theories and contradictory practices of 'development', both in the academy and outside, 'sustainability' soon evolved into what Egon Becker and Thomas Jahn have defined as a set of 'internationally accepted keywords for a political discourse committed to quality of life, the conservation of natural resources and a sense of obligation to future generations' (1999: 1). This notion focuses not only on the status of developing countries, but also on the 'limits of growth' in Western industrialized countries. The latter calls into question the limits of scientific and technological development, as well as a drastic critique of consumerism and economic exploitation. It specifically challenges the equation between development and economic growth.

According to Ignacy Sachs's witty formulation, 'sustainability' started originally as a debate between 'the doomsayers (apocalypse tomorrow, due to exhaustion of resources and/or by asphyxia from pollution) and the cornucopians (exponential growth of GNP extrapolated for centuries to come)' (Sachs 1999: 26). The notion of sustainability received its official definition in the Brundtland Report (1987), *Our Common Future*, which outlines four major components within this visionary concept: ecological, economic, social and cultural sustainability. The basic principles of sustainability are: inter-generational and intra-generational equity, so that present and future generations can inherit a liveable planet; the conservation of biodiversity, so that all species can prosper and endure; and the emphasis on the precautionary principle, which states that in case of doubt about the possible environmental implications of some projects, caution should definitely prevail. Sustainability implies therefore strong strategic and political concerns about the geopolitics of power. It also opens up the question of a planetary responsibility for the future, which intersects with discussions of global citizenship and governance.

Sustainability emerges consequently as a central concept in social theory and it raises suitably complex questions of methodology. One of the theoretical challenges here is how to think in terms of processes, not of entities or single substances, at both the social and the symbolic levels. Interdisciplinarity is an issue, but the very boundaries between the various disciplines also get questioned and need to be re-examined both conceptually and methodologically. New forms of cross-disciplinary cooperation seem absolutely necessary, as well as a form of 'self-reflexive transdisciplinarity' (Becker and Jahn 1999:13). 'Sustainability' as a concept in the social sciences, social theory and philosophy, can function as a bridge-builder which draws together areas of study that are not often connected. As such, it raises issues of ethical and political concern and value, which are best approached within the general framework of philosophical nomadism.

Sustainability attempts to come to terms with the complex, hybrid structure of contemporary social problems. Phenomena such as the environmental crisis, which is linked to technological development and to the techno-teratological social imaginary that sustains it (Braidotti 2002), or the loss of political energy and hope for progressive politics after the return of the master narratives, cannot be dealt with in the conventional language and methodology of social philosophy and of the social sciences. They are transversal phenomena that call into question a cluster of factors and of multiple effects. Thinking at the intersection of different domains, in terms of processes and interrelations, and trying to represent the ever speeding rate of transformations, are the main challenges thrown open by the issue of sustainability. Central among the lines that structure this 'hybrid' is the relationship between the natural and the social, the embodied and embedded material foundations of 'life' and the social and symbolic forms of mediation that sustain them (or not). A new unity is imposed on our ways of thinking, by the problems created by our very historicity. How to rethink the singular complexity of this unity is the challenge. The social and the natural are related but heterogeneous notions within a structure of mediation that is historically shaped. As such, they are internally differentiated and process-oriented. The assumption is that nature cannot be addressed apart from social practices of appropriation, perception and symbolization, but that nature is also more than that and different from any other social construction. 'We' are in *this* together.

Strategically, this condition of mutual dependence on a nature–culture continuum places an extra burden on critical theory to track the mutations and the constant flows or fluctuations, but one which meets with a double challenge. The first comes from the corporatist resistance against this fragmented vision of the subject on the part of many philosophers in the areas of both epistemology and moral philosophy. So much time wasted in polemics has delayed a more reasoned confrontation of genuine theoretical differences, as I argued in chapter 1. Contrary to the arrogance of Sokal and Bricmont, Becker and Jahn offer a far more intelligent and hence humble option. They argue that more methods of the natural sciences can be useful to understand the complex materiality of 'Life', provided they do not claim complete objectivity and contest independent truths. The best approach is a combination of transdisciplinary analytical tools. The second challenge is of a different nature as it concerns the methodological difficulty of accounting for a web of fast-changing, interrelated and yet potentially contradictory power effects related to *bios/zoe*, or 'Life'. More specifically, serious methodological issues emerge in trying to deal with the illogical, non-linear and often quite simply irrational structures of advanced, post-industrial systems and their networks of power.

This calls not only for a higher degree of transdisciplinarity, but also for a revision of the very category of subjectivity that underscores them. A non-unitary, open, dynamic subject in or of becoming is a far more adequate point of reference in the cartography of contemporary power-relations, than the unitary, humanistic vision of a fixed and self-transparent subject. A new community needs to be engendered, which cuts across the internal divides between scientific disciplines, but also the larger divide that separates science from other intellectual endeavours, artistic projects and community-based actions. A new model of kinship is needed, which moves beyond the subject–object distinction imposed by classical rational thought and induces instead new forms of empathy, a new sense of connection. Above all, more conceptual creativity is called for.

Sustainability is an ethics of affirmation which involves the transformation of negative into positive passions: resentment into affirmation, as Nietzsche put it. The notion of *amor fati* is crucial here: we have to be worthy of what happens to us and rework it within an ethics of relation. Of course, repugnant and unbearable events do happen. Ethics consists, however, in reworking these events in the direction of positive relations. Edouard Glissant provides a perfect example of this productive ethics in his work on race and racism, which I analysed in chapter 2. An ethical relation cannot be based on resentment or resignation, but rather on the affirmation of positivity. Every event contains within it the potential for being overcome and overtaken – its negative charge can be transposed. The moment of the actualization is also the moment of its neutralization. 'Every event is like death, double and impersonal in its double,' argues Deleuze (1990: 152). The free subject, the ethical subject is the one with the ability to grasp the freedom to depersonalize the event and transform its negative charge.

The point about life, as *zoe*, is that its monstrous energy transforms and transposes, hence it also destroys. 'Of course', argues Deleuze, 'all life is a process of breaking down' (1990: 154). This is expressed through the concept of the crack, the visible or invisible mark of unsustainability: the alcoholic, the drug-addict, the depressed or the burnt-out cruise on the crest of the wave of cracking-up. To dismiss these practices as merely self-destructive is to miss the point.

The point for nomadic processes of transformation is that perfectly good health is not only a rather unusual state, but also a rather precarious one. What is far more frequent and common is to be rather in average or poor health. Buchanan defines the concept of 'good health' in Deleuze in terms of 'the actual measurable capacity to form new relations, which can always be increased, and the concomitant determination of whether or not the newly formed relations between bodies lead to the formation of new compounds, or the decomposition of already existing ones' (Buchanan 1997: 82). According to this ethics of affirmative becoming, healthy relations are those which ensure a possible future. Unhealthy on the other hand are those relations which lead to the decomposition of the old relations without possible future lines of development. In my language, only the former are sustainable.

Elizabeth Grosz (1999a) stresses that in contrast to normalizing and homologizing practices and understandings of this notion in mainstream culture, 'health' expresses the body's capacity to continuing to enter relations and experience affects. This ability is a virtue in that it banks on and actively promotes a future. It is enduring and sustainable: it does go on. An unsustainable relation, on the other hand, stops the flow of relations to others and as a result the subject encounters the state of termination of its intensity. Given that intensity is the body's fundamental capacity to express its joy, positivity and desire, as I indicated in the previous chapter, to put a stop to it marks the death of desire. In the ethics of sustainable nomadic subjects, 'unhealthy' states are those which kill the affirmative powers of expression of positive passions (*potentia*). In other words, they are not sustainable and do not endure. By failing to endure, they short-circuit the possible future, that is to say: they do not actualize its virtual stock. The transcendental empiricism of the non-unitary subject is such that becoming is a forward-looking activity. The joyful expression of becoming is a way of writing the prehistory of possible futures, that is to say to take care of the unfolding of possible worlds.

In other words, futurity or possible futures are built into the logic of sustainable affirmative interrelations. The point is to allow the embodied self to express its powers of affirmation, by increasing his or her capacity to be affected and to affect in the positive sense of sustaining enriching encounters. This is not utopian, but rather a rigorous geometry of positive passions that expresses confidence in the sustainability of liveable futures.

On addiction

Practices that are commonly regarded as self-destructive, such as anorexia and bulimia, drugs, alcoholism, masochism, etc., are important for philosophical nomadism, though not in a moralistic or even normative mode. They rather express and bring to the point of implosion the complexities and inbuilt paradoxes of nomadic embodiment. As Buchanan points out: 'The major achievement of this reconfiguration is its opening the way for cultural analysts to think these practices of self for themselves, instead of interpreting them according to the dictates of a previously stipulated clinical condition' (Buchanan 1997: 75). By de-pathologizing these allegedly 'extreme' clinical cases, we can approach them not so much as indicators of disorder, but as markers of a standard condition, namely the human subjects' enfleshed exposure to the irrepressible and at times hurtful vitality of life (*zoe*) and hence also the familiarity with or proximity to the crack, the line of unsustainability. 'Flesh is only the thermometer of becoming. The flesh is too tender. The second element is not so much bone or skeletal structure, as house or framework. The body blossoms in the house' (Deleuze and Guattari 1992: 179). On a more positive note, they also express the subject's propensity for affective interaction and involvement with others. This is a complex issue, which connects states of heightened intensity to both thresholds of sustainability and the quest for adequate forms of expression. It is the very intensity of affectivity that often makes us implode into the black hole of negative, ego-indexed forces, which are likely to hurt the embodied entity. This is where drug users, alcoholics, anorexics and workaholics implode and self-destroy.

Deleuze discusses his own addiction to drinking extensively in *The Logic of Sense* with a praiseworthy degree of lucidity and unsentimentality. He also tracks down examples and accounts of addictions through 'high' cultural products, mostly literary works by Zola, Artaud and Blanchot. He rests on Blanchot's double structure of death as both personal and impersonal. In *The Instant of My Death*, Blanchot (2000) addresses the paradox of the impersonality of death. Death is implacable in its presence and immanent to every human life; we start dying from the word 'go'.

This does not mean, however, that life unfolds on the horizon of death. This classical notion is central to the metaphysics of finitude that, especially in the Heideggerian tradition, sacralizes death as the defining feature of human consciousness. I want to stress instead the productive differential nature of *zoe*, which means the productive aspect of *bios/zoe*. This is in opposition to Agamben who refers to 'bare life' as the negative limit of modernity and the abyss of totalitarianism that constructs conditions of human passivity. This point can be made all the more explicit if one compares Agamben's line on the horrors of modernity to the far more productive position taken by Edouard Glissant on this very same topic, starting from the transposition of the experience of slavery. The ethics of productive affirmation are quite a different way of handling the issue of how to operate in situations which are no less extreme, while bringing out the generative force of *zoe*.

Nothing could be further removed form the affirmative position of philosophical nomadism. In this perspective, death is not the teleological destination of life, a sort of ontological magnet that propels us forward: death is rather behind us. Death is the event that has always already taken place at the level of consciousness. As an individual occurrence it will come in the form of the physical extinction of the body, but as event, in the sense of the awareness of finitude, of the interrupted flow of my being-there, death has already taken place. We are all synchronized with death – death is the same thing as the time of our living, in so far as we all live on borrowed time. The time of death as event is the impersonal ever-present *aion*, not the individualized *chronos*. It is the time span of death in time itself, the totality of time.

This means that what we all fear the most, our being dead, the source of anguish, terror and fear, does not lie ahead but is already behind us, it has been. This death that pertains to a past that is forever present is not individual but impersonal; it is the precondition of our existence, of the future. This proximity to death is a close and intimate friendship that calls for endurance, in the double sense of temporal duration or continuity and spatial suffering or sustainability. Making friends with the impersonal necessity of death is an ethical way of installing oneself in life as a transient, slightly wounded visitor. We build our house on the crack, so to speak. We live to recover from the shocking awareness that this game is over even before it started. The proximity to death suspends life, not in transcendence, but rather in the radical immanence of just a life, here and now, for as long as we can and as much as we take.

Death frees us into life. Each of us is always already a 'has been'; we are a mortal being. Desire (as *potentia*) seduces us into going on living. Living just a life, therefore, is a project, not a given. If sustained long enough, it becomes a habit; if the habit becomes self-fulfilling, life becomes addictive, which is the opposite of necessary or self-evident, or even pleasurable. Life is beyond pleasure and pain – it is a process of becoming, of stretching the boundaries of endurance. There is nothing self-evident or automatic about life. It is not a habit, though it can become an addiction. One has to 'jump-start' into life each and every day; the electromagnetic charge needs to be renewed constantly. There is nothing natural or given about it.

Life, in other words, is an acquired taste, an addiction like any other, an open-ended project. One has to work at it. Life is passing and we do not own it, we just inhabit it, as a time-share location. I live in a world where some people kill in the name of the 'right to life'. Thus, in contrast to the mixture of apathy and hypocrisy that marks the habits of thought that sacralize 'life', I would like to cross-refer to a somewhat 'darker' but more lucid tradition of thought that does not start from the assumption of the inherent, self-evident and intrinsic worth of 'life'. On the contrary, I would like to stress the traumatic elements of life in their often unnoticed familiarity.

Deleuze connects the double structure of death to the crack, the line of addiction to the incorporeal, or becoming, but also to the thick materiality of a body that perishes. This generates an ethical line of reasoning which involves two elements. Firstly, a transposition of the issue of ethics in terms of what a body can do. This entails a reflection on the limits and thresholds of the processes of becoming, defined as actualizations of incorporeal or virtual possibilities. Secondly, this process displaces the subject of the ethical relation by making him or her an active participant in a process, not an evaluator of human failings. This requirement is all the more stringent for the philosopher who rejects the Kantian model of the judge or priest and replaces it with that of nomadic interaction with fellow others. Deleuze addresses this ethical dilemma in relation to the problem of alcoholism, of which he fully partakes:

> Well then, are we to speak always about Bousquet's wound, about Fitzgerald's and Lowry's alcoholism, Nietzsche and Artaud's madness while remaining on the shore? Are we to become the professionals who give talks on these topics? Are we to wish only that those who have been struck down do not abuse themselves too much? Are we to take up collections and create special journal issues? Or should we go a short way further to see for ourselves, be a little alcoholic, a little crazy, a little suicidal, a little of a guerrilla – just enough to extend the crack, but not enough to deepen it irremediably? Wherever we turn, everything seems dismal. Indeed, how are we to stay at the surface, without staying on the shore? (Deleuze 1990: 157–8)

Deleuze swims away from the shore to explore this issue. Approached rigorously, within the geometry of affects and the philosophy of time as sustainable becoming, alcoholism means a tightening up and hence a reduction of the flow of time: a fixation. It is not a search for pleasure, but an escape from it, which induces a hardening of the present: the memories of the sober life turn into the 'outside' of the alcoholic state. The hard past becomes the soft core of an unbearable present: 'the alcoholic does not live at all in the imperfect or the future; the alcoholic has only a past perfect – albeit a very special one', he has loved, he has lived, he is and has been (1990: 158). More importantly, he has drunk. This convergence of a hard past and a soft present totalizes the alcoholic's experience of time into a manic sense of omnipotence: 'the present has become a circle of crystal or of granite, formed about a soft core, a core of lava, of liquid or viscous glass' (Deleuze 1990: 158).

This tension also swallows the act itself. The alcoholic 'has drunk' always in the past perfect mode. He experiences his condition as the effect of an effect, always already lost. The present escapes the alcoholic and defies the imaginary identifications with his actual state. The past has fled, or is rather suspended in a fast-fading present and 'in the new rigidity of this new present in an expanding desert' (Deleuze 1969: 159). The present perfect expresses the infinite distance between the present (I have) and the effect of the flight of the past (drunk). This results in the loss of the object itself, in every sense and direction. This loss is at the heart of the depressive mood of alcoholism. Whereas in the affirmative ethical stance, the awareness that death has already occurred triggers the desire to live and make friends with the abyss, in negative states the horizon of time gets frozen in fear, anxiety and despair. The present perfect engenders no possible future, but rather implodes into a black hole. Every drink is the second last – and the next one never comes in the mode of presence. It can only be given as a has been. This effect goes on till the end, till death. Death is the last drink. That drink which coincides with the act and the perception of the act: that is the instant when death as event coincides with your being dead, with physical extinction.

This is why alcoholism is an addiction to life, not the courting of death: it determines the need to drink anew and drink again. Or rather 'of having drunk anew' (Deleuze 1990: 160), in order to triumph over the present that only signifies and subsists in death. The present is experienced as having been, as perpetual loss. It is a process of orchestrated demolition of the self – a long deep crack. The ethical position with relation to alcoholism, as in other similar states of self-destruction, is to take equal distance from two related pitfalls. One is the moralistic condemnation in the name of a belief in the intrinsic value of life. The other is the altruistic compassion for what is perceived as the alcoholic's inability to make something of him- or herself. Both miss the point that states of alleged self-destruction are a subject's way of coping with life; they are modes of living. This assumes that life is defined as *zoe* and hence as a negotiation with the line of cracking up. A nomadic ethics of sustainable becomings acknowledges this state and makes a powerful case for positive or affirmative states. It avoids, however, both normative injunctions and empathic condescension. It affirms with calm rigour that there is nothing compelling or necessary about life and staying alive, while strongly urging the subject to cultivate the kind of relations that can help us to develop sustainable paths of becoming, or possible futures.

The point for Deleuze is that poor health, or a dose of cracking up, is actually necessary for both ethical relations and the process of serious thinking. Thought is the shield against and the surfing board that rides the crest of the cracking wave. Marguerite Duras, a life-long alcoholic, knows this well. The message is clear and Deleuze sums it up as follows: 'better death than the health which we are given' (Deleuze 1990: 160). This is not self-destruction, this is a way of honouring and enduring life in its often unbearable intensity.

The ethical position is affirmative: we must endure the longest and not lose sight of the 'great health', which is not a question of survival (survival is a basic and minimal condition and hence cannot form the basis for an ethical relation). Ethics is rather a question of expanding the threshold of what we can endure and hence sustain, while not avoiding the effects of the crack upon the surface of our embodied selves. The crack is for Deleuze the indicator of poor health: the pain that necessarily accompanies the process of living under the overwhelming intensity of Life. Great(er) health would be the process of going to the extreme limit, without dying, but exploding the boundaries of the self to the uttermost limit. This point of evanescence of the self – to which I will return later on in this chapter – is also the experience of eternity within time, or becoming imperceptible.

The event is inscribed in the flesh, which is the thermometer of becoming. We must therefore labour towards the counter-actualization of painful events – *zoe* leaves its scars. 'We must accompany ourselves – first, in order to survive, but then even when we die' (Deleuze 1990: 161). This is a form of experimentation: 'It is to give to the crack the chance of flying over its own incorporeal surface area, without stopping at the bursting within each body; it is, finally, to give us the chance to go farther than we would have believed possible' (Deleuze 1990: 161). Ethics is about new incorporeal becoming, not new 'revelations', but the stretching of the thresholds of sustainability. Ethics is a matter of experimentation, not of control by social techniques of alienation.

The crack designates the generative emptiness of Death, as part of *zoe* and the swarming possibilities it expresses. The overcoming of Death as silence by an active frequentation of the line of cracking-up is, for Deleuze, the work of thought. We think to infinity, against the terror of insanity, through the horror of the void, in the wilderness of mental landscapes fit only for werewolves. We think with the shadow of death dangling in front of our eyes. Thought, however, is a gesture of affirmation and hope for sustainability and endurance not in the mode of liberal moderation, but rather as a radical experiment with thresholds of sustainability. This refers back to the point I made in chapter 2, about the necessity to acknowledge and feel compassion for pain and those who suffer it, but also to work through it. Moving beyond the paralysing effects of pain on self and others, working across it, is the key to nomadic sustainable ethics. It does not aim at mastery, but at the transformation of negative into positive passions. Putting the 'active' back into activism has an ethical, as well as a political dimension.

In other words, for the ethics of sustainability, it is always and already a question of life and death. Being on the edge of too-muchness, or of unsustainability, surfing on the borders of the intolerable is another way of describing the process of becoming. Becoming marks in fact a qualitative leap in the transformation of subjectivity and of its constitutive affects. It is a trip across different fields of perception, different spatio-temporal coordinates; mostly, it transforms negativity into affirmative affects: pain into compassion, loss into a sense of bonding, isolation into care. It is simultaneously a slowing down of the rhythm of daily frenzy and an acceleration of awareness, connection to others, self-knowledge and sensory perception.

Thinking is a creative acceleration; speed as heightened intensity and capacity to affect and be affected. When dosed correctly it can lead to shifts in one's sense and orientation in the world. This is akin to Huxley's drug-induced hope of throwing open the doors of perception. Drugs are accelerators. They achieve nothing that cannot be achieved by normal means. They are just considerably faster. Thinking is also a way of increasing the intensity of Life. The brain, after all, manufactures its own adrenaline. Contrary to pharmaceutical drugs, however, mental accelerations produce a humble process, like a quickening of one's perception, a being-there with and for other entities, forces, beings, so as to be transported fully into the magnificent chaos of life. It cracks open the shield of tedium and predictability in which we wrap ourselves up in order to get through the day.

The ethics of sustainability aims at making these processes of becoming into productive, life-enlarging events. Keep in mind that 'Life', in this context, is to be disengaged from the trappings of Christian morality, as much as from the deterministic certainties of genetic science. 'Life' is *bios/zoe* combined in flows of becoming. This implicit positivity is important in itself because it provides the sense of limits beyond which the potency of becoming cannot be sustained and thus collapses. It also implies, however, some added value in terms of existential performance. Sustainable ethics is really an ascetic kind of rule, which rests on a firm commitment to the principle of non-profit in the running of one's own life. This does not mean that one is not productive or useful to society, but simply that one refuses to accumulate. Stocking up and cashing in on the built-up capital of selfhood is the model of liberal individualism, which I criticized in chapter 1. The individual is a profit-minded entity; the nomadic subject, on the other hand, is strictly non-profit in that it gives itself away in a web of multiple belongings and complex interactions. Gratuitousness or non-profit, however, does not equate self-destruction. Succeeding in one's existential exploits is part and parcel of the project of finding and sustaining one's limits and, as such, it requires priority, attention and critical scrutiny.

It is indeed the case that, if *potentia* or joyful, affirmative energy suffers, the room for affirmative expression shrinks and negative passions fold in upon the subject, diminishing or even restraining him or her. These are all powerful indications of limits that should not be trespassed. Mutations, yes, but not into the nihilism of some of the 'narco-philosophers' of today, like Baudrillard, who celebrate altered states of simulation for their own sake. Nomadic subjectivity is a field of transformative affects whose availability for changes of intensity depends firstly on the subject's ability to sustain encounters with and the impact of other forces or affects. I am defending here a radically materialist, anti-essentialist vitalism attuned to the technological era, which could not be further removed from the illusion of eternal youth, perfect health and social success which is marketed by contemporary culture. The genetic multiplication of virtual embodiments promised by techno-culture boosts this imaginary. The nomadic, enfleshed, vitalist but not essentialist vision of the subject is a self-sustainable one that owes a great deal to the project of an ecology of the self. As I argued in chapter 4, the rhythm, speed and sequencing of the affects as well as the selection of the forces are crucial to the process of becoming. It is the pattern of reccurrence of these changes that marks the successive steps in the process, thus allowing for the actualization of forces that are apt to frame and thus express the singularity of the subject. Thinking through the body, and not in flight from it, means confronting boundaries and limitations and living with and through pain (Sobchack 1995).

Of limits as thresholds

The notion of 'life' as a vital force is crucial to the discussion of both health and the limit in philosophical nomadism.[1] Life is cosmic energy, simultaneously empty chaos and absolute speed or movement. It is impersonal and inhuman in the monstrous, animal sense of radical alterity: *zoe* in all its powers. Nomadic subjectivity loves *zoe* and sings its praises by emphasizing active, empowering forces against all negative odds. *Zoe*, or life as absolute vitality, however, is not above negativity and it can hurt. It is always too much for the specific slab of enfleshed existence that single subjects actualize. It is a constant challenge for us to rise to the occasion, to practise *amor fati*, to catch the wave of life's intensities and ride it on, exposing the boundaries or limits as we transgress them. We often crack in the process and just cannot take it anymore. The sheer activity of thinking about such intensity is painful because it causes strain, psychic unrest and nervous tension. If thinking were pleasurable, more humans may be tempted to engage in this activity. Accelerations or increased intensities of the intellectual or other kind are, however, that which most humans prefer to avoid.

Crucial to this ethics of affirmation is the concept of limit. For Spinoza and Deleuze the limit is built into the affective definition of subjectivity. Affectivity in fact is that which activates an embodied subject, empowering him or her to interact with others. This acceleration of one's existential speed, or increase of one's affective temperature, is the dynamic process of becoming. Because of this, it follows that a subject can think/understand/do/become no more that what she or he can take or sustain within his or her embodied, spatio-temporal coordinates. This deeply positive understanding of the human subject posits built-in, bio-organic limitations. It also inscribes diversity at the level of *potentia*, of what one is capable of: the degree, speed and extension of one's power to interact and produce affirmative ethical relations with others. Humans differ so radically on the ethical scale of *potentia*, that to impose a common norm, like a sort of moral average, does violence to human diversity and misses the ethical target.

[1] I am very grateful to Arnaud Villani for some very enlightening conversations on this topic at the Deleuze conference at Trent University, in May 2004.

Thus the ethical challenge, as Nietzsche had recommended, consists in cultivating joyful modes of confronting the overwhelming intensity of *bios/zoe*. This implies approaching the world as singularity, force, movement, through assemblages or webs of interconnections with all that lives. The subject is an autopoietic machine, fuelled by targeted perceptions, and it functions as the echoing chamber of *zoe*. This non-anthropocentric view expresses both a profound love for Life as a cosmic force and the desire to depersonalize subjective life and death. This is just one life, not *my* life. The life in 'me' does not answer to my name: 'I' is just transient.

To live intensely and be alive to the nth degree pushes us to the extreme edge of the crack of mortality. This has implications for the question of the limits, which are set to a very high degree by the embodied and embedded structure of the subject. The limits are those of one's endurance – in the double sense of lasting in time and bearing the pain of confronting 'Life' as *zoe*. The ethical subject is one that can bear this confrontation, cracking up a bit but without having its physical or affective intensity destroyed by it. Ethics consists in reworking the pain into thresholds of sustainability: cracking, but holding it, still.

What is ethics, then? Ethics is a thin barrier against the possibility of extinction. It is a mode of actualizing sustainable forms of transformation. This requires adequate assemblages or interaction: one has to pursue or actively create the kind of encounters that are likely to favour an increase in active becomings and avoid those that diminish one's *potentia*. It is an intensive ethics, based on the shared capacity of humans to feel empathy for, develop affinity with and hence enter in relation with other forces, entities, beings, waves of intensity. This requires dosage, rhythms, styles of repetition, and coordination or resonance. It is a matter of unfolding and enfolding in the complex and multi-layered forces of *bios/zoe* as a deeply inhuman force.

In other words, *potentia*, in order to fulfil its inherent positivity, must be 'formatted' in the direction of sustainability. Obviously, this means that it is impossible to set one standard that will suit all; a differential approach becomes necessary. What bodies are capable of doing or not, is biologically, physically, psychically, historically, sexually and emotionally *specific*: singular and hence partial. Consequently, the thresholds of sustainable becomings also mark their limits. In this respect 'I can't take it anymore' is an ethical statement, not the assertion of defeat. It is the lyrical lament of a subject-in-process who is shot through with waves of intensity, like a set of fulgurations that illuminate his self-awareness, tearing open fields of self-knowledge in the encounter of and configuration with others. Learning to recognize threshold, borders or limits is thus crucial to the work of the understanding and to the process of becoming. For Lacan limits are wounds or scars, marks of internal lacerations and irreplaceable losses and for liberal thoughts limits are frontiers that cannot be trespassed without the required visas or permissions. For Deleuze, however, limits are simultaneously points of passage or thresholds and markers of sustainability.[2]

Deleuze has an almost mathematical definition of the limit, as that which one never really reaches. In his *Abécédaire* (1996) Deleuze discusses with Claire Parnet the question of the limit in terms of addiction. Reminiscing on his own early alcoholism, Deleuze notes that the limit or frame for the alterations induced by alcohol is to be set with reference not so much to the last glass, because that is the glass that is going to kill you. What matters instead is the 'second-last' glass, the one that has already been and thus is going to allow you to survive, to last, to endure – and consequently also to go on drinking again. A true addict stops at the second-last glass, one removed from the fatal sip, or shot. A death-bound entity, however, usually goes straight for the last shot. That gesture prevents or denies the expression of the desire to start again tomorrow, that is to say to repeat that 'second-last shot', and thus to endure. In fact, there is no sense of a possible tomorrow: time folds in upon itself and excavates a black hole into which the subject dissolves. No future.

One of the images Deleuze uses to represent in a positive manner the notion of a frame of containment or the embodied and embedded nomadic subject is that of the house. The house protects and nurtures the sensitive enfleshed subject like an outer skin that sustains the impact with life forces. The house is not the Oedipalized 'home', but a complex and interactive mutual nestling by subjects who practise nomadic ethics and thus need limits, framing and nurturing. In *A Thousand Plateaus* Deleuze and Guattari speak out clearly against the unsustainable flows of transformation induced by drug-consumption. Before we go on to misread this as moralistic, we would do well to remember that both 'mind-expansion' and 'mood-enhancement' drugs are something that neither Deleuze nor Guattari are *a priori* against. What they are against is the addiction to drugs, which tips over the threshold of tolerance of the organism. Addiction is not an opening up, but a narrowing down of the field of possible becomings. It freezes time and locks the subject up in a black hole of inner fragmentation without encounters with others. The black hole is the point beyond which the line-of-flight of becoming implodes and disintegrates.

I want to stress that Deleuze's position on the thresholds of sustainability attempts to strike a new position that would coincide neither with the 'laissez-faire' ideology, nor with repression and moralism (which are synonymous). A Spinozist-nomadic notion of the limit, of 'not going too far', is a far cry from mainstream culture's appeal to moderation and savvy management of one's health. This renewed appeal to the individual's management of his or her bodily resources, health potential and life

[2] I am grateful to Donatella Barazetti, Marina D'Amelia, Serena Sapegno and Annamaria Tagliavini for this formulation, at the ATHENA Network meeting in Noordwijk, the Netherlands in March 1999.

capital is the distinctive feature of contemporary neo-liberalism. As Jackie Stacey (1997) has critically noted, it results in a misappropriation of the notion of 'responsibility' and a mistranslation of the term into styles of self-management based on 'prevention' and the pursuit of 'a healthy lifestyle'. This cultural obsession with health and with clean, functional bodies is the corollary of the fear of fatal diseases like cancer and AIDS and the monstrous imaginings they give rise to. The compulsive and consumerist pursuit of 'health' entails social, cultural and bodily practices which openly contradict one another. This is the normative force of contemporary bio-politics (Rose 2001).

The ethics of sustainability combines a flair for and a commitment to change with a critique of excess for its own sake. I specifically see in it a rejection of two related cultural phenomena. One is the ideology of excess on the far left of the political spectrum, in the various brands of counter-cultural movements that continue to posit intensity as an end in itself. The other is the commodification of transgression in the culture of spectacle, which emerged with the global MTV culture of 'sex, drugs and rock n' roll', and became integrated as a global commodity. In the swinging pendulum of postmodernity, de-territorializations are followed by reterritorializations, which means that yesterday's blasphemies constitute today's banalities, and boundaries that were transgressed by force or violence then, come to be held as the mainstream now. To construct this as 'progress' would be evidence of excessive optimism or a fatal case of Hegelian overdose. The question rather is what price we are prepared to pay for going through and even profiting from this chain of contradictory effects, wrongly rendered as 'progress'. The radical social theories and practices of the 1960s and 1970s have been reprocessed into consumerism of 'lifestyle' and 'infotainment'. Their subversive sting, namely the desire for in-depth transformation of the subject and of the public sphere, has been taken out. The extent to which advanced capitalism has simultaneously reduced all counter-cultures to objects of commodified consumption and re-established a conservative ethos that spells the death of all experiments aimed at transformative changes is one of the most perverse traits of contemporary culture, as I argued in the introduction.

The stress on the notion of sustainability refocuses this debate on the necessity to reappraise the desire for change and for transformation, so as to break through the infernal logic of commodified consumption of all that is allegedly 'new'. It is important to reiterate the importance and positivity of transformative experimentations: vitality and transgression, but without self-destruction. We need to take the time to enact and implement changes, because change is a precarious and painful experience. We need sustainable systems for change. This is not to fall back, however, into easy moralizing, or mainstream appeals to moderation. On the contrary, I think that 'whatever gets you through the day', whatever help and support one needs to get on with it, is just fine. We all need props to deal with the crack: the soft, aching pain of the soul that Virginia Woolf describes with such precision; the sharp pang at the back of your head that Marguerite Duras captures with cruel accuracy; the diabolical thumping ache in the belly that makes Kathy Acker run are states of frail intensity that require whatever shot of adrenaline or existential props one needs in order to cope and to get going. The point is to achieve some sense of sustainability and balance – for better or for worse and for some time.

Of course 'whatever gets you through the day' as a refrain may become the pretext to forms of addiction, to legal or illegal mood-enhancement systems. They include perfectly legal activities which post-industrial society values and rewards, such as: high levels of physical exercise, eighty-hour-a-week workaholism, or the standard intellectual assemblage: 'writing/books/the-friendly-purr-of-the-PC/e-mails/music/concentration/think think/crack crack'. We all have the patterns of dependency that we deserve. Even the standard line of assemblage of intellectual affects described above, however, can take hell-bent deviations at almost any point in the process. For instance, it can take a sudden turn towards excessive snacks (anorexia/bulimia variable) or drinks (alcoholism variable) or any other 'fix' (the narcotics variable). An overdose of writing is also not uncommon, however, as is bulimic reading. The boundaries between these and the other, 'normalized' life-support systems is therefore one of degree, not of kind. If life is not a self-evident category, in fact, if 'what's the point?' is an ethically viable question, then whatever gets you through the day is an ethically neutral statement which points to a viable option. Accepting the need for existential props is a suitable way of handling, as well as an adequate exemplification of, the problem of how to be an ethical subject-in-becoming.

'Whatever gets you through the day' as the melancholy *fin-de siècle* refrain covers the depression of suburban opulence, as much as the despair of homeless life in the streets. Both the centre and the periphery are shot through by profoundly destabilizing, perverse power-relations that engender sombre, albeit asymmetrical, social relations. Neither of them, therefore, is immune from or alien to the process of becoming-ethical.

The second last smoke/glass/shot/kiss . . .

The most effective implementation of this intensive ethics is a non-moralistic approach. This is expressed by the notion of the 'second last' glass/sniff/shot. The principle of 'stopping at the second last' is an active way of creating the threshold of sustainability, and thus of fostering moral health by cracking up a bit. This demonstrates a series of interrelated points. Firstly, that philosophical nomadism is an ethics, though it opposes dominant morality. Secondly that it rests on an intensive or affective vision of the subject as constituted in interaction and encounters with others. Thirdly, that it contains a concept of limits in terms of frames of containment for self and others. Lastly, that these limits are postulated not in relation to norms or dogmas, but with reference to a practice of experimental immanence and to transcendental empiricism. I want to start arguing this case with an example from literature.

A very clear, albeit ironical, illustration of the principle of the 'second last' can be found in Italo Svevo's masterpiece *Confessions of Zeno* (1962). In a typical Mittel-European twist, the main character Zeno is, literally, close to Zero. The fact that his name begins with the last letter of the alphabet is a clear signifier of his intrinsic and explicit worthlessness. Zeno is, in some ways, an earlier version of Woody Allen's Zelig in that his empathic connection to the rest of the world is so intense as to become boundless and borderless; so much so that it easily spills over into a merry sort of emotional and morphological anarchy. Like Alice in Wonderland, Zelig expands, contracts, alters himself and mutates to 'take in' and enter into contact with the many significant others that mark his existential territory. This kind of bodily empathy is of the same etymological root as both pathology and passion. Beyond metamorphic representation, it shows becomings as sympathic mergers between entities that are capable of deep impact upon each other. Svevo portrays Zeno as a relatively personality-free entity, with an acute sense of inconsequentiality. This, however, makes him extraordinarily available to others, extremely open to encounters. His 'id' is far more accessible than his weak 'ego', as Freud would have it. Aware of this ontological lack in the in-depth structure of his subjectivity, Zeno organizes his life as a set of variations on the theme of containing the original damage. Deeply influenced by Schopenhauer and Nietzsche, Svevo draws up the portrait of a subject who, because of the acute awareness of his 'crack', or shortcomings, lives with a permanent sense of illness and ill-at-ease-ness about himself. In what I can only describe as a transmutation of values, however, Zeno constructs himself as a social subject, a husband, lover, father, citizen, businessman, who shines for his concern for others.

In other words, Zeno transcends the deep sense of shame and inadequacy that he feels about himself and turns it into a source of strength and givenness. He gives what he perceives he is receiving from life, namely affects and intensities. His motivation for doing this is the opposite of the rational calculations of Kantian morality (don't do to others what you don't wish that they may do to you). Zeno's sense of ethics rather rests on two separate, but interconnected moments. Firstly, the recognition of his inadequacy, his ineptitude, his falling short of his own expected and desired standards. Secondly, and more importantly, his determination to transcend these negative emotions in order to express the best of himself to those who surround him and depend on him. In other words, it is the awareness of a deep-seated sense of shame about

himself that lays the conditions of possibility (the *a priori*) for a life where
generosity, concern for others, honesty and accountability provide the
guiding rules. He gives to others what he does not have, positive self-
esteem, in order to prop up his own existential journey. This is not just
altruism, but also clever self-styling through positive interaction with
others. The crucial point is the transcendence of the negativity (shame,
lack, insecurity, sense of ontological inadequacy, original sin, structural
guilt), which turns all the reactive passions into sources of affirmative
energy. The ethics consists in the production of joyful affects, not of falling
in a logic of ontological debts or unpayable losses, as stipulated in the
dominant Hegelian–Lacanian model.

Influenced by Freud's psychoanalysis, Svevo translates this problem
into the issue of the subject's structural dependence on others, that is to
say his incompleteness or lack. Because of this fundamentally flawed
structure, the subject tends to develop forms of dependence on what I
would define as the everyday life-support system of relatively innocent
addictions. This indicates a dense and highly complex network of mutually interrelated mechanisms that sustain the subject through the perilous
task of getting through another day. In Zeno's case that takes the form
of smoke addiction. Smoking – an environmental and health hazard – is
definitely a way of relating, but is rather a toxic way of relating to one's
world. It is in some way a self-contradictory mode of both connecting to
and separating from one's habitat.

Richard Klein has commented eloquently upon the symbiotic powers
of smoking:

> The smoke penetrates sharply, then exudes, softly envelops you in the
> experience of extending your body's limits, no longer fixed by the
> margin of your skin . . . Joining aside and out, each puff is like total
> immersion: it baptizes the celebrant with the little flash of a renewed
> sensation . . . An inhaling moment of concentration, centralizing the self
> to make it more dense, more opaquely present to itself, is trailed by a
> movement of evaporation, as the self exhales itself ecstatically, in a
> smoky jag – as it grows increasingly tenuous, progressively less differ-
> entiated from the exterior world it becomes. (Klein 1995: 51)

Not unlike breathing, smoking merges the smoker with his or her own
environment. Thus, smoke is a protective membrane that the subject
self-projects so as to affect and in some way create his or her habitat. Like
other legal mood-enhancement addictive substances – alcohol, coffee,
workaholism and chocolate – it constructs one's habitat. In this, it is analogous in its function, though clearly not on its health effects, to the personalized acoustic world that is created by the Walk and Disk-Man that most
of the urban humanoids stroll around with (but one should really say
'wrapped around') these days. Like all legal life-support systems, they

affect the nervous system, by pumping acoustic or biochemical addictives straight into the embodied subject's operational centres. Eardrums, lung tissues and blood vessels register and must sustain the strain. They also get injured accordingly.

The intimacy of these external props wraps one up in a protective, warm, nurturing envelope. In the case of smoke this is the kind of wrapping which is deeply positive for the subjects who find pure oxygen slightly overwhelming. Similarly, chocolate is beneficial to those who find wet food slightly nauseating. Props that help you get through the day are vital for people who labour on the edge of the crack. One could extend this argument – for the sake of provocation – and wonder how many inhabitants of the post-industrial urbanized world, who have been able to adapt to the ozone hole, the greenhouse effect and the increasing rate of car exhaust fumes, would even recognize fresh air if they ever came across it.

In this respect nothing could be more hypocritical than the moralistic position taken against smoking by advanced liberal democracies. The biggest polluters in the world, such as the United States and Australia, voracious consumers of the vast majority of the earth's resources, addicted to car culture to the point of ridicule, are now leading a crusade against smoking which borders on fanaticism. All the while the hard-hit tobacco corporations are multiplying their investments in the South (which includes sections of former Eastern Europe and, till recently, Ireland), to compensate for their losses in the health conscious 'North'. Younger women in these areas are especially targeted as potential new consumers of cigarettes. Thus, the spectacle of American smokers lined up on the pavements of the few cities where they are still allowed to exist, puffing ashamedly away as the traffic drives past in an uninterrupted flow of fume emissions, is enough to sum up the self-defeating hypocrisy of the anti-smoking position. Cutting down on car usage and therefore on car fumes would surely be a better way for liberal democracies to start making a contribution to a cleaner environment than by persecuting smokers as if they were responsible for the environmental crisis. Signing and implementing the Kyoto agreement would also help.

I have already suggested that 'Life' in the sense of '*bios/zoe*' is a fundamentally amoral force, the true nature of which is best expressed in its relentless generative power. Cells reproduce and carry on, no matter what. There is no implicit *a priori* difference between cancer and birth, or between a malignant proliferation of cells in cancer and the benign proliferation induced by pregnancy. Pursuing this problematic analogy further, for the sake of the argument, one could venture to suggest that existential props like cigarettes or other life-supporting devices 'lean on', or alternatively are grafted onto, the ruthless generative power of *bios/zoe*, as it is incarnated in the embodied subjects. Whatever else the function of smoking may be for the subject whose survival depends on lighting both the first and the second-last cigarette, the end result is a prop that sustains the acceleration without which 'life' is not tolerable. Another related effect is, of course, corporeal contamination, with the unwanted corollary of potential malignant cell proliferation. Thus, smoking ends up creating an intoxicating humus; it becomes a malignant placenta.

Moreover, it produces hostile effects not only on the smoker him- or herself, but also on the people around him- or herself. Smoking is an environmental and health hazard with a collective dimension. Witness the conditions of the offspring of chronic smokers, drug addicts or AIDS-afflicted babies. A communitarian dimension of mutuality is necessarily built into this discussion, namely how to reconcile conflicting desires and necessities. Non-smokers have the right to clean air, though it would be absurd to single out cigarette smoke as the main polluting agent in today's highly toxic world. While recognizing and acknowledging their right, I also want to look at the other side of the question. Kantian morality is a way of begging the question of how to sustain the burden of life's intensity.

In the case of adults who freely choose or cannot do without addictive substances, albeit ones which they know perfectly well can damage their health, for those who wilfully and purposefully choose or cannot do without these props, why would this extra 'wrapping' or protective frame provided by mood-enhancement substances be negative? Only a sacral-ized, metaphysical glorification of life for its own sake could argue that one must live at all costs and that life must be preserved at all costs. This fetishism of 'life' is what I want to argue against. My main reason for doing so is that the practices of life and death have been dislocated and redefined in fundamental ways by contemporary culture and technology. We already live and die in ways that were not programmed by humanistic philosophies, or envisaged by the ethics of care. Facing up to these con-tradictions seems to me an important step in the process of generating productive transformations of the ways in which we represent to our-selves our real-life condition.

This refers back to the discussion about the containment of others (see chapter 4) and the Kantian objection that the others set the boundaries of possible flows of affective interconnections. My response to this consists in rejecting the Self–Other distinction, and adopting instead a monistic and vitalistic vision of a non-unitary vision of nomadic subjectivity. Coupled with the idea of desire as plenitude and not as lack, this produces a more transformative approach to ethical values.

The quest for thresholds of sustainability is collective and it requires a transversal synchronization of our different modes of interaction with our habitats. Some need nicotine, some prefer oxygen, but because 'we' are in *this* eco-philosophical discussion together, negotiations have to be held, not in the name of a transcendent standard or a universal moral rule, but differentially. It is a question of cultivating the productive encounters that suit one's affective speed, rhythm and intensity. Moreover, to stay with the issue of smoking, a nomadic ethics requires that we look at the broader picture, avoiding scapegoating the smokers and considering environmental degradation as a serious attack on the structure of our being-in-the world in an age of integration and increased interconnection.

Zeno the smoker is no nihilist. On the contrary, his life is spent in constructing and deconstructing such interrelations with the outside world by smoking. Mostly, he tries to contain this addiction by deluding himself that he is about to give up, that is to say that this is his last cigarette. Zeno's existence is punctuated by a series of all-important '(second-) last-cigarettes', all of them comforting him in the illusion that he is about to change, that maybe this time is the right time to start a new phase. It just happens that this is never the case, that radical transformation is not on the agenda and that the many allegedly 'last cigarettes' are in fact merely a long series of second-last smokes. Given that smoking has to do with inhaling and both of them with breathing, it is hard to see that the 'last cigarette' easily translates into 'the last breath', 'the last time', 'the last chance' and thus expresses a generalized sense of death-in-life. Zeno's life is spent in trying to contain this addiction by deluding himself that he is about to give up, that is to say that this is his last cigarette. Like Deleuze's alcoholics, the compulsive smoker freezes the present into a hard slab of constant deferrals: 'not this', 'not now' – have another one!

Zeno's adventures confirm this as he moves on to apply his 'last cigarette' mode to a number of other salient experiences in his life. For example the 'last time' he makes love with his mistress, determined to put an end to the adulterous betrayal, turns out to be an exquisitely perfect moment, never to be savoured again. The strategy of 'just one last time' is not mere rhetoric, nor is it hypocritical self-delusion. It is a corrida against time, a game of incantation and a seduction into life. Like Zeno's paradox in classical Greek philosophy, time simultaneously stands still, eternally returns and rushes ahead. This relies on an atomistic vision of time, whereby distance between two points can never be bridged, but constitutes an absolute difference. Translated into my nomadic language: our experience of time is related to movement, the overall pattern of motion can be perceived as the simultaneity or synchronization of different time zones. Bergson's concept of duration means 'back to the future'. A fundamental instability can consequently be detected at the heart of existence, one which confirms Zeno's belief that nobody can truly claim to be normal and that degrees of tolerable abnormality and sustainable poor or average health are the best we can aspire to. Zeno achieves excellence within the category of inadequacy, thereby turning a minus into a plus, that is to say, transcending the negative. He is the ethical subject *par excellence*.

As signifier of this quality and safeguard of the moral order, Zeno elects his wife, whose name can only begin with the first letter of the alphabet, of course. The solid, safe, sane Augusta is the clearing house of Zeno's immanent ethics: she is the *conditio sine qua non*. She stands steady as a monument to tranquillity in the stormy waters of the eternal return in which Zeno regularly plunges, just that once, for the last time. She is the house, or frame of containment. Zeno lives life in a series of constantly deferred 'last times' which hinge upon the caring presence of – mostly female – others. With each repetition, however, he develops a higher degree of awareness of one's condition in terms of limitations but also responsibilities. Each mistake is the second last one.

It is the pursuit of joyful and life-giving passion that provides the underlying continuity in one's life. Thus, wanting to repeat the pleasurable experience is as normal as breathing. One enjoys it so much that one is tempted to intensify this pleasure, enhancing it by artificial means like, for instance, lighting a cigarette, but only for that last time, of course. This makes it a very, very special event: one last cigarette is not just any old smoke. It contains the desire for otherness, elsewhereness and otherwiseness. It expresses the desire for the new, the pure, the not-yet-played-out. Paradoxically, it is a gesture of confidence in the future: 'One last cigarette and then I must stop, or else I'll ruin my life'. It expresses care and the desire to endure, that is to say not to self-destroy or self-implode. Repetition is not the performance of a script, but rather a way of framing and engendering the future.

Thus, Zeno's 'last cigarettes' are always and only the second-last ones: they allow him to start again tomorrow, or immediately; they allow him to go on, to endure, in a sustainable manner. As Harvey Keitel expressed in the film *Smoke*: a puff of blue smoke to get you through the day, or the nights of your discontent, a puff for a breath, and the anxiety is released into thin air. Nicotine-tainted oxygen is a life-enhancement life-endangering mood-controlling drug. Legal in most countries for the moment, like coffee and alcohol, it just gets you through the day; till the next time, at a price, if the others comply.

If it is true that one's freedom ends where the freedom of the other begins, it is equally true that such interdependence is a form of social symbiosis that applies to all states, not only the altered or narcotic ones. An addiction to life is a collective endeavour. This ethics of stopping before one goes too far is collectively negotiated; it is variable in each and everyone; it is action-orientated; it is affirmative of *potentia*; it banks on empowerment but invites consideration for those who cannot sustain. It also asserts unrelenting hatred of the moralists. It is about a physics of forces and an ethical balance that selects and marks thresholds of sustainability. It is an eco-philosophy that asserts a simple truth: that a certain amount of chemical nourishment can help the soil, but too much of it will poison it. Knowing the difference means one has marked the threshold of sustainability. A notion of measure or limit is therefore enacted which refers to the internal forces and the necessities and drives of bodies and embodied subjects in interaction and relation to others. This is the implementation of the eco-philosophy of multiple belongings that I analysed in chapter 4. Such an ethics is not based on judgement, but rather on transversal negotiations with multiple others bent on the active creation of processes of change. Entering this field of active experimentation with others is the event itself, but this process of becoming is neither infinite nor self-imposed: it is limited by its very radical immanence. Death is one such event and one such limit. The aim of becoming is active creation, not dissolution; it is an evolutionary act that is expressed through disruption.

I want to develop this notion of sustainability into an ethics of differential sustainable subjects and propose a public discussion on this right across some of the problematic social issues which are dismissed as self-destructive by dominant morality. This agenda should be taken seriously. It is equally important at this stage to challenge any claim to purity by any conceptual, theoretical or philosophical school. No one has a monopoly over issues of ethics and moral values. To cultivate the ethical life means applying the principle of joyful transformation of negative into positive affects, in courteous but firm disagreement with the dominant neo-liberal brand of Kantian moral universalism.

For philosophical nomadism,[3] the problem with sustainability is that it has the feel of a qualitative (intensive) criterion, but in fact it is a quantitative one. Sustainability clashes with duration, which is not the same as pluralistic speed. Speed is a trajectory; it is spatialized and it deals with concepts like bodies or actualized entities. Duration, on the other hand, is an intensity, which deals with abstract diagrams or lines of becoming. Sustainability as a quantitative measure runs the risk of becoming effective and operational within the logic of advanced capitalism, which it aims to undermine, namely the liberal individual responsibility for one's well being. This is an axiomatic system capable of considering all qualities as quantities and of instrumentalizing them in order to feed itself. My response to this consists in adopting instead a non-unitary vision of nomadic subjectivity which, coupled with the idea of desire as plenitude and not as lack, produces a more transformative approach to ethical values. The stated criteria for this new ethics include: non-profit; emphasis on the collective; viral contaminations; and a link between theory and practice, including the importance of creation. Furthermore, the non-Hegelian notion of the limit which I propose as the threshold of sustainability means that limits are to be seen as dynamic connectors or attractors.

They need to be experimented with collectively, so as to produce effective cartographies of how much bodies can take, or thresholds of sustainability. They also aim to create collective bonds, a new affective community or polity. This must include an evaluation of the costs involved in

[3] I am very grateful to Yves Abrioux for clarifying this point to me at the Deleuze conference in Cologne in July 2004.

pursuing active processes of change and of recognition of the pain and the difficulty these entail. The problem of the costs within the schizoid logic of our times concerns mostly *potestas*, the quantitative, not *potentia*, or incorporeal intensities. Creation, or the invention of the new, can only emerge from the qualitative intensities and thus cannot apply to a notion that measures the tolerance of bodies as actualized systems. Hence the ethical question: if, in the name of encouraging (pre-human or individual) life (*zoe*), we value the incorporeal invention of quality and primarily affect and precept; if (again, following Deleuze) we insist on the incorporeal insistence of affects and precepts or becoming (as distinguished from affected bodies and perceptions of entities), then how can we use a concept of sustainability to argue against the cost of fidelity to the concept or the precept? That would involve a corporeal criterion to the incorporeal. This is a conceptual double bind and a true ethical dilemma.

How can we combine sustainability with intensity? One line I would propose, is to hold everyone, not only noticeable people like writers or thinkers, but just anyone (*homo tantum*) accountable for the ethical effort to be worthy of the production of affect and precept. It is a noble ethics of overcoming the self and stretching the boundaries of how much a body can take; it also involves compassion for pain, but also an active desire to work through it and find a way across it. The ethical question would therefore emerge from the absolute difference (or *différend*) between incorporeal affects, or the capacity to experiment with thresholds of sustainability and our corporeal fate as such and such an affected body. What ethical criterion can we invent in the context of this difference? How can one (simultaneously?) increase affectivities as the capacity to invent or capture affect and look after the affected bodies? What kind of synchronized effort could achieve this aim? In other words, what is the 'cost' of the capacity to be affected which allows us to be the vehicle of creation? What would a qualitative concept of cost be? This is the core of the nomadic ethics agenda. It includes interrelationality and a relation to otherness, on the model of mutual specification and collective becomings.

Against neo-liberal moderation

To measure the abyss that separates nomadic ethics from dominant morality (think of chapter one), let us consider neo-liberal morals. Fukuyama (2002), in his neo-liberal discussion of our post-human condition, does address the issue of drug addiction in relation to the staggering rate of development of pharmaceutical drugs that affect the biochemistry of the brain. Arguing that neuropharmacology is the single most potent means of controlling human behaviour, Fukuyama also stresses its addictive character, with some 28 million Americans currently on mood-enhancing drugs like Prozac or Ritalin (Fukuyama 2002: 43). The genderized structure of the usage of these drugs is also noted: Prozac is meant for low-esteem, depressed characters – mostly women – whereas Ritalin is supposed to curtail excessive aggression and thus tame teenage males. Unable to take in the ethical impact of feminist theorizations of gender as a factor that structures power-relations, Fukuyama falls into predictable platitudes about using drugs to 'androgynize our children' (Fukuyama 2002: 94). This is in keeping with his sexist definition of femininity as castration or devirilization, the only advantage of which is to position women as agents of civilization against testosterone-driven aggression. Ever mindful of the political implications of such patterns of social control of human behaviour, and yet loath to travel the road of coherence, Fukuyama proposes some *ad hoc* distinctions between legally prescribed drugs, like Prozac and Ritalin, and illegal ones, like Ecstasy. The neo-liberal theorist presents some convoluted and self-contradictory arguments in defence of his utterly untenable distinction: thus, ecstasy is charged with harmful side-effects, in spite of the growing mass of evidence concerning the negative long-term side-effects of Prozac and Ritalin. Admitting to confusion on the matter, Fukuyama provides a splendid example of meretricious neo-liberal thinking, by stating that 'We feel very ambivalent about substances that have no clear therapeutic purpose, and whose only effect is to make people feel good' (Fukuyama 2002: 55).

This ambivalence is all the greater if the drugs involved are heavily addictive, like heroine or cocaine, and if they cause clear damage to the body. When damage is done to one's *potentia*, however, or in terms of psychological effects, then Fukuyama is unwilling to take a stand. The option of being a coherent Kantian libertarian and thus of granting people the right to use whichever drugs they want, so long as they do not harm others, is discarded. Fukuyama evokes as a sort of paradox the interesting compromise of wanting to classify the unhappiness or depression (of the soul) as a pathology, to have it treated as such by the neurological and psychiatric professions and thus to make all psychotropic and mood-enhancing drugs legal and refundable on the national health scheme. But the gesture is merely rhetorical and Fukuyama does not endorse the ethical path he evokes: he upholds the mind–body distinction and uses it as a criterion by which to organize the allocation and legalization of phar-maceutical drugs. He does acknowledge the dramatic size of problems related to depression, aggression and other 'behavioural' problems, but also avoids the roots of the problems.

The heart of the matter is precisely the political economy of legalizing drugs, or of forcefully prescribing them. In turn this is related to the ethical weight that one is prepared to give to everyday misery, or unhap-piness, depression, burnout and general disfunctionality. These are the banal yet overwhelming difficulties encountered by millions of our co-citizens, mostly women and youths, actually to make it through the day and cope with social realities at times of disruptive changes. We may well

call them diseases of the soul, as Freud did a century ago and so opened
an alternative road which the neurologists have fought against ever since.
This is the line of cracking up, as philosophical nomadism suggests. These
phenomena should be addressed as serious social issues, of collective
importance and relevance. Indeed, I consider happiness a political issue,
as are well-being, self-confidence and a sense of empowerment. These are
fundamental ethical concerns, which should not be left in the hands of
the pharmaceutical companies, the managers of diversity and human
capital experts, or to the many apostles of 'new age' remedies and pop
psychology. The feminist movement has played the historical role of
placing these items at the centre of the social and political agenda: happiness as a fundamental human right and hence a political question. Neo-
liberals like Fukuyama are doing their best to sweep them under the
carpet again, in twists of moral convulsions that smack of hypocrisy. Our
times call for a more systematic approach to these issues because our
women and youth, among others, need more and deserve better.

I want to plead consequently for a less moralistic and conceptually
more rigorous agenda that combines a broader approach to the alterations
of 'human nature' with a serious commitment to think alongside contemporary culture and not against its grain. The rate of unhappiness and
dysfunctionality is part of it: we all live on the crack. For nomadic subjectivity, sustaining a state of well-being is crucial to the ethics of the
subject. Expressing his or her innermost essence means for the subject to
reach the utmost of what she or he is capable of: *conatus* propels us
towards self-enhancement (or not). Happiness, in this scheme of thought,
is a political question and the role of the state is to enhance and not to
hinder humans in their striving to become all they are capable of. Politics
must assist the ethical fulfilment of the human being's innermost freedom
in making the question of transformations the heart of the social agenda.
The ethology of forces proposed by nomadic revisitations of Spinoza
allows us to differentiate the molar from the molecular forms of transformation and mobility. Given that nomadism is about displacing and
stretching our boundaries, the ethics of sustainability are a powerful
means of negotiating different shifts and different intensive modes of
becoming. This is a political as well as an ethical project, in that it supports
a change of perspective that allows us to resist the unlimited erasures,
multiple evictions and enforced semioses of advanced capitalism, while
allowing for flow and mobility.

In her brave survey of the interconnection between writing and drug
taking, Sadie Plant (Plant 2000) argues passionately against the hypocrisy
that surrounds the public debate about addiction. Pointing to the long-
established and highly successful interaction between creative writing
and 'illegal psychotropic substances', Plant provides an exemplary cartography of both sustainable and unsustainable forces. The strength of
her case lies in its materialist approach: Plant offers a well-documented

historical account of the interaction between drugs and the production of culture, which encompasses the analysis of imperialism and of the role that drug cultivation and consumption has played in European culture, from the Opium War of the nineteenth century to the 'trade wars' and the hypocritical 'war on drugs' of today. As is often the case in European history, the industrial and the military developments were also woven into the colonial project. A parallel genealogy is thus set up between the development of drugs, colonial expansion, and the discovery and commercialization of new technologies. From the hypodermic needle to the nasal inhaler, pharmacology and war technologies have been working hand in hand since the nineteenth century.

One of the significant points of Plant's analysis is the way she challenges the distinction between legal and illegal addictions. First and foremost among the former is the addiction to writing, which is socially accepted and yet no less lethal than many of the unacceptable ones. Also, creative minds are keen experimenters and thus are prone to channel their high intensity towards alcohol and drugs. The point in common between the legal addiction (writing) and the illegal one (alcohol or drugs) is the desire to speed up, to accelerate one's senses. How to expand one's perception apparatus is the ultimate aim, as Sigmund Freud, Walter Benjamin, Aldous Huxley, Carlos Castaneda and all the 1960s hippie subculture knew all too well. It is almost impossible to imagine cultural progress without such leaps of the imagination and sudden accelerations. The list is not meant as some sort of narcotic 'outing', but rather as a way of challenging the widespread belief that drugs are the ultimate in wasteful consumption, and that they constitute the antithesis of productive behaviour. Plant's analysis demonstrates instead the innovative role they play in producing highly valuable, if not downright pathbreaking, work. Moreover, as major commodities in today's market economies, drugs are very much part of the labour-intensive system of production and distribution of wealth. A non-moralistic attitude is therefore of the utmost importance in approaching this subject.

The crucial point is the acceleration of the existential speed, a sort of flush of energy, which is the mark of desire in the sense of the expression of *potentia*. What is affirmed, asserted and empowered in the ethics of nomadic sustainable subjects is the positivity of *potentia* itself. That is to say the singularity of the forces that compose the specific spatio-temporal grid of immanence that composes one's life. This life is an assemblage, a montage, not a given; it is a set of points in space and time; a quilt of retrieved material. It is the project that makes for the uniqueness of one's life, not any deep-seated essence.

Many contemporary artists struggle with the idea that everyday reality is just a stratified data bank of sedimented habits and that inducing changes upon them is a question of setting mobility at the very heart of the subject. Many of them, from digital manipulator Inez van Lamsweerde to satellite data projects like Makrolab (Biemann 2003), rely on tactical decontextualization as their standard practice. This consists in removing the subject from the expected steam of experiential data to which she or he has grown accustomed. This dislocation of the subject opens up spaces where new modes of data intake can be implanted, and hence new sensorial, perceptual, conceptual and ethical insights. The tactic of sensorial decontextualization is not deprived of violence. Disintoxication clinics or any high security enclosed space reproduce exactly the same conditions of traumatic displacement. In the case of contemporary digital art culture, however, the touch of cruelty is set to the task of enlarging the range of what embodied, embedded and technologically enhanced subjects are actually capable of becoming. Which, in the ethical project of philosophical nomadism, can be translated into: how much can his or her body take?

Marko Pelijan of Makrolab encloses his subjects in a mobile laboratorium: 'an octagonal tube, 14 m. long, with a silver shining mantle and steel stilts, a couple of satellite dishes and a wind turbine for energy supply' (Biemann 2003: 148). He then subjects them to the reception of up to 600 data input sources: television, internet, satellite; 'electromagnetic frequencies and interstellar noise' (Biemann 2003: 149). Breaking open the doors of perception through sensorial intervention leads to the desegregation of bodily capacities by decoding the sedimented knowledge to which the subject is used. The result is as addictive as any legally prescribed drug.

A critical agenda for the next millennium, both in feminist theory and in mainstream social philosophy, cannot fail to address these issues. We need to talk about the simultaneity of opposite social and cultural effects, and to address them in a non-moralistic manner. 'Whatever gets you through the day' need not be the manifesto for self-destruction that it is often made to be. It can merely help us frame a threshold of sustainable patterns of transformative changes, of becomings as modes and moods of empowerment.

Bios/*zoe* ethics and Thanatos

Death is the ultimate transposition, though it is not final. I want to argue against the Christian-based belief in the alleged self-evidence and implicit worth of 'life'. The sacralization of life in Christian ethics is challenged by Deleuze's theory of the becoming animal/insect/imperceptible. *Zoe* carries on, relentlessly. This belief system has categorized as 'sin' or 'nihilism' bodily practices and phenomena which are of daily significance to my culture and society: disaffection of all kinds; addictions of the legal and of the illegal kind; suicide, especially youth suicide; birth control, abortion, and the choice of sexual practices and sexual identities; euthanasia and the agony of long-term diseases; life-support systems in hospitals and outside; depression, burnout and stress-related syndromes in post-industrial societies. Such practices tend to be read with reference to Christian morality and to a sacralized notion of both 'life' and the individual who inhabits it. This results in presenting such practices as pathologies, social problems or scandalous issues which get culturally coded as 'different' in the monstrous or anomalous sense.

Philosophical nomadism, on the other hand, is a more positive approach to these phenomena which would allow us to think alongside them and with them. My hypothesis is that a non-unitary vision of the subject, combined with an ethics of sustainability, allows us to bypass the habit that pathologizes self-destructive practices. This amounts to a radical redefinition of the boundaries of the human and of the terms of his or her embodiment. It also generates new and more complex forms of compassion or deeply shared affinity in others.

On suicide

As a consequence, I find that the labour intensive non-evidence of 'getting on with life' generates another relevant question: 'what is the point?' I do not mean this in the plaintive or narcissistic mode, but rather as the necessary moment of stasis that precedes action. It is the question mark that both prefaces and frames the possibility of ethical agency. When Primo Levi, who asked that question all his life, and struggled to answer it all his life, actually failed to find the motivation for raising the question once more, suicide followed. That gesture, however, was not the sign of moral defeat, or a lowering of one's standards. On the contrary, it expresses one's determination not to accept life at an impoverished or diminished level of intensity. As such, it is an ethically positive gesture.

Lloyd (1994) argues that on the issue of suicide Spinoza is very clear: the choice for self-destruction is neither positive, nor can it be said to be free. The self-preservation of the self is such a strong drive that destruction can only come from the outside. A *conatus* cannot wish its own self-destruction and if it does so it is due to some physical or psychical compulsion that negates the subject's freedom. The interconnectedness of entities means that self-preservation is a commonly shared concern. Joining forces with others so as to enhance one's enjoyment of life is the key to the ethical life; it is also the definition of a joyously lived rational life. Suicide and rationality are at odds with each other. Spinoza repudiates the 'ethic of noble suicide', as Lloyd (1996: 94) calls it but he equally refuses to make a virtue of self-denial. The greatest and perhaps the only sin for Spinoza is to succumb to external forces and thus diminish one's *potentia*.

Commenting on Primo Levi's and Virginia Woolf's suicides, Deleuze – who will himself choose this way to terminate his own existence – put it very clearly: you can suppress your own life, in its specific and radically immanent form, and still affirm the potency of life, especially in cases where deteriorating health or social conditions may seriously hinder your power to affirm and to endure joyfully. This is no Christian affirmation of life nor transcendental delegation of the meaning and value system to categories higher than the embodied self. On the contrary, it is the intelligence of radically immanent flesh that states with every single breath that the life in you is not marked by any signifier and it most certainly does not bear your name.

This is linked to the issue of costs, which I discussed earlier. The awareness of the absolute difference between intensities or incorporeal affects and the specific affected body that one happens to be is crucial to the ethics of choosing one's own death. Death is what is unsustainable. This type of argument, coupled with mercy for the suffering of terminally ill patients, is also at the heart of contemporary debates on euthanasia. They are marked in the public sphere by dramatically incompatible understandings of 'Life', as well as by often unspoken vested interests. Only as pragmatic and tolerant a culture as that of the Netherlands succeeded in striking a classical Dutch compromise and thus officializing some kind of euthanasia laws. Even there, however, the public debate would benefit from an injection of nomadic ethics.

André Colombat in his comment on Deleuze's death links the act of suppressing one's failing body, as in suicide or euthanasia, to an ethics of assertion of the joyfulness and positivity of life, which necessarily translates into the refusal to lead a degraded existence.

> This notion rests on a preliminary and fundamental distinction between personal and impersonal death. The former is linked to the suppression of the individualized ego, the latter is beyond the ego: a death that is always ahead of me. It is the extreme form of my power to become other or something else. An absolute and dynamic fissure that does not define the 'possible' but that which will never end, the virtual that never gets accomplished, the unending and unceasing through which 'I' lose the power to die. (Colombat 1996: 241)

In other words, in a nomadic philosophical perspective the emphasis on the impersonality of life is echoed by an analogous reflection on death. Life being an impersonal, or rather an apersonal force – *zoe* in its magnificent indifference to the interests of humans – also means that death is no less so. Death is not a failure or the expression of a structural weakness at the heart of life because it is part and parcel of its generative cycles. As such, it is a 'zero institution', to which I will return in the discussion on Lévi-Strauss and the Lacanian symbolic in the epilogue. It is the empty shape of all possible time as perpetual becoming that can become actualized in the present, but it flows back to past and future. It is virtual in that it has the generative capacity to engender the actual. Consequently, death is but an obvious manifestation of principles that are active in every aspect of life, such as the pre-individual or impersonal power of *potentia*; the affirmation of multiplicity and not of one-sidedness and the interconnection with an 'outside' which is of cosmic dimension, and thus infinite.

I would describe this as the flows of patterns of becoming in an unlimited space somewhere between the no longer and the not yet. It is a temporal brand of vitalism that could not be further removed from the idea of death as the inanimate and indifferent state of matter, to which the body is supposed to 'return'. Death, on the contrary, is the becoming-imperceptible of the nomadic subject and as such it is part of the cycles of becomings, yet another form of interconnectedness, a vital relationship that links one with other, multiple forces. The impersonal is life as *bios/zoe* in us, the ultimate outside as the frontier of the incorporeal.

In *Viroid Life*, Ansell-Pearson comments in a very illuminating manner on the distinction between personal and impersonal death in Deleuze's philosophy of becoming. The paradox of affirming life as *potentia*, energy, even in and through the suppression of the specific slice of life that 'I' inhabits, is a way of pushing anti-humanism to the point of implosion. It dissolves death into ever shifting processual changes, and thus disintegrates the ego, with its capital of narcissism, paranoia and negativity. Impersonal death from the specific and highly restricted viewpoint of the ego is just the manifestation of *zoe* or pre-human vitality:

> A positive, dynamical and processual conception of death, which would release it from an anthropomorphic desire for death (for stasis, for being), speaking instead only of a death that desires (a death that is desire, where desire is construed along the lines of a machine or a machinic assemblage), can only be arrived at by freeing the becoming of death from both mechanism and finalism. . . . This is to posit the world as a 'monster of energy' without beginning and without end, a Dionysian world of 'eternal' self-creation and 'eternal' self-destruction . . . a world of becoming that never attains 'being', never reaching a final death. (Ansell-Pearson 1997b: 62–3)

Death need not be the 'unproductive black hole' (Ansell-Pearson 1996: 68) that we all fear, but rather a point in a creative synthesis of flows, energies and becomings. As I argued above, death is behind us and this view is very removed from the metaphysics of finitude: it is neither the significant closure, nor the defining border of human existence. Relying on Spinoza, Deleuze emphasizes instead the multiplying of connections and the wealth of creativity of a self that unfolds in processes of becomings. This affirmative view of life and thought situates philosophical nomadism in a logic of positivity, rather than in the redemptive economy of classical metaphysical thought. This vision of death as process is linked to time understood as endurance and sustainability.

The ethics of this position in Deleuze's work are as much indebted to Nietzsche as to Spinoza. Philip Goodchild quotes Deleuze effectively on this point: 'Since destructive forces are always exchanged among people, it is much better to destroy oneself under agreeable conditions than to destroy others' (Goodchild 1996: 208). Because of this ethics of affirmation and positivity, a Deleuzian approach suggests that 'whatever gets you through the day', whatever life-support, mood-enhancement system one is dependent on, should not be the object of moral indictment, but rather a neutral term of reference: a prop in the process of becoming.

Life as a project that aims at affirming the intensity and positivity of desire rests on the materialist foundation of the enfleshed subject. This is a non-unitary, post-humanistic subject-in-becoming. The life in 'me' does not, indeed, bear my name; 'I' does not own it; 'I' is only passing through. In a culture saturated by egotism, 'I' is more often than not of hindrance to the project of affirming and empowering the unstoppable and triumphant return of the impersonality, or rather the apersonality, of becomings (eternal returns). These becomings do not privilege anthropocentric subjects, but rather emphasize assemblages of a heterogeneous kind. Animals, insects, machines are as many fields of forces or territories of becoming: the life in 'me' is not only human. Beyond the subject/object distinction that supports the paranoid-narcissistic empire of the ego-life as eternal becomings goes on, regardless and relentless.

In any case, the 'life' that is empowered by the nomadic ethics of sustainability is not the uniqueness of life as in the Christian dogma, nor is it the equally unchallenged scientific belief in the dictatorial powers of DNA. It is staggering to note to what an extent our understanding of the human subject is still tied up with a sense of the body as a container, or as an envelope, containing a divinely ordained soul, or an equally despotic genetic code. Distinct from it is the mind, governed by the black box of innately sovereign reason, or by a rationally regulated libido that knows what's right for you. These are humanistic conventions packaged as human essence. Nomadic subjectivity, however, suggests that the singularity of the subject rests in the project that animates one's becoming in the minoritarian consciousness that unfolds and expresses itself through multiple becomings.

The subject-in-becoming is the one for whom 'what's the point?' is an all-important question. A high-intensity subject is also animated by unparalleled levels of vulnerability. With nomadic patterns comes also a fundamental fragility. Processes without foundations need to be handled with care; *potentia* requires great levels of containment in the mode of framing.

ETERNITY WITHIN TIME

Lloyd (1994) argues that the eternity of the mind makes death an irrelevance for a Spinozist vision of the subject. To understand a thing as eternal for Spinoza means understanding it as actual. Eternity is not the same thing as 'duration' and thus it does not mean 'lasting forever'. Minds can understand themselves as partaking of a larger totality; for Spinoza this is the mind of God (*sub specie aeternitatis*), which is by definition eternal in the enjoyment of its perfection and love. The intellectual love for such a vision makes our own mind eternal as well. Wisdom is the contemplation of the eternity of the life forces, not the perenniality of death. Spinoza's thought is not free of contradictions on this point – notably on the distinction between the notions of 'eternity' and of 'duration' – which also affects his view of God, religion and salvation. Spinoza contests the orthodox view of God that is upheld by major religions and defends instead the existence of an infinite and eternal God, without whom nothing exists or can be understood, given that the human mind is only a mode in the attribute of the thought of God. The mind, according to Spinoza, strives to make itself into a unity in temporal as well as spatial terms. In doing so, it needs to accept its complex nature and thus accept internal complexities and differentiations. Setting limits to this internal complexity is the ethics of sustainability. Time itself sets some limits, in so far as it organizes experience in a sequence of past, present and future, thus limiting the complexities and the proliferation of associations by the memory and the imagination.

As Edwin Curley (1988) argues in his materialist reading of Spinoza, the idea of the parallelism between mind and body rests on the notion of soul (*anima*) as a life force through which things persevere in their being. Such a life force is present in all things, though in different degrees. The case for the immortality of the soul fits in with this parallelism. The point is not to think in terms of personal immortality, because as we saw in the previous chapter a person is necessarily embodied and inscribed in a temporal sequence guaranteed by his or her memory. A radical disruption of consciousness induced by death through the destruction of the body is such that the person could not survive. And yet, for Spinoza self-preservation is written into the essence of the subject and death can only occur through external causes. The scholarship on Spinoza's notion of immortality is quite extensive,[4] but it is a point of consensus that Spinoza's work is situated in-between the two dominant traditions in Western thought. One, Platonic, defines 'eternity' in the sense of timelessness and it consequently precludes any discussion of time. The other, Aristotelian, defines eternity simply as endless time or 'sempiternity'. Martha Kneale (1973) argues that Spinoza moves towards an Aristotelian view that she sums up as follows:

A given human mind . . . is that system of knowledge which has the existence of God as its first premises (this is common to all), the exist-

4 For an overview see Grene (1973).

ence of other parts of the universe as intermediate premises, and the existence of its own body as conclusion. Thus every human mind is in a way the same system as every other human mind, but it is the system arranged in a different way. Hence our individuality, not merely in this life but sempiternally.

The mind is embodied and part of 'nature' in the sense of living environment as I argued in chapter 3. This involves the realization of its interconnection with other modes of thought and forces, and it can thus also comprehend the rivalry with other minds and consequently external sources that can prove negative or destructive. But it cannot contemplate the possibility of its own death. As Lloyd outs it: 'death is the destruction of the conatus' (Lloyd 1994: 132). Dying means ceasing to partake of that vital flow of positive and negative interactions with others, which is the distinctive trait of the embodied subject. Something in our existence will go on after death, but it is not the continued existence of the self. The mind's eternity rests on its partaking of a larger reflexive totality. The existence of the mind, however, is contingent upon that of the body and exists only in so far as the body actually exists. So the mind does cease to exist with the death of the body, yet the idea of that mind/body entity is not wiped out with the disappearance of the body. The truth of what has been the case, the subject, cannot be lost. The past remains steadfast and self-assured and is thus the true object of becoming. For the subject to understand itself as part of nature means to perceive itself as eternal, that is to say both vulnerable and transient. It also involves, however, a temporal dimension: what we are, is bound up with things that existed before and after us and some of which go on after us. Death does affect it, of course, but 'death does not have the power to make it not have been' (Lloyd 1994: 132). Being dead does not reduce one to the status of a figment of other people's imagination, but it dissolves the self into an interconnected continuum with nature as One. Whatever happens – and death always does happen – we will have been and nothing can change that, not even death itself. The future perfect paves the road to the continuous present.

The embodied mind remains part and parcel of a larger and more articulated whole. The point of this is that one can come to this awareness during life, namely the awareness that there is something that transcends time. Once this insight is acquired, there is little to fear from actual death. I think this is a crucial passage, because the truth about the nature of the embodied self can and must be grasped from within existence. This is the higher form of thought that allows for eternity. It is anchored in memory and the imagination but it requires the clarity of reason in order to elucidate its workings. The awareness of the transcendence of death is something that must happen in life and not at the point of death itself. Lloyd explores this paradox admirably: 'The character of what is past is not altered by the passage of time . . . that an event is over, or that a thing has ceased to be, does not intrude on what it has been' (Lloyd 1994: 137).

How will life (*zoe*) in me go on after my physical extinction? Firstly, in my embodied and material frame, the organism will continue to produce and grow: nails and hair. But also bacteria, fluids of all kinds and third parties, such as worms and other parasites. Merging with the environment triggers a number of metamorphoses that are vital, even as they prove lethal. 'They had to call and call', writes Silvia Plath, 'and pick the worms off me like sticky pearls' (1965: 17), thus expressing the close proximity of the creative state of accelerated intensity with that of impersonal death. This is the same author who chose to terminate her spatio-temporal continuum by gassing herself in the kitchen.

Secondly, 'Life' in me will go on in the memories of others, in the multiple webs of interrelations and connections one built up in one's life. Affects and memories are the only afterlife most of us can aspire to (Phillips 1999). Connected to this is the degree of transformation of negative into positive affects that one managed to sustain and enact, and thus also share and distribute nomadically across the space-time of interrelations.

Life as process of becoming is a project, not a given. As such it is in and for the world, pursuing the positive encounters that actualize and increase our collective *potentia*, or desire to make a positive difference in the world. Death can terminate the specific slice of embodied existence that one is, but it cannot change the fact that one will have been a mortal (a 'has been'). The past perfect merges with the future anterior, opening a line of immortality in the sense of friendship with impersonal death in the here and now of just a life.

This vision of immortality within time refers to the awareness and friendly proximity of impersonal death as the always-already presence of an event that bypasses the individual. It is not the same as the eternity of the self, which is obviously a pathetic illusion. Immortality follows from the fact of having to become dead, sooner or later: immortality is not the eternity of the present, but the flow of time itself in its temporal and atemporal dimension. Time as endless becoming involves immortality as its core. This is not meant as a religious statement, but as a logical consequence of endurance as the affective heart of the nomadic subject. The joyfulness that comes from this awareness is a bond of recognition with other human immortals who share the finitude and the awareness of being able to become immortal only by and through dying.

The crucial aspect of this notion of death is that it is the opposite of transcendence because it does not locate eternity in 'the totality of omnipresent truths' (Lloyd 1994: 137), but in the actualization of specific patterns of forces which define each specific singularity. It makes the subject into something that 'will continue to have been' (Lloyd 1994: 138). The eternity of the mind not as duration but as the partaking of a continuing existence makes death powerless to intrude on what a subject has been. Thus, salvation occurs in the realization of eternity within time. What makes a mind eternal is precisely the knowledge of its eternity, which in turn is determined by its power of synthesis between reason, the memory and the imagination.

Beyond the entropic death-drive

To understand this redefinition of death, it is necessary to set it up against the psychoanalytic tradition of thinking of life in relation to the death drive. Laplanche (1976) argues that, as the prototypical modality of the negative, death knows no representation in the unconscious processes: it is beyond any possible representation. This is the source of its link with the feminine, on which Freud projects the full burden of both embodiment and mortality. One's own death is unrepresentable and only the death of the other can possibly be contemplated by the conscious subject. Thus, we can only accede to some intuition of our mortality by projecting it onto someone else or by identification or empathic connection to another, usually a loved one. This positions 'mourning' as a very central mode of relating to the other, and obliquely also to one's own death. In so far as sexuality is the most fundamental drive or mode of relation to others, the death drive is discussed by Freud in the framework of his overall theory of sexuality. The drive is the anti-instinct in that it provides fundamental mediation between the somatic and the psychic in a sort of energetic or libidinal 'delegation'. Freud recognizes the somatic or biological foundations of the subject, but his concern is to de-biologize and therefore to de-naturalize sexuality, so as to disengage it from anything instinctual.

The ethics of psychoanalysis rests precisely on this recognition of the ineluctably social and historical structure of human sexuality, that is to say its non-biological nature. As Laplanche argues, Freud destroys any pretence at 'naturalness' by stressing the wide range of 'perversions' displayed by human sexuality, which 'is only the precarious result of a historical evolution which at every stage of its development may bifurcate differently, resulting in the strangest aberrations' (Laplanche 1976: 15).

Freud gets round the issue of biology through a theory of the drives which describes how the libidinal forces 'lean' or get 'propped up' by some of the body's most essential or vital functions. The psychoanalytic idea is that of a doubling up of the somatic material into a psychic map of pleasures and desires, which bear only a distant relationship to bodily needs or instincts. The drives 'lean on' the instincts but transcend them at each and every step. The motor of the transcendence is pleasure itself. The traces of pleasures and of pain colour the psychic map of the body onto a landscape which has nothing natural in it, and which is subjected to great singular variations in each individual. For Freud, sexuality or desire fall under the Life force, also known as 'Eros'. This is a vital register of self-preservation and growth. Although sexuality depends on these vital needs, its entire course will lead it to dissociate itself from the somatic and the necessary, heading for the superfluous and the gratuitous, that is to say for pleasure. By implication, human sexuality has no predetermined aim or objects. It props itself up against any objects, for the purpose of achieving its aim: self-fulfilment as pleasure.

Here things get tricky, because psychoanalysis also wants to argue that every subject has as its primary object of the desire, the site of origin, that is to say the mother's body. Freud is quite materialistic about this and signals that, in terms of the infant's psychic development, the crucial term of reference is the breast, the provider of food and comfort. In a way the socialization process consists in allowing the mother to emerge as a significant other over and beyond the psychic function she fulfils as provider of 'Life'. Hence Freud's idea that there is no 'original' love object, but that each object has to be found again and is thus phantasmatic in structure. The phantasmatic means that the object that is desired is a substitute by displacement, which means that 'the object which has been lost is not the same as that which is to be rediscovered' (Laplanche 1976: 20). Sexuality is thus marked by the double movement of 'leaning' on the somatic, but also of deviation from it through displacement. By implication, there is no 'natural' sexual organ, but the body as a whole is invested by sexuality.

What Eros or sexuality is, according to Laplanche, is 'nothing but the transcription of the sexual repercussions of anything occurring in the body beyond a certain quantitative threshold' (Laplanche 1976: 22). Any vital function can therefore 'secrete' sexuality, which becomes diffused through the entire bodily self. Bodily orifices are privileged in so far as they are bridges opened out onto the world, points of passage and transition towards the 'outside' of the subject. These 'holes' are also the objects of care by the adults and consequently get sexualized by them as their own fantasy objects. To say that sexuality can be in anything does not, however, amount to a pansexualist position, that everything is sexuality. Freud argues that something always resists sexuality and that its expression is consequently marked by conflict, repression and denial. Why? Partly because the development of human sexuality is slow: after an intense phase in infancy it lies dormant till puberty, when it explodes again in hormonally derived outbursts. This disjointed temporal rhythm favours hindrances and repression.

In order to account for the phenomenon of resistance to sexuality, or the death drive, Freud relies on a full theory of psychic mediation. The point here is that the death drive functions by withholding or subtracting energy. It does not dispose of any libidinal energy of its own, but merely prevents, deviates or defers the libido itself. Hence the need to bring in forms of mediation that account for that which becomes subjected to the negativity of the death drive. To account for it, Freud turns to the fantasy of the primal seduction scene, which Laplanche calls 'the primal deceit'. What this amounts to is that the subject can only represent his or her sexuality to him or herself in passive terms of being seduced by another, rather than by taking full responsibility for one's active desire. Sexuality is thus experienced as a violent eruption, a traumatic impact with external agents. The violence is quite simply that of a degree of intensity or libidinal energy that goes beyond what one is normally accustomed to. I would sum this up in the cry: 'I can't take it any more'. Uttered in pleasure or in pain, this cry marks the boundary beyond which some extreme state of tension is reached, the borders of the self dissolve and the ego and bodily integrity collapse, causing consciousness to lose its hold. Bataille has constructed his entire theory of eroticism on a notion of 'excess' that stresses the porous nature of the border between pleasure and pain, Eros and Thanatos. The erotic imaginary of the late nineteenth and early twentieth centuries rotates round this metaphysically laden couple, desire and death, to which I have opposed the life (as in: *bios/zoe*) force and the positivity of desire, in an unholy mixture of Spinoza, Nietzsche and the early Freud, revisited with Deleuze and Irigaray. I have discussed this vitalist eroticism in chapter 4.

The interconnection between truth and fantasy about the primary seduction scene is such as to make it impossible to differentiate the two. In a move that many have criticized, but which I find of the utmost importance, Freud advances the hypothesis that, for all ends and purposes of the psychoanalytic account of human sexuality, it does not even matter to be able to tell the truth from the fantasy. The point is that the drive, or the libidinal level, has its own register of truth or of reality, which does not coincide with sociological parameters. The violence concerns all that is in excess of the subject's capacity to sustain it. This has a number of important implications.

Firstly, the libidinal drive or energetic change are neutral in terms of content: they merely mark a quantitative level of energy. More accurately: the drives are the ideational representative of a quantity of energy which gets inscribed or encrypted as a memory, that is to say a mnemic trace. This means that memories function as encryption codes which are very variable in each individual; their meaning lies not so much in the content, as in the 'specificity of the paths followed by the circulating quantity' (Laplanche 1976: 57). Significantly, the libido or life force is the one genuine vital force, whereas the death-drive disposes of no energy of its own. The basic principle of psychic life is that the mnemic traces, circulating affective quantities or libidinally driven memories aim to discharge themselves of the very energy that activates them. The drives aim only at self-fulfilment, but paradoxically their fulfilment means equating the zero level of energy, that is to say emptying out. This is consequently the primary definition of the death drive: equating the zero degree of energy.

Secondly, that the boundary of what can be taken as opposed to what is experienced as excessive, violent or painful is variable in each and everyone. It is a negotiable boundary that is not fixed on the same level or the same location for all. This means that standard morality more often than not fails to do justice to the complexity of human sexuality.

Thirdly, repression, denial or psychic defence is a major category of human sexuality. The active desire is transposed by the subject into the fantasy of his or her being seduced. This shift from activity to passivity relieves the subject from his or her responsibility. Freud argues that the psychoanalytic process of elaboration, or working through, allows for the attenuation of the over-charged material that was originally experienced as excessive or traumatic, which gets gradually reabsorbed into the ego. If, however, the ego is not in place at the time of the trauma, inhibition or blockage occurs, which means that the traumatic material cannot be worked through and attenuated in due course.

Fourthly, sexuality is experienced as aggression or as violence; it is therefore an intrinsically disruptive force because it threatens the unity, stability and integrity of the ego. The latter is an enveloping and synthetic unit that aims at capitalizing and totalizing the energy flows, so as to provide stability. Its function therefore is essentially inhibitive. Moreover, the ego, which far from encompassing the whole of the subject in fact merely reflects some specific formation within the psychic apparatus, nonetheless has the self-reflexive ability to pass itself off as a totality, representing the interests of the whole. Sexuality as an impetuous flow of energy threatens the conscious authority of the ego.

Confronted by the evidence that sexuality tends to be experienced as an invasion or a violation, as a disruption of the order guaranteed by the ego, Freud makes a double move. He connects the psychic mechanism of encryption of the affects upon their ideational representative or memory trace to the workings of language. A linguistic model of metaphorical displacement thus offers the basic hermeneutic model for the psychoanalytic idea of the Libido. Furthermore, Freud reinvests the model of rational consciousness as the unquestionable organizing principle of order, unity, stability and cohesion of the self. Over and against the persistence of the cry of agony and ecstasy, 'I can't take it any more', Freud reinstates the supervisory role of the conscious self, and of the ego.

This means that the highly specific and technical function of the ego becomes associated with the conscious, wilful, self-controlled vision of civilized selfhood against which the successive libidinal waves of intensity come to crash. In a titanic struggle of the will against desire, the idea of 'I can't take it any more' becomes simultaneously pathologized and moralized. It is important to stress this point because it is where both Irigaray and Deleuze part company with Freud. Deleuze and Guattari in particular retain from early psychoanalysis the theory of the drives, but actively dissociate it from the centrality of the ego and the necessity of positing the authority of an anonymous subject.

Another significant difference here is that: the ego is held together and also draws its self-retentive capacity from a narcissistic force. Narcissism means an internal reinvestment of the libido, which reduces the subject's exposure to external forces. This limiting capacity is one of the sources of the ego's binding force. As George Eliot (Spinoza's English translator) put it rather bluntly: 'if most of us were fully receptive to the whole range of intensity available to living beings, we would shudder.' Fortunately, 'most of us walk around well-wadded in stupidity' (Eliot 1973: 226). In what must surely feature as one of his most anti-humanistic turns, Freud argues that this dimming down and narrowing down of intensity is vital, necessary and beneficial. It is thanks to this scaling down that the ego can find its stability and thus partake of a vital order of prosperity. Hence Freud's final and in some ways contradictory reappraisal of the ego as a vital support in the formation of the subject.

Laplanche signals the paradox that is shaping up in Freud's thought here. The imaginary and libidinal inertia provided by the ego is beneficial in that it binds, holds and puts to good use and to hard work the libidinal energy. If you remember that the aim of the libido is to empty itself out, approximating to the zero level of affective intensity, then the paradox becomes flagrant. Freud presents us on the one hand with a notion of the libido as that which aims at its own death and, in opposition to it, the ego as that which longs for life and self-preservation. The paradox is that sexuality, which circulates through both, shares in the characteristics of the former rather than in the opaque stability of the latter. The implication is that the pleasure principle is not a vital, but rather a dissipative structure, a zero approximation machine that aims at shedding the very memory traces or ideational contents which it travels through. Sexuality is a perfect vampire, if you wish, or a viral infection that destroys the site that incubates it. Thanatos equals Libido. Laplanche emphasizes that this is the basic principle of psychic life. Hence the ballast-role played by the ego, which prevents complete dispersion and allows for some capitalization on the libidinal material.

Deleuze and Guattari's critique of Freud's conservative approach stresses the link to capitalism and the extent to which the ego sums up the historical and culture-specific features of a vision of the individual as serving the purpose of capitalist industrial economy. It also confirms the centrality of the social institution of the family in the form of the Oedipalized triangle, which in turn inscribes human sexuality within a very charged, confined social space where the adults' fantasies and the infants' need for care are potentially at odds with each other. Philosophical nomadism declares this to be a dated vision of the subject position and by extension of the shape of contemporary capitalism. The crux of the critique of psychoanalysis, however, is conceptual. There is no real necessity other than that given by the context to reattach the drives to a central governing principle guaranteed by the ego and the liberal bourgeois definition of the individual. In fact, Freud himself provides us with the tools to undo this vision, although he disowns it himself. Thus, the idea that the drives 'lean on' and are propped by vital functions but do not coincide with them means that sexuality develops in humans by detaching itself from any natural pre-given object. Sexuality can in fact turn upon itself and constitute some reflexive moments of extraordinary autonomy from the will of the individual.

Philosophical nomadism takes this point and develops the more radical conclusions from Freud's theory, namely that sexuality is flowing and nomadic, not stable and rooted. The libidinal rule is, as Laplanche points out, the primacy of zero over constancy, of the drives over the ego, so that free energy tends to diminish whereas bound energy tends to increase. Whereas Freud concludes from this the necessity of reasserting the biological organism as a necessary mediator, a store of energy ruled by the ego, he is downplaying the far more forceful fact that this coagulation or stratification of forces that get bundled up as an organism, a self, an individual or an ego, is merely a wrapper. What is at the core of it, however, is the death-drive as the most vital flow, that which aims at expressing its energy, exhausting it and emptying it out, spending to death, so to speak. Contrary to the common-sense, sentimental celebrations of 'Life', psychoanalysis could give us the conceptual means of explaining how, at the core of the bound mass of energy of the self, there is a principle of anti-life, a force that is not vital but dissipative. The death-drive is the constitutive principle of libidinal circulation.

Freud did not push his findings far enough: decency, expediency, fear and the need to survive in a hostile social environment made him hold back and celebrate the need for the self and the retentive function of the ego as that which fulfils the vital function. But what does this vital function consist of, ultimately? Laplanche's paradox is very illuminating here: it consists of blocking the flows, storing up energy (capital, profits, fats, money), fixing the subject in sedentary stability. In opposition to this binding force, the libido, operated by the death-drive, aims at reaching the state of pure movement, discharging its affects as it goes, moving within the chain till it is completely spent. Thus, the death principle which Freud says cannot be represented is relocated at the heart of the unconscious and hence of the subject, so as to become its most radical expression. By choosing to re-embrace standard morality, Freud leaves us a mixed legacy, because the 'Life' which this morality venerates is in psychoanalytic terms the denial of the very libidinal force which is the source of the subject's vitality. A perfect and therefore unsolvable paradox.

Philosophical nomadism exploits this paradox fully and it proceeds by depathologizing and demoralizing the discussion. The Life and death forces get recoded, with Spinoza, in terms of activity and passivity; these are expressed in morally neutral terms and simply refer to that which enhances the subject's *conatus* or *potentia* (affirmative or positive forces), as opposed to that which diminishes it (negative or reactive forces). The authority, centrality and significance of a central conscious subject dominated by the ego is reduced accordingly. Even more significant is the extent to which Deleuze disengages this ethology of forces from any dialectical scheme, rejecting the Hegelian approach in favour of a more cartographic one. Life and death can occur simultaneously and even overlap, thus they do not follow the 'either/or' scheme, but rather the 'and/and/and' scheme. In her critique of the vulgarity or commonness of Freud's notion of the death-drive, Dorothea Olkowski (1999) underlines the extent to which psychoanalysis indexes the Ego to powers of desexualization and the emptying out of unconscious libidinal forces. In opposition to this entropic mode, Deleuze proposes endless contractions and expansions or duration and extension in processual becomings or qualitative differentiations.

In philosophical nomadology, time is one. Becoming solidifies into moments of being, just as pure magma cools off and gains a shape and a vertical structure in a manner that is directly proportional to the loss of heat or intensity which it undergoes. The line of consolidation is always molar: it blocks and uses up energy without producing any in return. It is a form waiting to be filled by matter that is activated to higher and higher degrees of intensity and heat. Ansell-Pearson (1997a, 1997b) argues that in a Spinozist–Deleuzian perspective the positivity of difference and its unfolding through processes of becoming undercuts the claims of entropy. Entropy is the tendency of energy to cancel itself out, so as to evolve into something homogeneous and identical to itself. Through evolution, all differences would then get smoothed out, till everything resembles everything else – in a condition of death. The paradigmatic value of this notion of heat-death is contested by Deleuze as a typically nineteenth-century state of affairs, which installs 'reason' as 'the power which identifies and equalizes difference, concealing the diversity of existence by subjecting it to an entropic narrative in the form of a philosophy of history, establishing a politics of identity and, finally, branding the absurd or the irrational as that which resists appropriation to the common sense of humanity' (Ansell-Pearson 1997a: 11).

In other words, Deleuze argues for a non-entropic evolution of differences, which follows neither a linear logic nor one of recognition and identity, but rather evolves in a non-linear fashion through spontaneous self-organization and flows of becomings. Complexity is the key term here and it is reflected in the new scientific reasoning proposed among others by Prigogine, which opposes a view of 'life as evolving in contradistinction to the alleged laws of physics, constantly wrestling with inevitable destruction and decay at the hands of the demon of entropy' (Prigogine and Stengers 1980: 11). A new alliance of physics and biology is under way, which rests on and reasserts the positive logic of difference through repeated patterns of becoming.

Sustainability stresses the idea of continuity and assumes faith in a future, and also a sense of responsibility for 'passing on' to future generations a world that is liveable and worth living in. A present that endures is a sustainable model of the future. Hence the importance of stopping at the second-last drink/smoke/shot. 'Enough', or 'not going too far', expresses the necessity of framing, not the common-sense morality of the mainstream cultural orthodoxy. 'Enough' is a term that defines a cartography of sustainability.

Bio-centred egalitarianism depathologizes and demoralizes the flows of the drives, and reinstates circulation as the basic principle in the organization of the nomadic subject. Death, in such a framework, is merely a point, it is not the horizon against which the human drama is played out. The centre is taken by *bios/zoe* and its ever-recurring flows of vitality. In and through many deaths, *bios/zoe* lives on. Deleuze turns this also into a critique of the whole Heideggerian legacy that places mortality at the centre of philosophical speculation. Only the arrogance of a self-consciousness desperately seeking power and recognition could invest the individual self with such exorbitant and megalomaniac powers of control. It is against this self-glorifying image of a pretentious and egotistical narcissistic and paranoid consciousness that philosophical nomadism unleashes the multiple dynamic forces of *bios/zoe* that do not coincide with the human, let alone with consciousness. Irigaray does something analogous when she proposes the 'sensible transcendental' as the affirmative power of an embodied and sexualized subject that does not conform to the phallogocentric format. These are non-essentialist brands of vitalism.

This is not a way of denying death, or the importance of negativity in the constitution of the subject: it merely dislocates it and disengages it from the metaphysical heart of the subject. Accepting the centrality of the death-drive in the sense of the tendency for the affects or the drives to reach the zero approximation level is a critique of the bourgeois liberal view of the subject, not a rejection of subjectivity (as Hegel claimed in his critique of Spinoza). Such a position does not condemn us to nihilism, nor does it plunge us into the naive belief that the answer lies in something called 'spontaneity', a notion dear to all new age thinking. I disagree with these options. What follows from nomadic subjectivity is rather the need for a different type of ethical scale, one which would allow for a wider range of variations of intensity among individuals, while putting higher value not on the capitalization, stocking and binding of energy, but rather on a sustainable use of the whole lot.

Self-styling one's death

Dying
Is an art, like everything else.
I do it exceptionally well.
(Sylvia Plath, 'Lady Lazarus')

In poststructuralist ethics, both God and the principle of immortality undergo a fundamental critique in terms of the embodied, and consequently mortal and partial, structure of the subject. What matters is not death as the big gaping hole waiting at the edge of (our) time, but rather the modes in which we live, perceive and negotiate with dying in the course of life, by cultivating positive ethical encounters. Lest this be misunderstood for a Christian type of message, let me stress again the non-theist nature of this statement. Death is not entropy or the return to inert lifeless matter, but rather the opening up of new intensities and possibilities of the inhuman or non-human kind. Ansell-Pearson describes it as 'the immeasurable, the alogical, the unrepresentable' (1997b: 58). Death needs to be freed from the double burden of mechanism and finalism in order to be experienced as merging with the endless generative energy of a cosmos that is supremely indifferent to humans. Endorsing Blanchot against Freud, Deleuze inscribed death into life not as the dyad Eros–Thanatos, but rather as incorporeality, or the ultimate crack, perish consciousness, that we may experiment with this final leap.

As Adam Phillips (1999) notes in his remarkable cross-reading of Darwin and Freud, the notion of 'transience' comes firmly to the fore of their concerns. Phillips notes: 'If once we could think of ourselves as (sinful) animals aspiring to be more God-like, now we can wonder what, as animals without sin (though more than capable of choosing harm), we might aspire to' (Phillips, 1999: 17). In open contrast to traditional morality, this ethical approach is critical of the lofty idealism and the misplaced forms of perfectionism it engenders. High ideals are forms of escapism from the contingencies and the partialities of our existence. A sober and more secular brand of realism is proposed instead, one that emphasizes our ability to be part of our environment, part of 'nature', while being aware that the human is not at the centre of it. On the contrary, the relentless generative power of 'Life' is such that it is indifferent to the fate of humans as such. Pragmatic realism is the key to an ethical behaviour that stresses processes of active interaction in a bio-centred, egalitarian mode, as well as the instability and flux of individual identity.

The processes of thinking, or of theoretical representation of such an embodied and embedded subject, are not only partial, but also basically defensive in structure. Consciousness is an attempt to come to terms with the forces that have already made us who we are: it is external, other-driven, and *a posteriori*. More importantly, death or the transience of life (Phillips 1999) is written at the core of the subject and is integral to the life-processes. Life being desire which essentially aims at extinguishing itself, i.e. reaching its aim and then dissolving, the wish to die is another way to express the desire to live. Not only is there no dialectical tension between Eros and Thanatos, but also the two forces are really just one; *zoe* as a life-force aims to reach its own fulfilment. However, as Phillips astutely points out, the point is not that the human's innermost desire is to disappear, but rather that he or she wishes to do so in his or her own way. 'The organism wishes to die only in its own fashion. There is a death ... that is integral to, of a piece with, one's life: a self-fashioned, self-created death' (Phillips 1999: 77).

This is the paradox that lies at the heart of the post-humanist ethics I am exploring here. While at the conscious level all of us struggle for survival, at some deeper level of our unconscious structures all we long for is to lie silently and let time wash over us in the perfect stillness of not-life.

The self-styling of one's death is the logical complement of the notion of 'autopoiesis', or self-organization and construction, which I discussed in chapters 2 and 3. Self-styling one's death means cultivating an approach, a 'style' of conceptual creativity which sustains the impact with the line of cracking and engenders counter-habits, or alternative memories that do not repeat and confirm the dominant modes of representation. The aesthetic model drawn from painting or from the musical refrain is crucial to understanding this mixture of conceptual rigour and creativity. The main issue at stake here is to break the cycles of inert repetitions. The generative capacity of *bios/zoe*, in other words, cannot be bound or confined to the single, human individual. Rather it transversally trespasses such boundaries in the pursuit of its aim, which is self-perpetuation. 'Life' is understood here as aiming essentially at self-perpetuation and then, after it has achieved its aim, at dissolution. It can be argued that it also encompasses what we usually call 'death'. Just as the life in me is not mine in the appropriative sense espoused by liberal individualism, but is rather a time-sharing device, so the death in me is not mine, except in a very circumscribed sense of the term. In both cases all 'I' can hope for is to craft both my life and my death in a mode, at a speed and fashion which are sustainable and adequate: 'I' can self-style them autopoietically, thus expressing my essence as the constitutive desire to endure (*potentia*).

The same process of heat-death can also be rendered in a different set of representations drawn from music. The production of sounds, even the cultivated use of the singing voice, can produce effects that destabilize us, heighten our awareness and stimulate our perception. How to endure the impact without rejecting it as unbearable is a problem. In some ways, the pure expression of intensity is impossible. It is unattainable because the variations of intensity are infinite, contrary to the limited human capacity to express it and sustain it. This is why time is so crucial a factor. In music, time can be heard as a set of variations of speed or intensity: moments of being, beats and partitions, never one cosmic whole. Silence, stillness and the inaudible can also be made perceptible in music, which has the power to approximate infinity. To reduce this fundamental desire for the stillness of being ex-centric to life to mere nihilism or self-destruction, is to miss the point altogether. I would say rather that self-destructive forms of behaviour are the way – the only way – some of us humans have found to express and experience this constitutive longing for non-life, which lies at the heart of subjectivity. Actively to desire to die one's death is the same as wanting to live life as intensely as possible. My life is my story about dying in my own fashion – argues Phillips – thus expressing my desire as *potentia*, while *zoe* just aims to grow stronger and go further. We thus pursue what we are ultimately trying to avoid: 'we are essentially, idiosyncratic suicides, but not from despair, but because it is literally our nature to die' (Phillips 1999: 110).

The point of the ethics of joyful affirmation and becoming is to extract this awareness from the economy of loss, the logic of lack, and the moral imperative to dwell in never-ending and unresolvable states of mourning. We need to move beyond both nihilism and the tragic solemnity of traditional morality, to grow to appreciate instead that wishing to die is an affirmation of the *potentia* of that life in me which, by definition, does not bear my name.

The idea of styling your own life – in the autopoiesis sense – is far from a merely aesthetic gesture. In this, as in other cases, it is important to disengage this notion from the connotations it inherited from the nineteenth century. Autopoiesis is a far cry from the dandy-like posturing that it is often caricatured as. The 'practices of the self', which Foucault wrote extensively about, are rather an ethical and practical exercise. They involve constructing one's subjectivity without the reference to and hence the support of an essentialistic vision of human nature – as innately rational, or divinely ordained, or linked to liberal individualism. Without self-referentiality, but rather in relation to a number of 'others', whose otherness is not conceptualized or approached in a dualistic mode of binary oppositions, but in an open and non-hierarchical manner. Last but not least, for Foucault the self is constructed through concrete and material practices of accountability for one's self and one's position. In the classical mode of philosophical self-reflexivity, these tend to be practices of narration and writing. The spiritual diary or journal is the most established genre in what constitutes a well-established confessional mode. As is known, Foucault traces the genealogies of this genre from the Christian/Catholic practice of the religious confession, through the psychoanalytic speech and dialogue it entails, well into modernity's obsession with the self's sexuality as the alleged location of truth.

In his polemic with the foundationalism that sustains this vision of subjectivity, Foucault proposes as an alternative a subject-in-process that is inscribed in networks of relations of discursive production and hence of power (as *potestas/potentia*). Claire Colebrook[5] has argued forcefully that Foucault's biopolitics has a more limited range of applicability than Deleuze, in so far as Foucault stays within the Aristotelian position by postulating life on the horizon of the political, which reduces *zoe* to the biological. Foucault's reference to biopolitics is therefore an objection to

[5] In 'The meaning of life', a paper delivered at the Deleuze conference at Trent University, in May 2004.

modernity's increasing emphasis on and commercial and scientific interest in man's species being, that is to say his genetic life (in the sense of *zoe*). Foucault does offer a criticism of the mobilization of life forces by the polity, suggesting that ethics can only be normalized when it takes the site of *zoe* into view. He renders all in terms of the ethics/aesthetics of self-styling, or the art of self-creation, but does not fully think the material or corporeal side of this matter, namely that the subject is materially embedded, sexually embodied, historically located, interacting with others and productive or affirmative of his or her own vitality.

Agamben's subsequent work on *bios* and *zoe*, as I suggested in chapter 1, does not go much further. His position is deficient in many respects because he is nostalgic and sees the mobilization of *bios* in modernity as the loss of a more authentic thought of potentiality. Following the Heideggerian mode, he also makes etymological distinctions that we have now lost, which however turn out to be inaccurate. Deleuze, on the other hand, takes the politics of *zoe* to mean a world in which there can be no distinction between the socialized forces of the body politic and the corporeal forces of matter. Deleuze thinks it possible to account for power before its political coding, as in human desire or germinal flux. The problem for a vitalist ethics consequently is how to explain the syntheses that emerge from this encounter between personal and pre-personal forces (genealogically and geologically). Foucault on the other hand insists that desire can only be thought through norms and regulations. This indicates residual doses of Kantianism in Foucault's notion of biopolitics.

Deleuze develops a rigorous conceptual critique of Kantian moral imperatives, and hence of law and lack. Following Spinoza, Deleuze proposes instead a more materialistic, a geometrical pattern of interrelationality, a geometrical pattern of multiple connections, as a web of multiple connections, as befits his non-unitary vision of the subject.

The missing link in this argument about self-styling or the practices of the self is feminist theory. As both Foucault and Deleuze acknowledge – albeit in secondary and often indirect ways – the best example of a social practice of the self, in the transformative and radical sense they intend to give it, is provided by the women's movements. Local, yet global in inspiration and reach; theoretically informed, yet practically minded; political in every aspect, in so far as they have politicized everyday life and the entire sphere of the personal, the women's movements are the best enactment of that molecular way of practising a politicized version of what Deleuze and Guattari theorize in more abstract terms.

The feminist practice of the politics of locations, later to become situated knowledge, provides the missing link between the theory and the practice of a non-unitary, relational and outward-bound definition of the subject. Self-styling, in this framework, is both an epistemological standpoint which deals with the difficulties of providing adequate cartographic accounts of one's locations, and an ethic political one. To learn to know oneself in terms of the politics of locations requires a lucid materialist approach, and hence familiarity with the ways in which power – positive as well as negative – stimulates one's existence. It also rests upon a collective structure, a community or a group. Locations are not determined by self-naming, but rather through dialogues, clashes and encounters with others. The kind of 'self' that is 'styled' in and through such a process is not one, nor is it an anonymous multiplicity: it is an embedded and embodied set of interrelations, constituted in and by the immanence of his or her expressions, acts and interactions with others and held together by the powers of remembrance: by continuity in time. The 'self' that is 'styled' in this manner needs an inbuilt ethical barometer to stay on the only course worth pursuing, that of sustainability. Lest this be confused with the Christian morality of carefully chosen moderation, it is important to stress that exactly the same exercise in self-styling, or the practice of the self, is at work in the far less evident exercise of styling one's own death. 'Life' is not to be understood here as the Christian notion of the self-evidence of being or staying alive. Survival is not the point, but sustainability is.

Death, or the evanescence of the subject

How does all this relate to the project of ethics as a qualitative evaluation of the costs involved in experimenting with boundaries of sustainability?

In keeping with the deep materialism of his Spinozist roots, Deleuze stresses not only the importance of shame and proximity to the crack as the motors of ethical behaviour, but also the relevance of transience for the subject. What we truly desire as humans is to disappear, to step on the side of life and let it flow by, without actually stopping it: becoming-imperceptible. And yet our fundamental drive (*conatus*) is to express the potency of life (*potentia*), by joining forces with other flows of becoming. The great animal-machine universe is the horizon of becoming that marks the eternity of life as *bios/zoe* and its resilience, its generative power expressed also through what we humans call death: becoming a skeleton, larvae, bacteria.

Indeed, what we humans truly yearn for is to disappear by merging into this eternal flow of becomings, the precondition for which is the loss, disappearance and disruption of the self. The ideal would be to take only memories and to leave behind only footsteps. What we most truly desire is to surrender the self, preferably in the agony of ecstasy, thus choosing our own way of disappearing, our way of dying to and as our self. This can be described also as the moment of dissolution of the subject; the moment of its merging with the web of non-human forces that frame him or her. Call it death, this point of evanescence has to do with radical immanence, with the totality of the moment in which, as Lacan cynically and wittily put it, you coincide completely with your body; you become a corpse. In the perspective of sustainable ethics, the same issue is treated with more subtlety and considerably more compassion by distinguishing death along the majority-line (*Chronos*) from the impersonal death which occurs along the minority-line of Becoming (*Aion*).

At the point of their evanescence or dissolution, subjects are enfleshed entities that are immersed in the full intensity and luminosity of becoming. Theirs, however, is the brightness of phosphorescent worms, not the light of the eternal rays of some monotheistic God. This, therefore, is the glorious expression of the life force that is *zoe*, and not the emanation of some divine essence. Radical immanence as a mode of thinking the subject, and as a philosophical style, deflates the pretence of grandiose eternity that marks the Christian religious values. Life is eternal, but this eternity is postulated on the dissolution of the self, the individual ego, as the necessary premise. The life in me does not bear my name: 'I' inhabits it as a time-share.

Whereas Christianity, even in its postmodern variations (I am thinking of Gianni Vattimo), turns this vitality into the preface to the reaffirmation of a higher order, a totalizing One into which all fragments will reassemble and find a harmonious reallocation, the philosophy of radical immanence remains resolutely attached to *zoe* – the life force of recurrent waves of positive differences. Life endures in or as bio-centred egalitarianism in the ruins of the self-representation of a unified, controlling individual subject allegedly motivated by a self-reflexive consciousness. Becoming imperceptible is the ultimate stage in a process that, at *some* point, must go through a becoming-women, but *not* stop there. Deleuze does argue that all processes of becoming aim at the becoming-imperceptible, but he thinks within the flat ontology on immanence, which encompasses both the embodiment of mind and the 'embrainment of matter'. There is no collapse of being into non-being, or ontological implosion, but rather a reversal of all negativity into the great animal, the Body-without-Organs, the cosmic echoing chamber of infinite becomings.

What is at stake in the ethics of sustainable nomadic subjects, ultimately, is an acceleration that would allow us to jump over the high fence of the ruins of metaphysics. Not in a utopian mode, but in a very embodied and embedded way, actualized in the here and now. The swift exhilaration that emanates from texts that are clearly indexed on the *potentia* of life, and not on its diminishment, or negation – has to put wings on our feet and infuse joyfulness. If it doesn't have the right beat, it will not work. But if it blasts off our minds with excessive intensity, it will not be much good either. Let us just opt for the staggering intelligence of 'just a life' as Deleuze put it in the last text he wrote before ending his own slice of life. Just a life in its radical immanence, in affirmation and sets of discontinuous but sustainable becomings. It may be a way of returning the subject to the specific complexity of his or her singularity, and returning the activity of 'thinking' to a lightness of touch, a speed which many of us passionately aspire to.

Post-secular spirituality

Nomadic sustainable ethics treads a secular path within the Western philosophical tradition of critical theory. This is crucial to scientific debates because most scientists, thinking people and critical thinkers today are atheistic or non-religious and thus secularism facilitates dialogue. Of course, as I indicated in chapter 1, some scientists are militantly secular and thus often turn out to be as dogmatic as the religions they are committed to fighting.

Secular thought is also important in so far as it is the backbone of Western feminism and human rights activism and it stretches all the way back to the Enlightenment. These historical roots are crucial to me in terms of both cartography and accountability. Last but not least, a non-religious approach is important because I find present-day religions are dogmatic and reactionary in their approach to issues both of technology and of sexuality and gender. By extension, contemporary religiously defined women's rights movements are feminist in their support of issues affecting the status of women, but quite defensive about the Western feminist agenda on sexuality, homosexuality and reproductive rights. As second-class citizens women have to fight for basic human rights, such as the right to have rights, that is to say issues of entitlement and access to ethical and political subjectivity. My aim is to avoid moralism but also fight cultural relativism: we need transversal alliances that do not stop on the border of cultural, religious or any other form of identity.

I want to defend secular thinking because the contemporary world order is too global to fit into any one religious system. We consequently need to develop the skills necessary to live with all of them and to try to create a consensus among all of them. In conclusion, I want to take seriously the kind of mutations that have occurred in the structure of human subjectivity under the impact of advanced, opulent post-industrial social conditions, which I have analysed extensively in chapter 2. They include the collapse of the humanist paradigm of human nature; the decline of the humanist view of 'Man' and his 'others'; the decline of self-evident, 'natural' visions of life and of values aimed at the respect and defence of 'Life'; the multiple processes of racialization; the need to reconsider self-destructive practices in terms of the difficulties involved in coping with the challenges of our times and the need to base ethics on practices of accountability and a forward-looking, non-nostalgic sense of what 'Life' is worth. I believe that such a need is best served by a non-unitary, non-linear mode of nomadic subjectivity that unfolds towards issues of general concern in a rigorously secular mode.

The rhizomatic web of glocalized claims for new forms of universalism which aim at regrounding the values which animate the non-unitary subject inevitably raises issues that are usually and hastily classified under the heading of spirituality. Such a claim needs to be qualified critically, considering the popularity of neo-eschatological visions of catastrophe and redemption that circulate nowadays. The resurgence of 'new age' spiritual practices is also a salient feature of the contemporary landscape. There is also an urgent need to contextualize and take into account the return of religious movements of all kinds, including the fundamentalists, as a geopolitical force at the start of the new millennium. It is just because of these phenomena that the issue of spirituality needs to be rethought from within the post-Enlightenment tradition of secularity. This is not the residual mysticism of a notion of life as pure becoming, empty of meaning, but rather a concrete plan for embedding and embodying new formations of living subjects. Not an evolutionary tale, but a qualitative leap of values.

Edward Said (1978) in his influential work on orientalism first alerted critical theorists in the West to the need to develop a reasoned and secular account of Enlightenment-based humanism. Following Said the 'post-colonial' movement argued for and documented the extent to which the Enlightenment ideals of reason, secular tolerance, equality under the law and democratic rule, need not and indeed historically have not excluded European practices of violent domination, exclusion and systematic and instrumental use of terror. To acknowledge that reason and barbarism are not self-contradictory, nor Enlightenment and horror, need not result in either cultural relativism or moral nihilism. As the poststructuralist left has been arguing in the aftermath of colonialism, Auschwitz, Hiroshima and the Soviet Gulag, we need to be historically accountable both for the promises of the Enlightenment as an ideal and for its shortcomings. On the basis of this location of historical accountability a revised and more critical brand of humanistic thought and practice needs to be developed, on the debris of unkept promises. This practice is a form of resistance against the horrors that have been bred by the West's arrogant assumption that the motor of human evolution is the progressive historical implementation of rational premises which emerge – like the goddess Athena – fully clad and armed for battle, from the father's head. Phallocentrism and Eurocentrism need to be dislodged, if Western humanism is to regain any ethical credibility at all.

Said's formulation of the role of post-colonial intellectuals located in one of the many diasporas that mark the contemporary globalized world, has proved influential in preserving a deeply secular and non-romanticized understanding of both 'home culture' and 'exile'. As I argued in chapter 2, most post-colonial theory has a strong humanistic leaning, as does African humanism in the form of *Ubuntu*, sustained by secular saints such as Nelson Mandela.

Homi Bhabha's idea of 'subaltern secularism' is of great relevance here. He borrows the term 'subaltern' from Gramsci's theory of hegemonic power and he extends it to all those who are excluded from it because of race, gender, class, generation, etc. Very keen to retain the key values of the Enlightenment such as secularism, tolerance and solidarity, but equally determined to disengage them from their ethno-specific and Eurocentric roots, Bhabha wants to relocate these notions within a transnational context, thus making them accountable for the colonial and imperial aspects of that very Enlightenment era which produced them. In keeping with this legacy, and in opposition to liberal neo-humanism, Homi Bhabha supports a revisitation of the notion of secularism, which he wants to attach to the subalterns' existence and experience. With reference to Nussbaum (see chapter 1), he argues that secularism, like all the key concepts of the Enlightenment – individualism and liberalism – appears more self-evident than it is. Bhabha wants to broaden the relevance and applicability of this concept to cover the 'colonial and imperial enterprise which was an integral part of that same Enlightenment' (Bhabha 1996: 209). Bhabha argues that we need to separate secularism from its Western roots and its 'unquestioned adherence to a kind of ethnocentric and Eurocentric belief in the self-proclaimed values of modernization' (Bhabha 1996: 209). In other words, it is important to address the issue of religious belief and of spiritual values in a transnational mode. In this endeavour, the notion of individualism is not helpful in that it implies a 'freedom of choice' which bears no relation to the history of marginalized and oppressed people of colonial descent. This amounts to making liberalism broader and to extend it to those very subjects who historically never enjoyed the tolerance and solidarity that it preaches. Bhabha shrewdly points out that a secular space is the only social location that would allow for a serious and peaceful confrontation of the conflicting understandings of secularism itself, let alone of the comparative values of different religions. Fighting for such subaltern secular spaces is a priority for a postmodern quest for secular spirituality.

Subaltern secularism is especially relevant as a critique of the facile liberal idea of 'free choice' – a notion that disregards the asymmetries in power-relations among colonial and other marginalized subjects. The point is to extend liberal values to those who historically have been excluded from it, without falling prey to the conflicting brands of fundamentalism that are structuring the geopolitical landscape of the age of globalization. A subaltern brand of secularism allows for spiritual and religious practices to develop in an ethical space of freedom that needs to be constructed and not be taken for granted as an _a priori_ condition for liberal exchanges. Only a secular space can grant such social freedom and thus create subject positions that empower a freedom of choice. But only a transnational space based not on the assumption of sameness but rather on the recognition of difference can disengage this practice from ethnocentrism. Bhabha argues that groups like the UK-based Women Against Fundamentalism, the Southall Black Sisters, and Gita Sahgal's work with Asian Women are examples of subaltern secularism in that they both posit and test the boundaries of alternative social spaces that engender the recognition of multiple differences, which can found a notion of 'freedom of choice' which is taken as a duty to society. Bhabha concludes:

> Secularism at its best, I believe, enshrines this public, ethical duty of choice precisely because it often comes from the most private experience of suffering, doubt and anxiety. We need to 'secularize' the public sphere so that, paradoxically, we may be free to follow our strange gods or pursue our much-maligned monsters, as part of a collective and collaborative 'ethics' of choice. (Bhabha 1996: 211)

Nomadic subjectivity as an eco-philosophy contains a post-secular spirituality, redefined as a topology of affects, based on the selection of these forces. This process of unfolding affects is central to the composition of radically immanent bodies and thus it can be seen as the actualization of enfleshed materialism. The selection of the forces of becoming is regulated by an ethics of joy and affirmation which functions through the transformation of negative into positive passions (see chapter 4). The selection is essentially a matter of affinity: being able to enter into a relation with another entity whose elements appeal to one produces a joyful encounter. They express one's *potentia* and increase the subject's capacity to enter into further relations, to grow and to expand. This expansion is time-bound: the nomadic subject by expressing and increasing its positive passions empowers itself to last, to endure, to continue through and in time. By entering into relations, nomadic becomings engender possible futures. They construct the world by making possible a web of sustainable interconnections. This is the point of becoming: a collective assemblage of forces that coalesce around commonly shared elements and empower them to grow and to last. Deleuze attempts to disengage biology from the structural functionalism and neo-determinism of DNA-driven linearity and to veer it instead towards the zigzagging patterns of nomadic becoming.

I want to steer a course between the renewed Christian spirituality and sacralization of 'Life' on the one hand, and the new determinism and dogmatic self-assurance of genetic biosciences on the other. Both hold themselves up as the sole holders of eternal truths and of rationally demonstrable beliefs. Yet, throughout, I have upheld and defended secular thinking, in the spirit of the philosophical materialism that I see as the tradition to which my work belongs. Materialism and secular thought go well together and the positivity of their interaction needs to be stressed at the dawn of the third millennium, when the return of religious fundamentalisms of all kinds coincides with a rebirth of new age practices. In such a social context, it is important to think critically about the notion and the ideal of spirituality, in the spirit of the materialist philosophical nomadism which I favour.

Spiritual practices are embodied and embedded. They do not take place in a flight from the flesh, but through it. Nomadic subjectivity as radical immanence implies a practice of spirituality of the non-theistic, post-humanist, non-Christian kind. This practice has to do with the ultimate phase of the process of becoming, namely the becoming-imperceptible. This notion needs to be rescued from the tradition of transcendence in Christian metaphysics and be transposed into the idea of radical imma-nence. This implies a politics of location, i.e. an embodied and embedded grounding of the subject in becoming. It also involves an ethics of affirma-tion, i.e. the effort to cultivate and enhance the relations that sustain one's empowerment (potential), so as to work towards transforming pain and negative passions into active, as in activating, affects. Last but not least, nomadic spirituality expresses faith in the future and thus contributes to the creation of social horizons of hope (see epilogue).

The sense of endurance I want to defend as the process of becoming-imperceptible is less grandiose and considerably less narcissistic because it is not interested in capitalizing on well-placed moral investments in the ever-after. Capitalism is the religion that mirrors and supports the ethos of profits. Nomadic spirituality, on the other hand, is profit-free and even anti-profit. It is beyond the ego and its metaphysical life-insurance poli-cies. It enjoys and experiences joy in giving everything away in what used to be called a mystical merging with the cosmos. The same suspension or erasure of the boundaries of the self can also be found in eroticism, in that *jouissance* which, for Lacan, was best expressed by the ecstasy of Saint Teresa as depicted by Bernini. It is feminine in its fluidity, its empathy and yearning for otherness in a non-appropriative mode, in non-closure and intensity. Becoming-imperceptible is the ultimate stage in the becoming-woman, in that it marks the transition to a larger, 'natural' cosmic order. Clarice Lispector describes it as an *oratorio*, a song of praise and of accep-tance of all that is. Which, for nomadism, means being worthy of all that happens to us, in a pragmatic version of *amor fati*. All that ever happens is the recurrence of difference in successive waves of repeated, successive and excessive becomings, in which 'I' participates and gets formatted, whereas *zoe* acts as the motor.

If life is not human, however – it cannot be divine, either – certainly not in the Christian mode which is the inflated projection of the paranoia and narcissism of the Western subject in his molar formation. Nomadic becoming-imperceptible leans towards a spirituality, which is the opposite of mysticism in the sentimental mode dear to Christianity. It is definitely not a stepping stone to the data bank in the sky, the final cashing-in-point for our existential frequent flyer programme to get an upgrade to the VIP lounge in the heavens. Nomadic ethics is not inter-ested in capitalizing on well-placed moral investments. Nomadic post-secular spirituality is not a morality of fringe benefits, but rather an ethics of non-profit. It is beyond metaphysical life-insurance politics. It enjoys gratuitous acts of kindness in the mode of a becoming-world of the subject. Joy in giving something away for free – even if you're not sure of having it; give it for the hell of it, let it go for the love of the world.

This profound generosity, which in Christianity used to be one with a mystical merging with the cosmos, entails the evanescence of the subject in a process of amplification of the field of being. I want to plead for a secular sense of respect or the singularity of embodied subjects that are non-unitary, that is to say creative compounds of composite forces. Respecting this heterogeneity while acknowledging the diversity is the balancing act that a nomadic subject needs to accomplish. This is where the ethics of sustainability emerges as a way of doing justice to the complexities within, while providing a cartographic account of the external power-relations. Nomadic spirituality as radical immanence proposes becoming-imperceptible as transcendental empiricism. It is far closer to the full void of meditation in the Buddhist sense of the term, propelled towards the ultimate threshold, a cosmic echoing chamber that resonates like a web of interconnected, post-human, molecular and viral types of relations. It is the monstrous energy of the cosmos, the great animal, the machinic production of gods. It is indeed the case that the Life in me will go on, but it is *zoe*, not the rational conscious, sovereign individual, without a 'self' that could even claim to supervise, let alone control, the process. It will go on in the superior generative powers of a Life that is relentlessly not human in its power to endure, in its obscene capacity to fulfil the vitality that animates it. *Zoe* can be cruel: cells split and multiply in cancer as in pregnancy. The logic is the same, as is the vitality, although the effects on the psycho-social entity that supports them – the actual subject – can be dramatically different. But Life will go on, as *zoe* always does; so much so that the injunction is not the classical 'give me life (*bios*) or give me death', but rather 'give me life (*zoe*) and hence give me death'.

ON BECOMING-IMPERCEPTIBLE

The qualitative leap necessary to induce a positive ethics of sustainability is a creative process, a praxis, an activity. As such it simply needs to be performed: just do it! What's in a maxim, after all?

It is a statement or expression of my desire in the sense of *potentia*, akin to the 'yes I will' of James Joyce's Molly Bloom. It is also an act of faith in our capacity to make a difference and as such it is an expression of generosity and love of the world. It is also a plea, an open question, a reaching out, or an invitation to the dance ('let's do it'). It is an imperative, an injunction to endure in the sense both of lasting and of suffering, but also a declaration of love; a gesture of defiance of social norms and resistance against the inertia of habits and settled conventions. More importantly, it is an act of autopoiesis, or affirmative self-creation not of an atomized self, or a separate individual, but rather of a nomadic subject of different speeds and intensity of becoming. As such, it is a refusal of the Oedipalized position and an assertion of firm detachment ('you're on your own now, so get on with it, at your own speed and for as long as you can stand it!'). It is an injunction in which endurance and sustainability intersect in producing an impersonal mode of singularity; the stark and imperative tone cuts down the sentimentality of dominant visions of the subject, as well as the overstated authority of the leader whose dogmatism and presence are sources of veneration. In this respect, the injunction to do it is the opposite of the '*mots d'ordre*' or the political slogan. There is no assurance here of a teleologically ordained trajectory, just the urge to get on with it, just do it, though the final destination may not be very clear. All that matters is the going, the movement.

It just so happens that, in the perverse logic of advanced capitalism, 'Just do it!' is also the chief slogan of the transnational global corporation Nike (Naomi Klein 1999). Advanced capitalism, the great nomad, markets this slogan as an incitement to individual over-achievement and self-construction. Philosophical nomadism, as a critique of this logic, introduced a different inflexion into this maxim, thus setting limits to its profit-making tendency. It also challenges the perverse temporality of capitalism, fighting against the theft of the present to construct sustainable paths of becoming. The addressee of this injunction is anybody, the generic anybody (*homo tantum*) that is the opposite of the universalized other: it is a singularity that intersects with others, not for the sake of profit, but for that of empowerment to resistance.

Let us try to connect the injunction to 'just do it!' to the process of becoming-imperceptible, or merging with one's environment. This marks a different time sequence; it is a qualitative shift of coordinates which is a pure process of becoming. It is the flooding of the present by possible futures, in a clean break from the past if by past we mean a sedimentation of habits, the institutionalized accumulation of experience whose authority is sealed by molar or dominant memory and the identities it engenders. Becoming-imperceptible is a sort of transcendence that plunges us into the impossible, the unheard-of: an affirmative present. This is what Deleuze calls 'an event' – or the eruption of the actualization of a sustainable future (see chapter 3).

Acoustic environments in our technologically driven world have the capacity to approximate to and evoke infinity. They have a 'post-human', insect-like quality (Braidotti 2002) in the speed, the intensity of pitch and variation they produce. Ranging from the inaudible to the unheard-of, technomusic stretches the boundaries of our collective perception to the extreme. Contemporary music enacts the de-centring of the human subject and thus produces sounds that reflect the heterogeneous structure of nomadic subjects. By mapping acoustically the shifts and mutations of intensities and multiplicities, rhizomic music replaces the Platonic ideal of harmony or the modernist representational model with a more daring quest for unlikely synchronizations with human and inhuman forces. This expresses the ethical endeavour of challenging us to produce the conditions for sustainable transpositions in the era of *bios/zoe*-power.

Not the least paradox involved in this process is that in order to trigger a process of becoming-imperceptible, quite a transformation needs to take place in what we could call the self. Becoming-imperceptible is the point of fusion between the self and his or her habitat, the cosmos as a whole. It marks the point of evanescence of the self and its replacement by a living nexus of multiple interconnections that empower not the self, but the collective, not identity, but affirmative subjectivity, not consciousness, but affirmative interconnections. It is like a floodgate of creative forces that make it possible to be actually fully inserted into the *hic et nunc* defined as the present unfolding of potentials, but also the enfolding of qualitative shifts within the subject. The paradoxical price to pay for this is the death of the ego understood as social identity, as the labels with which *potestas* has marked our embodied location. This opens the possibility of a proliferation of generative options of an altogether different kind. Ultimately all one has is what one is propelled by, namely affects. One is constructed in these transitions and through these encounters. It is the ultimate delegation of selfhood to something that you may call transcendence, except that it takes you into embodied and embedded perspectives, into radical immanence, not into further abstractions.

In terms of time, this strategy amounts to a qualitative leap to a sustainable future, like writing the prehistory of a future, thus fixing us at last in a present that is neither nostalgic, nor backward-looking, nor euphorically confident, but is actualized here and now. In this sense, Deleuze's 'becoming-imperceptible' is Deleuze's conceptual and affirmative answer to Foucault's much celebrated and grossly misunderstood 'death of the subject'. You have to die to the self in order to enter qualitatively finer processes of becoming. To do that, to be able to sustain it, you can draw the strength from the future, and thus engender an event here and now.

Becoming-imperceptible is an eruption of desire for the future which reshapes the present. Maybe it is a mistake to call it 'the future', also because it smacks of new age optimism. So let me rephrase this: it is a time sequence based on *aion*, not on *chronos*; it marks the time of becoming. It is a qualitative leap that precipitates a change of existential gear, acceleration, a creative speed. All of this is literally invisible and cannot be perceived by the naked eye and yet in philosophical nomadism this movement can be conceptualized in terms of immanence.

Deleuze describes this in terms of 'assemblages', that is to say *agencements*', which indicates modes of perception which are not subject-based, but are rather beyond intentionality and identification. Nonetheless, they constitute agency (as in *agencement* or assemblages). These processes push the subject to deferral, they are inescapable, ungraspable and beyond reflexivity; the becoming-imperceptible opens up towards the unexpected and unprogrammed. The process of becoming-imperceptible is cosmic, but not in any sentimental or holistic sense of the term. In philosophical nomadism this mode of becoming is rather linked to a sense of interconnectedness that can be rendered in terms of an ethics of eco-philosophical empathy and affectivity which cuts across species, space and time (see the previous chapter). Bio-centred egalitarianism is an ethics of sustainable becomings, of affirmative qualitative shifts that decentre and displace the human. Becoming-imperceptible is about reversing the subject to face the outside: a sensory and spiritual stretching of our boundaries. It is a way of living more intensely and of increasing one's *potentia* with it, but in a manner which aims at framing, sustaining and continuing these processes by pushing them to the limit of endurance. It is the absolute form of deter-ritorialization and its horizon is beyond the immediacy of life.

Becoming-imperceptible is the event for which there is no immediate representation and hence no identification. In this sense it marks the death of the self to any notion of identity. It cannot be recognized because it is a radical displacement that traces patterns of estrangement and deterri-torialization. All one can aspire to is the recording of the experience which cannot be located either in relation to the past or the future as one may know it. In this state of becoming the individual that desired (to undergo this process) is already gone and the one who would welcome it is not yet there. Such is the paradox of nomadic subjectivity at the height of its process of becoming other-than-itself.

The eruption of a sustainable future in the present actualizes virtual possibilities in the present. It marks a qualitative transformation, the non-place where the 'no longer' and the 'not yet' reverse into each other, unfolding-out and enfolding-in their respective 'outsides'. This short-circuits linear time and causes a creative conflagration. It propels a leap of faith in the world, but it is not an act that can be understood apart from the transformations and the connections it produces. 'Becoming' is a way of configuring this leap itself – the actual transmutation of values which will propel us out of the void of critical negativity, into the paradoxically generative void of positivity, or full affirmation. It is a seduction into life that breaks with the spectral economy of the eternal return of the Same, and involves friendship with impersonal death.

At that point of becoming-imperceptible, all a subject can do is mark his or her assent to the loss of identity (defined as a by-product of *potestas*) and respectfully merge with the process of *potentia* itself, and hence with one's environment. You may call it, for want of a better word, the untimely presence of death; some call it 'adoration', but that would be an altogether different trip.

EPILOGUE

Transmissions, or Transposing the Future

What we most lack is a belief in the world, we've quite lost the world, and it's been taken from us. If you believe in the world you precipitate events, however inconspicuous, that elude control, you engender new space-times, however small their surface or volume. It's what you call *pietas*. Our ability to resist control, or our submission to it, has to be assessed at the level of our every move. We need both creativity and a people.

Gilles Deleuze, *Negotiations*

This book marks a major stop-over in my long journey across the multiple tracks of nomadic subjectivity, which started as I listened – dazed and amazed – to Deleuze, Foucault and Irigaray in Paris in the late 1970s. I perceived clearly then what I can opaquely think now, namely that non-unitary subjectivity, complexity and multiplicity will have been the key terms for the next millennium. As will fear, terror, ethical and political panic as well as staggering technological and cultural advances. Instead of falling back on the sedimented habits of thought, which past philosophical traditions have institutionalized, I have proposed a leap forward into the complexities and paradoxes of our times. The project of creating new concepts and practices of ethical subjectivity at the end of postmodernism, amidst the return of master narratives of genetic determinism and neo-liberalism, is a challenge which projects humanity in-between a future that cannot be guaranteed and a fast rate of progress which demands one.

Issues of power are central to discussions of ethics in a globally mediated world. Advanced capitalism as globalized cash flow rests on the convergence of information and bio-technologies and activates a proliferation of differences aimed at commercial exploitation. It blurs boundaries and enforces mobility of goods and people, the former circulating far more freely than the latter. The three case studies of feminism, racism and environmentalism demonstrate the extent to which the classical figures of otherness (woman, natives, earth others) have undergone major transpositions in the new world order. The axes of sexualization, racialization and naturalizations have shifted and no longer coincide with the real-life presence and the lived experience of the traditional empirical referents. They are dematerialized and delinked from dichotomous oppositions and dialectical dynamics.

This process, however, does not eliminate negative power-relations – sexism, racism or disregard for the environment – but merely relocates them along complex lines of transposition. Advanced capitalism as the era of commercialization of *bios/zoe*-power will push relentlessly towards the commercialization of all that lives. As such it may well become an ally in the struggle against the old symbolic system with its inbuilt taboos and restrictions. The logic of 'anything goes, so long as you can pay for it', however limited, has some deterritorializing force in the advanced post-industrial world. In this logic, gay families, the black middle classes and genetically engineered companion species may well become the new 'post-natural' denizens and citizens of the global economy. It is the task of critical theory to track down these shifting locations and account for them through adequate figurations in politically informed cartographies that combine accountability with the quest for possible sites of resistance. The key terms in this exercise are: the feminist politics of locations, the importance of processes as opposed to identities and the need for a materialist approach that combines issues of embodiment with the analysis of power-relations. Power as *potestas* (hindering) or as *potentia* (enabling), power as a circulation of complex and dynamic, albeit contradictory, effects, simply cannot be left out of the discussion on ethics and democratic values. This *bios/zoe*-centred vision of the technologically mediated subject of postmodernity or advanced capitalism is fraught with internal contradictions. In this respect all kinds of experimentations at the empirical and social level are necessary and important. In order to be able to think through this web of strategically located relations, we need a flair for complexities and a focus on processes and in-between states, rather than on any one notion or concept.

The first step to take is to confront the challenge of our historicity, thus resisting the traditional move that disconnects philosophical thought from its context. This move entails the assumption of responsibility or accountability so that one can engage actively with the social and cultural conditions that define one's location. The ultimate aim is to negotiate spaces of resistance to the new master narratives of the global economy, in a less frenzied or paranoid mode than contemporary techno-culture allows: a more productive manner. Bodily materialism that is promoted by philosophical nomadism offers some powerful alternatives to the neo-determinism of the geneticists, the euphoria of their commercial and financial backers, and the techno-utopianism of their academic apologists.

The transposition of the dialectical Self–Other relation produces a number of paradoxical side effects. The most relevant for my argument is the emergence of *zoe*, or of 'life' itself, as a political subject in advanced, genetically backed capitalism. Whereas 'life' as *bios* has been conceptualized as a discursive and political notion ever since Aristotle, *zoe* is the non- or pre-human 'outside' of the polity. It has been rendered in figurations of pejorative alterity as the 'other of the living human', which means the inhuman or divine and the dead. I have criticized the extent to which *zoe* gets coded in negative terms, for instance in the post-Heideggerian work of Agamben, as a liminal state of extreme vulnerability of being human: a becoming-corpse. Against this forensic turn in contemporary philosophy, I stressed instead the need to cultivate positive political passions and an ethics of affirmation. Revisiting Spinoza and Nietzsche with Deleuze and anti-racist feminist theory allows us to posit the project of constructing positive values. We need to rethink ethics, politics and representation in view of the non-unitary subjects in process, which we have already become. Conceptual creativity and vision are needed, as is the love of *zoe*. This in turn raises complex issues related to the status of death as the inhuman but all too human event par excellence. *Zoe* as the ultimate echoing chambers of the specific slice of life that we embody is larval, but also cosmic. Questions linked to post-secular spirituality arise as a consequence of the politics of life and an ethics that takes *zoe* seriously as a productive category.

The potency of *zoe* as the defining trait of the subject displaces the unitary vision of consciousness and the sovereignty of the 'I'. Both liberal individualism and classical humanism are accordingly disrupted at their very foundations. Far from being merely a 'crisis' of values, I think this situation confronts us with a formidable set of new opportunities. Renewed conceptual creativity and a leap of our collective imagination are needed to meet the challenge. A post-humanistic brand of non-anthropocentric vitalism, inspired by philosophical nomadism, is one possible response to this challenge. My quarrel with humanism, in such a context, has to do with the limitations of its own historical relevance in the present context. Classical humanism needs to be reviewed and opened up to the challenges and complexities of our times. A politics of life defined as *bios/zoe* power opens the possibility of the proliferation of highly generative post-humanities.

A non-unitary vision of the subject endorses a radical ethics of transformation, thus running against the grain of contemporary neo-liberal conservatism, but it also asserts an equally strong distance from relativism or nihilistic defeatism. A sustainable ethics for a non-unitary subject proposes an enlarged sense of interconnection between self and others, including the non-human or 'earth' others, by removing the obstacle of self-centred individualism. Far from entailing the loss of values and a free fall into relativism, this rather implies a new way of combining self-interest with the well-being of an enlarged sense of community, which includes one's territorial or environmental interconnections. It is a nomadic eco-philosophy of multiple belongings. In this perspective, an exclusive focus on unitary identity, especially in the liberal tradition of individualism, is of hindrance rather than assistance. Identity involves a narrowing down of the internal complexities of a subject for the sake of social conventions. Transposing the subject out of identity politics into a non-unitary or nomadic vision of selves as interrelational forces is a more useful approach. Consciousness is redefined accordingly not as the core of the humanistic subject, but at best as a way of synchronizing the multiple differences within everyone, which constitute the ethical core of nomadic subjects. The return of the master narratives of genetic determinism and market capitalism today provide a perverse equation of individualism with the multiple inter-connective capacities of advanced technologies. This results is simultaneously containing and narrowing down the enormous potential of the technologies themselves, which are advanced enough to redesign our cosmological views as well as social relations. They also prevent humans from active experimentations with new thresholds of sustainability: how far we can go without cracking, how much our bodies can take on the current transformations. As Glissant puts it:

> Thought of the Other is the moral generosity disposing me to accept the principle of alterity, to conceive of the world as not simple and straightforward, with only one truth – mine. But thought of the Other can dwell within me without making me alter course, without 'prizing me open', without changing me within myself. An ethical principle, it is enough that I do not violate it. (Glissant 1997: 154)

A subject of *bios/zoe* power raises therefore questions of ethical urgency: given the acceleration of processes of change, how can we tell the difference among the different flows of changes and transformations? This calls for a revision of the subject in terms of an eco-philosophical integration into his or her environment. The shift to bio-centred egalitarianism posits the subject as a post-identity site, or an embodied and embedded entity, which exists in the interaction with a number of external forces and others, not all of them human, social or historical others. Such a vision of the subject transposes both humanism and social constructivism and calls for a revision of vitalism as a major theoretical issue. All the more so as *zoe* is not neutral: the play of complexities it introduces does not eliminate power differentials, but multiplies them along multiple axes. *Zoe* is sexualized, racialized and rendered anthropocentrically. Thinking through these complexities means radicalizing our relationship to power. The nomadic social critic in the era of *bios/zoe* aims at resisting the schizoid pull of euphoria or over-optimism on the one hand and nostalgia or melancholia on the other. Before we mistake a shift of scale for a qualitative shift of perspective, we need to develop more accurate cartographies, to stay focused on the potential for qualitative changes (becoming-minor), not just quantitative proliferations. In order to answer these challenges, the specific time-sequences and temporality of nomadic subjectivity need to be accounted for. The non-linear time of becoming accomplishes a number of productive transpositions of life into *zoe* and of death into atemporal and incorporeal becomings. How to synchronize some modes of continuity and stability across the multiple complexities that constitute the nomadic subject has been a central theme of this book.

The eco-philosophical dimension, or multiple ecologies of belonging

This environmentally bound subject is a collective entity that moves beyond anthropocentrism. The human organism is an in-between that is plugged into and connected to a variety of possible sources and forces. It may be useful to define it as a machine, which does not mean an appliance or anything with a specifically utilitarian aim, but rather something that is simultaneously more abstract and more materially embedded. My minimalist definition of a body-machine is: an embodied affective and intelligent entity that captures, processes and transforms energies and forces. An embodied and embedded nomadic entity feeds upon, incorporates and transforms its environment (be it 'natural', 'social', 'human', or whatever) constantly. Being embodied in this high-tech ecological manner means being immersed in fields of constant flows and transformations. Not all of them are positive, of course, although in such a dynamic system this cannot be known or judged *a priori*. The starting point is the relentless generative force of *bios*/*zoe* and the specific brand of trans-species egalitarianism, which they establish with the human. The ecological dimension of philosophical nomadism is a matter of forces, and of ethology.

In this book I have addressed this problem through the issue of sustainability. Ethics includes the acknowledgement of and compassion for pain, as well as the activity of working through it. Any process of change must do some sort of violence to deeply engrained habits and dispositions which got consolidated in time.

Overcoming these engrained habits is a necessary disruption, without which there is no ethical awakening. Consciousness-raising is not free of pain. The utterance 'I can't take it any more!', far from being an admission of defeat, marks the threshold and hence the condition of possibility for creative encounters and productive changes. This is how the ethical dimension appears through the mass of fragments and shreds of discarded habits that are characteristic of our times. The ethical project is not the same as the implementation of ruling standards of morality. It rather concerns the norms and values, the standards and the criteria that can be applied to the quest for sustainable, that is to say for newly negotiated, limits. Limits are to be rethought in terms of an ethics of becoming, through a non-Hegelian notion of 'limits' as thresholds, that is to say points of encounter and not of closure: living boundaries and not fixed walls.

The joint necessity for both the pursuit of social change and in-depth transformation, as well as for an ethics of endurance and sustainability, is important to stress because critical and creative thinkers and activists who pursue change have often experienced the limits or the boundaries like open wounds or scars. The generation that came of age politically in the 1970s has taken enormous risks and has enjoyed the challenges they entailed. A lot was demanded and expected from life and most ended up getting it, but it was not merely a joy ride. An ethical evaluation of the costs involved in pursuing alternative visions, norms and values is important in the present context where the alleged 'end of ideology' is used as a pretext for neo-liberal restoration that terminates all social experiments. It is necessary to find a way to combine transformative politics with sustainability and confront the conceptual and social contradictions such an approach inevitably entails.

Sustainable ethics allows us to contain the risks while pursuing the original project of transformation. This is a way to resist the dominant ethos of our conservative times that idolizes the *new* as a consumerist trend, while thundering against those who believe in change. Cultivating the art of living intensely in the pursuit of change is a political act. In this regard, I have insisted on the importance of endurance – in the double sense of learning to last in time, but also to put up and live with pain and suffering. Again, it is a question of dosage and of balance. Thresholds of sustainability need to be mapped out, so that a rate and speed of change can be negotiated and set, which will allow each subject to endure, to go on, to stop at the second-last smoke, shot, drink, book.

This implies a differential type of ethics, which clashes with dominant morality. It has nothing to do with relativism either. Rather it contains clearly set limits that are activated by careful negotiations. The embodied structure of the subject is a limit in itself. To accept differential boundaries does not condemn us to relativism, but to the necessity to negotiate each passage. In other words: we need a dialogical mode. We need future-oriented perspectives, which do not deny the traumas of the past but transform them into possibilities for the present. It is not the heavenly future at which we aim, but rather a more sustainable one, situated here and now.

Difference as the ethical principle of not-one

One of the points I highlighted in this book is not so much that sexualized, racialized and naturalized differences are over, as that they no longer coincide with sexually, racially and naturally differentiated bodies.

Advanced capitalism has delinked the empirical referents of otherness (woman/native/earth other) from the imaginary institutions of sexuality/race/nature, which traditionally framed them. Genetic engineering and biotechnologies have seen to it that a qualitative dislocation has taken place. The sexualized, racialized and naturalized others are no longer the boundary markers of categorical distinctions. Genetic engineering and contemporary molecular biology have located the markers for the organization and distribution of differences in micro-instances like the cells of living organisms. We have come a long way from the gross system that used to mark difference on the basis of visually verifiable anatomical differences between the sexes, the races and the species. We have moved from the bio-power that Foucault exemplified by comparative anatomy to the sort of molecular *bios/zoe* power of today. In postmodernity, under the impact of the technological revolution, the political economy of the Panopticon is no longer adequate and has been replaced by the molecular informatics of domination. By extension it follows that the classical others are no longer the necessary point of reference for the organization of a symbolic division of labour between the sexes, the races and the species. Today, they have been transformed in the spectral economy of the dematerialization of difference.

This is not to say, however, that the function which difference was called to perform is over. The collapse of the former system of marking difference makes it all the more urgent to reassert the principle of alterity, of not-One, as constitutive of the subject and to elaborate nomadic forms of ethical accountability to match it. What is needed is an ethics of embodied differences that can sustain this challenge: an undifferentiated grammar of gender simply will not do. To critique the content of the socio-symbolic myth of difference, therefore, is not the same as dismantling or even displacing its structural function. Difference, understood as the principle of not-One, in Lévi-Strauss's sense of 'zero institution', fulfils the function of marking a fundamental break as the site of origin of the subject. What needs to be broken is the fantasy of unity, totality and One-ness. This is what the psychoanalytic idea of the original loss stands for: it is the pound of flesh one needs to hand over in order to enter the socio-symbolic contract. What is knocked out from the subject's psychic landscape is the delusion of One-ness, the phantasy of omnipotence. To recognize this basic, ego-deflating principle is the ground zero of subject-formation. The recognition of alterity in the sense of incommensurable loss and an unpayable outstanding debt to others entails the awareness that one is the effect of irrepressible flows of encounters, interactions, affectivity and desire, which one is not in charge of. This humbling experience of not-Oneness, which is constitutive of the non-unitary subject, far from opening the doors to relativism, anchors the subject in an ethical bond to alterity, to the multiple and external others that are constitutive of that entity which, out of laziness and habit, we call the 'self'. The split, or non-unitary nature of the subject, entails the recognition of a pre-discursive structure of the 'self', of a necessary loss of that which is always already there – an affective, interactive entity endowed with intelligent flesh and an embodied mind. Zoe is the generative flux of transversal connections to others.

'Life' as zoe or generative inhuman energy emerges in its own right. My affinity for zoe as generative pre-human vitality, against the negative rendition made of it by Agamben and others who are influenced by Heidegger, rests on the fact that zoe has historically been feminized. Women were classified alongside natives, animals and others as referents of a generative force that was reduced to a mere biological function and deprived of political and ethical relevance. The politics of Life itself today redesigns this Relation: we need to attend to the forces of life and matter that are traversed by and not exhausted by politics. This implies giving centre stage to zoe as relations or flows of interaction; production or generative power and the inhuman. Accepting the bio-egalitarianism of zoe-politics means that each subject, no matter the sex, race or species, has to be rethought according to the positivity of difference, i.e. the notion of difference as the principle of non-One as zero-institution. This has two major implications. The first one is ethical: we need to rethink responsibility in terms of eco-philosophical principles. A diffuse sort of ontological gratitude is needed in the post-human era, towards the multitude of non-human agents that is supporting us through the present anthropological mutation. This is exactly the opposite of what Teilhard de Chardin had in mind, with his Christian-revivalist reading of evolutionary theory for the sake of an anthropocentric appropriation of scientific progress. Bio-centred egalitarianism aims instead at dispersing and transcending anthropocentrism by dissolving it into a network of bio-agencies in the viral and symbiotic sense of the term. Sustainable ethics can be based on this, as can a secular version of spirituality which aims at acknowledging this radical shift without giving in either to nihilism, or to new age holism. We need instead a rigorous answer in the mode of a spiritual bond, an affirmative and empowering bond to our eco-sphere, our habitat and our world. This is not techno-paganism, but radical immanence in its ethical version, its most concrete form: it points to the becoming-imperceptible of the former anthropocentric subject.

The second implication is political: we need to organize communities that reflect and enhance this vision of the subject. This is a community that acknowledges difference as the principle of not-Oneness as its founding myth of origin. Anti-Oedipal, post-humanist, vitalist, non unitary and yet accountable. Not bound together by the guilt of shared violence, or irreparable loss, or unpayable ontological debts – but rather by the compassionate acknowledgement of our common need to negotiate thresholds on sustainability with and alongside the relentless and monstrous energy of a 'Life' that does not respond to our names. A political economy of non-compensation needs to be installed, that is to say a fundamental principle of non-profit. This rejects the psychoanalytic scheme of the subject, which inscribes the political economy of capitalism at the heart of subjectivity in terms of losses, savings, discounts, long-term investments, interest rates, and the surplus value of *jouissance*. Acknowledging instead the proximity of the crack, the margins of unspeakableness, the traumatized nature of our being-in-the-world and hence a great fragility is the starting point for philosophical nomadism. It is a choice for stillness, deceleration and sustainability. It is a form of *amor fati*; against the Kantian model of judgement. It is a way of living up to the intensities of life, to be worthy of all that happens to us – to live fully the capacity to affect and to be affected.

Such a position encourages and supports the project of laying the foundation for sustainable futures, in terms of endurance. We have to learn to endure the principle of not-One at the in-depth structures of our subjectivity. Becoming-nomadic, by constructing communities where the notion of transience, of passing, is acknowledged in a sober secular manner that binds us to the multiple 'others' in a vital web of complex interrelations. Kinship systems and social bonding, like flexible citizenship, can be rethought differently and differentially, moving away from the blood, sweat and tears of the classical social contract. Given the extent of the transpositions brought about by advanced capitalism and the dislocations of traditional values and social bonding they have triggered, the conditions for a renegotiation of our being in *this* together are timely.

My choice of a nomadic style of thinking is also a matter of affectivity, temperament and sensibility, which is not deprived of a sort of impatience with the ever-deferred fulfilment of the promises of humanism as a set of intellectual and moral ideals. I have no more time for the wishful thinking and the rhetorical gestures that predictably occur whenever constituted authorities are confronted with the obvious historical manifestations of the failure of humanistic values. Other modes of representation of the subject and a different style of ethical expectation are needed, which do not defer to an unlikely future the fulfilment of its promises, but rather works actively in the present. I would rather replace the weight of traditional habits, which I see as forms of legalized addiction, with a more disloyal, creative and forward-looking practice of theoretical thought. Positive metamorphoses are indeed my political passion: the kinds of becoming that destabilize dominant power-relations, deterritorialize Majority-based identities and values, and infuse a joyful sense of empowerment into a subject that is in-becoming. This passion is political as well in that it associates these creative deterritorializations with resistance against monolithic and centralized power systems. This critical freedom mobilizes the work of the creative imagination as well as more traditional intellectual resources.

I want to defend transformations as transpositions of positive energy and forces, as a sustainable enterprise, not as a recipe for fashionable border crossing. The point is to achieve successful transformations by striking sustainable interconnections. For the purposes of academic and scholarly discussions on ethics, several constituencies need to be involved, from the science and technology corners as well as from ecology, culture and social theory. A transdisciplinary type of balance needs to be struck, by rigorously non-linear transpositions. We need to ground this in a sort of post-humanist rejection of the arrogance of anthropocentrism. This should also include the sense of the recognition of proximity to the onco-mice, the mad cows, the multiple Dollies, the genetically modified foods, the missing seeds and the unmentionable number of technologically mediated micro-organisms that have come to constitute our eco-sphere.

Transfigured futures, or the prophetic intellectuals

Those who inhabit the paradoxes of technologically mediated societies need new cosmologies and world-views that are appropriate to our own high level of technological development and to the global issues that are connected with it. We also need political analysis that does justice to the ferocious and insidious sets of structural injustices and repeated modes of dispossession or eviction that mark the global economy. New forms of transcendence are needed to cope with the new global civilization we have entered and which encompasses all the earth and also beyond it, our immediate cosmic space. We need cultural, spiritual, ethical values, be it myths, narratives or representations, that are adequate to this new civilization we inhabit. These need not be modelled on the universalism that is so dear to moral philosophers, especially those of the Kantian tradition. More creativity is needed to refigure this ethical interconnection. This does not reject universalism, but rather expands it, to make it more inclusive.

We need to define the parameters of this new eco-philosophy of belonging in terms of sharing ethical sensibility: a new *zoe*-etho-politics is in the making. On a more positive note, there is no doubt that 'we' are in *this* together. Any nomadic philosophy of sustainability worthy of its name will have to start from this assumption and reiterate it as a fundamental value. The point, however, is to define the 'we' part and the '*this*' content, that is to say the community in its relation to singular subjects and the norms and values for a political eco-philosophy of sustainability. Far from being a symptom of relativism, I see them as asserting the radical immanence of the subject. They constitute the starting point for a web of intersecting forms of situated accountability, that is to say an ethics. An ethics of sustainable forces that takes life (as *bios* and as *zoe*) as the point of reference not for the sake of restoring unitary norms, or the celebration of the master-narrative of global profit, but for the sake of sustainability.

This project requires more visionary power or prophetic energy, qualities which are neither especially in fashion in academic circles, nor highly valued in these times of commercial globalization. Yet, the call for more vision is emerging from many predictable and some unexpected quarters. Cornel West, for instance, prefers prophetic criticism, which he sees as the most effective way of addressing both power-relations and more textually based questions of methodology. This combination of sensitivity to representational issues and awareness of the materialist workings of power is, for West, the force of the demystificatory intellectuals. He also refers to this strategy as 'prophetic criticism', because it does not stop at the critical side of the matter, but rather moves towards issues of norms, ethical evaluation and practical action. It is both crisis-centred and ethically charged.

Hardt and Negri (2000) relay the call for more conceptual creativity in order to confront the challenges of the new global power-relations. They also stress the role that a prophetic visionary insight plays in sustaining such creative inspiration. Deleuze's neo-Spinozist theoretical legacy supports such pleas for the courage, the strength and the intelligence necessary to make creativity happen. Feminists have a long and rich genealogy of pleading for increased visionary insight. From the very early days, Joan Kelly (1979) typified feminist theory as a double-edged vision, with a strong critical and an equally strong creative function. Faith in the creative powers of the imagination is an integral part of feminists' appraisal of embodiment and the bodily roots of subjectivity. Nomadic subjects attempt to valorize the cognitive, theoretical and political importance of inventing modes of representation, which adequately express the complex singularities that feminist women have become. The prophetic dimension is alive and well not only in the formidable tradition of feminist theology and spirituality, and in the environmental and ecological feminist movements, but also in epistemology. Donna Haraway's work provides the best example of this kind of epistemological and political respect for a dimension where creativity is unimaginable without some visionary or spiritual fuel.

Prophetic or visionary minds are thinkers of the future. The future as an active object of desire propels us forth and we can draw from it the strength and motivation to be active in the here and now of a present that hangs on in-between the 'no longer' and the 'not yet' of advanced postmodernity. The present is always the future present: it will have made a positive difference in the world. Only the yearning for sustainable futures can construct a liveable present. The sheer thinkability of the future is the necessary precondition for inhabiting creatively the present. The anticipation of endurance, of making it to a possible 'tomorrow', transposes energies from the future back into the present. This is how sustainability enacts modes of creative becoming. This is a non-entropic model of energy-flow and hence of transferral of desire. Drawing energy from the thinkability of the future means that our desires are sustainable to the extent that they engender the conditions of possibility for the future. In order to get there, a nomadic subject position of flow and multi-layeredness is a major facilitator. This is not a leap of faith, but an active transposition, a transformation at the in-depth level, a change of culture akin to genetic mutations, but registered also at the ethical level.

Philosophies of radical immanence help us understand this ethical-genetic mutation of cultural values: Deleuze's empirical transcendental and Irigaray's virtual feminine, or sensible transcendental, because they join forces to produce a qualitative shift of perception. They represent a culture of affirmative difference that is virtual and therefore actualizable and hence 'real', and just waiting to enfold and unfold. They affirm a non-hierarchical role of vision, imagination and desire. This mutation is bio-genetic as well as ethical: it redefines what it means to be human through nomadic practices of transpositions of differences in the sense of practices of the not-One, of affinities and viral contaminations, interde-pendence and non-entropic economies of desire. It is in some ways an evolutionary move, but not in a narrow Darwinian sense and not in a hierarchical model. It rather moves towards the construction of possible and hence sustainable futures by enforcing the notion of intra-species and intra-generational justice. As Deleuze put it: we need both a future and a people.

This transformative ethics affirms the positivity of difference by cleans-ing it of its hegemonic and exclusionary connotations, thus laying the foundations for the present unfolding of sustainable futures. In a nomadic Spinozist frame, this is in fact a tautology, because the future can only be sustainable in so far as it can produce generative unfolding. As such it actualizes the positivity of desire because it carries within it the possibility and the promise of the future, that is to say of sustainability.

In order to enforce this project, transversal alliances are needed and active public debates about the limits of sustainability and their political implications in the age of *bios/zoe*-power. This assumes that the increasing unthinkability of the future is already depriving us, here and now, of the only time we have: the present. The narrowing of the temporal horizon is already pushing many of us back to the entropic embrace of a universe that is running out of steam and of inspiration. We, not unlike our endan-gered planet, are running out of breath. A prophetic or visionary dimen-sion is necessary in order to secure the one element that advanced capitalism is systematically depriving us all of – namely sustainable becoming or transformations. A qualitative and creative leap induced by a prophetic, visionary dimension is the only way to repair and compen-sate that which we are running out of: time.

What has posterity ever done for me?[1]

The subject is an evolutionary engine, endowed with his or her own embodied temporality, in the sense of both the specific timing of the genetic code and the more genealogical time of individualized memories. If the embodied subject of bio-power is a complex molecular organism, a bio-chemical factory of steady and jumping genes, an evolutionary entity endowed with its own navigational tools and an inbuilt temporality, then we need a form of ethical values and political agency that reflects this high degree of complexity. What is at stake in nomadic ethics is a non-linear model of genealogy and hence of evolution that expresses a non-Oedipal kinship system. Evolution needs to be approached as a productive and creative force, in a way that demystifies the transcendental illusions of the subject. Ansell-Pearson lists among these illusions: entropy, nihilism, linear evolution and the myth of individualistic autonomy under capitalism. It is important to accept that techno-culture is an evolutionary culture in the autopoietic machinic model that I exposed in chapter 4. Techno-culture has its own model of development and temporal scale, which does not conform to the Darwinian model. Multiple forces that displace it and transpose it again traverse the subject that is situated in such a world. This is a non-linear evolutionary model.

Modernity, as an ideology of progress founded on the historical unfolding of rational principles of truth and goodness, was a universalizing force. Its universality was based on a double pull: on the spatial level it flattened out all differences, especially the anomalous or wild ones. On the temporal front, however, universality postulated boundless faith in the future. Bauman quotes one of my favourite writers, Diderot, who stated that modern man is in love with posterity (Bauman 1993: 42), that is to say that the ultimate destination of the human is located in a future, which is still waiting to unfold. Postmodernity, on the other hand, sets as its horizon the globalization process in terms of technological and economic interdependence. As early as 1913 Rosa Luxemburg, in her celebrated dispute with Lenin, argued that capitalism had no inbuilt teleological purpose, historical logic or structure, but was rather a self-imploding system that would stop at nothing in order to fulfil its aim: profit. This inherently self-destructive system feeds on and thus destroys the very conditions of its survival. Capitalism is omnivorous. It is an unsustainable system, whose way of existing becomes the main cause of its self-destruction.

Bio-genetic capitalism, with its entropic power of hybridization, simultaneously establishes new hegemonies and denies the structural power differentials that constitute it. It lacks both a critical self-reflexive approach

[1] I owe this expression to Robert Heilbroner, in Pojman (1994: 217).

and genuine powers of invention. It is a hybridizing machine *par excellence*, structurally deprived of visionary insight. It has no blueprint for the future because it is not grounded anywhere; it coincides with the turbulent, homogenizing flows of capital that market hybridity and mixity and thus promotes the proliferation of differences for the sake of profit. The spectral economy of capital desynchronizes time and introduces the phenomenon of systematic jet lag. Being nothing more than this all-consuming entropic energy, capitalism lacks the ability to create anything new: it can merely promote the recycling of spent hopes, repackaged in the rhetorical frame of the 'new'. The superficial optimism, which characterizes it, is the opposite of an affirmative force in the sustainable sense of the term.

In the globalized world order, the question 'what is to be done?' arises with particular urgency. It was, of course, Lenin's watchword in the good old days when the social consensus – at least in the political left – was that the philosopher's task had always been to interpret the world, but the point now was to change it. Much has happened to the world and to people's desire for change since such an imperative saw the red light of day. In the climate of fear and anxiety that marks the post-industrial societies of the global era since the end of the Cold War in 1989, the question 'what is to be done?' tends to acquire a far less imperial and definitely more pathetic tone. What can we do to cope with the fast rate of change? With the crumbling of established certainties and values? The evaporation of dear and cherished habits? How far can we go in accepting the changes? How far are we capable of stretching ourselves? Or, to paraphrase the neo-Spinozist leanings of Deleuze, 'how much can our bodies – our embodied and embedded selves – actually take?'

In so far as the axiomatics of capitalism oppose the eco-philosophy of sustainability, the political economy of fear and the impending extinction of our biosphere, capitalism destroys the future. Resistance to it entails the collective endeavour to construct horizons of hope. This micro-political level of action is vulnerable because the Majority threatens it and appropriates its strategies. Yet, the diagonal line of flight aims at the actualization of a sustainable future. Sustainability expresses the desire to endure and as such it is the maker of possible futures. It is a present-based practice, which reactivates both past and present into producing 'futurity'. That means that sustainable presents generate possible futures. The future is the virtual unfolding of the affirmative aspect of the present (*potentia*). It takes a firm stand against the 'future eaters' (Flannery 1994) and honours our obligations to the generations to come. This acts as an equalizer among generations. By targeting those who come after us as the rightful ethical interlocutors and assessors of our own actions, we are taking seriously the implications of our own situated position and of our practices within it. This form of inter-generational justice is crucial and it both illustrates and supports the temporal continuum.

This pragmatic point about inter-generational fairness need not, however, be expressed or conceptualized within the phallogocentric imaginary as an Oedipal narrative. To be concerned about the future need not result in linearity, i.e. in restating the unity of space and time as the horizon of subjectivity. On the contrary, I would take inter-generational decency as a way of displacing the Oedipal hierarchy. It is a becoming-minoritarian of the elderly, the senior, and the parental figures; in turn this implies the de-Oedipalization of the inter-generational bond of the young to those who preceded them. As such, it calls for new ways of addressing and of solving inter-generational conflicts. We should join forces across the generational divide by working together towards sustainable futures.

As Keith Ansell-Pearson put it, the problem now is 'how to think trans-humanly the future' (1997b: 7). Life in you does not bear your name; it is only a time-share. Those who are inscribed in life under the sign of the desire for change may be more mortal or vulnerable than most because they need to live more intensely. They need accelerations, those bursts of energy, and those sudden and at times violent rushes. They need to be jolted out of a set habits in so far as they are passionately committed to writing the prehistory of the future, that is to say: to change the present. This is the productive side of *amor fati*: a desire to go on becoming, to effect multiple modes of belonging to complex and heterogeneous lines of specification, interaction, negotiations. These constitute our world as one world, in its immanence. To be up to the intensity of life, the challenge, the hurt of all that happens to us entails great faith in the connection to all that lives. This is the love for the world that frames a horizon of sustainability and hence of hope.

Ernst Bloch has described Hope as 'dreaming forward'. It is an anticipatory virtue that permeates our lives and activates them. It is a powerful motivating force grounded not only in social and political utopias, but also in the imagination, dreams, religion and art. Hope constructs the future in that it opens the spaces onto which to project active desires; it gives us the force to emancipate ourselves from everyday routines and structures that help us dream ahead. Hope carves out active trajectories of becoming and thus can respond to anxieties and uncertainties in a productive manner. It requires awareness of the past, or memory and the knowledge needed to handle its transitions into a possible future. Ideologies of all kinds have always traded on hope, manipulating it to their ends, often with dramatic consequences.

Why would subjects hope for change? For no particular reason at all: it is a gratuitous act of confidence that Hannah Arendt described admirably as 'for the love of the world', not as an abstract universal, but as the grounded concerns for the multitude of 'anybody' (*homo tantum*) that composes the human community. The pursuit and the sharing of hope is an end in itself in that it intensifies one's involvement in and enjoyment of life defined as the expression of a passionate desire, *potentia* or becoming. It is also a strong act of faith in the future, in that it works to create the conditions to leave behind for posterity a better world than was found in the first place. Lest our greed and selfishness destroy or diminish it. Given that posterity per definition can never pay us back, this gesture is perfectly generous.

The ethical subject of sustainable becoming practises a humble kind of hope, rooted in the ordinary micro-practices of everyday life: simple strategies to hold, sustain and map out thresholds of sustainable transformations. The motivation for it is completely gratuitous: the struggle for the social construction of hope takes place for no reason at all, other than profound shame at the mess we made of it and our accountability for it. A fundamental gratuitousness is part of the principle of non-profit that marks contemporary neo-asceticism. Working through the shame towards a more positive approach helps the nomadic subjects to synchronize themselves with the changing world in which they try to make a positive difference. Co-synchronizations constitute communities. Fitting in with the world in order to help it along the horizon of hope and sustainability indicates *amor fati* as an evolutionary talent. It is about the ability to adapt and develop suitable navigational tools within the fast-moving techno- and ethno- and gender-scapes of a globally mediated world. Against the general lethargy on the one hand and the rhetoric of selfish genes and possessive individualism on the other, hope rests with a non-rapacious ethics of sustainable becoming: for the hell of it and for love of the world.

Call it, if you will, *pietas*.

Bibliography

Acker, Kathy (1988) *Bodies of Work*. London and New York: Serpent's Tail.

Acker, Kathy (1995) 'The End of the World of White Men', in J. Halberstam and Ira Livingston (eds) *Posthuman Bodies*. Bloomington: Indiana University Press.

Adams, Carol (1990) *The Sexual Politics of Meat: A Feminist-Vegetarian Critical Theory*. New York: Continuum.

Adams, Carol (2000) 'Caring about Suffering: A Feminist Exploration', in Josephine Donovan and Carol Adams (eds) *Beyond Animal Rights: A Feminist Caring Ethic for the Treatment of Animals*. New York: Continuum.

Agamben, Giorgio (1998) *Homo Sacer: Sovereign Power and Bare Life*. Stanford: Stanford University Press.

Agarwal, Bina (1992) 'The Gender and Environmental Debate: Lessons from India', *Feminist Studies*, vol. 18, no. 1, pp. 119–58.

Agarwal, Bina (1997) 'Gender Perspectives on Environmental Action: Issues of Equity, Agency and Participation', in J. Scott, K. Caplan and D. Keates (eds) *Transitions, Environments, Translations: Feminisms in International Politics*. London and New York: Routledge.

Alcoff, Linda (2000) 'Philosophy Matters: A Review of Recent Work in Feminist Philosophy', *Signs*, vol. 25, no. 3, pp. 841–82.

Alexander, Jacqui M. and Mohanty, Chandra (eds) (1997) *Feminist Genealogies, Colonial Legacies, Democratic Futures*. New York and London: Routledge.

Amis, Martin (1997) *Einstein's Monsters*. London: Penguin.

Anon. (2003) Anonymous announcement, *Guardian Weekly*, 14–20 August.

Ansell-Pearson, Keith (1997a) *Deleuze and Philosophy: The Difference Engineer*. London and New York: Routledge.

Ansell-Pearson, Keith (1997b) *Viroid Life: Perspectives on Nietzsche and the Transhuman Condition*. London and New York: Routledge.

Ansell-Pearson, Keith (1999) *Germinal Life: The Difference and Repetition of Deleuze*. London and New York: Routledge.

Appadurai, Arjan (1994) 'Disjuncture and Difference in the Global Cultural Economy', in P. Williams and L. Chrisman (eds) *Colonial Discourse and Post-colonial Theory: A Reader*. New York: Western University Press, pp. 324–39.

Appiah, Anthony (1991) 'Is the Post- in Postmodernism the Post- in Postcolonial?', *Critical Inquiry*, 17 (Winter), pp. 336–57.

Arendt, Hannah (1963) *Eichmann in Jerusalem: A Report on the Banality of Evil*. New York: Viking.

Arendt, Hannah (1968) *Men in Dark Times*. New York: Harcourt Brace.

Badinter, Elisabeth (2003) *Fausse Route*. Paris: Odile Jacob.

Balibar, Étienne (2001) *Nous, citoyens d'Europe? Les frontières, l'état, le peuple*. Paris: Éditions de la Découverte.

Balibar, Étienne (2002) *Politics and the Other Scene*. London: Verso.

Balsamo, Anne (1996) *Technologies of the Gendered Body: Reading Cyborg Women*. Durham, NC and London: Duke University Press.

Barad, Karen (2003) 'Posthumanist Performativity: Toward an Understanding of How Matter Comes to Matter', *Signs*, vol. 28, no. 3 (Spring), pp. 801–32.

Bauman, Zygmunt (1993) *Postmodern Ethics*. Oxford: Blackwell.

Bauman, Zygmunt (1998) *Globalization: The Human Consequences*. Cambridge: Polity.

Beauvoir de, Simone (1949) *Le deuxième sexe*. Paris: Gallimard. English translation: *The Second Sex*, trans. H. M. Parshley. New York: Vintage, 1989.

Beck, Ulrich (1992) *Risk Society*. London: Sage.

Beck, Ulrich (1999) *World Risk Society*. Cambridge: Polity.

Becker, Egon and Jahn, Thomas (eds) (1999) *Sustainability and the Social Sciences: A Cross-disciplinary Approach to Integrating Environmental Considerations into Theoretical Reorientation*. London: Zed Books and UNESCO.

Bendikt, Michael (ed.) (1991) *Cyberspace: First Steps*. Cambridge, MA: MIT Press.

Benhabib, Seyla (1992) *The Situated Self*. Cambridge: Polity.

Benhabib, Seyla (1996) *The Reluctant Modernism of Hannah Arendt*. Thousand Oaks: Sage.

Benhabib, Seyla (1999) 'Sexual Difference and Collective Identities: The New Global Constellation', *Signs*, vol. 24, no. 2, pp. 335–62.

Benhabib, Seyla (2002) *The Claims of Culture: Equality and Diversity in the Global Era*. Princeton and Oxford: Princeton University Press.

Benjamin, Jessica (1988) *The Bonds of Love: Psychoanalysis, Feminism and the Problem of Domination*. New York: Pantheon Books.

Berardi, Franco (1997) *Exit. Il nostro contributo all'estinzione della civiltà*. Milan: Costa & Nola.

Berlant, Lauren (1997) *The Queen of America goes to Washington City: Essays on Sex and Citizenship*. Durham, NC: Duke University Press.

Bhabha, Homi K. (ed.) (1990) *Nation and Narration*. London and New York: Routledge.

Bhabha, Homi K. (1994) *The Location of Culture*. London and New York: Routledge.

Bhabha, Homi K. (1996) 'Unpacking my Library . . . Again', in Iain Chamber and Lidia Curti (eds) *The Post-colonial Question: Common Skies, Divided Horizons*. New York and London: Routledge.

Biemann, Ursula (ed.) (2003) *Geography and the Politics of Mobility*. Vienna: General Foundation.

Blanchot, Maurice (2000) *The Instant of my Death*. Stanford: Stanford University Press.

Boer, Inge (1996) 'The World beyond our Window: Nomads, Travelling Theories and the Function of Boundaries', *Parallax*, no. 3, pp. 7–26.

Bogue, Ronald (1996) 'Deleuze's Style', *Man and World*, vol. 29, no. 3, pp. 251–68.

Bordo, Susan (1986) 'The Cartesian Masculinization of Thought', *Signs*, vol. 11, no. 3, pp. 439–56.

Brabeck, Peter (2003) 'Trade', *Guardian Weekly*, 11–17 September.

Brah, Avtar (1993) 'Re-framing Europe: En-gendered Racisms, Ethnicities and Nationalisms in Contemporary Western Europe', *Feminist Review*, no. 45 (Autumn), pp. 9–28.

Brah, Avtar (1996) *Cartographies of Diaspora – Contesting Identities*. New York and London: Routledge.

Braidotti, Rosi (1991) *Patterns of Dissonance*. Cambridge: Polity; New York: Routledge.

Braidotti, Rosi (1994) *Nomadic Subjects: Embodiment and Sexual Difference in Contemporary Feminist Theory*. New York: Columbia University Press.

Braidotti, Rosi (2002) *Metamorphoses: Towards a Materialist Theory of Becoming*. Cambridge: Polity.

Braidotti, Rosi, Charkiewicz, Ewa, Hausler, Sabine and Wieringa, Saskia (1994) *Women, the Environment and Sustainable Development: Towards a Theoretical Synthesis*. London: Zed Books and INSTRAW.

Bray, Abigail (2004) *Hélène Cixous*. Basingstoke and New York: Palgrave Macmillan.

Brodkin Sacks, K. (1994) 'How Did Jews become White Folks?' in Steven Gregory and Roger Sanjek (eds) *Race*. New Brunswick and New Jersey: Rutgers University Press, pp. 78–102.

Brundtland Commission (1987) *Our Common Future*. Oxford: Oxford University Press.

Bryld, Mette and Lykke, Nina (1999) *Cosmodolphins: Feminist Cultural Studies of Technologies, Animals and the Sacred*. London: Zed Books.

Buchanan, Ian (1997) 'The Problem of the Body in Deleuze and Guattari, or, What can a Body Do?', *Body & Society*, vol. 3, no. 3, pp. 73–92.

Buchanan, Ian (2000) *Deleuzism: A Metacommentary*. Edinburgh: Edinburgh University Press.

Buchanan, Ian and Colebrook, Claire (eds) (2000) *Deleuze and Feminist Theory*. Edinburgh: Edinburgh University Press.

Bukatman, Scott (1993) *Terminal Identity: The Virtual Subject in Post-modern Science Fiction*. Durham, NC: Duke University Press.

Butler, Judith (1991) *Gender Trouble*. New York and London: Routledge.

Butler, Judith (1993) *Bodies that Matter*. New York and London: Routledge.

Butler, Judith (2000) *Antigone's Claim: Kinship between Life and Death*. New York: Columbia University Press.

Butler, Judith (2002) 'Is Kinship Always Already Heterosexual?', *Differences*, vol. 3, no. 1, pp. 14–44.

Butler, Judith (2004a) *Undoing Gender*. London and New York: Routledge.

Butler, Judith (2004b) *Precarious Life: Powers of Violence and Mourning*. New York: Verso.

Butler, Judith, Laclau, Ernesto and Žižek, Slavoj (2000) *Contingency, Hegemony, Universality: Contemporary Dialogues on the Left*. London: Verso.

Cacciari, Massimo (1994) *Geo-filosofia dell'Europa*. Milan: Adelphi.

Carlston, G. Erin (1998) *Thinking Fascism: Sapphic Modernism and Fascist Modernity*. Stanford: Stanford University Press.

Castells, Manuel (1996) *The Rise of the Network Society*. Oxford: Blackwell.

Chakrabarty, Dipesh (2000) *Provincializing Europe: Post-colonial Thought and Historical Difference*. Princeton: Princeton University Press.

Chambers, Iain and Curti, Lidia (eds) (1996) *The Post-colonial Question: Common Skies, Divided Horizons*. New York and London: Routledge.

Cheney, Jim (1994) 'Nature/Theory/Difference: Ecofeminism and the Reconstruction of Environmental Ethics', in Karen J. Warren (ed.) *Ecological Feminism*. London and New York: Routledge.

Cixous, Hélène (1997) 'Mon Algeriance', *Les Inrockuptibles*, 20 August, magazine archive no. 115, p. 70. English translation: 'My Algeriance, in Other Words, to Depart not to Arrive from Algeria', *Tri-Quarterly*, 100 (Fall 1997), pp. 259–79.

Clifford, James (1994) 'Diasporas', *Cultural Anthropology*, vol. 9, no. 3, pp. 302–38.

Cohen, Robin (1997) *Global Diasporas: an Introduction*. London: UCL Press.

Cohn-Bendit, Daniel (1995) 'Transit Discussion', *Newsletter of the Institute for Human Sciences* (Vienna), no. 50 (June–August), pp. 1–4.

Colebrook, Claire (2000a) 'Is Sexual Difference a Problem?', in Ian Buchanan and Claire Colebrook (eds) *Deleuze and Feminist Theory*. Edinburgh: Edinburgh University Press, pp. 110–27.

Colebrook, Claire (2000b) 'From Radical Representation to Corporeal Becomings: The Feminist Philosophies of Lloyd, Grost and Gateus', *Hypatia*, vol. 15, no. 2, pp. 76–91.

Colebrook, Claire (2002) *Understanding Deleuze*. Crows Nest, NSW: Allen & Unwin.

Colebrook, Claire (2004) 'Postmodernism is a Humanism: Deleuze and Equivocity', *Women: A Cultural Review*, vol. 15, no. 3, accessed 23 September.

Colette (1979) *Le Pur et l'impur*. Paris: Hachette.

Colombat, André (1996) 'Deleuze's Death as an Event', *Man and World*, vol. 29, no. 3, pp. 235–49.

Connolly, William (1999) *Why am I not a Secularist?* Minneapolis: University of Minnesota Press.

Coward, Rosalind and Ellis, John (1977) *Language and Materialism*. London: Routledge & Kegan Paul.

Creed, Barbara (1993) *The Monstrous Feminine: Film, Feminism and Psychoanalysis*. New York and London: Routledge.

Crenshaw, Kimberlé (1989) *Demarginalizing the Intersection of Race and Sex: A Black Feminist Critique of Antidiscrimination Doctrine, Feminist Theory and Antiracist Politics*. Chicago: University of Chicago Legal Faculty.

Crenshaw, Kimberlé (1995) 'Intersectionality and Identity Politics: Learning from Violence against Women of Colour', in Kimberlé Crenshaw, Neil Gotanda, Gary Peller and Kendall Thomas (eds) *Critical Race Theory*. New York: New Press, pp. 178–93.

Cresswell, Tim (1997) 'Imagining the Nomad: Mobility and the Postmodern Primitive', in Georges Benko and Ulf Strohmeyer (eds) *Space and Social Theory*. Oxford: Blackwell.

Curley, Edwin (1988) *Beyond the Geometrical Method: A Reading of Spinoza's Ethics*. Princeton: Princeton University Press.

Dahrendorf, R. (1990) *Reflections on the Revolution in Europe in a Letter intended to have been sent to a gentleman in Warsaw*. London: Chatto & Windus.

Davion, Victoria (1994) 'Is Ecofeminism Feminist?' in Karen J. Warren (ed.) *Ecological Feminism*. London and New York: Routledge.

Dawkins, Richard (1976) *The Selfish Gene*. Oxford: Oxford University Press.

Delanda, Manuel (2002) *Intensive Science and Virtual Philosophy*. London: Continuum.

Deleuze, Gilles (1953) *Empirisme et subjectivité*. Paris: Presses Universitaires de France. English translation: *Empirism and Subjectivity: An Essay on Hume's Theory of Human Nature*, trans. C. V. Boundas. New York: Columbia University Press, 1991.

Deleuze, Gilles (1962) *Nietzsche et la philosophie*. Paris: Presses Universitaires de France. English translation: *Nietzsche and Philosophy*, trans. Hugh Tomlinson and Barbara Habberjam. New York: Columbia University Press, 1983.

Deleuze, Gilles (1964) *Proust et les signes*. Paris: Presses Universitaires de France. English translation: *Proust and Signs*, trans. R. Howard. New York: G. Braziller, 1972.

Deleuze, Gilles (1966) *Le bergsonisme*. Paris: Presses Universitaires de France. English translation: *Bergonism*, trans. Hugh Tomlinson and Barbara Habberjam. New York: Zone Books, 1988.

Deleuze, Gilles (1968a) *Différence et répétition*. Paris: Presses Universitaires de France. English translation: *Difference and Repetition*, trans. Paul Patton. London: Athlone, 1968.

Deleuze, Gilles (1968b) *Spinoza et le problème de l'expression*. Paris: Minuit. English translation: *Expressionism in Philosophy: Spinoza*, trans. M. Joughin. New York: Zone Books, 1990.

Deleuze, Gilles (1969) *Logique du sens*. Paris: Minuit. English translation: *The Logic of Sense*, trans. M. Lester and C. Stivale. New York: Columbia University Press, 1990.

Deleuze, Gilles (1972a) *Un nouvel archiviste*. Paris: Fata Morgana. English translation: 'A New Archivist', in Peter Botsman (ed.) *Theoretical Strategies*. Sydney: Local Consumption, 1982.

Deleuze, Gilles (1972b) 'Les intellectuels et le pouvoir. Entretien Michel Foucault–Gilles Deleuze', *L'arc*, no. 49, pp. 3–10. English translation: 'Intellectuals and Power', in D. Bouchard (ed.) *Language, Counter-memory, Practice*, trans. D. Boudiano. Ithaca: Cornell University Press, 1973, pp. 205–17.

Deleuze, Gilles (1973a) *La pensée nomade*. Paris: Union Générale d'Édition.

Deleuze, Gilles (1973b) 'La pensée nomade', in *Nietzsche Aujourd'hui*, vol. 1. Paris: Union Générale d'Édition, pp. 159–74. English translation: 'Nomad Thought', in David B. Allison (ed.) *The New Nietzsche: Contemporary Styles of Interpretation*. Cambridge MA: MIT Press, 1985.

Deleuze, Gilles (1978) 'Philosophie et minorité', *Critique*, no. 369, Paris, pp. 154–5.

Deleuze, Gilles (1981) *Francis Bacon: Logique de la sensation 1*. Paris: Éditions de la Différence.

Deleuze, Gilles (1983) *Cinéma I: L'Image-mouvement*. Paris: Minuit. English translation: *Cinema I: The Movement-Image*, trans. Hugh Tomlinson and Barbara Habberjam. Minneapolis: University of Minnesota Press, 1986.

Deleuze, Gilles (1985) *Cinéma II: L'Image-temps*. Paris: Minuit. English translation: *Cinema I: The Time-Image*, trans. Hugh Tomlinson and Robert Galeta. Minneapolis: University of Minnesota Press, 1989.

Deleuze, Gilles (1986) *Foucault*. Paris: Minuit. English translation: (1988) *Foucault*, trans. Sean Hand. Minneapolis: University of Minnesota Press.

Deleuze, Gilles (1988a) *Le pli*. Paris: Minuit. English translation: *The Fold: Leibniz and the Baroque*. Minneapolis: University of Minnesota Press, 1992.

Deleuze, Gilles (1988b) *Périclès et Verdi. Le philosophie de François Châtelet*. Paris: Minuit.

Deleuze, Gilles (1989) 'Qu'est-ce qu'un dispositif?', in *Michel Foucault Philosophe*. Paris: Seuil, pp. 185–95.

Deleuze, Gilles (1990) *Pour parlers*. Paris: Minuit. See also English translation at Deleuze 1995b.

Deleuze, Gilles (1995a) 'L'immanence: une vie . . .', *Philosophie*, no. 47, pp. 3–7.

Deleuze, Gilles (1995b) *Negotiations. 1972–1990*, trans. Martin Joughin. New York: Columbia University Press. Translation of Deleuze 1990.

Deleuze, Gilles (1996) *Abécédaire*. 3 videotapes. Paris: Sodaperaga.

Deleuze, Gilles and Guattari, Felix (1972a) *L'anti-Oedipe. Capitalisme et schizophrénie I*. Paris: Minuit. English translation: *Anti-Oedipus: Capitalism and Schizophrenia*, trans. R. Hurley, M. Seem and H. R. Lane. New York: Viking Press/Richard Seaver, 1977.

Deleuze, Gilles and Guattari, Felix (1972b) 'Capitalisme énurgumène', *Critique*, no. 306 (Nov).

Deleuze, Gilles and Guattari, Felix (1975) *Kafka. Pour une litérature mineure*. Paris: Minuit. English translation: *Kafka: Toward a Minor Literature*, trans. Dana Polan. Minneapolis: University of Minnesota Press, 1986.

Deleuze, Gilles and Guattari, Felix (1976) *Rhizome*. Paris: Minuit. English translation: 'Rhizome', trans. Paul Foss and Paul Patton, *Ideology and Consciousness*, no. 8 (Spring, 1981), pp. 49–71.

Deleuze, Gilles and Guattari, Felix (1980) *Mille plateaux. Capitalisme et schizophrénie II*. Paris: Minuit. See also English translation at Deleuze and Guattari 1987.

Deleuze, Gilles and Guattari, Felix (1986) *Nomadology*, trans. Brian Massumi. New York: Semiotexte.

Deleuze, Gilles and Guattari, Felix (1987) *A Thousand Plateaus: Capitalism and Schizophrenia*, trans. Brian Massumi. Minneapolis: University of Minnesota Press. Translation of Deleuze and Guattari 1980.

Deleuze, Gilles and Guattari, Felix (1992) *What is Philosophy?* New York: Columbia University Press. Translation of *Qu'est-ce que la philosophie?* Paris: Minuit, 1991.

Deleuze, Gilles and Parnet, Claire (1987) *Dialogues*, trans. Hugh Tomlinson and Barbara Habberjam. New York: Columbia University Press. Translation of *Dialogues*. Paris: Flammarion, 1977.

Derrida, Jacques (1994) *Specters of Marx*. New York and London: Routledge.

Derrida, Jacques (1997) *Cosmopolites de tous les pays, encore un effort!* Paris: Galilée.

Derrida, Jacques (2001) *The Work of Mourning*. Chicago: University of Chicago Press.

DeSalvo, L. and Leaska, M. A. (eds) (1984) *The Letters of Vita Sackville-West to Virginia Woolf*. London: Macmillan.

Deschaumes, Ghislaine Glasson (2002) 'Journal of the Caravan' in Ghislaine Glasson Deschaumes and Svetlana Slapsak (eds) *Balkan Women for Peace: Itineraries of Cross-border Activism*. Paris: Transeuropéennes, Réseaux pour la Culture en Europe, pp. 9–84.

Deschaumes, Ghislaine Glasson and Slapsak, Svetlana (eds) (2002) *Balkan Women for Peace: Itineraries of Cross-border Activism*. Paris: Transeuropéennes, Réseaux pour la Culture en Europe.

Deutscher, Penelope (2003) 'Between East and West and the Politics of Cultural Ingenuity', *Theory, Culture & Society*, vol. 20, no. 3, pp. 65–75.

Donovan, Josephine (1996) 'Animal Rights and Feminist Theory', in Josephine Donovan and Carol Adams (eds) *Beyond Animal Rights: A Feminist Caring Ethic for the Treatment of Animals*. New York: Continuum.

Dyer, Richard (1997) *White*. New York and London: Routledge.

Eisenstein, Zillah (1998) *Global Obscenities: Patriarchy, Capitalism and the Lure of Cyberfantasy*. New York: New York University Press.

Eliot, George (1973) *Middlemarch*. London: Penguin.

Epps, Brad (1996) 'Technoasceticism and Authorial Death in Sade, Kafka, Barthes and Foucault', *differences: A Journal of Feminist Cultural Studies*, vol. 8, no. 3, pp. 79–127.

Essed, Philomena (1991) *Understanding Everyday Racism: An Interdisciplinary Theory*. London: Sage.

Faiola, Anthony (2001–2) 'Animal Trafficking Sucks Life from Amazon Rain Forest', *Guardian Weekly*, 27 December 2001–2 January 2002.

Fausto-Sterling, Anne (2000) *Sexing the Body: Gender Politics and the Construction of Sexuality*. New York: Basic Books.

Felski, Rita (1997) 'The Doxa of Difference', *Signs*, vol. 23, no. 1, pp. 1–22.

Fitzpatrick, Peter (2001) 'Bare Sovereignty: *Homo Sacer* and the Insistence of Law', *Theory and Event*, 5, 2, at http://muse.jhu.edu/journals/tae.

Flannery, Tim (1994) *The Future Eaters*. Sydney: Reed New Holland.

Foucault, Michel (1975a) *Les mots et les choses*. Paris: Gallimard. English translation: *The Order of Things*. New York: Pantheon Books, 1980.

Foucault, Michel (1975b) *Surveiller et punir*. Paris: Gallimard. English translation: *Discipline and Punish*. New York: Pantheon Books, 1977.

Foucault, Michel (1976) *Histoire de la sexualité I: La volonté de savoir*. Paris: Gallimard. English translation: *The History of Sexuality*, vol. I, trans. Robert Hurley. New York: Pantheon, 1978.

Foucault, Michel (1977) *L'ordre du discours*. Paris: Gallimard.

Foucault, Michel (1984a) *Histoire de la sexualité II: L'usage des plaisirs*. Paris: Gallimard. English translation: *History of Sexuality, vol. II: The Use of Pleasure*, trans. Robert Hurley. New York: Pantheon Books, 1985.

Foucault, Michel (1984b) *Histoire de la sexualité III: Le souci de soi*. Paris: Gallimard. English translation: *History of Sexuality, vol. III: The Care of the Self*, trans. Robert Hurley. New York: Pantheon Books, 1984.

Foucault, Michel and Hélène Cixous (1979) 'A propos de Marguérite Duras', in *Cahiers Renaud Barrault*, pp. 8–22.

Frankenberg, Ruth (1994a) 'Introduction: Points of Origin, Points of Departure', in *White Women, Race Matters: The Social Construction of Whiteness*. Minneapolis: University of Minnesota Press, pp. 1–22.

Frankenberg, Ruth (1994b) 'Questions of Culture and Belonging', in *White Women, Race Matters: The Social Construction of Whiteness*. Minneapolis: University of Minnesota Press, pp. 191–235.

Franklin, Sarah, Lury, Celia and Stacey, Jackie (2000) *Global Nature, Global Culture*. London: Sage.

Fraser, Nancy (1996) 'Multiculturalism and Gender Equity: The US "Difference" Debates Revisited', *Constellations*, vol. 1, pp. 61–72.

Fukuyama, Francis (2002) *Our Posthuman Future: Consequences of the Biotechnological Revolution*. London: Profile Books.

Fuss, Diana (1989) *Essentially Speaking*. London and New York: Routledge.

Galas, Diamanda (1993) *Vena Cava*. Mute Records, 61459-2.

Gatens, Moira (1996) *Imaginary Bodies: Ethics, Power and Corporeality*. London: Routledge.

Gatens, Moira and Lloyd, Genevieve (1999) *Collective Imaginings: Spinoza, Past and Present*. London and New York: Routledge.

Gedalof, Irene (1996) 'Can Nomads Learn to Count to Four? R. Braidotti and the Space for Difference in Feminist Theory', *Women: A Cultural Review*, vol. 7, no. 2, pp. 189–201.

Gedalof, Irene (2000) 'Identity in Transit, Nomads, Cyborgs and Women', *European Journal of Women's Studies*, vol. 7, pp. 337–54.

Geertz, Clifford (1984) 'Anti Anti-relativism', *American Anthropologist*, vol. 86, no. 2 (June), pp. 263–78.

Gellner, Ernest (1992) *Postmodernism, Reason and Religion*. London and New York: Routledge.

Gibson, William (1984) *Neuromancer*. London: Victor Gollancz. Edition used: London: Voyager/HarperCollins, 1995.

Giddens, Anthony (1994) *Beyond Left and Right: The Future of Radical Politics*. Cambridge: Polity.

Gilligan, Carol (1982) *In A Different Voice: Psychological Theory and Women's Development*. Cambridge, MA: Harvard University Press.

Gilroy, Paul (1987) *There Ain't No Black in the Union Jack: The Cultural Politics of Race and Nation*. London: Hutchinson.

Gilroy, Paul (1993) *The Black Atlantic: Modernity and Double Consciousness*. Cambridge, MA: Harvard University Press.

Gilroy, Paul (1996) 'Route Work: The Black Atlantic and the Politics of Exile', in Iain Chambers and Lidia Curti (eds) *The Post-colonial Question: Common Skies, Divided Horizons*. New York and London: Routledge.

Gilroy, Paul (2000) *Against Race: Imaging Political Culture beyond the Colour Line*. Cambridge, MA: Harvard University Press.

Glissant, Edward (1997) *Poetics of Relation*, trans. Betsy Wing. Ann Arbor: University of Michigan Press. Translation of *Poétique de la relation*. Paris: Gallimard, 1990.

Goodchild, Philip (1996) *Deleuze and Guattari: An Introduction to the Politics of Desire*. London: Sage.

Gould, Stephen Jay and Wolff Purcell, Rosamond (2000) *Crossing Over: Where Art and Science Meet*. New York: Three Rivers Press.

Gray, Cris Hables (2001) *Cyborg Citizen: Politics in the Posthuman Age*. New York and London: Routledge.

Grene, Marjorie (ed.) (1973) *Spinoza: A Collection of Critical Essays*. Notre Dame, IN: University of Notre Dame Press.

Grewal, Inderpal and Kaplan, Caren (eds) (1994) *Scattered Hegemonies: Postmodernity and Transnational Feminist Practices*. Minneapolis: University of Minnesota Press.

Griffin, Gabriele and Braidotti, Rosi (2002) *Thinking Differently: A Reader in European Women's Studies*. London: Zed Books.

Griggers, Camilla (1997) *Becoming-Woman*. Minneapolis: University of Minnesota Press.

Grossberg, Lawrence (1997) *Dancing in Spite of Myself: Essays on Popular Culture*. Durham, NC and London: Duke University Press.

Grosz, Elizabeth (1994a) 'A Thousand Tiny Sexes: Feminism and Rhizomatics', in C. V. Boundas and D. Olkowski (eds) *Gilles Deleuze and the Theatre of Philosophy*. London and New York: Routledge.

Grosz, Elizabeth (1994b) 'The Hetero and the Homo: The Sexual Ethics of Luce Irigaray' in C. Burke, N. Schor and M. Whitford (eds) *Engaging with Irigaray*. New York: Colombia University Press.

Grosz, Elizabeth (1995a) *Space, Time and Perversion: The Politics of Bodies*. Sydney: Allen & Unwin.

Grosz, Elizabeth (1995b) 'Animal Sex: Libido as Desire and Death', in Elizabeth Grosz and Elspeth Probyn (eds) *Sexy Bodies: The Strange Carnalities of Feminism*. London and New York: Routledge.

Grosz, Elizabeth (ed.) (1999a) *Becomings: Explorations in Time, Memory and Futures*. Ithaca: Cornell University Press.

Grosz, Elizabeth (1999b) 'Darwin and Feminism: Preliminary Investigations for a Possible Alliance', *Australian Feminist Studies*, vol. 14, no. 29, pp. 31–45.

Grosz, Elizabeth (2000) 'Deleuze's Bergson: Duration, the Virtual and a Politics of the Future', in Ian Buchanan and Claire Colebrook (eds) *Deleuze and Feminist Theory*. Edinburgh: Edinburgh University Press.

Grosz, Elizabeth and Probyn, Elspeth (eds) (1995) *Sexy Bodies: The Strange Carnalities of Feminism*. London and New York: Routledge.

Gruen, Lori (1994) 'Toward an Ecofeminist Moral Epistemology', in Karen J. Warren (ed.) *Ecological Feminism*. London and New York: Routledge.

Guattari, Felix (1992) *Chaosmose*. Paris: Galilée (French original).

Guattari, Felix (1995) *Chaosmosis: An Ethico-Aesthetic Paradigm*. Sydney: Power.

Guattari, Felix (2000) *The Three Ecologies*. London: Athlone.

Habermas, Jürgen (1992) 'Citizenship and National Identity: Some Reflections on the Future of Europe', *Praxis International*, vol. 12, no. 1, pp. 1–34.

Habermas, Jürgen (2003) *The Future of Human Nature*. Cambridge: Polity.

Halberstam, Judith (1991) 'Automating Gender: Postmodern Feminism in the Age of the Intelligent Machine', *Feminist Studies*, no. 3, pp. 439–60.

Halberstam, Judith and Livingston, Ira (eds) (1995) *Posthuman Bodies*. Bloomington: Indiana University Press.

Hall, Stuart (1996) 'When was the "Post Colonial"?', in Iain Chambers and Lidia Curti (eds) *The Post-colonial Question: Common Skies, Divided Horizons*. New York and London: Routledge.

Haraway, Donna (1985) 'A Manifesto for Cyborgs: Science, Technology, and Socialist Feminism in the 1980s', *Socialist Review*, vol. 5, no. 2, pp. 65–108.

Haraway, Donna (1988) 'Situated Knowledges: The Science Question in Feminism as a Site of Discourse on the Privilege of Partial Perspective', *Feminist Studies*, vol. 14, no. 3, pp. 575–99.

Haraway, Donna (1992) 'The Promises of Monsters: A Regenerative Politics for Inappropriate/d Others', in L. Grossberg, C. Nelson and A. Treichler (eds) *Cultural Studies*. London and New York: Routledge.

Haraway, Donna (1997) *Modest_Witness@Second_Millennium. FemaleMan©_Meets_ OncoMouse™*. London and New York: Routledge.

Haraway, Donna (2000) *How Like a Leaf: An Interview with Thyrza Nichols Goodeve*. New York and London: Routledge.

Haraway, Donna (2003) *The Companion Species Manifesto: Dogs, People and Significant Otherness*. Chicago: Prickly Paradigm Press.

Harding, Luke (2001) 'Delhi Calling', *Guardian Weekly*, 15–21 March.

Harding, Sandra (1986) *The Science Question in Feminism*. London: Open University.

Harding, Sandra (1987) *Feminism and Methodology*. London: Open University.

Harding, Sandra (1991) *Whose Science? Whose Knowledge?* Milton Keynes: Open University.

Hardt, Michael (1992) *Gilles Deleuze: An Apprenticeship in Philosophy*. Minneapolis: University of Minnesota Press.

Hardt, Michael (1998) 'The Withering Of Civil Society', in Eleanor Kaufman and Kevin Jon Heller (eds) *Deleuze and Guattari: New Mappings in Politics, Philosophy and Culture*. Minneapolis: University of Minnesota Press.

Hardt, Michael and Negri, Antonio (2000) *Empire*. Cambridge, MA: Harvard University Press.

Hayles, Katherine (1999) *How We Became Posthuman: Virtual Bodies in Cybernetics, Literature and Informatics*. Chicago: University of Chicago Press.

Herrnstein-Smith, Barbara (1988) *Contingencies of Value: Alternative Perspectives for Critical Theory*, Cambridge, MA: Harvard University Press.

Hill Collins, Patricia (1991) *Black Feminist Thought: Knowledge, Consciousness and the Politics of Empowerment*. New York and London: Routledge.

Hirschman, Albert (1993) 'Exit, Voice and the Fate of the German Democratic Republic: An Essay in Conceptual History', *World Politics*, vol. 45, no. 2, pp. 173–202.

Hirschman, Albert (1994) *Passaggi di Frontiera. I luoghi e le idee di un percorso di vita*. Roma: Donzelli.

Hirschman, Albert (1995) 'Introduction', in V. Fry, *Assignment: Rescue. An Autobiography*. New York: Scholastic Inc., pp. v–viii.

Hirschmann, Ursula (1993) *Noi senza patria*. Bologna: Il Mulino.

Hobsbawm, Eric and Ranger, Terence (eds) (1983) *The Invention of Tradition*. Cambridge: Cambridge University Press.

Holland, Eugene (1999) *Deleuze and Guattari's Anti-Oedipus*. New York and London: Routledge.

hooks, bell (1990) 'Postmodern Blackness', in *Yearning: Race, Gender and Cultural Politics*. Toronto: Between the Lines.

hooks, bell (1992) 'Representations of Whiteness in the Black Imagination', in *Black Looks: Race and Representation*. Boston: South End, pp. 165–79.

Huntington, Samuel (1996) *The Clash of Civilizations and the Remaking of World Order*. New York: Simon & Schuster.

Irigaray, Luce (1974) *Spéculum. De l'autre femme*. Paris: Minuit. English translation: *Speculum of the Other Woman*, trans. Gillian Gill. Ithaca: Cornell University Press, 1985.

Irigaray, Luce (1977) *Ce sexe qui n'en est pas un*. Paris: Minuit. English translation: *This Sex Which Is Not One*, trans. Catherine Porter. Ithaca: Cornell University Press, 1985.

Irigaray, Luce (1980) *Amante marine. De Friedrich Nietzsche*. Paris: Minuit. English translation: *Marine Lover of F. Nietzsche*, trans. Gillian Gill. New York: Columbia University Press, 1991.

Irigaray, Luce (1983) *L'oubli de l'air chez Martin Heidegger*. Paris: Minuit. English translation: *The Forgetting of Air in Martin Heidegger*, trans. Mary Beth Mader. Austin: University of Texas Press, 1999.

Irigaray, Luce (1984) *L'éthique de la différence sexuelle*. Paris: Minuit. English translation: *An Ethics of Sexual Difference*, trans. Carolyn Burke and Gillian Gill. Ithaca: Cornell University Press, 1993.

Irigaray, Luce (1987a) 'Égales à qui?', *Critique. Revue générale des publications Françaises et étrangères*, vol. 43, pp. 480, 420–37. English translation: 'Equal to Whom?', *differences. A Journal of Feminist Cultural Studies*, vol. 1, no. 2 (1988), pp. 59–76.

Irigaray, Luce (1987b) *Sexes et parentés*. Paris: Minuit. English translation: *Sexes and Genealogies*, trans. Gillian C. Gill. Ithaca and New York: Cornell University Press, 1993.

Irigaray, Luce (1989) *Le temps de la différence. Pour une révolution pacifique*. Paris: Hachette. English translation: *Thinking the Difference: For a Peaceful Revolution*, trans. Karin Montin. London: Athlone, 1994.

Irigaray, Luce (1990) *Je, tu, nous. Pour une culture de la différence*. Paris: Grasset. English translation: *Je, Tu, Nous: Towards a Culture of Difference*, trans. Alison Martin. New York and London: Routledge, 1993.

Irigaray, Luce (1991) 'Love Between Us' in E. Cadava, P. Connor and J. L. Nancy (eds) *Who Comes after the Subject?* New York and London: Routledge, pp. 167–77.

Irigaray, Luce (1997) *Entre l'est et l'ouest. De la singularité à la communauté*. Paris: Minuit. English translation: *Between East and West: From Singularity to Community*, trans. Stephen Pluhacek. New York: Columbia University Press, 2002.

Jaggar, Alison Marion (1995) 'Caring as a Feminist Practice of Moral Reason', in Virginia Held (ed.) *Justice and Care: Essential Readings in Feminist Ethics*. New York: Westview Press/HarperCollins.

Jaggar, Alison Marion and Young, Iris Marion (eds) (1998) *A Companion to Feminist Philosophy*. Malden, MA: Blackwell.

Jameson, Fredric (1993) 'Postmodernism, or the Cultural Logic of Late Capitalism' in *Postmodernism: A Reader*. New York and Chichester, West Sussex: Columbia University Press. Original: (1984) in *New Left Review*, no. 46, pp. 111–25.

Jokinen, Eeva and Veijola, Soile (1997) 'The Disoriented Tourist: The Figuration of the Tourist in Contemporary Cultural Critique', in Chris Rojek and John Urry (eds) *Touring Cultures: Transformations of Travel and Theory*. London and New York: Routledge.

Kappeler, Susan (1987) *The Pornography of Representation*. Cambridge: Polity.

Keller, Evelyn Fox (1983) *A Feeling for the Organism: The Life and Work of Barbara McClintock*. New York: W. H. Freeman.

Keller, Evelyn Fox (1992) *Secrets of Life, Secrets of Death: Essays on Language, Gender and Science*. New York and London: Routledge.

Keller, Evelyn Fox (1995) *Reflections on Gender and Science*. New Haven: Yale University Press.

Kelly, Joan (1979) 'The Double-Edged Vision of Feminist Theory', *Feminist Studies*, vol. 5, no. 1 (Spring), pp. 216–27.

King, Ynestra (1989) 'Healing the Wounds: Feminism, Ecology, and Nature/ Culture Dualism' in Alison Jaggar and Susan Bordo (eds) *Gender/Body/Knowledge: Feminist Reconstructions of Being and Knowing*. New Brunswick: Rutgers University Press.

Klein, Naomi (1999) *No Logo: Taking Aim at the Brand Bullies*. New York: Picador.

Klein, Richard (1995) 'The Devil in Carmen', *differences. A Journal of Feminist Cultural Studies*, vol. 5, no. 1, pp. 51–72.

Kneale, Martha (1973) 'Eternity and Sempiternity', in Marjorie Grene (ed.) *Spinoza: A Collection of Critical Essays*. Notre Dame, IN: University of Notre Dame Press.

Kristeva, Julia (1980) *Pouvoirs de l'horreur*. Paris: Seuil. English translation: (1982) *Powers of Horror*, trans. Leon S. Roudiez. New York: Columbia University Press.

Kristeva, Julia (1981) 'Women's Time', *Signs*, vol. 7, no. 1, pp. 13–35.

Kristeva, Julia (1991) *Strangers to Ourselves*, trans. Leon S. Roudiez. New York: Columbia University Press. Translation of *Étrangers à nous-mêmes*. Paris: Fayard, 1988.

Kroker, Arthur (1987) 'Panic Value: Bacon, Colville, Baudrillard and the Aesthetics of Deprivation', in John Fekete (ed.) *Life after Postmodernism: Essays on Value and Culture*. New York: St Martin's Press.

Kroker, Arthur and Kroker, Marilouise (1987) *Body Invaders: Panic Sex in America*. New York: St Martin's Press.

Kung, Hans (1998) *A Global Ethic for Global Politics and Economics*. Oxford: Oxford University Press.

Lacey, A. R. (ed.) (1996) *A Dictionary of Philosophy*. London and New York: Routledge.

Laclau, Ernesto (1995) 'Subjects of Politics, Politics of the Subject', *differences*, vol. 7, no. 1, pp. 146–64.

Laplanche, Jean (1976) *Life and Death in Psychoanalysis*. Baltimore and London: Johns Hopkins University Press.

Lee, Hermione (1996) *Virginia Woolf*. London: Chatto & Windus.

Lefanu, Sarah (1988) *In the Chinks of the World Machine*. London: Women's Press.

Lichtenberg-Ettinger, Bracha (1992) 'Matrix and Metamorphosis', *differences*, vol. 4, no. 3, pp. 176–207.

Lloyd, Genevieve (1985) *The Man of Reason*. London: Methuen.

Lloyd, Genevieve (1994) *Part of Nature: Self-knowledge in Spinoza's Ethic*. Ithaca and London: Cornell University Press.

Lloyd, Genevieve (1996) *Spinoza and the Ethics*. London and New York: Routledge.

Lovibond, Sabina (1994) 'The End of Morality', in Kathleen Lenno and Margaret Whitford (eds) *Knowing the Difference: Feminist Perspectives in Epistemology*. London and New York: Routledge.

Lutz, Helma, Yuval-Davis, Nira and Phoenix, Ann (1996) *Crossfires: Nationalism, Racism and Gender in Europe*. London: Pluto Press.

Lyotard, Jean-François (1979) *La Condition postmoderne*. Paris: Minuit.

Lyotard, Jean-François (1983) *Le Différend*. Paris: Minuit.

Lyotard, Jean-François (1988) *L'Inhumain. Causeries sur le temps*. Paris: Galilée. English translation: *The Inhuman: Reflections on Time*, trans. Geoffrey Bennington and Rachel Bowlby. Oxford: Blackwell, 1989.

MacCannell, Dean (1992) *On Empty Meeting Grounds*. London and New York: Routledge.

MacCormack, Patricia (2000) 'Pleasure, Perversion and Death: Three Lines of Flight for the Viewing Body'. Ph.D. Dissertation, Monash University, Melbourne.

Makrolab (2003) in Ursula Biemann (ed.) *Geography and the Politics of Mobility*. Vienna: General Foundation.

Margulis, Lynn and Sagan, Dorion (1995) *What is Life?* Berkeley and Los Angeles: University of California Press.

Massumi, Brian (1992a) *First and Last Emperors, the Absolute State and the Body of the Despot*. Brooklyn: Autonomedia.

Massumi, Brian (1992b) 'Anywhere You Want to Be: An Introduction to Fear', in Joan Broadhurst (ed.) *Deleuze and the Transcendental Unconscious*. Coventry: Warwick Journal of Philosophy.

Massumi, Brian (1992c) *A User's Guide to Capitalism and Schizophrenia*. Boston: Massachusetts Institute of Technology Press.

Massumi, Brian (1998) 'Requiem for our Prospective Dead! (Toward a Participatory Critique of Capitalist Power)', in Eleanor Kaufman and Kevin Jon Heller (eds) *Deleuze and Guattari: New Mappings in Politics, Philosophy and Culture*. Minneapolis: University of Minnesota Press.

Massumi, Brian (2002) *Parables for the Virtual: Movement, Affect, Sensation*. Durham, NC: Duke University Press.

Maturana, Humberto and Varela, Francisco (1972) *Autopoiesis and Cognition: The Realization of the Living*. Dordrecht: Reidel.

May, Todd (1995) *The Moral Theory of Poststructuralism*. University Park: Pennsylvania State University Press.

Meek, James (2000) 'Mighty Mouse', *Guardian Weekly*, 27 April–3 May.

Meny, Yves (2000) *Tra Utopia e Realtà. Una costituzione per l'Europa*. Florence: Possigli Editore.

Midgley, Mary (1996) *Utopias, Dolphins and Computers: Problems of Philosophical Plumbing*. London and New York: Routledge.

Mies, Maria and Shiva, Vandana (1993) *Ecofeminism*. London: Zed Books.

Mohanty, Chandra Talpade (1994) 'Under Western Eyes: Feminist Scholarship and Colonial Discourses', in P. Williams and L. Chrisman (eds) *Colonial Discourse and Post-colonial Theory*. New York: Colombia University Press, pp. 196–220.

Mohanty, Chandra T., Russo, Ann and Torres, Lourdes (eds) (1991) *Third World Women and the Politics of Feminism*. Bloomington: Indiana University Press.

Morin, Edgar (1987) *Penser l'Europe*. Paris: Gallimard.

Morrison, Toni (1992) *Playing in the Dark*. Cambridge, MA: Harvard University Press.

Mouffe, Chantal (1994) 'For a Politics of Nomadic Identity', in G. Robertson, M. Mash, L. Tickner, J. Bird, B. Curtis and T. Putnam (eds) *Travellers' Tales: Narratives of Home and Displacement*. London and New York: Routledge.

Moulier Boutang, Yann (1986) 'Resistance to the Political Representation of Alien Population: The European Paradox', *International Migration Review*, Special issue: Civil Rights and Socio-political Participation of Migrants, vol. 19, no. 71, pp. 485–92.

Naess, Arne (1977a) 'Spinoza and Ecology', in Siegfried Hessing (ed.), *Speculum Spinozanum, 1877–1977*. London: Routledge & Kegan Paul.

Naess, Arne (1977b) 'Through Spinoza to Mahayana Buddhism or through Mahayana Buddhism to Spinoza?', in Jon Wetlesen (ed.) *Spinoza's Philosophy of Man*. Proceedings of the Scandinavian Spinoza Symposium, Universitetsforlaget, Oslo.

Negri, Antonio (1981) *The Savage Anomaly: The Power of Spinoza's Metaphysics and Politics*. Minneapolis: University of Minnesota Press.

Nessman, Ravi (2002) 'Cut-off Afghans Forced to Eat Grass', *Guardian Weekly*, 3–5 January.

Nicolson, N. (ed.) (1992) *Vita and Harold: The Letters of Vita Sackville-West and Harold Nicolson*. New York: G. P. Putnam's Sons.

Nicolson, N. and Trautmann, J. (eds) (1975) *The Letters of Virginia Woolf. Vol. III, 1923–1928*. New York and London: Harvest Books.

Nietzsche, Friedrich (1994) *Human, All Too Human*, trans. Marion Faber and Stephen Lehmann. London: Penguin.

Norris, Christopher (1991) *Spinoza and the Origins of Modern Critical Theory*. Oxford: Blackwell.

Noske, Barbara (1989) *Humans and Other Animals: Beyond the Boundaries of Anthropology*. London: Pluto Press.

Nussbaum, Martha C. (1986) *The Fragility of Goodness*. Cambridge: Cambridge University Press.

Nussbaum, Martha C. (1994) 'Patriotism and Cosmopolitanism', *Boston Review* (October/November).

Nussbaum, Martha C. (1999a) *Cultivating Humanity: A Classical Defense of Reform in Liberal Education*. Cambridge MA: Harvard University Press.

Nussbaum, Martha C. (1999b) 'The Professor of Parody: The Hip Defeatism of Judith Butler', *New Republic*, 22 February, pp. 37–45.

Olkowski, Dorothea (1999) *Gilles Deleuze and the Ruin of Representation*. Berkeley: University of California Press.

Oliver Bell, A. (ed.) (1979) *The Diary of Virginia Woolf. Vol. II, 1920–1924; Vol. III, 1925–1930*. New York and London: Harvest.

Ong, Aihwa (1993) 'On the Edge of Empires: Flexible Citizenship among Chinese in Diaspora', *Positions*, vol. I, no. 3, pp. 745–78.

Outlaw, Lucius (1996) *On Race and Philosophy*. London and New York: Routledge.

Parisi, Luciana (2004a) *Abstract Sex: Philosophy, Bio-Technology, and the Mutation of Desire*. London: Continuum Press.

Parisi, Luciana (2004b) 'For a schizogenesis of sexual difference', *Identities*, vol. 3, no. 1, pp. 67–93.

Parks, Lise (2003) 'Plotting the Personal: Global Positioning Satellites and Trajective Mapping', in Ursula Biemann (ed.) *Geography and the Politics of Mobility*. Vienna: General Foundation.

Parsons, F. Susan (1992) 'Feminism and the Logic of Morality: A Consideration of Alternatives', in Elisabeth Frazer, Jennifer Hornsby and Sabine Lovibond (eds) *Ethics: A Feminist Reader*. Oxford: Blackwell.

Passerini, Luisa (ed.) (1998) *Identità culturale europea. Idee, sentimenti, relazioni*. Florence: La Nuova Italia Editrice.

Patton, Paul (2000) *Deleuze and the Political*. New York and London: Routledge.

Pels, Dick (1999) 'Privileged Nomads: On the Strangeness of Intellectuals and the Intellectuality of Strangers', *Theory, Culture & Society*, vol. 16, no. 1 (February), pp. 63–86.

Phillips, Adam (1999) *Darwin's Worms*. London: Faber & Faber.

Pisters, Patricia (1997) 'Cyborg Alice; or, Becoming-Woman in an Audio-visual World', *Iris*, 23 (Spring), pp. 148–63.

Pisters, Patricia (ed.) (2001) *Micropolitics of Media Culture: Reading the Rhizomes of Deleuze and Guattari*. Amsterdam: Amsterdam University Press.

Plant, Sadie (2000) *Writing on Drugs*. New York: Farrar Straus & Giroux.

Plath, Sylvia (1965) *Ariel and Other Poems*. London: Faber & Faber.

Plumwood, Val (1993) *Feminism and the Mastery of Nature*. London and New York: Routledge.

Plumwood, Val (1998) 'The Environment', in Alison Jaggar and Iris Young (eds) *A Companion to Feminist Philosophy*. Oxford: Blackwell.

Plumwood, Val (2002) *Environmental Culture*. New York and London: Routledge.

Pojman, Louis P. (ed.) (1994) *Environmental Ethics: Readings in Theory and Application*. Boston and London: Jones & Bartlett.

Post-human (1993) Catalogue of the exhibition at Deichtorhallen, Germany.

Preuss, Ulrich K. (1996) 'Two Challenges to European Citizenship', *Political Studies*, vol. 44, pp. 534–52.

Prigogine, Ilya and Stengers, Isabelle (1980) *La Nouvelle Alliance*. Paris: Gallimard. English translation: *Order out of Chaos*, trans. Alvin Toffler. London: Heinemann, 1984.

Probyn, Elspeth (1990) 'Travels in the Postmodern: Making Sense of the Local', in Linda Nicholson (ed.) *Feminism/Postmodernism*. London and New York: Routledge.

Probyn, Elspeth (1996) *Outside Belongings*. New York and London: Routledge.

Raqs Media Collective (2003) 'A/S/L', in *Geography and the Politics of Mobility*. Vienna: General Foundation.

Rich, Adrienne (1976) *Of Women Born: Motherhood as Experience and Institution*. New York: Norton.

Riefenstahl, Leni (1992) *The Sieve of Time*. New York: Quartet Books.

Rose, Hilary (2001) 'Nine Decades, Nine Women, Ten Nobel Prizes: Gender Politics on the Apex of Science', in Mary Wyer, Mary Barbercheck, Donna Geisman, Hatice Orun Otzurk and Marta Wayne (eds) *Women, Science and Technology: A Reading in Feminist Science Studies*. New York and London: Routledge.

Rose, Nicholas (2001) 'The Politics of Life Itself', *Theory, Culture & Society*, vol. 18, no. 6, pp. 1–30.

Rouch, Hélène (1987) 'La Placenta comme tiers', *Langages*, no. 85, pp. 71–9.

Roy, Arundhati (2001) *Power Politics*. Cambridge, MA: South End Press.

Sachs, Ignacy (1999) 'Social Sustainability and Whole Development: Exploring the Dimensions of Sustainable Development', in Egon Becker and Thomas Johan (eds) *Sustainability and the Social Sciences: A Cross-Disciplinary Approach to Integrating Environmental Considerations into Theoretical Reorientation*. London: Zed Books and UNESCO.

Said, Edward (1978) *Orientalism*. London: Penguin.

Sassen, Saskia (1994) *Cities in a World Economy*. Thousand Oaks and London: Pine Forge Press/Sage.

Sassen, Saskia (1996) 'Toward a Feminist Analytics of the Global Economy', *Indiana Journal of Global Legal Studies*, vol. 4, no. 1, pp. 7–41.

Sassen, Saskia (1997) 'Electronic Space: Embedded and Segmented', *International Planning Studies*, vol. 2, no. 2, pp. 229–40.

Schrift, Alan (1995) *Nietzsche's French Legacy: A Genealogy of Poststructuralism*. New York: Routledge.

Sevenhuijsen, Selma (1998) *Citizenship and the Ethics of Care*. New York and London: Routledge.

Shiva, Vandana (1988) *Staying Alive: Women, Ecology and Development*. London: Zed Books.

Shiva, Vandana (1993) *Monocultures of the Mind*. London: Zed Books.

Shiva, Vandana (1997) *Biopiracy: The Plunder of Nature and Knowledge*. Boston: South End Press.

Slater, David (1992) 'Theories of Development and Politics of the Post-modernism', *Development and Change*, vol. 23, no. 3, pp. 283–320.

Sloterdijk, Peter (2000) *Regels voor het mensenpark*. Amsterdam: Boom. Originally published as *Regeln für den Menschenpark*. Frankfurt: Suhrkamp, 1999.

Smith, Bonnie G. (1998) *The Gender of History: Men, Women and the Historical Practice*. Cambridge, MA: Harvard University Press.

Smith, D. W. (2000) 'The Place of Ethics in Deleuze's Philosophy', in Eleanor Kaufman and Kevin Jon Heller (eds) *Deleuze and Guattari: New Mappings in Politics, Philosophy and Culture*. Minneapolis: University of Minnesota Press.

Sobchack, Vivian (1995) 'Beating the Meat/Surviving the Test or How to Get Out of this Century Alive', *Body & Society*, vol. I, no. 3–4 (November), pp. 209–14.

Sokal, Alan and Bricmont, Jean (1998) *Intellectual Impostures*. London: Profile Books.

Spinelli, Altiero (1979) 'La vie politique d'Ursula Hirschmann, fondatrice de Femmes pour l'Europe', *Textes et Documents*, numéro spécial. Brussels: Ministère des Affaires Étrangères, du Commerce Extérieur et de la Coopération au Développement, pp. 11–15.

Spinelli, Altiero (1988) *Come ho tentato di diventare saggio*. Bologna: Il Mulino.

Spinelli, Altiero (1992) *Diario europeo*. Bologna: Il Mulino.

Spivak, Gayatri Chakravorty (1983) 'Displacement and the Discourse of Woman', in Mark Kupnick (ed.) *Displacement: Derrida and After*. Bloomington: Indiana University Press, pp. 169–95.

Spivak, Gayatri Chakravorty (1987) *In Other Worlds*. New York: Routledge.

Spivak, Gayatri Chakravorty (1988) 'Can the Subaltern Speak?', in Cary Nelson and Lawrence Grossberg (eds) *Marxism and the Interpretation of Culture*. Basingstoke: Macmillan. Reprinted in Patrick Williams and Laura Chrisman (eds) *Colonial Discourse and Post-colonial Theory*. New York: Columbia University Press, 1994, pp. 66–111.

Spivak, Gayatri Chakravorty (1989) 'In a Word', *differences. A Journal of Feminist Cultural Studies*, vol. 1, no. 2, pp. 124–56.

Spivak, Gayatri Chakravorty (1992) 'French Feminism Revisited: Ethics and Politics', in Judith Butler and Joan Scott (eds) *Feminists Theorize the Political*. New York: Routledge.

Spivak, Gayatri Chakravorty (1999) *A Critique of Postcolonial Reason: Toward a History of the Vanishing Present*. Cambridge, MA: Harvard University Press.

Springer, Claudia (1996) *Electronic Eros: Bodies and Desire in the Postindustrial Age*. Austin: University of Texas Press.

Sprinker, Michael (1995) 'The War against Theory' in Jeffrey Williams (ed.) *PC Wars: Politics and Theory in the Academy*. New York: Routledge, pp. 149–71.

Squier, Susan (1995) 'Reproducing the Posthuman Body: Ectogenetic Fetus, Surrogate Mother, Pregnant Man', in Judith Halberstam and Ira Livingston (eds) *Posthuman Bodies*. Bloomington: Indiana University Press, pp. 113–34.

Stacey, Jackie (1997) *Teratologies: A Cultural Study of Cancer*. London and New York: Routledge.

Stengers, Isabelle (1997) *Power and Invention: Situating Science*. Minneapolis: University of Minnesota Press.

Stimpson, Catharina (1988) 'The Female Sociograph: The Theater of V. Woolf's Letters', in *Where the Meanings Are*. New York: Methuen.

Strathern, Marilyn, *After Nature: English Kinship in the Late Twentieth Century*. Cambridge: Cambridge University Press, 1992.

Svevo, Italo (1962) *Confessions of Zeno*. London: Secker & Warburg. Translation of *La coscienza di Zeno*. Milan: Garzanti, 1985.

Teilhard de Chardin, Pierre (1959) *The Future of Man*. New York and Evanston: Harper & Row.

Théâtre de Complicité (1999) *Mnemonic*. London: Methuen.

Theweleit, Klaus (1987) *Male Fantasies I: Women, Floods, Bodies, History*. Minneapolis: University of Minnesota Press.

Theweleit, Klaus (1989) *Male Fantasies II: Male Bodies: Psychoanalyzing the White Terror*. Minneapolis: University of Minnesota Press.

Thompson, Tony (2005) 'All Work and No Play in the Virtual Sweatshop', *Guardian Weekly*, 25–31 March.

Tong, Rosemarie (2001) *Globalizing Feminist Bioethics*. Oxford: Western Press.

Touraine, Alain (2001) *Beyond Neoliberalism*. Cambridge: Polity.

Tronto, Joan (1989) 'Women and Caring: What Can Feminists Learn about Morality from Caring?' in Alison Jaggar and Susan Bordo (eds) *Gender/Body/Knowledge*. New Brunswick and London: University of Rutgers Press.

Tronto, Joan (1993) *Moral Boundaries: A Political Argument for an Ethic of Care*. New York and London: Routledge.

Tronto, Joan (1995) *Caring for Democracy: A Feminist Vision*. Utrecht: University of Humanistic Studies, Inaugural Lecture.

Urry, John (1990) *The Tourist Gaze: Leisure and Travel in Contemporary Societies*. London: Sage.

Vidal, John (2002) 'Half a Million Animals Genetically Modified in Labs' *Guardian Weekly*, 23–29 May.

Virno, Paolo (1994) *Mondanità*. Rome: Manifesto Libri.

Virno, Paolo (2001) *Grammatica della Moltitudine*. Rome: Derive Approdi.

Walzer, Michael (1992) *What it Means to be an American*. New York: Marsilio.

Ware, Vron (1992) *Beyond the Pale: White Women, Racism and History*. London and New York: Verso.

Warren, J. Karen (ed.) (1994) *Ecological Feminism*. London and New York: Routledge.

West, Cornel (1990) 'The New Cultural Politics of Difference', in Russell Ferguson, Marthe Gever and Trinh Minh-ha (eds) *Out There: Marginalization and Contemporary Cultures*. Cambridge, MA: MIT Press.

West, Cornel (1992) 'The Postmodern Crisis of the Black Intellectuals', in L. Grossberg, C. Nelson and P. Treichler (eds) *Cultural Studies*. London and New York: Routledge, pp. 689–96.

West, Cornel (1994) *Prophetic Thought in Postmodern Times*. Monroe, ME: Common Courage Press.

White, Eric (1995) 'Once They Were Men, Now They're Landcrabs: Monstrous Becomings in Evolutionist Cinema', in Judith Halberstam and Ira Livingston (eds) *Posthuman Bodies*. Bloomington: Indiana University Press.

Williams, Jeffrey (1995) 'Introduction', in Jeffrey Williams (ed.) *PC Wars: Politics and Theory in the Academy*. New York: Routledge, pp. 1–10.

Williams, Patricia (1991) *The Alchemy of Race and Rights*. Cambridge, MA: Harvard University Press.

Wilson, Elizabeth A. (1998) *Neural Geographies: Feminism and the Microstructure of Cognition*. New York and London: Routledge.

Witchalls, Clint (2003) 'A Nose for Sniffing out Signs of Disease', *The Times*, 2 June.

Wittig, Monique (1992) *The Straight Mind*. New York and London: Harvester Wheatsheaf.

Woolf, Virginia (1938) *Three Guineas*. London: Hogarth Press.

Woolf, Virginia (1977) *The Waves*. London: Grafton.

Woolf, Virginia (1978) *The Diary of Virginia Woolf, volume 2 (1920–1924)*. New York and London: Harcourt Brace Jovanovich.

Woolf, Virginia (1980) *The Diary of Virginia Woolf, volume 3 (1925–1930)*. New York and London: Harcourt Brace Jovanovich.

Woolf, Virginia (1993) *Flush*. London: Penguin.

Wright, Elizabeth (1992) *Feminism and Psychoanalysis: A Critical Dictionary*. Oxford: Blackwell.

Young, Robert (1990) *White Mythologies: Writing History and the West*. London and New York: Routledge.

Yuval-Davis, Nira (1997) 'National Spaces and Collective Identities: Borders, Boundaries, Citizenship and Gender Relations'. Inaugural Lecture, University of Greenwich, 22 May.

Yuval-Davis, Nira and Anthias, Floya (eds) (1989) *Woman-Nation-State*. London: Macmillan.

Žižek, Slavoj (1999) *The Žižek Reader*, ed. Elizabeth Wright and Edmond Wright. Oxford: Blackwell.

Index